KU-602-446

SOUTHERN SPAIN
ANDALUCÍA & GIBRALTAR

Cadogan Books plc
Letts House, Parkgate Road, London SW11 4NQ

The Globe Pequot Press
6 Business Park Road, PO Box 833, Old Saybrook, Connecticut 06475–0833

Book design by Animage
Cover design by Ralph King
Cover illustration by Povl Webb
Maps © Cadogan Guides, drawn by RJS Associates

Proofreading: Eric Smith
Indexing: Ann Hall
Macintosh: Jacqueline Lewin & Typography 5

Series Editors: Rachel Fielding, Vicki Ingle
Editor: Peter Casterton

First published in 1991. Fully revised and updated in 1994

A catalogue record for this book is available from the British Library.
ISBN 0–947754–60–1

Library of Congress Data available
ISBN 1·56440·463·3

The author and publishers have made every effort to ensure the accuracy of the information in this book at the time of going to press. However, they cannot accept any responsibility for any loss, injury or inconvenience resulting from the use of information contained in this guide.

Typeset in Weidemann and entirely produced on Apple Macintosh with Quark XPress, Photoshop, Freehand and Word software.
Printed and bound in Great Britain by Redwood Books, Trowbridge, Wiltshire.

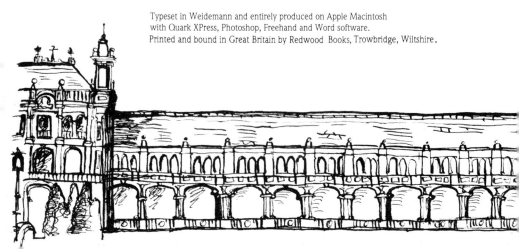

About the Authors

Dana Facaros and **Michael Pauls** are professional travel writers. Over the past 12 years they have lived in several countries, concentrating mainly on the Mediterranean area, and have written 11 highly successful Cadogan guides. They lived in Granada for a year researching the guide to Spain, visiting its distant corners and seldom-frequented villages, and trying not to eat too many *churros*. Now they have moved with their children, computer and library to an idyllic, if draughty, retreat somewhere in France.

About the Updater

Sue Nelson, who updated the practical information in this edition, is a freelance journalist and broadcaster. She has presented travel reports for Channel 4's *Travelogue*, and Radio 4's *Breakaway*. She writes travel articles for the *Independent on Sunday*, the *Guardian* and *The Sunday Times*. She was a finalist for the *Observer's* Young Travel Writer of the Year Award.

Acknowledgements

We would like to thank, once again, all those who made possible the previous edition of this guide, in particular Michael Davidson and Brian Walsh. From the publishers, a big thank you to Alex, Horatio, Kicca, Veronica, and especially to Jacqueline, for their hard work and amazing juggling skills. Thanks also to Anne Greenshields, Stuart Wild and Robert Smith, to Eric Smith for proof-reading the book and to Ann Hall for indexing it.

Please help us to keep this guide up to date

We have done our best to ensure that the information in this guide is correct at the time of going to press. But places and facilities are constantly changing, and standards and prices in hotels and restaurants fluctuate. We would be delighted to receive any comments concerning existing entries or omissions, as well as suggestions for new features. All contributors will be acknowledged in the next edition, and will receive a copy of the Cadogan Guide of their choice.

Contents

Topics 61–72

Andalucía: the Guadalquivir Valley 73–120

Andalucían Coasts 121–74

Andalucían Interior 175–210

Gibraltar 211–26

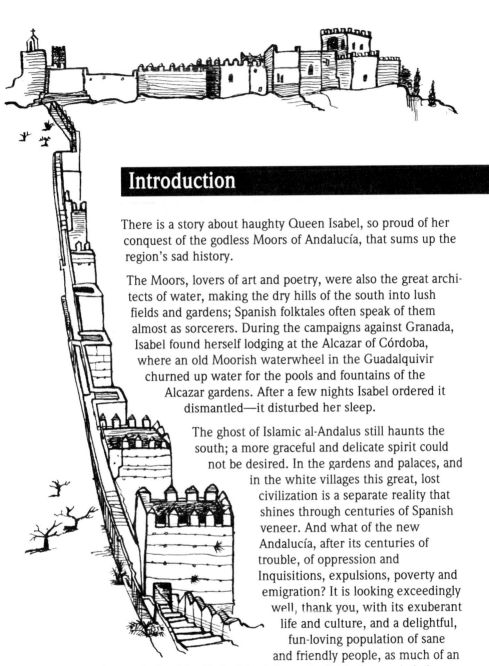

Introduction

There is a story about haughty Queen Isabel, so proud of her conquest of the godless Moors of Andalucía, that sums up the region's sad history.

The Moors, lovers of art and poetry, were also the great architects of water, making the dry hills of the south into lush fields and gardens; Spanish folktales often speak of them almost as sorcerers. During the campaigns against Granada, Isabel found herself lodging at the Alcazar of Córdoba, where an old Moorish waterwheel in the Guadalquivir churned up water for the pools and fountains of the Alcazar gardens. After a few nights Isabel ordered it dismantled—it disturbed her sleep.

The ghost of Islamic al-Andalus still haunts the south; a more graceful and delicate spirit could not be desired. In the gardens and palaces, and in the white villages this great, lost civilization is a separate reality that shines through centuries of Spanish veneer. And what of the new Andalucía, after its centuries of trouble, of oppression and Inquisitions, expulsions, poverty and emigration? It is looking exceedingly well, thank you, with its exuberant life and culture, and a delightful, fun-loving population of sane and friendly people, as much of an attraction as the land itself. Andalucía is a minefield of unexploded stereotypes: sequined matadors and strumming guitars, torrid flamenco and hot-blooded gypsies, orange blossoms and jasmine. They may be hard to avoid, but then again, why try? Few regions of Europe have been blessed with such stereotypes. Visitors never weary of them, and the Andalucíans certainly don't either; they cultivate and polish them with the greatest of care.

Today, with its green and white flag flying proudly on every public building, autonomous, democratic Andalucía may have the chance to rediscover itself. With a fifth of Spain's population, its biggest tourist industry, and potentially its richest agriculture, it has great promise for the future. And as the part of Spain with the longest and most brilliant artistic heritage—not only from the Moors, but from the troubled, creative, post-Reconquista Andalucía that has given Spain Velázquez, García Lorca and Manuel de Falla—the region may find it still has the resources once more to become the leader in Spain's cultural life.

For its size, Andalucía contains a remarkable diversity of landscapes— from Spain's highest mountains to endless rolling hills covered with olive trees, Europe's biggest marshland preserve and even some patches of desert. And no other part of Spain can offer so many interesting large cities. Andalucía is a world unto itself; it has as many delights to offer as you have time to spend on it.

How This Guide is Organized

The guide begins with **Travel** and **Practical A–Z** chapters, which are packed with information to help you plan both your journey to southern Spain or Gibraltar, and you itinerary once you get there. The next two chapters offer an anthropological background. **History** begins in the caves around Gibraltar, and the develops over 50,000 years to rest a while in the pavilions of Sevilla. **Topics** provide a random glimpse at the region's culture through a potpourri of short essays. The gazetteer begins where History left off—in Sevilla.

For convenience, we've divided Andalucía's complicated geography into three parts: Sevilla, Córdoba, and the **Guadalquivir Valley**; then the **Coasts**, of which the famous Costa del Sol is only a small part; then the **Interior**, including the inimitable white villages of the mountains between the Guadalquivir and the sea, and Granada and the Sierra Nevada. Finally, we deal with Iberia's geographical appendix, **Gibraltar**.

The Gazetteer is divided into sections which focus on a key city or town and the area around it, or on a journey between two featured places. Each section is topped and tailed with practical information, providing points of first reference and recommendations: Getting Around and Tourist Offices at the beginning, and Where to Stay and Eating Out at the end.

The book concludes with **Art and Architecture**, **Further Reading** and an **Index**. On the final page, the authors have given an admittedly subjective guide to the **Best of Southern Spain**.

Travel

By air

From the UK, you can fly direct to Spain from Heathrow to Alicante, Bilbao, Santiago, Málaga, Sevilla or Valencia, or from Manchester direct to Madrid or Barcelona. There is an astounding variety of flight options; even Spain's national airline, **Iberia**, offers tempting discounts—bargain fly-drive deals, as well as an unlimited domestic flight option for purchasers of regular flight tickets. **British Airways** offers many of the same services as Iberia. **GB Airways** has daily flights from London to Gibraltar, and several times a week from Manchester.

APEX fares, purchased at least two weeks in advance and for a stay of 7–180 days, offer a discount, especially if you're travelling mid-week. Ask, too, about Iberia's 'Bravo' fares and offers: options available include second-ticket discounts to Sevilla, and discounts for children under 12. Discounts are also available for domestic flights.

Iberia Offices in Europe

France: 14 Boulevard des Capucines, 75009 Paris,
℡ (1) 47 42 14 87

Germany: Kurfürstendamm 207–8, 1000 Berlin 15,
℡ (30) 01 30 63 63

Ireland: 54 Dawson Street, Dublin 2,
℡ (1) 779 846

Italy: Via Bertoloni 3D (Angolo Piazza Pitagora), Rome 00197,
toll free ℡ 1678 31055

Netherlands: Aurora Building, Stadhouderskade 2, 1054 Amsterdam,
℡ (20) 685 0401

UK: 11–12 Haymarket, London SW1Y 4BP,
℡ (071) 830 0011 (open Mon–Fri, 8–8, Sat and Sun
9–5.30)

Other Airlines with Direct Routes to Spain

Air France: flights from Paris: information,
℡ (1) 44 08 24 24; reservations, ℡ (1) 44 08 22 22

Alitalia: flights from Rome,
℡ (6) 65642/3

British Airways: information and reservations if calling from within London,
℡ (081) 897 4000; from outside London, ℡ (0345)
222111

GB Airways: flights from London,
℡ (081) 759 1818; from Manchester, ℡ (061) 489 2510

KLM:	flights from Amsterdam, ℡ (20) 474 7747
Lufthansa:	flights from Frankfurt, ℡ (69) 255 255;
	flights from Dusseldorf, ℡ (211) 868 686

charter flights

These can be incredibly cheap, and offer the added advantage of departing from local airports. Companies such as **Thomson**, **Airtours** and **Unijet** offer return flights ranging from £130–220. This theoretically includes *basic* accommodation, but nobody expects you to make use of this facility. Some of the best deals have return dates limited strictly to one week or two; sometimes four, the maximum allowed under the regulations. In many cases a return charter ticket is a big saving over a one-way regular fare, even if your itinerary means you have to let the return-half lapse. Check it out at your local economy travel agent, bucket shop, or in your local paper; in London, also look in *Time Out*.

Get your ticket as early as possible, but be doubly sure of your plans, as there are no refunds for missed flights—most travel agencies sell insurance, so that you don't lose all your money if you become ill. Students and anyone under 26 have the additional option of special discount charters, departing from the UK, but make sure you have proof of student status. An STA Youth card costs £4; if you teach at a recognized educational institution, an STA Academic card is available for £6.

Discount and Youth Travel Specialists

| **STA Travel:** | 117 Euston Road, NW1 and 86 Old Brompton Road, SW7 are the main London centres, ℡ (071) 937 9921. |
| **Campus Travel:** | 52 Grosvenor Gardens, London SW1, ℡ (071) 730 3402. |

By Sea

The last sea link between Spain and the UK is the **Plymouth–Santander Ferry**, operated by Brittany Ferries. This is a good way to go if you mean to bring your car or bicycle. Prices for passengers are just a bit less than a charter flight; children of 4–13 go for half-price, under-4s free. Prices for vehicles vary on size and season—it's most expensive from 22 June–2 September; an adult without vehicle pays £44–73 one way, an adult with vehicle pays £122–217, depending on length and type of vehicle. In the high season, on-board accommodation goes from £5.50 for a simple Pullman seat, and £23 to share a four-berth cabin, to £110 for a deluxe twin-berth cabin. There are also 8-day return specials, where one adult plus car comes to £174–309. The 24-hour crossing is made twice a week. **Information**: contact your travel agent or Brittany Ferries in Plymouth, Millbay Docks, Plymouth PL1 3EW, ℡ (0752) 221321. In Santander the address is the Estación Marítima, ℡ (942) 21 45 00.

By Rail

From London to Andalucía takes at least a day and a half and requires a change of trains in Paris and Madrid or Barcelona. A two-month return, London–Madrid costs £163; London–Sevilla, £175. Students, those under 26 and holders of a Senior Citizen's Railcard can get reductions.

If you've been a resident in Europe for the past 6 months and are under 26, you can take advantage of the **InterRail Pass**, available at British Rail or any travel agents, giving you a month's rail travel for £249, as well as half-price discounts on Channel crossings and ferries to Morocco, where the pass is also valid. **Bookings**: rail tickets to Spain from England, or vice versa, can be obtained from British Rail International, Ticket and Information Office, PO Box 29, Victoria Station, London SW1V 1JX, ✆ (071) 834 2345. Take your passport. Tickets for local Spanish services can be obtained from certain UK travel agents, but bookings must be made weeks in advance. For *couchette* and sleeper reservations in France, contact French Railways, 179 Piccadilly, London W1, ✆ (071) 495 4433. If you're taking a car, ✆ (071) 409 3518. French Railways are also agents for the American EurRail pass.

By Bus or Coach

One major company, Eurolines, offers departures several times a week in the summer (once a week out of season) from London to Spain, along the east coast as far as Alicante, or to Algeciras via San Sebastián, Burgos, Madrid, Córdoba, Granada and Málaga. Buses take nearly two days to reach Algeciras, a couple of hours longer than the train. An adult single costs £64–85, a return £114–143. There are discounts for anyone under 26, senior citizens and children under 12. The national coach companies operate services that connect with the continental bus system. In the summer, the coach is the best bargain for anyone over 26; off-season you'll probably find a cheaper charter flight. **Information and booking**: Eurolines, 52 Grosvenor Gardens, London SW1, ✆ (071) 730 8235; National Express, ✆ (071) 730 0202; Caledonian Express, ✆ (041) 332 4100. Details of all UK–Spain bus services can be obtained from the Spanish Tourist Office in London.

By Car

From the UK via France you have a choice of routes. Ferries from Portsmouth cross to Cherbourg, Caen, Le Havre and St Malo. From any of these ports the most direct route takes you to Bordeaux, down the western coast of France to the border at Irún, and on to San Sebastián, Burgos and Madrid, from where you can choose your entry point into Andalucía. An alternative route is Paris to Perpignan, crossing the border at the Mediterranean side of the Pyrenees, then along the coast to Barcelona, where the E15 will take you south. Both routes take an average of two days' steady driving. You may find it more convenient and less tiring to try the ferry from Plymouth to Santander, which cuts out driving through France and saves expensive *autoroute* tolls. For the scenery, opt for one of the routes over the Pyrenees, through Puigcerdá or Somport-Canfranc or Andorra, but expect heavy traffic; if you're not in a hurry, take the classic route through Roncesvalles, Vall d'Arán, or through Tarbes and Aragnouet through the tunnel to Parzán.

Getting There from the US and Canada

By Air

There are numerous carriers that serve Spain. Most regular flights from the US or Canada are to Madrid or Barcelona. **Iberia**, the national airline, offers fly-drive deals and discounts: inquire about the 'Visit Spain' offer. From anywhere in the US, you can use Iberia's toll-free line, ✆ 800 772 4642.

Iberia Offices in the US and Canada

Florida:	Suite 1308, 150 South East Second Avenue, Miami, FL 33131, ✆ (305) 358 88
Illinois:	205 North Michigan Ave, Chicago, IL 60601, ✆ (312) 819 2900
Mass.:	20 Park Plaza, Boston, MA 02116, ✆ (617) 426 8335
New York:	509 Madison Ave, NY 10022, ✆ (212) 644 8843
Texas:	8111 LBJ Freeway, Suite 941, Dallas, TX 75251, ✆ (214) 669 3336
Washington:	1725 K. Street NW, DC 20006, ✆ (202) 293 6970
Ontario:	102 Bloor St West, Toronto, M5S IM8, ✆ (416) 964 6625
Quebec:	2020 University St, Montreal H3A 2A5, ✆ (514) 849 3352

Other Airlines with Direct Routes to Spain

American Airlines:	toll free ✆ 800 433 7300
Continental Airlines:	toll free ✆ 800 231 0856
TWA:	toll free ✆ 800 892 4141
United Airlines:	toll free ✆ 800 538 2929
Air Canada:	toll free ✆ 800 268 7240

Other Airlines with Routes Via Europe

British Airways :	toll free ✆ 800 247 9297
KLM:	toll free ✆ 800 777 5553
Lufthansa:	toll free ✆ 800 645 3880

| TAP: | toll free © 800 221 7370 |
| **Virgin Atlantic** | toll free © 800 862 8621 |

charter flights

These require a bit more perseverance to find, though you can save considerably on the cost of a regular or APEX flight—currently a charter from New York to Madrid varies between $400–700 depending on the season. You may want to weigh this against the current trans-atlantic fares to London, where in most cases you can get a low-cost flight to Spain departing within a day or two of your arrival. This is an especially cheap way to go in the off season. The Sunday *New York Times* has the most listings.

Some Major Charter Companies and Consolidators

Council Charters:	205 East 42nd Street, New York, NY 10017, toll free © 800 800 8222; uses Air Europa
DER:	toll free © 800 782 2424
Spanish Heritage Tours:	116–47 Queens Blvd, Forest Hills, NY 11375, © (718) 520 1300; uses Air Europa
TFI:	34 West 32nd Street, New York, NY 10001, © (212) 736 1140, toll free © 800 745 8000

By Rail

The American **EurRail Pass**, which must be purchased before you leave the States, is a good deal only if you plan to use the trains every day in Spain and else-where—though it's not valid in the UK, Morocco or countries outside the European Union. A month of travel is around $508 for those under 26; those over 26 can get a 15-day pass for $460, a 21-day pass for $598 or a month for $728. **Contact**: CIT Tours, 342 Madison Avenue, Suite 207, New York 10173, © (212) 697 2100, or toll free © 800 248 7245.

In Spain you'll have to pay supplements for any kind of express train and the EurRail pass is not valid on Spain's numerous narrow-gauge (FEVE) lines.

Special Interest Holidays

Andaluz cuisine

The region's centre for culinary research is housed in a charming renovated old mill on a river near Granada. There is a restaurant offering Andaluz, Moorish and Sephardic dishes, besides the cookery training centre and workshops, conducted in a very practical way. **Contact**: Centro Andaluz de Investigaciones Gastronómicas, Plaza del Carmen 2, 18009 Granada, © (958) 22 71 23.

flamenco

Albeit 'flamenco players are not born, they are made in heaven', you may nevertheless consider a course from the *maestro* himself, Paco Peña. The Peña home is in the Plaza del Potro, in the historic and picturesque centre of Córdoba. Students from as far as Japan and the USA come here for the lectures in classical guitar, flamenco dancing and flamenco guitar. **Contact**: Centro Flamenco Paco Peña, Plaza del Potro 15, 14002 Córdoba.

golf

There are more than 50 golf courses on the Costa del Sol. Most hotels cater specifically for the golfer and there are numerous specialist golf operators, some of which are listed below. Green fees are a touch expensive, starting at about 3,000 pts. **Contact**: the Royal Spanish Golf Federation, Calle Capitán Haya 9, Madrid, ✆ (91) 555 26 82 or 555 27 57.

language and arts

Courses generally last from 2–12 weeks, beginners to advanced. Course fees average 30,000 pts for 2 weeks; private tuition costs around 2,500 pts per hour. Accommodation can be arranged, whether boarding with families (50–70,000 pts per week) or sharing an apartment (20–26,000 pts per week). **Contact**, for more information and complete listings: the Instituto Cervantes, 102 Eaton Square, London SW1, ✆ (071) 235 1484.

Some Specialist Centres

Granada: Espalengua, Calle Nueva de Cartuja 24, 18012 Granada, ✆ (958) 20 77 82.

Escuela de Español de las Alpujarras, Calle Natalio Rivas 1, 18001 Granada. Language courses integrated with activities in the Alpujarras area, including cycling, hiking, horseriding, cooking and flamenco dancing.

Málaga: Instituto de Español Picasso, Plaza de la Merced 20, 29080 Málaga, ✆ (95) 221 3932.

Nerja: Escuela de Idiomas, Almirante Ferrandiz 73, 29780 Nerja, Málaga.

Sevilla: Hispalis Center, Instituto de Lenguas y Cultura Española, Amor de Dios 31–2, 41002 Sevilla.

outdoors

Benamonarda Cooperativa offers nature activity holidays in the Serrania de Ronda: hiking, cycling, horse trekking, photography. They also have complete programmes for children, starting at 3 years old. **Contact**: Benamonarda, Calle Postigo 66, 29492 Jubrique, Málaga; contact in UK, ✆ (0532) 686147.

In Andalucía there's a spa to cater to every complaint, from allergies to rheumatism.

Major Centres

Almería: Balneario San Nicolás, Ctra Almería–Granada, Km 18, 04400 Alhama de Almería, ✆ (950) 10 01 58.

Cádiz: Balneario Fuente Amarga, Avenida de Fuente Amarga s/n, 11130 Chiclana de la Frontera, ✆ (956) 40 05 20.

Granada : Balnearios Alhama de Granada, 18120 Alhama de Granada, ✆ (958) 35 00 11.

Jaén: Balneario de Marmolejo, Ctra Balneario s/n, 23770 Marmolejo, ✆ (953) 54 01 03 or 54 04 04.

Málaga: Balneario de Carratraca, Baños 1, 29551 Carratraca, ✆ (95) 245 80 20.

Specialist Operators

Abercrombie & Kent International, 1520 Kensington Road, Oak Brook, Illinois, IL 60521, toll free ✆ 800 323 7308, specializes in a wide range of up-market FIT holidays throughout Spain.

ACE Study Tours, Sawston Road, Babraham, Cambridge CB2 4AP, ✆ (0223) 835055, organizes art, architecture, archaeology and natural history tours, with accommo-dation, usually in three-star hotels or higher. A 10-day tour of Moorish Spain costs £790 per person and includes the services of a tour leader and entrance fees.

Andrew Brock Travel, 54 High Street East, Uppingham, Rutland LE15 9PZ ✆ (0572) 821 330. Walking holidays in southern Andalucía; accommodation in hotels and safari-style camps.

Arblaster & Clarke, 104 Church Road, Steep, Petersfield GU32 2DD, ✆ (0730) 266883, will be organizing wine tours throughout Andalucía from 1995.

Aventura, Apartado 21, Orgiva, Granada, ✆ (958) 78 52 53. Long distance riding holi-days in the Sierra Nevada. Groups of 8–10; accommodation in local inns along the way.

British Museum Tours Ltd, 46 Bloomsbury Street, London WC1B 3QQ, ✆ (071) 323 8895. An escorted tour of Islamic Spain, beginning in Granada and continuing through Ronda, Sevilla and Córdoba.

Cadogan Travel, 10 Portland Street, Southampton SO9 1ZP, ✆ (0703) 332661. Up-market inclusive holidays in four- and five-star hotels in Gibraltar, southern Spain and Morocco. Flights included; optional car rental.

Cortijo Romero, 24 Grange Avenue, Chapeltown, Leeds LS7 4EJ, ✆ (0532) 374 015. Personal and spiritual 'growth' vacations in Las Alpujarras: vegetarian meals are available and workshops for yoga, tai-chi, shiatsu and meditation. Course fees average £190 per week.

Cox & King's Travel Ltd, St James Court, 45 Buckingham Gate, London SW1E 6AF, ✆ (071) 873 5002. Natural history tours of the Parque Nacional del Coto de Doñana. It is also agent for the Al Andalus Expreso.

Explore Worldwide, 1 Frederick Street, Aldershot GU11 1LQ, ✆ (0252) 319448, do tours to the Sierra Nevada and Las Alpujarras and small escorted tours to Moorish Andalucía' which include walks in Parque Natural de Cazorla and visits to Sevilla, Córdoba and Granada.

Lessaggro Golfing Holidays, Calle Huertos 78, Nerja, Málaga, ✆ (95) 252 46 99, fax (95) 252 42 99.

Longshot Golf Holidays, Meon House, College House, Petersfield GU32 3JN, ✆ (0730) 268 621.

Magic of Spain, 227 Shepherds Bush Road, London W6 7AF, ✆ (081) 748 7575, which organizes touring, walking, painting and horse-riding holidays in Andalucía.

Marketing Ahead, 433 Fifth Avenue, New York, NY 10016, ✆ (212) 686 9213, specializes in *parador* holidays throughout Spain.

Mundi Color Holidays, 276 Vauxhall Bridge Road, London SW1V 1BE, ✆ (071) 828 6021, specializes in golfing holidays in the Costa del Sol.

Plantagenet Tours, 85 The Grove, Moordown, Bournemouth BH9 2TY, ✆ (0202) 521895, organizes an Isabelline tour of Medieval Andalucía during the Spring.

Unicorn Holidays, 2 Place Farm, Wheathampstead, Herts. AL4 8SB, ✆ (0582) 834400, specializes in tailor-made holidays to the *real* Spain, focusing on high quality character hotels and *parador* accommodation in particular.

Entry Formalities

Passports and Visas

There are no formal entry requirements for EU passport holders travelling to Spain, regardless of the purpose or duration of the visit. If you intend staying for more than 3 months, you must report to the Foreign Nationals Office (*Oficina de Extranjeros*) at the local police station and apply for a community resident's card (*tarjeta de residente comunitario*). If you fly to Gibraltar you'll have no trouble getting into Spain.

Holders of US or Canadian passports can enter Spain for up to 90 days without a visa; holders of Australian or New Zealand passports need a visa, available from any Spanish consulate.

For Gibraltar there are no extra visa requirements for US citizens, and EU nationals have the same rights and status as in the UK.

Spanish Consulates

Canada: 1 West Mount Square, 1456 Montreal, H3Z 2P9, ✆ (514) 935 5235
1200 Bay Street, Toronto, Ontario, M5R 2A5, ✆ (416) 967 4949

France: 165 Blvd Malesherbes, 75840 Paris, ✆ (1) 46 22 10 34

Germany: Lichtensteinallee 1, 1000 Berlin 30, ✆ (30) 261 60 81/2

Ireland: 17a Merlyn Park, Ballsbridge, Dublin 4, ✆ (1) 691 640

Italy: Via Campo Marzio 34, 00186 Roma, ✆ (6) 687 1401

Netherlands: Frederiksplein 34, 1017XN Amsterdam, ✆ (20) 620 3811

UK: 22–23 Manchester Square, London W1M 5AP (from May 1994,
20 Draycott Place, London SW3 2RZ), ✆ (071) 581 5921–5

1a Brooks House, 70 Spring Gardens, Manchester M22 2BQ, ✆ (061)
236 1233

63 North Castle Street, Edinburgh EH2 3LJ, ✆ (031) 220 1483

US: 545 Boylston Street, Boston, MA 02116, ✆ (617) 536 2506

180 North Michigan Avenue, Chicago, IL 60601, ✆ (312) 782 4588

1800 Berins Drive, Houston, TX 77057, ✆ (713) 783 6200

6300 Wilshire Blvd, Los Angeles, CA 90048, ✆ (305) 446 5511

2102 World Trade Centre, 2 Canal Street, New Orleans, LA 70130,
✆ (504) 525 4951

150 East 58th Street, New York, NY 10155, ✆ (212) 355 4090

2080 Jefferson Street, San Francisco, CA 94123, ✆ (415) 922 2995

2700 15th Street NW, Washington, DC 20009, ✆ (206) 265 0190

Customs

Customs are usually polite and easy to get through—unless you come in through Morocco, when they'll search through everything you own. EU limits of duty free are 1 litre spirits or 2 litres liquors (port, sherry or champagne) plus 2 litres wine and 200 cigarettes. Much larger quantites, bought locally and provided you are travelling between EU countries (up to 10 litres spirits, 90 litres wine, 110 litres beer), can be taken through customs if you can prove that they are for private consumption only. If coming from the UK or USA, don't bother to pick up any duty-free alcohol—it's cheaper on the supermarket shelves in Spain. It may be worth buying cigarettes if you are fussy about the flavour of your tobacco.

By Air

Internal flights in Spain are on Iberia, Aviaco, Viva and Binter. These are nationally run and all operate under the Iberia Group umbrella. In Andalucía you'll find airports in Almería, Córdoba, Granada, Jerez (Cádiz), Málaga, Sevilla, together with Melilla in North Africa.

Prices are inexpensive compared to most of Europe, and if you shop around and are willing to travel at night on slow days you can pick up some bargains, especially if you're going on a round trip. Also, check out the national charters in Spanish travel agencies.

Iberia Offices in Southern Spain

Almería:	Paseo de Almería 44, ℂ (950) 23 09 33
Córdoba:	Ronda de los Tejares 3, ℂ (957) 47 89 28
Granada:	Plaza Isabel la Católica 2, ℂ (958) 22 14 52
Jerez:	Plaza Reyes Católicos 2, ℂ (956) 34 40 54
Málaga:	Molina Lario 13, ℂ (95) 213 61 66/7
Sevilla:	Almirante Lobo 2, ℂ (95) 422 89 01
Gibraltar:	Commercial Centre, 24 Main Street, ℂ (350) 77 666

By Sea

The *Transmediterránea* line operates services from the Spanish mainland to the Balearic Islands, North Africa and the Canary Islands. **Agents:** Southern Ferries, 179 Piccadilly, London W1V 9DB, ℂ (071) 491 4968.

By Rail

Mister Traveler, take the Spanish Train!

RENFE brochure

If you're using public transportation, there is usually an even choice between the bus and train. The slight difference in price usually favours the train, while buses are usually a bit faster and run more frequently.

Democracy in Spain has made the trains run on time, but Western Europe's most eccentric railway, **RENFE**, still has a way to go. The problem isn't the trains themselves; they're almost always clean and comfortable, and do their best to keep to the schedules, but the new efficient RENFE remains so phenomenally complex it will foul up your plans at least once if you spend much time in Spain.

To start with, there are no fewer than 13 varieties of train, from the luxury **TEE** (Trans-Europe Express) to the excruciating *semidirecto* and *ferrobús*. Watch out for these; they stop at every conceivable hamlet to deliver mail. The best are the **Talgo** trains, speedy and stylish beasts in gleaming stainless steel, designed and built entirely in Spain; the Spaniards are very proud of them. **TER** trains are almost as good. Note that a majority of lines are still, incredibly, single-track, so whatever train you take, you'll still have to endure delays for trains coming the other way.

Every variety of train has different services and a different price. RENFE ticket people and conductors can't always get them straight, and confusion is rampant. Prices are never consistent. There are discounts for children (under 4 years old, free; 4–12 pay 50 per cent), large families, senior citizens (50 per cent) and regular travellers, and 25 per cent discounts on *Días Azules* ('blue days') for *round-trip tickets only*. 'Blue days' are posted in the RENFE calendars in every station—really almost every day is a 'blue day'. Interpretations of the rules for these discounts differ from one ticket-window to the next, and you may care to undertake protracted negotiations over them like the Spaniards do. There is a discount pass for people under 26, the *tarjeta joven*, and BIGE or BIJ youth fares are available from TIVE offices in the large cities.

Every city has a **RENFE travel office** in the centre (*see below*), and you can make good use of these for information and tickets. Always buy tickets in advance if you can; one of RENFE's little tricks is to close station ticket-windows 10 minutes before your train arrives, and if you show up at the last minute you could be out of luck. Other stations don't open the ticket-windows until the train is a couple of minutes away, causing panic and confusion. Don't rely on the list of trains posted; always ask at the station or travel office. There may well be an earlier train that makes an obscure connection. Fares average 500 pts for every 100km (63 miles)—750 pts first class—but there are supplements on the faster trains that can raise the price by as much as 80 per cent.

RENFE has plenty of services you'll never hear about—like car transport to all parts of Spain. If you plan to do a lot of riding on the rails, buy the *Guía RENFE*, an indispensable government publication with all the schedules, tariffs and information, available for a pittance from any station newsagent.

rail excursions

Southern Spain's answer to the famous *Transcantábrica* which operates in northwest Spain, is the *Al Andalus Expreso*, a luxury tour taking passengers from Sevilla to Córdoba, Granada, Málaga and Jerez. Although expensive, the trip is a memorable experience—the carriages are done out in fancy period decor and the cuisine is superb. The trip takes 4–5 days, depending on which 'cruise' you take.

Contacts for Al Andalus Expreso

Spain: Al Andalus Iberrail, Calle Capitán Haya 55, Madrid 28020, ✆ (91) 571 58 15

UK: Cox & King's Travel Ltd, St James Court, 45 Buckingham Gate, London SW1E 6AF, ✆ (071) 873 5002

US: Marketing Ahead, 433 Fifth Avenue, New York, NY 10016, ✆ (212) 686 9213

RENFE Offices

Almería:	Alcalde Muñoz 1, ✆ (950) 25 11 35
Cádiz:	Nuevo Edificio Estación, ✆ (956) 25 43 01
Córdoba:	Ronda de los Tejares 10, ✆ (957) 49 02 02
Granada:	Reyes Católicos 63, ✆ (958) 27 12 72
Huelva:	Vestíbulo Estación, ✆ (955) 24 66 66
Jaén:	Paseo Estación s/n, ✆ (953) 25 56 07
Málaga:	Strachan 2, ✆ (95) 236 02 02
Sevilla:	Zaragoza 29, ✆ (95) 441 41 11

By Car

This is probably the most pleasurable way of getting about, though the convenience is balanced by a considerably greater cost: petrol is as expensive in Spain as anywhere else in Europe, and unlike Italy, there are no petrol concessions or coupons for tourists. In cities, parking is always difficult; another problem is that only a few hotels—the more expensive ones—have garages or any sort of parking. Spain's highway network is adequate and in good repair. Signs along the carreteras (highways) indicate, in kilometres, the point you have reached along the route. Many major cities are now linked by dual carriageways. Government investment and Expo 92 resulted in numerous new roads and upgrading, particularly around Sevilla. Málaga also has a new by-pass, which considerably reduces congestion within the city and work is due to start on a Málaga–Nerja dual carriageway in 1994.

Once you venture off the beaten track, be prepared for a few surprises; some roads in Andalucía wind tortuously up mountainsides, with steep drops into gorges below. The N340 along the coast is much safer with the addition of frequent lane changing slip roads although don't mistake the highway for a motorway: it goes through towns; there are unexpected traffic lights; Spaniards tend to join the N340 at dangerously slow speeds before overtaking you minutes later; and then there are the occasional cyclists and joggers! Pay particular attention when driving on the notorious section between Málaga and Gibraltar, also known as 'mortuary mile'.

To drive in Spain you'll need a pink EU driving licence or an **International Driver's Permit** (IDP), available through the AA or RAC or any auto club in the US, and a **Green Card** proving limited liability insurance. In some parts of Spain, particularly away from the centres, local police may not recognize the EU driving licence so you are advised to take an IDP in any case. Though it's not compulsory, you are also advised to extend your motor insurance to include a bail bond. Should you be unfortunate enough to have an accident, without a bail bond your car will be impounded and you are just as likely to find yourself in jail for the night. Americans should not be intimidated by driving in Europe. Learn the international road-sign system (charts available to members from most auto clubs), brush up on your gear-stick shift technique, and get used to the idea of few signals, and traffic constantly converging from all directions. Seat belts are mandatory. The speed limit is 100km (62 miles) per hour on national highways, unless otherwise marked, and 120km (75 miles) per hour on motorways. Drive with the utmost care at all times—having an accident will bring you untold headaches, and to make matters worse, many Spaniards drive without insurance.

Hitchhiking is likely to involve a long, hot wait. Drivers in Andalucía are less inclined to give lifts and temperatures in midsummer can soar; few Spaniards ever hitchhike.

car hire

This is moderately cheaper than elsewhere in Europe. The big international companies are the most expensive but **ATESA**, the government-owned Spanish firm, is cheaper if you pre-book. Prices for the smallest cars begin at about £116–132 ($174–198) per week according to season, with unlimited mileage, insurance extra. Small local firms can sometimes offer a better deal, but these should be treated with some caution. On the Costa del Sol you may find some slightly better deals, but often with a stipulation that you limit your driving to the coastal region between Málaga and Algeciras. Local firms also rent **mopeds** and **bicycles**, especially in tourist areas. For the best deals you should make your car-hire arrangements before you leave the UK. Try Transhire, © (071) 978 1222; Holiday Autos, © (071) 491 1111; or Suncars, © (0444) 456446.

taxis

Taxis are still cheap enough for the Spaniards to use them regularly on their shopping trips. The average fare for a ride within a city will be 500–700 pts. Taxis are not always metered, but the drivers are usually quite honest; they are entitled to certain surcharges (for luggage, night or holiday trips, to the train or airport, etcetera), and if you cross the city limits they can usually charge double the fare shown. It's rarely hard to hail a cab from the street, and there will always be a few around the stations. If you get stuck where there are none, call information for the number of a radio taxi.

By Bus

With literally dozens of companies providing services over southern Spain, expect confusion. Not all cities have bus stations; in some there may be a dozen little offices spread around town for each firm. Buses, like the trains, are cheap by northern European standards, but still no bargain; if you're travelling on the cheap, you'll find that transportation is your biggest expense. Usually, whether you go by train or bus will depend on simple convenience: in some places the train station is far from the centre, in others the bus station is. Like the habit at some RENFE stations, tickets on the inter-city bus routes are sometimes sold at the last minute.

Small towns and villages can normally be reached by bus only through their provincial capitals. Buses are usually clean, dependable and comfortable, and there's plenty of room for baggage in the compartment underneath. On the more luxurious buses you even get air conditioning and a movie (*Rambo*, *Kung Fu*, sappy Spanish flicks from the Franco era or locally produced rock videos). **Tourist information offices** are the best sources for information.

city buses

Every Spanish city has a perfectly adequate system of public transportation. You won't need to make much use of it, though, for in almost every city all attractions are within walking distance of each other. City buses usually cost 85 pts or 100 pts, and if you intend to use them often there are books of tickets called *abonamientos* or *bono-Bus* or *tarjeta* cards to punch on entry, available at reduced rates from tobacco shops. Bus drivers will give change but don't give them a 1,000 pta note. In many cities, the bus's entire route will be displayed on the signs at each stop (*parada*).

Travellers with Disabilities

Facilities for disabled travellers are limited within Spain and public transport is not particularly wheelchair-friendly, though RENFE usually provides wheelchairs at main city stations. You are advised to contact the Spanish Tourist Office, which has compiled a two-page fact sheet and can give general information on accessible accommodation, or any of the organizations that specifically provide services to people with disabilities.

Some Specialist Organizations in Spain

ONCE (Organización Nacional de Ciegos de España), Paseo de la Castellana 95, Planta 28, Madrid, ✆ (91) 597 47 27, is the Spanish association for blind people.

ECOM, Balmes 311, Barcelona, ✆ (93) 200 19 80, the federation of private Spanish organizations offering services for disabled people. Ask for Emilio Grande who speaks good English.

Some Specialist Organizations in the UK

Holiday Care Service, 2 Old Bank Chambers, Station Road, Horley, Surrey RH6 9HW, ✆ (0293) 774535, for travel information and details of accessible accommodation and care holidays. All sites have been visited and assessed by Holiday Care representatives.

Mobility International, 8 Borough High Street, London SE1 1JX, ✆ (071) 403 5688, can offer some direct advice and runs seminars; it will certainly be able to put you in touch with specialist organizations in the UK or Spain,.

RADAR (The Royal Association for Disability and Rehabilitation), 25 Mortimer Street, London W1N 8AB, ✆ (071) 637 5400, has a wide range of travel information.

Royal National Institute for the Blind, 224 Great Portland Street, London W15 5TB, ✆ (071) 388 1266. Its mobility unit offers a 'Plane Easy' audio-cassette which advises blind people on travelling by plane. It will also advise on accommodation.

Triscope, The Courtyard, Evelyn Road, London W4 5JL, © (081) 994 9294 (also minicom), offers practical advice and information on every aspects of travel and transport for elderly and disabled travellers. On request, information can be provided by letter or tape.

Some Specialist Organizations in the US

American Foundation for the Blind, 15 West 16th Street, New York, NY 10011, © (212) 620 2000; toll free © 800 232 5463. The best source of information in the US for visually impaired travellers.

Federation of the Handicapped, 211 West 14th Street, New York, NY 10011, © (212) 747 4262. Organizes summer tours for members; there is a nominal annual fee.

Mobility International USA, PO Box 3551, Eugene, OR 97403, © (503) 343 1248, offers a service similar to that of its sister organization in the UK.

SATD (Society for the Advancement of Travel for the Disabled), Suite 610, 347 5th Avenue, New York, NY 10016, © (212) 447 7284, offers advice on all aspects of travel for the disabled, on an ad hoc basis for a $3 charge, or unlimited to members ($45, concessions $25).

Travel Information Center, Moss Rehabilitation Hospital, 1200 West Tabor Road, Philadelphia, PA 19141, © (215) 456 99 00.

Practical A–Z

The depressed property markets in northern Europe have predictably affected sales in southern Spain, and real bargains are to be found. A re-sale villa on the coast with two bedrooms can cost as little as £30,000, apartments considerably less. Buying property in Spain usually causes few serious problems, but there are some unpleasant and expensive exceptions, so inform yourself fully, and liaise constantly with your lawyer. For example, if you don't follow the correct legal procedures, you could end up with either no house or a demand for payment of back debts existing on the property. This happens when a developer sells off apartments to the public, pockets the cash and neglects to pay the outstanding building taxes to the local authorities. The developer then changes the name of his company and liquidates the old one, thereby *legally* avoiding payment. The tax authorities then come to the new owner, and ensure that the debt is paid by putting a lien on the property. This happens with surprising frequency. So, before you sign *anything,* get an English-speaking lawyer to do a 'search' on the property, a standard practice in other countries. This will show whether there are any outstanding debts or creditors waiting in the wings. (Unbelievably enough, this legal situation applies equally to cars—pending traffic and parking violations stay with the car, not the owner!) If your lawyer has done his homework, and all goes smoothly, the buyer and seller meet at the notary's office to sign the contract and hand over the loot. After that there is a wait of a couple of months before you receive the *escritura*, or title deeds; needless to say there are numerous administrative costs to cover, based on the sale price. In some cases, if the sale price is suspiciously low, costs will be worked out according to an assumed market value.

If buying an apartment or villa on an *urbanización*, you have to contribute to upkeep costs, pool maintenance, etcetera. This is done through an administrative *comunidad*, voted in by the owners. Once a year a general meeting is held to decide on a budget for the coming year. Annual costs for a two-bedroom apartment average around £700, including house and contents insurance.

A new law obliges non-residents to pay a wealth tax. Although not a very significant amount, it is designed to stop non-declaration of funds received by owners for real or theoretical holiday rentals in their absence. Now all property owners must obtain a fiscal number, or *NIE*, available from the foreigners department of the local police station. It is used to log all transactions, including the opening of a convertible current account at the bank, which allows you to deposit both pesetas and foreign currencies.

You and the Law in Spain, by David Baird, published by Lookout Publications, gives in-depth information and advice on all aspects of living (legally) in Spain.

Buying property in **Gibraltar** presents no special difficulties; you only need plenty of cash—house prices are on a par with those in England.

timeshares

In the coastal resorts of the Costa del Sol there lurks a demon that will pounce brazenly in broad daylight—the timeshare tout. This jeans-clad smile-toting charmer of the street has antennae for married couples of 20–65, out for a leisurely morning stroll. These unsuspecting innocents are bundled into taxis and taken off to 'resort clubs', from which many emerge elated with the free gifts of alcohol, bus trips or T-shirts, but thousands of pounds poorer.

The system works like this: the touts sweet-talk the eligible into a 'no obligation' guided tour of a resort development, with the dangled carrot of gifts or cash. The free taxi-ride delivers them into the claws of the waiting 'closers', guys who persuade the couple to part with a few thousand pounds (contract signed, on the spot) in exchange for two weeks a year, every year for the rest of their lives, in one of the resort's apartments. Whilst in theory the idea of timeshare must appeal to many, what most don't realize is the relatively enormous costs involved. Many timeshare owners, when they arrive back to move into 'their' apartment, find not only that they have been allocated quite a different one, but also that their yearly quota for maintenance fees is astronomical.

Children

Spaniards adore children, and they'll welcome yours almost everywhere. Baby foods, etc. are widely available, but don't expect to find babysitters except at the really smart hotels; Spaniards always take their children with them, even if they're up until 4am. Nor are there many special amusements for children, though these are beginning to spring up with Spain's new prosperity, for better or worse; traditionally Spaniards never thought of their children as separate little creatures who ought to be amused. Ask at a local tourist office for a list of attractions in its area geared towards children

Climate and When to Go

Andalucía is hot and sunny in the summer, brisk and sunny in the winter—in fact you can count on more sunshine here than anywhere else in Europe. The mild winters in coastal regions give way to pleasant, warm springs with minimal rainfall. Temperatures inland can be considerably lower, especially in the mountainous regions. Autumn weather can pack a few surprises: while normally warm and comfortable, recent years have seen torrential rains, causing landslides and extensive flooding. On the Atlantic coast, the *Levante* wind can make life uncomfortable, even in summer, when it will not only blow your beach umbrella away, but might even make you a bit kooky.

For comfort, spring and autumn are the best times to visit, by far; winter is generally pleasant on the Mediterranean coast, though damp and chilly inland. You'll probably feel more uncomfortable inside than out: Spanish homes—and hotel rooms—are not made for the winter.

The chart below shows the highest and lowest temperatures you're likely to encounter in each season. The Spanish care little for means, medians or averages, but they've always been fond of extremes.

	Jan		April		July		Oct	
	max	min	max	min	max	min	max	min
Sevilla	15(59)	6(43)	23(74)	11(52)	35(95)	21(69)	26(79)	14(58)
Málaga	17(63)	9(49)	21(70)	13(56)	29(84)	21(70)	23(74)	16(61)
Cádiz	15(59)	8(47)	21(70)	12(54)	29(84)	20(68)	23(74)	15(59)

average monthly rainfall in mm (ins.)

	Jan	April	July	Oct
Sevilla	99 (4)	80 (3)	0 (0)	37 (2)

climate in Gibraltar

Gibraltar's climate is of course Mediterranean, but appropriately enough it also manifests that most characteristic feature of British weather—cloud and rain. The moisture-laden *Levante* batters Gibraltar's shores and is forced up the sheer face of the rock, to condense in the lower temperatures at the top, forming a dense cloud that can be seen for miles, and in winter months letting fall a sometimes relentless shower on all beneath—pack your brolly.

Electricity

Current is 225 AC or 220 V, the same as most of Europe. Americans will need converters, and the British will need two-pin adapters for the different plugs. If you plan to stay in the less expensive *hostales*, it may be better to leave your gadgets at home. Some corners of Spain, even some big cities, have pockets of exotic voltage—150 V for example—guaranteeing a brief display of fireworks. Big hotels always have the standard current.

Embassies and Consulates

Australia:	Paseo de la Castellana 143, Madrid, ✆ (91) 279 85 04
Canada:	Núñez de Balboa 35, Madrid ✆ (91) 431 43 00
	Plaza de la Malagueta, Málaga, ✆ (95) 222 33 46
France:	Salustiano Olózaga 9, Madrid, ✆ (91) 435 55 60
Germany:	Fortuny 8, Madrid, ✆ (91) 319 91 00
Ireland:	Claudio Coelle 73, Madrid, ✆ (91) 576 35 00
Italy:	Joaquín Costa 29, Madrid, ✆ (91) 262 55 46
Netherlands:	Paseo de la Castellana 178, Madrid, ✆ (91) 359 09 14
New Zealand:	Go to either the British or the Australian embassy

UK:	Calle de Fernando el Santo 16, Madrid, ✆ (91) 319 02 00
	Plaza Nueva 8, Sevilla, ✆ (95) 422 88 75
	Edificio Duquesa, Calle Duquesa de Parcent 8, Málaga, ✆ (95) 221 75 71
	Avenida de las Fuerzas Armadas 11, Algeciras, ✆ (956) 66 16 00
	Gibraltar: (Vice Consulate) 65 Irish Town, ✆ (350) 78 305
US:	Calle Serrano 75, Madrid, ✆ (91) 577 40 00; consular office for passports, around the corner at Paseo de la Castellana 52
	Paseo de las Delicias 7, Sevilla, ✆ (95) 423 18 85
	Calle Martínez Catena, Portal 6, Apt 5B, Complejo Sol Playa, Fuengirola (Málaga), ✆ (95) 247 98 91

Festivals

One of the most spiritually deadening aspects of Francoism was the banning of many local and regional fiestas. These are now celebrated with gusto, and if you can arrange your itinerary to include one or two you'll be guaranteeing an unforgettable holiday. Besides those listed below, there are literally thousands of others, and new ones spring up all the time.

Many village patronal fiestas feature *romerías* (pilgrimages) up to a venerated shrine. Getting there is half the fun, with everyone in local costume, riding on horseback or driving covered wagons full of picnic supplies. Music, dancing, food, wine and fireworks are all necessary ingredients of a proper fiesta, while the bigger ones often include bullfights, funfairs, circuses and competitions. *Semana Santa* is a major tourist event, especially in Sevilla, but unless you're prepared to fight the crowds to see the *pasos* (ornate floats depicting scenes from the Passion) carried in an excruciating slow march to lugubrious tuba music, and accompanied by children and men decked out in costumes later copied by the Ku Klux Klan, you may want to skip it; the real revelry takes place after Easter.

Fiestas or *ferias* are incredibly important to Andalucíans, no matter what the cost in money and lost sleep; they are a celebration of being alive in a society constantly aware of the inevitability of death. There are festivities for every stratum of society—from the elite of Sevilla to the humble fieldworker.

Dates for most festivals tend to be fluid, flowing towards the nearest weekend; if the actual date falls on a Thursday or a Tuesday, Spaniards 'bridge' the fiesta with the weekend to create a four-day whoopee. Check dates at the tourist office in advance.

Spanish calendar

January

1–2   **Granada**: commemoration of the city's capture by the Catholic Kings.

5   **Málaga**: Epiphany parade of Los Reyes Magos.

February

mid-month   **Cádiz**: perhaps the best *carnival* in Spain and certainly the oldest, with parades, masquerades, music and fireworks in abundance.

March

Easter week   **Sevilla** sees the most important *Semana Santa*: celebrations, with over 100 processions, broken by the singing of *saetas* (weird laments). **Málaga**, **Granada** and **Úbeda** also put on major 'dos'.

April

last week   **Sevilla's** *Feria*, originally a horse-fair, now grown into the greatest festival of Andalucía. Costumed parades of the gentry in fine carriages, lots of flamenco, bullfights, and drinking.

                 Andújar (Jaén) hosts the *Romería de la Virgin de la Cabeza*, a pilgrimage from all over Andalucía which culminates in the procession to the sanctuary nearby in the Sierra Morena.

end of month   **Jerez** Horse Fair: equestrian events and sherry tasting.

May

1–2   **Navas de San Juan** (north of Úbeda): in honour of *Nuestra Señora de la Estrella*, one of the most important pilgrimages in the province of Jaén. During the night, the popular *mayos* are sung in front of the church.

first Friday   **Jaca** re-enacts the victory over the Moors by local women.

first week   **Jerez de la Frontera**, much like the *Feria* in Sevilla.

                 Granada: everyone dresses up and decorates the streets with carpets and flowers for the *Fiesta de la Santa Cruz*.

second week   **Córdoba**: every third year the *Concurso Nacional de Arte Flamenco* takes place, with 100 singers, guitar players and dancers.

Pentecost   **El Rocío** (Huelva): the biggest *romería* in Spain. Pilgrims converge on this tiny spot in Las Marismas, south of Sevilla, in gaily decorated wagons for a week of wild carrying-on. The religious aspect is secondary.

May (continued)

27–31   **Sanlúcar de Barrameda**: the *Manzanilla* wine fair. Vast quantities of fried fish and shellfish are consumed, helped down by equally copious amounts of *Manzanilla*; dancing, singing and sporting events.

end of month   **Zahara de la Sierra** (Cádiz) in particular sees four days of festivities begin on the Thursday after Trinity Sunday, celebrating *Corpus Christi.*

June

15   **Granada**: start of the month-long *Festival Internacional de Música y Danza,* which attracts some big names from around the world; classical music, jazz and ballet; also flamenco competitions in odd-numbered years.

second week   **Marbella**: *Feria de San Bernabé,* with big-name events.

23–26   **Alhaurín de la Torre** (Málaga): fair and festival in honour of the patron St John; entertainment includes a parade of giant figures and the *torre del cante,* one of the best flamenco gatherings in the region.

July

first Sunday   **Córdoba**: International Guitar Festival—classical, flamenco and Latino.

16   **Málaga**: *Virgen del Carmen*—decorated boats along waterfront with firework display.

last two weeks   **Lebrija**: flamenco festival.
     La Línea: summer fair.

end of month   **Almería**: festival, including jazz concerts.

August

3   **Huelva**: *Colombinas*—bullfights and other sporting events.

5   **Trevélez** (Granada) has a midnight pilgrimage up Mulhacén, Spain's highest mountain, so that pilgrims arrive exhausted but in time for prayers at midday.

first two weeks   **Ronda**: Pedro Romero festival—bullfights, equestrian parades and folk groups.

15   **Cómpeta** wine festival.

15–16   **Vejer** (Cádiz): Assumption of the Virgin and San Roque festivities, with flamenco.

mid-month   **Málaga**: its *feria* is gaining a reputation as one of the best in Europe, with a week of concerts, bullfights, dancing and singing in the streets of the old town.

last week   **Sanlúcar de Barrameda** (Cádiz): exaltation of the Río Guadalquivir and major flamenco events.
     Toro: *Fiesta de San Agustín,* with bulls and a 'fountain of wine'.

September

first week	**Jerez** has a *Vendimia* wine festival.
8	**Alájar** (Huelva) in particular, and many other places, celebrates The Virgin's Birthday. Far livelier and more popular than most pilgrimages; carriages and riders dressed in typical Andalucían costumes.
	Ronda, around this date, puts on an 18th-century-style bullfight in its historic ring.
second week	**Chipiona**: flamenco singing and dancing, running of the bulls, and bullfights.
turn of month	**Úbeda**: fair, stalls, and bullfights.

October

| 15–23 | **Jaén**: festival of St Luke, bullfights, cultural and sporting events. |
| second week | **Fuengirola**: *Feria del Rosario*. |

Gibraltar calendar

January 5	Three Kings Cavalcade.
April–June	Gibraltar Festival.
October 21	Trafalgar Day.
Nov/Dec	Drama Festival.

Food and Drink

Read an old guidebook to Spain, and when the author gets around to the local cooking, expressions like 'eggs in a sea of rancid oil' and 'mysterious pork parts' or 'suffered brain damage through garlic excess' pop up with alarming frequency. One traveller in the 18th century fell ill from a local concoction and was given a purge 'known on the comic stage as angelic water. On top of that followed four hundred catholic pills, and a few days later... they gave me *escordero* water, whose efficacy or devilry is of such double effect that the doctors call it ambidexter. From this I suffered agony.'

You'll fare better; in fact, the chances are you'll eat some of the tastiest food you've ever had at half the price you would have paid for it at home. The massive influx of tourists has had its effect on Spanish kitchens, but so has the Spaniards' own increased prosperity and, perhaps most significantly, the new federalism. Each region, each town even, has come to feel a new interest and pride in the things that set it apart, and food is definitely one of those; the best restaurants are almost always those that specialize in regional cooking.

Andaluz Cuisine

The greatest attraction of Andaluz cuisine is the use of simple, fresh ingredients. Seafood plays a big role, and marinated or fried fish is a speciality. (The traditional marinade, or *adobo*, is a mixture of water, vinegar, salt, garlic, paprika, cumin and marjoram.) Other specialities include the wholesome broth made with fish, tomato, pepper and paprika, and the famous cured hams of Jabugo and Trevélez. Almost everybody has heard of *gazpacho*; there are literally dozens of varieties, ranging from the *pimentón* of Antequera made with red peppers, to the thick Córdoban version, *salmorejo*. Olives, preserved in cumin, wild marjoram, rosemary, thyme, bay leaves, garlic, savoury fennel and vinegar are a treat, especially the plump green ones generally known as Sevilla olives.

In **Granada** an unappetizing mixture of brains, bulls' testicles, potatoes, peas and red peppers results in a very palatable *tortilla Sacromonte*; and many restaurants in the city work wonders with slices of beef *filete* or loin larded with pork fat and roasted with the juice from the meat and sherry. However, watch out for odd little dishes like *revoltillos*, whose name gives you a fair warning of what flavours to expect in this subtle dish of tripe, rolled and secured with the animal's intestines, mercifully lined with ham and mint.

The province of **Cádiz** takes the place of honour in Andaluz cuisine and some specialities to look out for are *cañailles* (sea snails), *pastel de pichones* (pigeon pâté), *calamares con habas* (squid with beans), *archoba* (a highly seasoned fish dish) or *bocas* (small crab).

Córdoba, too, has a fine culinary tradition, including dishes with a strong Arab and Jewish influence, like *calderetas*, lamb stew with almonds. But Córdoba is really the home of one of the most famous Andaluz dishes, *rabo de toro*, a spicy concoction of oxtail, onions and tomatoes. Try also the *buchón* (rolled fish filled with ham, dipped in bread-crumbs, then fried).

As one might expect, the **Sierras** offer dishes based on the game and wild herbs found in the mountains. Here freshwater lakes teem with trout, and on the slopes wild asparagus grows. The town of Jaén is particularly well known for its high-quality oil and vinegar, and delectable salads are a feature of most menus (try the *pipirrana*).

The **Costa del Sol's** traditional beachside delicacy is sardines, speared on a stick and cooked over a wood fire—best when eaten with a good salad and washed down with chilled white wine. *Boquerones* (fresh fried whitebait) feature widely in restaurants and tapas bars, along with *pijotas*, small hake that suffer the indignity of being sizzled with tail in mouth. All over the region you will find *pinchitos*, a spicier version of its Greek cousin the *souvlaki*, a mini-kebab of lamb or pork marinated in spices. To finish off your meal there are any number of desserts (*postres*) based on almonds and custards, and the Arab influence once again shows through, for example, the excellent sweetmeats from Granada and the *alfajores* from Huércal, Almería.

Ethnic Cuisine

The presence of 1.5 million foreign residents, mainly clustered along the southern coast, has had an effect on the Costa del Sol culinary scene, although Spanish restaurants still manage to hold their own. A bewildering choice of Indonesian, Belgian, Swedish, Chinese, French, Italian and numerous other nationalities' cuisines confront the tourist. The standard is in fact quite high in most 'ethnic' restaurants, and prices are reasonable because of the fierce competition. A host of British establishments (mostly pubs) offer the whole shebang: roast beef, Yorkshire pudding and three veg, apple pie and custard that would put your granny to shame, and all for under 850 pts.

eating out

Sticklers for absurd bureaucracy and measurement, the Spanish government rates **restaurants** by forks (this has become a bit of a joke—a car repair shop in Granada has rated itself two wrenches). The forks have nothing to do with the quality of the food, though they hint somewhat at the prices. Unless it's explicitly written on the bill (*la cuenta*), service is *not* included in the total, so tip accordingly.

Be careful, though. Spain still has plenty of bad restaurants. The worst offenders are often those with the little flags and 10-language menus in the most touristy areas. In general, rather than throw away your pesetas in these, you'd do better to buy some bread, Manchego cheese and a bottle of Valdepeñas red and have a picnic. If you dine where the locals do, you'll be assured of a good deal, if not necessarily a good meal. Almost every restaurant offers a *menú del día*, or a *menú turístico*, featuring an appetizer, a main course, dessert, bread and drink at a set price, always a certain percentage lower than if you had ordered the items *à la carte*. These are always posted outside the restaurant, in the window or on the plywood chef at the door; decide what you want before going in if it's a set-price menu, because these bargains are hardly ever listed on the menu the waiter gives you at the table.

One step down from a restaurant are **comedores** (literally, dining-rooms) often tacked on to the backs of bars, where the food and decor are usually drab but cheap, and **cafeterías**, usually those places that feature photographs of their offerings of *platos combinados* (combination plates) to eliminate any language problem. **Asadores** specialize in roast meat or fish; **marisqueras** serve only fish and shellfish—you'll usually see the sign for 'pescados y mariscos' on the awning. Keep an eye out for **ventas**, usually modest family-run establishments offering excellent *menús del día* for working people. They specialize in typical Andaluz dishes of roast kid or lamb, rabbit, *paella*, game (partridge crops up often) and many pork dishes, *chorizo* sausage and varieties of ham. Try and visit one on a Sunday lunchtime when all the Spanish families go out—with a bit of luck things may get out of hand, and guitars and castanets could appear from nowhere, in which case abandon all plans for the rest of the day.

If you're travelling on a budget, you may want to eat one of your meals a day at a **tapas bar** or *tasca*. Tapas means 'lids', since they started out as little saucers of goodies served on top of a drink. They have evolved over the years to become of the world's greatest snack cultures. Bars that specialize in them have platter after platter of delectable titbits—shellfish, slices of omelette, mushrooms baked in garlic, vegetables in vinaigrette, stews. All you have to do is pick out what looks best and order a *porción* (hors d'oeuvre), or a *ración* (big helping) if it looks really good. It's hard to generalize about prices, but on average 500 pts of *tapas* and wine or beer really fill you up. You can always save money in bars by standing up; sit at that charming table on the terrace and prices jump considerably.

Another advantage of tapas is that they're available at what most Americans or Britons would consider normal dining hours. Spaniards are notoriously late diners; 2pm is the earliest they would consider sitting down to their huge 'midday' meal, which can often turn into a marathon affair, then after work at 8pm a few tapas at the bar hold them over until supper at 10 or 11pm. After living in Spain for a few months this makes perfect sense, but it's exasperating to the average visitor. On the coasts, restaurants tend to open earlier to accommodate foreigners (some as early as 5pm) but you may as well do as the Spaniards do.

Prices in the guide are an average for two courses, without wine. Portions are usually so large that often a main course is more than enough. For menu and restaurant **vocabulary** *see* Language (pp. 239–42).

drink

No matter how much other costs have risen in Spain, **wine** (*vino*) has remained awesomely inexpensive by northern European or American standards; what's more, it's very good and there's enough variety from the regions for you to try something different every day. If you take an empty bottle into a *bodega*, you can usually bring it out filled with the wine that suits your palate that day. A *bodega* can be a bar, wine cellar or warehouse, and is worth a visit whatever its guise. If you want to learn how to discern a *fino* from an *amontillado*, go to one of the warehouse *bodegas* of Jerez where you can taste the sherry as you tour the site. While dining out, a restaurant's *vino del lugar* or *vino de la casa* is always your least expensive option; it usually comes out of a barrel or glass jug and may be a surprise either way. Some 20 Spanish wine regions bottle their products under strict controls imposed by the *Instituto Nacional de Denominaciones de Origen* (these almost always have the little maps of their various regions pasted on the back of the bottle). In many parts of Andalucía you may have difficulty ordering a simple bottle of white wine, as, on requesting *una botella de vino blanco de la casa*, you will often be served something resembling diluted sherry. To make things clear, specify a wine by name or by region—for example *una botella de Rioja blanco*—and the problem should be solved. Spain also produces its own champagne, known as *cava*, which is often just as good as the French, and notably cheaper.

Some Andaluz wines have achieved an international reputation for high quality. Best known is the *jerez*, or what we in English call **sherry**. When a Spaniard invites you to have a *copa* (glass) it will nearly always be filled with this Andalucían sunshine. It comes in a wide range of varieties: *manzanillas* are very dry, *fino* is dry, light and young (the famous *Tío Pepe*); *amontillados* are a bit sweeter and rich and originate from the slopes around Montilla in Córdoba province; *olorosos* are very sweet dessert sherries, and can be either brown, cream, or *amoroso*. The white wines of Córdoba grown in the Villaviciosa region are again making a name for themselves, after all but being wiped out by phylloxera in the last century. In Sevilla, wine is produced in three regions: Lebrija; Los Palacios (white table wines); and Aljarafe, where full-bodied wines are particular favourites. Jaén also has three wine-producing regions—take your bottle along to the local *bodega* when you are here, as many wines are on tap only. In Bailén, the white, rosé and red table wines resemble those of the more famous La Mancha vineyards. Torreperogil, east of Úbeda, produces clarets, but only a limited number are bottled. In the west of the province, Lopera white wines are also sold from the barrel. Málaga and Almería do not produce much wine, although the sweet, aromatic wines of Málaga are famous, especially the *Málaga Virgen*.

Many Spaniards prefer **beer** *(cerveza)*, which is also good, though not quite the bargain wine is. The most popular brands are *Cruzcampo* and *San Miguel*—most bars sell it cold in bottles or on tap; try *Mahón* Five Star if you see it. Imported whisky and other spirits are pretty inexpensive, though even cheaper are the versions Spain bottles itself, which may come close to your home favourites. Gin, believe it or not, is often drunk with Coca-Cola. Bacardi and Coke is a popular thirst-quencher; with a flourish worthy of a *matador* the barman will zap an ice-filled tumbler in front of you, and heave in a quadruple measure.

Coffee, tea, all the international soft-drink brands and *Kas,* the locally made orange drink, round out the average café fare. If you want tea with milk, say so when you order, otherwise it will probably arrive with a piece of lemon. Coffee comes with milk (*café con leche*) or without (*café solo*). Spanish coffee is good and strong, and if you want a lot of it order a *doble* in a *vaso*; one of those will keep you awake even through the guided tour of any museum.

food and drink in Gibraltar

This doesn't just mean sausage, chips and beans, though there are plenty of establishments serving such honest fare. Restaurants have become more competitive and people more selective, to the extent that you can find some excellent varieties of southern Mediterranean dishes in particular, some French classics and a healthy choice of many other nations' cuisines, at prices admittedly higher than in southern Spain, but lower than the average in other European countries. Pub grub can be good, too, but beware the fast-food alternatives unless your pockets are empty and your taste buds dead.

You can drink to your heart's delight in Gibraltar, but your liver may be happy to know that costs are about double the Spanish equivalent. Pub opening times follow Britain—open all day till 11pm; wines and spirits are cheap in the supermarkets and off-licences, but no bargain in restaurants or pubs.

Homosexuality was made legal in Spain in 1978. Since then, Spanish gays and lesbians have established a confident and communicative network, which should be relatively easy to tap into. The largest gay communities in Andalucía are in Cádiz and Torremolinos. Condoms are widely available from *farmacias* and less widely from vending machines. The age of consent is 12.

The gay guide to Spain, *Spartacus España* (Bruno Gmünder) is stocked by most good bookshops in the UK, and in the US by Giovanni's Room, 1145 Pine Street, Philadelphia, PA 19107, © (215) 923 2960.

Geography

Andalucía covers the southern fifth of the Iberian Peninsula, occupying an area slightly more than half of Portugal. Its natural border to the north is the rugged Sierra Morena mountain chain; the wild Atlantic batters its western shores and the timid Mediterranean laps its southern coast. The Sierra Morena mountains, although reaching barely 4,000ft, were for a long time a deterrent to northern invaders. The only natural interruption is the Pass of Despeñaperros, or the 'gateway to Andalucía'. Numerous early travellers spoke with awe of the first time they traversed this pine-clad gorge; the frontier that separated 'the land of men from the land of gods'. Arriving in Andalucía at this point provides a strong contrast indeed from the barren plains of La Mancha to the north. These peaks, rich in minerals, sweep down to the fertile Guadalquivir plain, widening as it proceeds to the western coast to form broad salt marshes and mud flats—including the Coto de Doñana National Park, one of the largest bird sanctuaries in Europe. From here, the coast as far as the Portuguese border is virtually one long sandy beach, its hinterland undulating farming terrain and the gentle mountains of Huelva province. South of the Guadalquivir valley the land rises again to form the craggy, spectacular Serranía de Ronda mountain range, home to bandits and smugglers for centuries; the terrain then descends sharply to meet the balmy palm-lined shores of the Mediterranean, with Tarifa, the furthest south you can go on mainland Europe, and Gibraltar, that geological oddity of a rock, whose outline resembles one of the sentinel lions on guard at the foot of Nelson's column. From the Serranía de Ronda the land dips and rises as it goes east till it joins the heights of the snow-capped Sierra Nevada, the highest peaks on mainland Spain, below which lie long beaches, tiny coves and crystal-clear water.

Dry as it is, Andalucía when properly tended has been the garden of Spain. The soil in most areas, *argiles de montmorillionite*, holds water like a sponge. The Romans first discovered how to irrigate it; the Moors perfected the system, and also introduced the palm and such crops as cotton, rice, oranges and sugar. Today most of the inhabitants of the region live in cities—it's traditionally one of the most urbanized regions in Europe—but its farmers have discovered the modern delights of tractors and of owning their own land. Unless the Hapsburgs or the Francoists come back, the region will have no excuse for not making a good living. Between the towns, spaces seem vast and empty, endless hillsides of olives, vineyards, wheat and sunflowers. Come in the spring, when the almond trees are in blossom, the oranges turn orange and wild flowers surge up along the road-sides—the unforgettable splash of colour that characterizes cheerful Andalucía and its warm, vibrant people.

Health and Insurance

There is now the standard agreement for citizens of EU countries, entitling them to a certain amount of free medical care, but it's not straightforward. You must complete all the necessary paperwork before you go to Spain, and allow a couple of months to make sure it comes through in time. Ask for a leaflet entitled *Before You Go* from the Department of Health and fill out form E111, which on arrival in Spain you must take to the local office of the *Instituto Nacional de Seguridad Social* (INSS), where you'll be issued with a Spanish medical card and some vouchers enabling you to claim free treatment from an INSS doctor. At time of writing, the government is trying to implement a much easier system. If you have a particular diet or need special treatment then obtain a letter from your doctor and get it translated into Spanish before you go. In an emergency, ask to be taken to the nearest *hospital de la seguridad social*. Before resorting to a *médico* (doctor) and his £20 ($30) fee (ask at the tourist office for a list of English-speaking doctors), go to a pharmacy and tell them your woes. Spanish *farmacéuticos* are highly skilled, and if there's a prescription medicine that you know will cure you, they'll often supply it without a doctor's note. (*El País* and the other national newspapers list *farmacias* in large cities that stay open all night.)

No inoculations are required to enter Spain, though it never hurts to check that your tetanus jab is up to date, as well as some of the more exotic inoculations (typhoid and cholera) if you want to venture on into Morocco. The tap water is safe to drink in Spain, but at the slightest twinge of queasiness, switch to the bottled stuff.

insurance

You may want to consider travel insurance, available through most travel agents. For a small monthly charge, not only is your health insured, but your bags and money as well. Some will even refund a missed charter flight if you're too ill to catch it. Be sure to save all doctor's receipts (you'll have to pay in cash on the spot), pharmacy receipts, and police documents (if you're reporting a theft).

Left Luggage

Since terrorists stopped leaving bombs in rail stations, RENFE has started to reintroduce *consignas*, or left-luggage facilities; you'll have about an even chance of finding one in a bus station or small bus company office, and sometimes bars near train or bus stations are willing to let you leave your bags.

Media

The Socialist *El País* is Spain's biggest and best national **newspaper**, though circulation is painfully low at under 400,000; Spaniards just don't read newspapers (the little magazine

Teleprograma, with television listings is by far and away the best-selling periodical). *El País* has the best regional **film** listings, indicating where you can see some great films subtitled instead of dubbed (look out for *versión original* or its abbreviation 'vo'). English films are occasionally shown on the Costa del Sol and dozens of shops rent English-language video releases. Films are cheap and Spaniards are great cinema-goers; there are lots of inexpensive outdoor movie theatres in the summer. Look for new films by Carlos Saura (*Carmen, Blood Wedding, El Dorado*), who is regarded as Buñuel's natural successor, or Victor Erice, or, most incredibly, Marx Brothers movies dubbed in Spanish The bright new light is Pedro Almódovar (*Women on the Verge of a Nervous Breakdown*).

The other big papers are *Diario 16* (centrist), *ABC* (conservative, in a bizarre 60s magazine format), and the *Alcázar* (neo-fascist). Major British papers are available in all tourist areas and big cities; the American *Herald Tribune*, the *Wall Street Journal*, and the awful *USA Today* are readily available where Americans go. Most hit the newsstands a day late; issues of *Time* and *Newsweek* often hang about until they find a home. There are also publications in English on the Costa del Sol, notably *Sur in English*, a translation of a Málaga paper with general items of news; *Lookout*, a glossy monthly general consumer magazine; *The Entertainer*, for local news, events and classified ads; and the *Marbella Times*, another slick mag for expats.

All British newspapers are flown daily to **Gibraltar**.

Money

Spanish **currency** comes in notes of 1,000, 2,000, 5,000, 10,000 *pesetas* (pts), all in different colours, and coins of 1, 5, 10 , 25, 50, 100, 200 and 500 pts. Don't be surprised to see Generalísimo Franco's scowling mug staring at you from the older coins—but do watch out for the old, ornately decorated notes larger than the standard size. These went out of use in 1986. At street markets, and in out-of-the-way places, you may hear prices given in *duros* or *notas*. A *duro* is a 5-pta piece, and a *nota* is a 100-pta note.

Exchange rates vary, but until any drastic changes occur £1 is 200 pts, and $1 equivalent to 135 pts. Think of 100 pts as about 50p or 75 cents—so those green 1,000-pta notes, the most common, are worth about £5.00 or $7.50. Spain's city centres seem to have a bank on every street corner, and most of them will exchange money; look for the *cambio* or *exchange* signs and the little flags. There is a slight difference in the rates, though usually not enough to make shopping around worth while. Beware of exchange offices as they can sometimes charge a hefty commission on all transactions. You can often change money at travel agencies, fancy hotels, restaurants or the big department stores. There are 24-hour *cambios* at the big train stations in Barcelona and Madrid. A Eurocheque card will make your British bank cheques good, though it may not be easy. **Traveller's cheques**, if they are from one of the major companies, will pass at most bank exchanges. Wiring money from overseas entails no special difficulties; just give yourself two weeks to be on the safe side, and work through one of the larger institutions (Banco Central, Banco de Bilbao, Banco Español de Crédito, Banco Hispano Americano, Banco de Santander, Banco de Vizcaya). All transactions have to go through Madrid.

Plastic money will not necessarily be helpful unless you rent cars, fly a lot, or patronize the most expensive hotels and restaurants. Nevertheless, major credit cards are recognized, so do take them along as they can be lifesavers in emergencies. Direct debit cards are also useful ways of obtaining money, though you should check with your bank before leaving to ensure your card can be used in Spain. But do not rely on a hole-in-the-wall machine as your only source of cash; if, for whatever reason, the machine swallows your card, it usually takes 10 days to retrieve it.

money in Gibraltar

In Gibraltar you can use local currency, UK sterling or pesetas, though you'll lose considerably on the exchange rate with pesetas. Spanish banks in Gibraltar tend to give a better rate of exchange from sterling to pesetas.

Opening Hours

banks

Most banks are open Mon–Thurs 8.30–4.30, Fri 8.30–2 and Sat (sometimes) 8.30–1.

churches

Most of the less important churches are always closed. Some cities probably have more churches than faithful communicants, and many are unused. If you're determined to see one, it will never be hard to find the *sacristán* or caretaker. Usually they live close by, and would be glad to show you around for a tip. Don't be surprised when cathedrals and famous churches charge for admission—just consider the costs of upkeep.

shops and museums

Shops usually open from 9.30am. Spaniards take their main meal at 2pm, and except in the larger cities most shops shut down for 2–3 hours in the afternoon, usually from 1pm or 2pm. In the south, where it's hotter, the siesta can last from 1pm to 5pm. In the evening most establishments stay open until 7pm or 8pm.

Museums and historical sites tend to follow shop opening hours too, though abbreviated in the winter months; nearly all close on Mondays. We have tried to list the hours for the important sights. Seldom-visited ones have a raffish disregard for their official hours, or open only when the mood strikes them. Don't be discouraged: bang on doors and ask around. We haven't bothered to list admission prices for all museums and sites; usually the sum is trivial—hardly anything will cost more than 250 pts, usually much less. The Alhambra in Granada, La Mezquita in Córdoba and La Giralda in Sevilla, all at 600 pts, are the most notable exceptions.

opening hours in Gibraltar

Shops in Gibraltar are generally open 9–7 on weekdays, and 9–1 on Saturdays; banks are open 9–3.30 weekdays only.

The Spaniards, like the Italians, try to have as many public holidays as possible. And everything closes. The big holidays, celebrated throughout Spain, are *Corpus Christi* in late May, *Semana Santa* during the week before Easter, the *Asunción* on 15 August and *Día de Santiago* on 25 July, celebrating Spain's patron, Saint James. No matter where you are there are bound to be fireworks or processions on these dates, especially for *Semana Santa* and *Corpus Christi*. But be aware that every region, town, and village has at least one of its own holidays as well (*see* Festivals above).

National Holidays in Spain

1 Jan:	Año Nuevo (New Year's Day)
6 Jan:	Epifanía (Epiphany)
March:	Viernes Santo (Good Friday)
1 May:	Día del Trabajo (Labour Day)
May/June:	Corpus Christi
25 July:	Día de Santiago (St James' Day)
15 Aug:	Asunción (Assumption)
12 Oct:	Día de la Hispanidad (Columbus Day)
1 Nov:	Todos los Santos (All Saints' Day)
6 Dec:	Día de Constitución (Constitution Day)
8 Dec:	Inmaculada Concepción (Immaculate Conception)
25 Dec:	Navidad (Christmas Day)

National Holidays in Gibraltar

1 Jan:	New Year's Day
mid-March:	Commonwealth Day
March:	Good Friday and Easter Monday
1 May:	May Day
May:	Spring Bank Holiday (last Monday of month)
mid-June:	Queen's Birthday
Aug:	August Bank Holiday (last Monday of month)
12 Sept:	Gibraltar Day
25–26 Dec:	Christmas Day and Boxing Day

Photography

Film is quite expensive everywhere; so is developing, but in any city there will be plenty of places—many in optician's shops (ópticas) or big department stores—where you can get processing done in a hurry. Serious photographers must give some consideration to the strong sunlight and high reflectivity of surfaces (pavements and buildings) in towns. If you're there during the summer use ASA100 film.

Police Business

Crime is not really a big problem in Spain and Spaniards talk about it perhaps more than is warranted. Pickpocketing and robbing parked cars are the specialities; in Sevilla they like to take the whole car. The big cities are the places where you should be careful, especially Málaga and Sevilla. Crime is also spreading to the tourist areas, particularly the Costa del Sol. Even on the Costa, though, you're probably safer in Spain than you would be at home: the crime rate is roughly a quarter of that in Britain. Note that in Spain less than 8 grams of reefer is legal; anything else may easily earn you the traditional 'six years and a day'.

There are several species of **police**, and their authority varies with the area. Franco's old goon squads, the Policía Armada, have been reformed and relatively demilitarized into the *Policía Nacional*, whom the Spaniards call 'chocolate drops' for their brown uniforms; their duties largely consist of driving around in cars and drinking coffee. They are, however, more highly thought of than the Policía Armada, and their popularity increased when their commander, Lt General José Antonio Saenz de Santa María, ordered his men to surround the Cortes to foil Tejero's attempted coup in 1981, thereby proving that he and his *Policía Nacional* were strongly on the side of the newly born democracy.

The *Policía Municipal* in some towns do crime control, while in others they are limited to directing traffic. Mostly in rural areas, there's the *Guardia Civil*, with green uniforms, but no longer do they don the black patent-leather tricorn hats. The 'poison dwarfs of Spain', as Laurie Lee called them, may well be one of the most efficient police forces in the world, but after a century and a half of upholding a sick social order in the volatile countryside, they have few friends. They too are being reformed; now they're most conspicuous as a highway patrol, assisting motorists and handing out tickets (ignoring 'no passing' zones is the best way to get one). Most traffic violations are payable on the spot; the traffic cops have a reputation for upright honesty.

police business in Gibraltar

Gibraltar has no serious crime to speak of, and given its military status, security is very tight. Gibraltarians like to forget the incident in which members of the armed forces shot dead suspected IRA terrorists in the late 80s.

Post Offices

Every city, regardless of size, seems to have one post office (correos) and no more. It will always be crowded, but unless you have packages to mail, you may not need ever to visit one. Most tobacconists sell stamps (*sellos*) and they'll usually know the correct postage for whatever you're sending. The standard charge for sending a letter is 45 pts (European Union) and 90 pts (North America). Send everything air mail (*por avión*) and don't send postcards unless you don't care when they arrive. Mailboxes are bright yellow and scarce. The post offices also handle telegrams, which normally take 4 hours to arrive within Europe but are very expensive—a one-word message plus address costs around 2,000 pts. There is also, of course, the poste restante (general delivery). In Spain this is called *lista de correos*, and it is as chancy as anywhere else. Don't confuse post offices with the Caja Postal, the postal savings banks, which look just like them.

Gibraltar

Post Offices in Gibraltar are open 9.30–6, and mail sent from here arrives much faster than from Spain.

Shopping

There are some delightful tacky tourist wares—Toledo 'daggers', plastic bulls and flamenco dolls ad nauseam. There are also some excellent buys of quality items like **leather**, most notably from Córdoba and the town of Ubrique, which has been producing leather-work since Roman times. Moorish craftsmen later had a major influence on the method of treating the cured skin for export. While Córdoba is better known for its ornate embossed leather for furniture decoration and **filigree jewellery**, Ubrique specializes in handmade items such as diaries, suitcases, bags and wallets. If you want an everlasting memory of Andalucía, have your boots made to measure in Valverde del Camino, Huelva province—guaranteed to last a lifetime. **Ceramic** plates, pottery and colourful *azulejo* tiles are made all over Andalucía; the quality varies enormously, from the shoddy factory-made products adorning tourist shop shelves, to the sophisticated ceramic ware of Sevilla. Granada is well known for its **inlaid wood** *taracea* work (chests, chessboards and music boxes). Spanish **woven goods** are reasonably priced; Sevilla produces exquisite *mantillas* and embroidered shawls, and is the centre for the extraordinary designs that adorn the bullfighter's costume. In the Alpujarras a concentrated effort is being made to revive old skills, using the wooden loom particularly, to produce the typical **woollen blankets** and **rugs** which this area had long been known for—a fascinating mixture of ancient Christian and Arab designs. Brightly coloured handwoven blankets are the claim to fame of Grazalema, a village less than 20km to the west of Ronda. In the province of Almería, the village of Níjar produces colourful *jarapas*—woven blankets and mats.

To encourage the nation's craftsmen, the government has organized a kind of cooperative, *Artespaña*, with various outlets selling their work. In Andalucía these can be found at Rodríguez Jurado 4, Sevilla; Corral del Carbón, Granada; and Ricardo Soriano 54, Marbella.

The major **department store** chains in Spain, El Corte Inglés and Galerías Preciados, often have good selections of crafts. All of the above will ship items home for you. You can also get some good buys at the **weekly markets** where Spaniards do a good deal of their shopping. Local tourist offices will have details. Good-quality **antiques** aren't the great finds they once were—Spaniards have learned what they're worth and charge accordingly. Guitars, mandolins and bagpipes, fine wooden furniture and Goya tapestries are some of the bulky, more expensive items you'd like shipped home. EU citizens are not entitled to tax refunds.

Sports and Activities

Bars and cafés collect much of the Spaniards' leisure time. They are wonderful institutions, where you can eat breakfast or linger over a glass of beer until 4 in the morning; in any of them you could see an old sailor delicately sipping his camomile tea next to a young mother, baby under her arm, stopping in for a beer break during her shopping. Some have music—jazz, rock or flamenco; some have great snacks, or tapas, some have games or pinball machines. Every Spaniard is a gambler; there seem to be an infinite number of lotteries run by the State (the *Lotería Deportiva*), for the blind (ONCE), the Red Cross, or the church, and there are casinos in all major resorts. Every bar has at least one slot machine, doling out electronic versions of *La Cucaracha* whenever it gets lonely.

Discos, night clubs, etc. are easily found in the big cities and tourist spots; most tend to be expensive. Ask around for the current favourites. Watch out for posters for **concerts, ballets**, and especially for **circuses**. The little travelling Spanish troupes with their family acts, tents, tinsel and names like 'The National Circus of Japan' will charm you; they often gravitate to the major fiestas throughout the summer.

Football has pride of place in the Spanish heart, and **bullfighting** (*see* Topics, p. 62) and cycling vie for second place; all are regularly shown on television, which, despite a heavy fare of dubbed American shows, everyone is inordinately fond of watching. Both channels are state-run, but with satellite dishes outnumbering *bodegas*, who watches them anyway? Certainly not the expat coastal residents, who tune in to BSkyB, Super-Channel and even the spectacularly tedious Gibraltar TV network.

cricket and rugby

Where there are concentrations of British residents, cricket has taken root and rugby enthusiasts are predictably asked to call some bar or other for information on their sport; try the Micadela Bar, Calle Camilo José Cela 4, Marbella, © (95) 282 92 95 (ask for Danny).

cycling

Cycling is taken extremely seriously in Spain and you don't often see people using a bike as a form of transport. Instead, Lycra-clad enthusiasts pedal furiously up the steepest of hills, no doubt trying to reach the standards set by Miguel Indurain, the Spanish winner of the *Tour de France* for three years running. If you do want to bring your own **bicycle** to Spain, you can make arrangements by ferry or train; by air, you'll almost always have to dismantle it to some extent and pack it in some kind of crate. Each airline seems to have its own policy. The south of Spain would be suicide to bike through in summer, though all right in winter. **Information**: call the Cycling Federation of Andalucía; in Jerez, © (956) 34 88 12; in Fuengirola, © (95) 247 70 75; in Nerja © (95) 252 43 97.

fishing and hunting

Fishing and hunting are long-standing Spanish obsessions, and you'll need to get a licence for both. Freshwater fishing permits (*permiso de pesca*) are issued on a fortnightly basis from the municipal ICONA office, or from the Jefatura Provincial del ICONA, Licencia Nacional de Caza y Pesca, Jorge Juan 39, Madrid, ✆ (91) 225 59 85. **Information:** for a list of the best trout streams (there are many), write to the Spanish Fishing Federation, Navas de Tolosa 3, 28013 Madrid, ✆ (91) 532 83 52; or to the Instituto Andaluz de Reforma Agraria de la Junta de Andalucía, Avenida República Argentina 25, Sevilla, ✆ (95) 427 00 73.

Deep-sea fishermen need to obtain a 5-year licence from the provincial Comandancias de Marina. **Information** on the best fishing waters and boat rentals can be obtained from the Directorate General of Sea Fishing, Subsecretaria de la Marina Mercante, Ministerio de Comercio, Calle Ruiz de Alarcón 1, Madrid.

You may bring sporting guns to Spain, but you must declare them on arrival and present a valid firearms certificate with a Spanish translation bearing a consulate stamp. Hunters (boar and deer are the big game, with quail, hare, partridges and pigeons, and ducks and geese along the coasts in the winter) are obliged to get a licence as well (*permiso de caza*) from the local autonomous community, presenting their passports and record of insurance coverage. **Information:** the Spanish tourist office, or the Spanish Hunting Federation, Avenida Reina Victoria 72, 28003 Madrid, ✆ (91) 253 90 17.

football

Soccer is the most popular sport throughout Spain, and the Spaniards play it well: FC Barcelona and Real Madrid are the best teams to watch; fans of Sevilla FC and Real Betis will each argue that their team is the best in Andalucía. The season lasts from September to June, and matches are usually trouble free. **Information:** Spanish Football Federation, Alberto Bosch 13, 28014 Madrid, ✆ (91) 420 33 21; fax (91) 420 20 94.

golf

English settlers built Spain's first golf course at the Rio Tinto mines in the 19th century, and since the advent of Severiano Ballesteros Spaniards too have gone nuts for the game. The sunny warm winters, combined with greens of international tournament standard, attract golfing enthusiasts from all over the world throughout the year. Any real-estate agent on the coast hoping to sell villas to foreigners, especially Scandinavians and the latest newcomers, the Japanese, stands little chance of closing a deal unless his property is within 10 minutes of a golf course. It's a rage in the Costa del Sol that's unlikely to diminish now that the 1997 **Ryder Cup** is to be held in Andalucía. By 1995 there will be 40 golf courses in the Málaga region; the Marbella area alone boasts over two dozen fine courses, some so exclusive that if you manage to get in you could find yourself teeing off next to Sean Connery. On the other hand, there is an abundance of humbler clubs where a mere 3,000 pts will get you a round. Most places hire out clubs. Inland you'll find courses around the big cities and, at the last count, there were 56 courses along the

Costa del Sol, over a third of all golf courses in Spain. Many hotels cater specifically for the golfer and there are numerous specialist tour operators (some are listed on p. 9). **Information**: the Spanish tourist office, or the Royal Spanish Golf Federation, Capitán Haya 9–5, 28020 Madrid, © (91) 555 27 57.

hiking and mountaineering

Spain's sierras attract thousands of hikers and mountaineers. There are paths in the Sierra Nevada above Granada and the Serranía de Ronda. The tourist office or the Spanish Mountaineering Federation provide a list of *refugios*, which offer mountain shelter in many places. Some are well equipped and can supply food. Most, however, do not, so take your own sleeping bags, cooking equipment and food with you. Hiking boots are essential, as is a detailed map of the area, issued by the Instituto Geográfico Nacional, or the Servicio Geográfico Ejército (*see* Maps, p. 41). **Information**: Spanish Mountaineering Federation, Alberto Aguilera 3, 28015 Madrid, © (91) 445 13 82.

horse racing

Horse racing is centred in Madrid, but there is a winter season at the Pineda racecourse in Sevilla. **Information**: Spanish Horse Racing Federation, Calle Montesquinza 8, 28010 Madrid, © (91) 319 02 32

horse riding

Andalucía has some perfect terrain for horse riding, whether exploring the Serranía de Ronda, the smugglers' trails around Cádiz, or following in the hoofprints of Sir John Betjeman's wife, Penelope Chetwode, who experienced one bosom-heaving emotion after another as she trekked boldly through the Sierra Nevada on horseback in the 1960s, an odyssey so delightfully recorded in her journal *Two Middle Aged Ladies in Andalucía*. There are a number of stables offering organized treks. **Information**: Caminos and Caballos, Duque de Liria 3, Madrid, © (91) 242 31 25.

pelota

Pelota, although a Basque game by origin, has a following in Andalucía. This is a fast, thrilling game, where contestants wearing long basket-like gloves propel a hard ball with great force at high walls; rather like squash. The fast action on the *jai-alai* court is matched by the wagering frenzy of the spectators.

skiing

Many of the mountains popular with hikers and mountaineers at other times of the year attract ski crowds in the winter. An hour from Granada you can be among the Iberian Peninsula's highest peaks and Europe's southernmost ski resorts, whose après-ski life can rival anything in the Alps. The Sierra Nevada will host the **World Alpine Ski Championships** in 1995. In preparation for this, new roads are being laid and new facilities, including artificial snowmaking machines, are already in place. In Spain, it's easy to arrange all-inclusive ski packages through a travel agent. A typical deal would include six nights' accommodation in a three- or four-star hotel with half board, unlimited use of ski lift for the week, at a cost of just under 100,000 pts. With instruction fees, count on 10–15,000 pts extra per week. **Information**: write to the tourist office or the Spanish Ski Federation, Claudio Coello 32, 28001 Madrid, ℂ (91) 575 89 43.

tennis

There is equal fervour for tennis as for golf, inspired by international champion Arantxa Sánchez Vicario, and more recently by Conchita Martínez, both of whom can be mentioned in the same breath as Graf, Seles and Sabatini. Again, the best clubs are to be found on the coast, and every resort hotel has its own courts; municipal ones are rare or hard to get to. The most famous tennis school in Andalucía lies just behind Fuengirola on the Mijas road, and is owned by Australian Lew Hoad, the Wimbledon favourite of the 50s and 60s. If you're looking for a game in Marbella, call Los Monteros Tennis Club, ℂ (95) 282 38 46, but expect to pay much more. **Information**: Royal Spanish Tennis Federation, Avenida Diagonal 618, 08021 Barcelona, ℂ (93) 201 08 44.

water sports

Water sports are the most popular activities in the summer. You can rent a windsurf board and learn how to use it at almost any resort; *aficionados* head for Tarifa, Europe's wind-surfing mecca and the continent's southernmost tip. If you're bringing your own boat, get the tourist office's literature on marinas before setting out. You have a choice of 30 along the coasts of Andalucía. There's a full calendar of sailing events and races, as well as sailing schools and rentals. A number of reservoirs have become quite popular as well for water sports. **Information**: write to the Royal Spanish Sailing Federation, Luis de Salazar 12, 28002 Madrid, ℂ (91) 519 50 08, fax (91) 416 45 04.

Underwater activists flock to the Almería coast in particular for its sparkling water and abundant marine life. **Information**: write to the Spanish Sub-Aqua Federation, Santaló 15, 08021 Barcelona, ℂ (93) 200 67 69; or contact the Federación Española de Esquí Náutico, Sabino de Arana 30, 08028 Barcelona, ℂ (93) 330 89 03.

Gibraltar

Gibraltar has a number of sports clubs and associations, many of them private. For further information ask at the tourist office.

Telephones

Emergency Numbers

Spain:	*protección civil* ℂ 006	police ℂ 091
Gibraltar:	ambulance and police ℂ 199	fire ℂ 190

Spain has long had one of the best telephone systems in Europe. During the civil war it kept running no matter what; commanders used it to keep in touch with their troops, and called towns on the front during offensives to check if they had fallen to the enemy.

Today, calls within Spain are comparatively cheap (15–25 pts for a short local call), and Spain is one of the few countries where you can make an international call conveniently from a phone booth—within Europe at least. In newer phone booths there are complete instructions (in English) and the phone itself has a little slide on top that holds coins; keep it full of 25 pts pieces—the newer ones also take 100 pts—and you can gab all day like the Spaniards do. This can be done to the US too, but take at least 3,000 pts in change with you in 100s. Overseas calls from Spain are among the most expensive in Europe: calls to the UK cost about 250–350 pts a minute, to the US substantially more. There are central telephone offices (*telefónica*) in every big city, where you call from metered booths (and pay a fair percentage more for the comfort); they are indispensable, however, for reversed-charge or collect calls (*cobro revertido*). Telefónicas are generally open from 9–1pm and 5–10pm and closed on Sundays. Expect to pay a big surcharge if you do any telephoning from your hotel or any public place that does not have a coin slot. Cheap rate is from 10pm–8am Monday–Saturday and all day Sunday and public holidays.

For calls to Spain from the UK, dial 010 followed by the country code, the area code (remember that if you are calling from outside Spain you drop the '9' in the area code) and the number. For international calls from Spain, dial 07, wait for the higher tone and then dial the country code, etcetera. Telephoning abroad from **Gibraltar**, dial 00 followed by country and area code.

Some Country Codes

Australia:	61	Netherlands:	31
Canada:	1	New Zealand:	64
France:	33	Spain:	34
Germany:	49	UK:	44
Italy:	39	US:	1

Toilets

Outside bus and train stations, public facilities are rare in Spain. On the other hand, every bar on every corner has a toilet; don't feel uncomfortable using it without purchasing something—the Spaniards do it all the time. Just ask for *los servicios* and take your own paper.

Tourist Information

After receiving millions of tourists each year for the last two decades, no country has more information offices, or more helpful ones, or more intelligent brochures and detailed maps. Every city will have an office, and about two-thirds of the time you'll find someone who speaks English. Sometimes they'll be less helpful in the big cities in the summer. More often, though, you'll be surprised at how well they know the details of accommodation and transportation. Don't mistake tourist offices for the new **consumer information** booths the Socialist government is setting up everywhere. Many large cities also maintain

municipal tourist offices, though they're not as well equipped as those run by the Ministry of Tourism, better known as **Turismo**. Hours for most offices are Monday to Friday, 9.30–1.30 and 4–7, Saturday mornings and closed on Sundays.

Spanish National Tourist Offices

Australia:	203 Castlereagh Street, Suite 21a, PO Box A-685, Sydney, ✆ (2) 264 79 66
Canada:	102 Bloor Street West, Toronto, Ontario, M5S 1M8, ✆ (416) 61 3131
France:	43 Avenue Pierre I de Serbie, Paris, ✆ (1) 47 23 37 75
Germany:	Kurfürstendamm 180, Berlin, ✆ (30) 882 60 36
	Myliusstrasse 14, Frankfurt, ✆ (69) 72 50 33
	Post Fach No. 151940, Schuberterstrasse 10, München, ✆ (89) 538 90 75
Italy:	Piazza di Spagna 55, Roma, ✆ (6) 679 82 72
	Piazza del Carmine 4, Milano, ✆ (2) 72 00 43 13
Netherlands:	Laan Van Meerdervoort 8, 2517 's-Gravenhage, ✆ (70) 346 59 00
UK:	57 St James's Street, London SW1A 1LD, ✆ (071) 499 0901
US:	845 North Michigan Ave, Chicago, Illinois, IL 60611, ✆ (312) 642 19 92
	4800 The Galleria, 5085 Westheimer, Houston, Texas, TX 77056, ✆ (713) 840 7411
	8383 Wilshire Boulevard, Suite 960, Beverly Hills, California, CA 90211, ✆ (213) 658 7188
	665 Fifth Avenue, New York, NY 10022, ✆ (212) 759 8822

Gibraltar Information Bureau

UK:	179 The Strand, London WC2R 1EH, ✆ (071) 836 0777

maps

Cartography has been an art in Spain since the 12th-century Catalans charted their Mediterranean empire in Europe's first great school of map-making. The tourist offices hand out beautifully detailed maps of every town; ask for their *Mapa de Comunicaciones,* an excellent general map of the country. The best large-scale maps are produced by *Almax Editores*. Topographical maps for hikers and mountaineers can be obtained from Instituto Geográfico Nacional, Calle General Ibáñez de Ibero 3, Madrid, ✆ (91) 533 31 21; Servicio Geográfico Ejército, Calle Dario Gazapo, Madrid, ✆ (91) 518 11 19; or the bookshop Libreria Quera, Petritoxl 2, Barcelona, ✆ (93) 318 07 43.

If you can't wait until you get to Spain, specialist shops in London include Stanfords at 12 Long Acre, WC2, ℂ (071) 836 1321; and in the US, The Complete Traveler, 199 Madison Avenue, New York, NY 10022, ℂ (212) 685 9007.

Where to Stay

Hotels in Spain are still bargains—though, as with prices for other facilities, Spain is gradually catching up with the rest of Europe. One thing you can still count on is a consistent level of quality and service; the Spanish government regulates hotels more intelligently, and more closely, than any other Mediterranean country. Room prices must be posted in the hotel lobbies and in the rooms, and if there's any problem you can ask for the complaints book, or *Libro de Reclamaciones*. No one ever writes anything in these; any written complaint must be passed on to the authorities immediately. Hotel keepers would always rather correct the problem for you.

The prices given in this guide are for double rooms with bath (unless stated otherwise) but do not include Vat (IVA) charged at 15 per cent on five-star *hoteles*, and 6 per cent on other *hoteles*. No Vat is charged on other categories of accommodation. Prices for single rooms will average about 60 per cent of a double, while triples or an extra bed are around 35 per cent more. Within the price ranges shown, the most expensive are likely to be in the big cities, while the cheapest places are always provincial towns. On the whole, prices throughout Andalucía are surprisingly consistent. No government, however, could resist the chance to insert a little bureaucratic confusion, and the wide range of accommodation in Spain is classified in a complex system. Look for the little **blue plaques** next to the doors of all *hoteles*, *hostales*, etcetera which identify the classification and number of stars. If you're travelling around a lot, a good investment would be the government publication *Guía de Hoteles*, a great fat book with every classified hotel and *hostal* in Spain, available for only 750 pts in many bookshops. The government also publishes similar guides to holiday flats (*apartamentos turísticos*) and campsites. Local tourist information offices will have a complete accommodation list for their province, and some can be very helpful with finding a room when things are tight.

paradores

The government, in its plan to develop tourism in the 1950s, started this nationwide chain of classy hotels to draw some attention to little-visited areas. They restored old palaces, castles and monasteries for the purpose, furnished them with antiques and installed fine restaurants featuring local specialities. *Paradores* for many people are one of the best reasons for visiting Spain. Not all *paradores* are historical landmarks; in resort areas, they are as likely to be cleanly designed modern buildings, usually in a great location with a pool and some sports facilities. As their popularity has increased, so have their prices; in most cases both the rooms and the restaurant will be the most expensive in town. *Paradores* are classed as three- or four-star hotels, and their prices range from 8,000 pts in remote provincial towns to 17,000 pts and upwards for the most popular. They are open all year round and offer substantial off-season discounts. If you can afford a *parador*, there is no better place to stay. We've mentioned most of them throughout this book.

Advance Booking

Spain: Head office, Calle Velázquez 18, Madrid ✆ (91) 435 97 00

UK: Keytel International, 402 Edgware Road, London W2 1ED,
✆ (071) 402 8182

US: Marketing Ahead, 515 Madison Avenue, New York, NY 10016,
✆ (212) 686 9213

hoteles

Hoteles (H) are rated with from one to five stars, according to the services they offer. These are the most expensive places, and even a one-star hotel will be a comfortable, middle-range establishment. *Hotel Residencias* (HR) are the same, only without a restaurant. Many of the more expensive hotels have some rooms available at prices lower than those listed. They won't tell you, though; you'll have to ask. You can often get discounts in the off season but will be charged higher rates during important festivals. These are supposedly regulated, but in practice hotel-keepers charge whatever they can get. If you want to attend any of these big events, book your hotel as far in advance as possible.

Price Ranges

rating	high	average	low
★★★★★	40,000	25,000	17,000
★★★★	30,000	20,000	12,000
★★★	18,000	12,000	8,000
★★	9,000	6,000	4,000
★	6,000	4,000	3,500

hostales and pensiones

Hostales (Hs) and *Pensiones* (P) are rated with from one to three stars. These are more modest places, often a floor in an apartment block; a three-star *hostal* is roughly equivalent to a one-star hotel. *Pensiones* may require full- or half-board; there aren't many of these establishments, only a few in resort areas. *Hostal Residencias* (HsR), like *hotel residencias*, do not offer meals except breakfast, and not always that. Of course, *hostales* and *pensiones*, with one or two stars will often have rooms without private baths at considerable savings. Be warned: small cheap *hostales* in ports (such as Málaga, Cádiz and Algeciras) can be crummy and noisy beyond belief—as you lie there unable to sleep, you can only marvel at the human body's ability to produce such a wealth of unidentifiable sounds, coming through the paper-thin walls of the room next door.

Price Ranges

rating	high	average	low
★★★	9,000	5,000	3,500
★★	7,000	4,000	3,000
★	4,000	3,000	2,500

fondas, casas de huéspedes and camas

The bottom of the scale is occupied by the *fonda* (F) and *casa de huéspedes* (CH), little different from a one-star *hostal*, though generally cheaper. Off the scale completely are hundreds of unclassified cheap places, usually rooms in an apartment or over a bar and identified only by a little sign reading *camas* (beds) or *habitaciones* (rooms). You can also ask in bars or at the tourist office for unidentified *casas particulares*, private houses with a room or two; in many villages these will be the best you can do, but they're usually clean—Spanish women are manic housekeepers. The best will be in small towns and villages, and around universities. Occasionally you'll find a room over a bar, run by some- body's grandmother, that is nicer than a four-star hotel—complete with frilly pillows, lovely old furnishings, and a shrine to the Virgin Mary. The worst are inevitably found in industrial cities or dull modern ones. It always helps to see the room first. In cities, the best places to look are right in the centre, not around the bus and train stations. Most inex- pensive establishments will ask you to pay a day in advance.

Price Ranges (without bath)

high	average	low
3,000	2,000	1,500

alternative accommodation

Youth hostels exist in Spain, but they're usually not worth the trouble. Most are open only in the summer; there are the usual inconveniences and silly rules, and often hostels are in out-of-the-way locations. You'll be better off with the inexpensive *hostales* and *fondas*—sometimes these are even cheaper than youth hostels—or ask at the local tourist office for rooms that might be available in **university dormitories**. If you fancy some peace and tranquillity, the national tourist office has a list of 64 **monasteries** and **convents** that welcome guests. Accommodation starts at about £10 a night, meals are simple and guests can usually take part in the religious ceremonies.

camping

Campsites are rated with from one to three stars, depending on their facilities, and in addi- tion to the ones listed in the official government handbook there are always others, rather primitive, that are unlisted. On the whole camping is a good deal, and facilities in most first-class sites include shops, restaurants, bars, laundries, hot showers, first aid, swimming pools, telephones and, occasionally, tennis court. Caravans (campers) and trailers converge on all the more developed sites, but if you just want to pitch your little tent or sleep out in some quiet field, ask around in the bars or at likely farms. Camping is forbidden in many forest areas because of fears of fire, as well as on the beaches (though you can often get close to some quieter shores if you're discreet). If you're doing some hiking, bring a sleeping bag and stay in the free **refugios** along the major trails (*see* p. 38).

Price range (per day)

Adult	275–500 pts
Caravan	300–650 pts
Child	200–350 pts
Tent	250–650 pts
Car	300–400 pts

Information: the government handbook *Guía de Campings* can be found in most bookstores and at the Spanish tourist office; further details can be obtained from the Federación Española de Campings, Gran Vía 88, Grupo 3 10–8, Madrid, © (91) 242 31 68; or Camping and Caravan Club, Greenfields House, Westwood Way, Coventry CV4 8JH, © (0203) 422 024 (membership necessary £24–8). **Reservations** for sites can be made through Federación Española de Empresarios de Camping, General Oraa 52, 2° d, 28006 Madrid. © (91) 562 99 94; or its regional office, Angel Ganivet 5, 4° a, 18009 Granada, © (958) 22 14 56.

resort accommodation

Almost everything along the coasts of Andalucía has been built in the last 25 years, and anonymous high-rise buildings abound. Lately the trend has turned towards low-rise 'villages' or *urbanizaciones* built around a pool, usually on or near the beach. We've tried to include places that stand out in some way, or which are good bargains for their rating. Resorts offer a choice of hotels in every price range, though the best bargains tend to be in the places where foreigners seldom tread—the Costa de la Luz west of Cádiz, or the small resorts west of Almería. If you intend to spend a couple of weeks on the Costa del Sol, your best bet is to book an all-inclusive package deal from the UK or US. Most hotels in the big resorts cater for package tours, and may not even answer a request for an individual reservation during the peak season. This stretch of coast has some ritzy hotels, particularly down near Marbella, the millionaires' playground. However, all sorts of bargains are to be had, especially if you plan a long-term stay in winter, a practice often followed by cold pensioners from the north. Incidentally, no beaches in Spain are private.

where to stay in Gibraltar

Gibraltar doesn't have the same range of accommodation, and there are no official categories; the only guide to quality is price—unfortunately not an accurate guarantee of standards anywhere. Based on Spanish categories, most hotels would fall into the two- or three-star bracket, with one or two exceptions, but don't expect any bargains—£50 is about average for a double room with bath, and there's little cheaper than that unless you go on a package deal.

There are no camping facilities in Gibraltar, but plenty on the Spanish side of the border, from where you can make a daytrip. Note that if you are travelling in a caravan (camper), you will not be allowed to take it in, as the streets are narrow and congested at the best of times. You can, of course, leave it on the Spanish side, but mind where you park—you could return to find it displaying a ticket, or clamped, or simply towed away.

On the whole, the horror stories of sexual harassment in Spain are a thing of the past—unless you dress provocatively and hang out by the bus station after dark. All Spaniards seem to melt when they see blondes, so if you're fair you're in for a tougher go. Even Spanish women sunbathe topless these days at the international *costa* resorts, but do be discreet elsewhere, especially near small villages. Apart from the coast, it often tends to be the older men who comment on your appearance as a matter of course. Whether you can understand what is being said or not, best to ignore them.

The Women's Travel Advisory Bureau © (0386) 701 082, has recently been launched in the UK. It provides information for women travelling alone and can research a specific destination or provide contact names and numbers recommended by other women travellers. The service costs between £6 and £30.

History

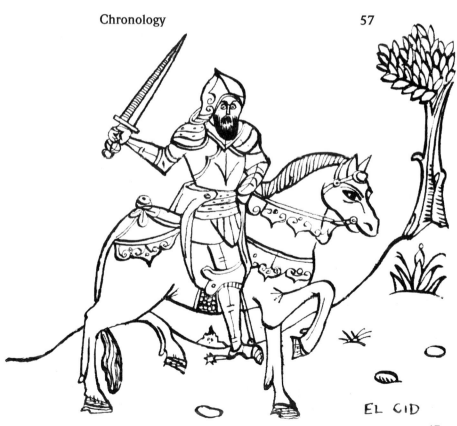

EL CID

Prehistory

Southern Spain has been inhabited since the remotest antiquity. Neanderthal man lived in Gibraltar some 50,000 years ago, and later peoples contributed cave paintings around Ronda. Neolithic cultures, with their dolmens and burial mounds begin to appear around the Iberian coasts *c.* 4000 BC. About 800 BC, the native Iberians were joined by other peoples, notably the Celts from over the Pyrenees, who occupied much of the north and centre of Spain. The great mystery of this era is the fabled kingdom of Phoenician **Tartessos**, roughly modern Andalucía, the only place where the anarchistic Iberians ever founded a state. Phoenician records mention it, and in the *Book of Kings* it appears as 'Tarshish', its great navy bringing wares of Spain and Africa to trade with King Solomon. With great wealth from the mines of the Río Tinto and the Sierra Morena, Tartessos reached its height about 800–700 BC, just in time to be digested by more high-powered civilizations from the east.

Phoenicians, Carthaginians, Romans: 1100 BC–AD 50

The Phoenicians 'discovered' Spain perhaps as early as 1100 BC, founding *Gades* (Cádiz), claimed to be the oldest city in Western Europe. They were after Spain's mineral resources—copper, tin, gold, silver and mercury, all in short supply in the Middle East at this time—and their successful exploitation of Spain made the Phoenicians the economic masters of the Mediterranean. Their rivals, the Greeks, arrived about 636 BC, founding a trading post at Mainake near Málaga.

By this time, the Phoenicians of the Levant were in decline, and **Carthage**, their western branch office, was building an empire out of their occupied coasts in Spain and North Africa. About 500 BC, the Carthaginians gobbled up the last remains of Tartessos and stopped the Greek infiltration. The Carthaginians contributed little to Spain, but they maintained the status quo until 264–241 BC, when **Rome** drubbed them in the First Punic War. In the rematch, the Second Punic War (begun in 218 BC), the Romans under Scipio Africanus conquered Spain while Hannibal was chasing rainbows in Italy (with a largely Spanish army).

Unlike their predecessors, the Romans were never content to hold just a part of Spain. Relentlessly, they slogged over the peninsula, subjugating one Celtic or Iberian tribe after another, a job that was not completed until about AD 50. Rome had to send its best—Cato, Pompey, Julius Caesar and Octavian (Augustus) were all commanders in the Spanish conquest. Caesar, in fact, was governor in Andalucía, the most prosperous part of the peninsula, and the one that adapted most easily to Roman rule and culture.

Roman Bætica: AD 50–409

At first, the Romans called the region simply 'Further Spain', but eventually it settled in as *Bætica*, from the Bætis, the ancient name for the Guadalquivir river. For the next four centuries, it would be a prosperous, contented place; by grace of its mineral and agricultural wealth it was the richest Roman province west of Tunisia. Besides wine, oil and metals, another export was dancing girls—Bætica's girls were reputed to be the hottest in the empire. And for the choicer Roman banquets, there was *garum*, a highly prized condiment made of fish guts. Modern gourmets have been trying to guess the recipe for centuries.

New cities grew up to join Cádiz, Itálica and Málaga. Of these the most important were *Hispalis* (Sevilla) and *Corduba* (Córdoba). Among the cosmopolitan population were Iberians, Celts, Phoenicians, Italians, and a sizeable minority of Jews. Rome settled them here in great numbers in the Diaspora as far from home as they could possibly put them; they were to play an important and constructive role in Spanish life for the next 1500 years. The province also had a talent for keeping in the mainstream of imperial politics and culture. Vespasian had been governor here, and Bætica gave birth to three of Rome's best emperors: Trajan, Hadrian and Theodosius. It also contributed almost all the great figures of the 'silver age' of Latin literature—Lucan, both Senecas, Martial and Quintilian.

Roman Twilight and the Visigoths: 409–711

By the 4th century, the crushing burden of maintaining the defence budget and the government bureaucracy sent Spain's economy into a permanent regression. Cities declined, and in the countryside the great landowners gradually squeezed the majority of the population into serfdom or outright slavery. Thus when the bloody, anarchic **Vandals** arrived in 409, they found bands of rural guerrillas, or *bagaudae*, to help them in smashing up the remnants of the Roman system. The Vandals moved on to Africa in 428, leaving nothing behind but, maybe, the name Andalucía—perhaps originally *Vandalusia*.

The next uninvited guests were the **Visigoths**, a ne'er-do-well Teutonic folk who had been pushed westwards by the Huns. After sacking Rome in 410, they found their way into Spain four years later. By 478 they had conquered most of it, including Andalucía, and they established an independent kingdom stretching from the Atlantic to the Rhône.

The Visigoths were illiterate, selfish and bloody-minded, but persistent enough to endure, despite endless dynastic and religious quarrels; like most Germans, they were Arian heretics. There weren't many of them, only a warrior elite that never formed more than a small fraction of the population. For support they depended on the landowners, who were making the slow but logical transition from Roman *senatores* to feudal lords.

Despite all the troubles, Andalucía at least seems to have been doing well—probably better than anywhere else in Western Europe—and there was even a modest revival of learning in the 7th century, the age of St Isidore (*c.* 560–636), famous scholar of Sevilla. King Leovigild (573–86) was an able leader; his son Reccared converted to orthodox Christianity in 589; both brought their state to the height of its power as much by internal reform as military victories. Allowing the grasping Church a share of power, however, proved fatal to the Visigoths. The Church's depredations against the populace, and its persecutions of Jews and heretics made the Visigothic state as many enemies within as it ever had across its borders.

The Muslim Conquest: 711–756

The great wave of Muslim Arab expansion that began in Muhammad's lifetime was bound to wash up on Spain's shores sooner or later. A small Arab force arrived in Spain in 710, led by **Tarif**, who gave his name to today's Tarifa on the straits. The following year brought a larger army—still only about 7,000 men—under **Tariq ibn-Ziyad** who quickly defeated the Visigoths near Barbate, a battle in which King Roderick was killed. Within five years, the Arabs had conquered most of the peninsula.

The ease of the conquest is not difficult to explain. The majority of the population was delighted to welcome the Arabs and their Berber allies. The overtaxed peasants and perse-cuted Jews supported them from the first. Religious tolerance was guaranteed under the new rule; since the largest share of taxes fell on non-believers, the Arabs were happy to refrain from seeking converts. The conquest, however, was never completed. A small Christian enclave in the northwest, the kingdom of Asturias, survived following an obscure but symbolic victory over the Moors at Covadonga—by the beginning of the 10th century the Christians had recaptured León and most of Galicia—but at the time the Arabs could barely have noticed. Muslim control of most of Spain was solid, but hampered by dissension almost from the start between the Arabs and the neglected Berbers, and between the various tribes of the Arabs themselves.

The Emirate of al-Andalus: 756–1031

Far away in Damascus, the political struggles of the caliphate were being resolved by a general massacre of the princes of the Ummayyad dynasty, the successors of Muhammad, as the Abbasids replaced them on the throne. One Ummayyad escaped—**Abd ar-Rahman**; he fled to Córdoba, and gained the support of Ummayyad loyalists there. After a battle in May 756, he proclaimed himself emir, the first leader of an independent **emirate of al-Andalus**.

Under this new government, Muslim Spain grew strong and prosperous. Political unity was maintained only with great difficulty, but trade, urban life and culture flourished. Though their domains stretched as far as the Pyrenees, the Ummayyad emirs referred to it all as *al-Andalus*. Andalucía was its heartland and Córdoba, Sevilla, and Málaga its greatest cities, unmatched by any others in western Europe. Abd ar-Rahman began the Great Mosque in Córdoba, a brilliant and unexpected start to the culture of the new state.

After Abd ar-Rahman, the succession passed without difficulty through Hisham I (788–96), Al-Hakam I (796–822), and Abd ar-Rahman II (822–52). One of Abd ar-Rahman's innovations, the creation of a professional army and palace secretariat, helped considerably in maintaining stability. The latter, called the *Saqaliba*, a civil service of imported slaves, was made up largely of Slavs and black Africans. The new dynasty seems also to have worked sincerely to establish justice and balance among the various contentious ethnic groups. One weakness, shared with most early Islamic states, was the personal, non-insti-tutional nature of rule. Individuals and groups could address their grievances only to the emir, while governors in distant towns had so much authority that they often began to think of themselves as independent potentates—a cause of frequent rebellions in the reign of Muhammad I (852–86).

In the tenth century, al-Andalus enjoyed its golden age. **Abd ar-Rahman III** (912–61) and **al-Hakam II** (961–76) collected tribute from the Christian kingdoms of the north, and from North African states as far as Algiers. In 929, Abd ar-Rahman III assumed the title of caliph, declaring al-Andalus entirely independent of any higher political or religious authority. When the boy Caliph Hisham II came to the throne in 976, effective power was seized by his chamberlain Ibn Abi-'Amir, better known as **al-Mansur** ('the victorious'), who recaptured León, Pamplona and Barcelona from the Christians, and even raided the great Christian shrine of Compostela, in Galicia, stealing its bells to hang up as trophies in the Great Mosque of Córdoba.

A more resounding al-Andalus accomplishment was keeping in balance a diverse, sophisticated population—Latinized Bæticans and residual Celtiberians, Yemenites, Jews, Arabs, Syrians, Slavs, Berbers, black Africans—all the while accommodating three religions and ensuring mutual tolerance. At the same time, they made it pay. Al-Andalus cities thrived, far in advance of any of their neighbours, Muslim or Christian, and the countryside was more prosperous than it has been before or since. The Arabs introduced cotton, rice, dates, sugar, oranges and much else. Irrigation, begun under the Romans, was perfected, and even parched Almería became a garden.

At the height of its fortunes, al-Andalus was one of the world's great civilizations. Its wealth and stability sustained an impressive artistic production—obvious today, even from the few monuments that survived the Reconquista. Córdoba, with al-Hakam's great library, became a centre of learning; Málaga was renowned for its singers, and Sevilla for the making of musical instruments. Art and life were also growing closer. About 822, the famous Ziryab had arrived in Córdoba from Baghdad. A great musician and poet, Ziryab also revolutionized the manners of the Arabs, introducing eastern fashions, poetic courtesies, and the proper way to arrange the courses of a meal. It wasn't long before the elite of al-Andalus became more interested in the latest graft of Shiraz roses than in riding across La Mancha to bash swords with the malodorous Asturians.

When backward Christian Europe was just beginning to blossom, al-Andalus and Byzantium were its exemplars and schoolmasters. Religious partisanship and western pride have always obscured the relationship; how much we really owe al-Andalus in scholarship—especially the transmission of Greek and Arab science—in art and architecture, in technology, and in poetry and the other delights of civilization, has never been completely explored. Contacts were more common than is generally assumed. Christian students were not unknown in Toledo or Córdoba—like the French monk who became Pope Sylvester II in 997.

Throughout the 10th century, the military superiority of al-Andalus was great enough to have finally erased the Christian kingdoms, had the caliphs cared to do so; it may have been a simple lack of aggressiveness and determination that held them back. The Muslim–Christian wars of this period cannot be understood as a prelude to the Crusades, or to the bigotry of Fernando and Isabel. Religious fanaticism, in fact, was lacking on both sides. Frontier chiefs could switch sides more than once without switching religions. The famous **El Cid** spent more time working for Muslim rulers than Christians; all the kings of León had some Moorish blood, and the mother of Abd ar-Rahman III was a Basque.

After the death of al-Mansur in 1002, the political situation began to change dramatically. His son, Abd al-Malik, inherited his position as vizier and *de facto* ruler and held the state together until his death in 1008, despite increasing tensions. All the while, Hisham II remained a pampered prisoner in the sumptuous palace-city of Madinat az-Zahra, outside Córdoba. The lack of political legitimacy in this ministerial rule, and the increasing distance between government and people, symbolized by Madinat az-Zahra, contributed to the troubles that began in 1008. Historians also suggest that the great wealth of al-Andalus had made the nation a bit jaded and selfish, that the rich and powerful were scarcely inclined to compromise or sacrifice for the good of the whole.

Whatever the reason, the caliphate disintegrated with startling suddenness after 1008. Nine caliphs ruled between that year and 1031, most of them puppets of the Berbers, the *Saqaliba* or other factions. Civil wars and city riots became endemic. Madinat az-Zahra itself was destroyed, and Córdoba sacked, by Berber troops in 1013. By 1031, when the caliphate was formally abolished, an exhausted al-Andalus had split into some 30 squabbling states called the *taifas.*

The Reconquista: 1031–1492

The years after 1031 are known as the age of the **taifas**, or 'Party Kings', so-called because most of them owed their position to one of the political factions. Few of these self-made rulers slept easily, in an era of constant intrigues and revolts, shifting alliances and pointless wars. The only relatively strong state was that of Sevilla, founded by former governor Muhammad ibn-Abbad and continued by his sons, who managed to annex Córdoba and several other towns.

The total inability of these rulers to work together made the 11th century a party for the Christians. **Alfonso VI**, King of Castile and León, collected tribute from most of the *taifas*, including even Sevilla. In 1085, with the help of the legendary warrior El Cid, he captured Toledo. The loss of this key fortress-city alarmed the *taifas* enough for them to request assistance from the **Almoravids** of North Africa, fanatical Berbers who had recently established an empire stretching from Morocco to Senegal. The Almoravid leader, Yusuf, crossed the straits and defeated Alfonso in 1086. Yusuf liked al-Andalus so much he decided to keep it, and by 1110, the Almoravids had gobbled up the last of the surviving *taifas*. Under their rule, al-Andalus became more of a consciously Islamic state than it had ever been before, uncomfortable for the Christian Mozarabs and even for the cultured Arab aristocrats, with their gardens and their poetry.

Popular rebellions put an end to Almoravid rule in 1145, and two years later their power in Africa was defeated and replaced by that of the **Almohads**, a nearly identical military-religious state. By 1172, the Almohads had control of most of southern Spain. Somewhat more tolerant and civilized than the Almoravids, their rule coincided with a cultural reawakening in al-Andalus, a period that saw the building of La Giralda in Sevilla. Literature and art flourished, and in Córdoba lived two of the greatest philosophers of the Middle Ages: Ibn Rushd (Averroës) and Moses Maimonides. The Almohads nevertheless shared many of the Almoravids' limitations. Essentially a military regime, with no deep support from any part of the population, they could win great victories over the Christians (as at Alarcos in 1195) but were never able to take advantage of them.

At the same time, the Christian Spaniards were growing stronger and gaining a new sense of unity and national consciousness. The end for the Almohads, and for al-Andalus, came with the **Battle of Navas de Tolosa** in 1212, when an army from all Christian Spain under Alfonso VII destroyed Almohad power forever. Alfonso's son, **Fernando III**, captured Córdoba (1236) and Sevilla (1248), and was made a saint for his trouble. **Alfonso X** (the Wise), noted for his poetry and the brilliance of his court, completed the conquest of western Andalucía in the 1270s and 1280s.

In the conquest of Sevilla, important assistance had been rendered by one of Fernando's new vassals, **Muhammad ibn-Yusuf ibn-Nasr**, an Arab adventurer who had conquered Granada in 1235. The **Nasrid Kingdom of Karnattah** (Granada) survived partly from its cooperation with Castile, and partly from its mountainous, easily defensible terrain. For the next 250 years it was the only remaining Muslim territory on the peninsula. As a refuge for Muslims from the rest of Spain, Granada became al-Andalus in miniature, a sophisticated and generally peaceful state, stretching from Gibraltar to Almería. It produced the last brilliant age of Moorish culture in the 14th century, expressed in its poetry and in the art of the Alhambra.

In the rest of Andalucía, the Reconquista meant a profound cultural dislocation, as the majority of the Muslim population chose to flee the rough northerners and their priests. The Muslims who stayed behind (the Mudéjars, meaning those 'permitted to remain') did not fare badly at first. Their economy remained intact, and many Spaniards remained fascinated by the extravagant culture they had inherited. In the 1360s, King Pedro of Castile was signing his correspondence 'Pedro ben Xancho' in a flowing Arabic script, and spending most of his time in Sevilla's Alcázar, built by artists from Granada. Throughout the period, though, this culture and the society that created it were becoming increasingly diluted, as Muslims either left or converted, while the Castilians imported large numbers of Christian settlers from the north. Religious intolerance, fostered by the Church, was a growing problem.

Los Reyes Católicos: 1479–1516

The final disaster, for Andalucía and for Spain, came with the marriage in 1469 of **King Fernando of Aragon** and **Queen Isabel of Castile**, opening the way, 10 years later, for the union of the two most powerful states in Spain. The glory of the occasion has tended to obscure the historical realities. If Fernando and Isabel did not invent genocide, they did their hypocritical best to sanctify it, forcing a maximalist solution to a cultural diversity they found intolerable. In 1481, they began the final war with Granada. In 1492, the capital fell, completing the Reconquisita; Fernando and Isabel expelled the Jews from

Spain; their Inquisition was in full swing, terrorizing converted Jews and Muslims and effectively putting an end to all differences of opinion, religious or political. The same year Columbus sailed from Andalucía to the New World, initiating the Age of Discovery.

Under the conditions of Granada's surrender in 1492, the Mudéjars were to be allowed to continue their religion and customs unmolested. Under the influence of the Church, however, Spain soon reneged on its promises and attempted forced conversion, a policy cleverly designed to justify itself by causing a revolt. The First Revolt of the Alpujarras, the string of villages near Granada in the Sierra Nevada, in 1500, resulted in the expulsion of all Muslims who failed to convert—the majority of the population had already fled—as well as decrees prohibiting Moorish dress and customs such as public bathhouses.

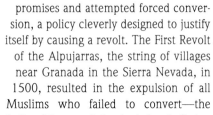

THE CREST
of FERDINAND
AND YSABELLA

Beyond that, the Spanish purposely impoverished the Granada territories, ruining their agriculture and bankrupting the important silk industry with punitive taxes and a ban on exports. The Inquisition enriched the Church's coffers, confiscating the entire property of any converted Muslims who could be found guilty of backsliding in the faith. A second revolt in the Alpujarras occurred in 1568, after which Felipe II ordered the prohibition of the Arabic language and the dispersal of the remaining Muslim population throughout the towns and cities of Castile. In the same year, the Inquisition began incinerating suspected Protestants in Sevilla. Intolerance had become the way of life.

The Age of Rapacity: 1516–1700

In the 16th century, the new nation's boundless wealth, energy and talent were squandered by two rulers even more vile than *Los Reyes Católicos*. Carlos I, a Habsburg who gained the throne by marriage when Fernando and Isabel's first two heirs died, emptied the treasury to purchase his election as Holy Roman Emperor. Outside Spain he is better known by his imperial title, **Charles V**, a ghoulish, sanctimonious tyrant who had half of Europe in his pocket and dearly wanted the rest. His megalomaniac ambitions bled Spain dry, a policy continued by his son **Felipe II**, under whom Spain went bankrupt twice.

Throughout the century, Andalucía's ports were the base for the exploration and exploitation of the New World. Trade and settlement were planned from Sevilla, and gold and silver poured into the city each year from the Indies treasure fleet. What did not immediately go to finance the wars of Carlos and Felipe was gobbled up by the nobility, the Genoese bankers, or by inflation—the 16th-century 'price revolution' caused by the riches from America. The historical ironies are profound: amidst all this opulence, Andalucía was rapidly declining from one of the richest and most cultured provinces of Europe to one of the poorest and most backward. Fernando and Isabel had begun the process, distributing the vast confiscated lands of the Moors to their friends, or to the Church and military orders; from its birth the new Andalucía was a land of huge estates, exploited by absentee landlords and worked by sharecroppers—the remnants of the original population as well as the hopeful colonists from the north, reduced in a generation or two to virtual serfdom.

By the 17th century, the destruction of Andalucía was complete. The Church's terror had done its work, eliminating any possibility of intellectual freedom and reducing the population to the lowest depths of superstition and subservience. Their traders and manufacturers ruined, the cities stagnated; agriculture suffered as well, as the complex irrigation systems of the Moors fell into disrepair and were gradually abandoned. The only opportunity for the average man lay with emigration, and Andalucía contributed more than its share to the American colonies. The shipments of American bullion peaked about 1610–20, and after that the decline was precipitous.

Bourbons, on the Rocks: 1700–1931

For almost the next two centuries, Andalucía has no history at all. The perversions of Spain's rulers had exhausted the nation. Scorned for its backwardness, Spain was no longer even taken seriously as a military power. The War of the Spanish Succession, during which the English seized Gibraltar (1704), replaced the Habsburgs with the **Bourbons**, though their rule brought little improvement. The one bright spot in the 18th century was the reign of **Carlos III** (1759–88), a reformer who expelled the Jesuits, attempted to revive trade and resettled the most desolate parts of Andalucía. New towns were founded—the *Nuevas Poblaciones*—such as La Carolina and Olavide.

Despite three centuries of decay, Andalucíans responded with surprising energy to the French occupation during the Napoleonic Wars. The French gave them good reason to, stealing as much gold and art as they could carry, and blowing up castles and historical buildings just for sport. As elsewhere in Spain, irregulars and loyal army detachments assisted the British under Wellington. In 1808, a force made up mostly of Andalucíans defeated the French at the Battle of Bailén. In 1812, a group of Spanish liberals met in Cádiz to declare a constitution, and under this the Spanish fitfully conducted what they call their **War of Independence**.

With victory, however, came not reforms and a constitution, but reaction and the return of the Bourbons. The confusing century that followed would see the loss of the American colonies, coups, counter-coups, civil wars on behalf of pretenders to the throne (the two Carlist Wars of the 1830s and 1870s), a short-lived First Republic in 1874 and several *de facto* dictatorships. Andalucía, disappointed and impoverished as ever, contributed many liberal leaders. The desperate peasantry, meanwhile, had become one of the most radicalized rural populations in Europe.

At first, this manifested itself as simple outlawry, especially in the Sierra Morena. In 1870, an Italian agitator and associate of Bakunin (the Russian writer and anarchist) named Fanelli brought **Anarchism** to Andalucía. In a land where government had never been anything more than institutionalized oppression, the idea was a hit. Anarchist-inspired guerrilla warfare and terrorism increased steadily, reaching its climax in the years 1882–6, directed by a secret society called the *Mano Negra*. Violence continued for decades, met with fierce repression by the hated but effective national police, the *Guardia Civil*.

The Second Republic and the Civil War: 1931–9

The coming of the democratic Second Republic in 1931 brought little improvement. Peasant rebellions intensified, especially under the radical right-wing government of 1934–6, when attempted land seizures led to incidents like the massacre at Casas Viejas in 1934. Spain's alarmed Left formed a Popular Front to regain power in 1936, but street fighting and assassinations were becoming daily occurrences, and the new government seemed powerless to halt the country's slide into anarchy. In July 1936 the army uprising, orchestrated by Generals Francisco Franco and Emiliano Mola, led to the **civil war**. The Army of Africa, under Franco's command, quickly captured eastern Andalucía, and most of the key cities in the province soon fell under Nationalist control. In Sevilla, a flamboyant officer named Queipo de Llano (later famous as the Nationalists' radio propaganda voice) singlehandedly bluffed and bullied the city into submission, and in arch-reactionary Granada, the authorities and local fascists massacred thousands of workers and republican loyalists. Thereafter Andalucía saw little fighting, though its people shared fully in Nationalist reprisals and oppression.

1939 to the Present

After the war, in the dark days of the 1940s, Andalucía like the rest of Spain knew widespread destitution and, at times, conditions close to famine. Emigration, which had been significant ever since the discovery of America, now became a mass exodus, creating the huge Andalucían colonies in Madrid and Barcelona, and smaller ones in nearly every city of northern Europe.

Economic conditions improved in the 1950s, with American loans to help get the economy back on its feet, and the birth of the Costa del Sol, on the empty coast west of Málaga. A third factor, often overlooked, was the quietly brilliant economic planning of Franco's economists, setting the stage for Spain's industrial take-off of the 1960s and 70s. In Andalucía, their major contributions were industrial programmes around Sevilla and Cádiz, and a score of dams, providing cheap electricity and ending the endemic, terrible floods.

When King Juan Carlos ushered in the return of democracy, Andalucíans were more than ready. Felipe González, the Socialist charmer from Sevilla, has been running Spain since 1982, and other Andalucíans are well represented in every sector of government and society. They took good advantage of the revolutionary regional autonomy laws of the late 1970s, building one of the most active regional governments, and giving Andalucía some control over its destiny for the first time since the Reconquista. Five centuries of misery and misrule cannot be redeemed in a day. The average income is less than half of that in Catalunya or the Basque country; the unemployment rate is brutal. The recession is affecting Spain in much the same way as the rest of Europe. None of this will be readily apparent, unless you go through the more dismal suburbs of Sevilla or Málaga, or in the mountain villages of Almería province, where the new prosperity is still a rumour. In the flashy, vibrant cities and the tidy whitewashed villages, Andalucíans hold fast to their ebullient, extrovert culture, living as if they were at the top of the world.

Chronology

BC

*c.*50,000	Earliest traces of man in Andalucía.
*c.*25,000	Paleolithic Proto-Spaniards occupy and decorate region's caves.
*c.*7000	Arrival of Iberians, probably from North Africa.
*c.*2300	Bronze-Age settlement at Los Millares, largest in Europe.
*c.*1100	**Phoenicians** found Cádiz.
*c.*800	Celts from over the Pyrenees join the Iberians; period of the kingdom of Tartessos in Andalucía.
*c.*636	**Greeks** found trading colony near Málaga.
*c.*500	**Carthage** conquers Tartessos.
241	Carthage loses **First Punic War** to Rome.
227	Rome and Carthage sign treaty, assigning lands south of the Ebro to Carthage.
219	**Second Punic War** breaks out when Hannibal besieges Roman ally Sagonte.
218	Hannibal takes his elephants and the war to Italy.
211–206	**Romans** under Proconsul Scipio Africanus take the war back to Spain, defeating Carthage.
206	Founding of Itálica, a Roman veterans' colony, near Sevilla.
55	The elder Seneca born in Córdoba.
46	During the ups and downs of the wars and colonizations of Spain, Caesar intervenes, riding from Rome to Obulco (60km from Córdoba) in 27 days; founds veterans' colony at Osuna.
27	Octavian divides Iberian peninsula into Interior Spain, Lusitania (Portugal) and Further Spain, soon better known as Bætica (Andulucía).

AD

39	Roman poet Lucan born in Córdoba.
50	All of Spain finally conquered by Romans, who lay out the first road network.
54	Trajan, future Roman emperor, born at Itálica.
70	Romans under Titus destroy the Temple in Jerusalem; in the subsequent diaspora thousands of Jews ended up in Spain.
76	Hadrian, Trajan's successor in 117, born at Itálica.
306	Council of Iliberis (Elvira, near Granada) consolidates the Christianization of Spain; votes for the celibacy of priests and bans Christians from wedding pagans.
409–28	**Vandals** vandalize Bætica and change its name to Vandalusia.

478	**Visigoths**, followers of the Arian heresy, control most of Spain, including Andalucía.
554	Byzantine Emperor Justinian sends troops to take sides in Visigoth civil war, and overstays welcome.
573	King Leovigild of the Visigoths chases the Greeks out of their last footholds in Andalucía.
589	Leovigild's son, Reccared, converts to orthodox Chritianity.
602–35	St Isidore, Bishop of Sevilla, whose writings provide main link between the ancient and medieval worlds.
711	**Arabs** and **Berbers** under Tariq ibn-Ziyad defeat Roderick, the last Visigoth king.
718	Pelayo, in Asturias, defeats Muslims at Covadonga, marking the official beginning of the Reconquista.
756	**Abd ar-Rahman**, of the Ummayyad dynasty, first emir of al-Andalus; begins the Great Mosque of Córdoba.
844	**Abd ar-Rahman II** begins the Alcázar in Sevilla.
880–917	Revolt against Ummayyads by Ibn-Hafsun, at Bobastro.
912–76	**Abd ar-Rahman III** declares himself caliph of Córdoba and begins the magnificent palace-city of Madinat az-Zahra.
977	Last enlargements of the Great Mosque by al-Mansur.
994	Birth of Ibn-Hazm of Córdoba (Abernhazam), greatest scholar of century and author of famous treatise on love, *The Ring of the Dove* (d. 1064).
1003	Birth of love poet Ibn-Zaydun in Córdoba (d. 1070).
1008	Caliphate starts to unravel.
1013	Berbers destroy Madinat az-Zahra.
1031	Caliphate abolished as al-Andalus dissolves into factions of the Party Kings.
1085	**Alfonso VI** of Castile and El Cid capture Toledo from the Muslims.
1086	*Taifa* kings summon aid of the Berber Almoravids.
1105	Birth of philosopher Ibn-Tufayl (Abubacer) in Guadix, author of charming narrative romance *Hayy ibn-Yaqzan* (The Awakening of the Soul), one of the masterworks of al-Andalus.
1110	**Almoravids** gobble up the *taifa* kingdoms.
1126	Birth of Ibn-Rushd in Códoba, philosopher and commentator on Aristotle, better known in the west as Averroës (d. 1198).
1135	**Alfonso VII** of Castile and León takes the title of Emperor of Spain.
1145	Uprisings against the Almoravids.
1172	**Almohads** conquer Sevilla, rounding off defeat of Almoravids.
1195	Completion of La Giralda in Sevilla.
1212	Alfonso VII's victory at Las Navas de Tolosa opens the gate to al-Andalus.
1231	Muhammad ibn-Yusuf ibn-Nasr carves out a small realm around Jaén.
1236	**Fernando III** (the saint) captures Córdoba.

1238	Muhammad ibn-Yusuf ibn-Nasr takes Granada, founding the Nasrid dynasty, and begins construction of the Alhambra.
1248	Fernando III takes Sevilla with the help of his vassal, Muhammad ibn-Yusef ibn-Nasr.
1262	**Alfonso X** (the Wise) picks up Cádiz.
1292	**Sancho IV** takes Tarifa.
1309	Guzmán el Bueno seizes Gibraltar.
1333	**Alfonso XI** loses Gibraltar to the king of Granada.
1350–69	Reign of **Pedro the Cruel** of Castile.
1 415	Ceuta captured by Portuguese, though it remained in Spanish hands after the division of the two kingdoms.
1462	**Enrico IV** gets Gibraltar back for Castile.
1479	**Isabel** and **Fernando** unite their kingdoms of Castile and Aragon.
1480	Spanish Inquisition sets up a branch office in Sevilla.
1492	Fernando and Isabel complete the Reconquista with the capture of Granada and expel Jews from Spain; Columbus sets off from Sevilla to discover the New World.
1500	First Revolt of the Alpujarras.
1516	Birth of lyric poet Luis de Góngora in Córdoba.
1516–56	Isabel and Fernando's grandson becomes King **Carlos I**.
1519	Carlos is promoted and becomes Holy Roman Emperor **Charles V**.
1528	Sculptor Pietro Torrigiano dies in the Inquisition's prison in Sevilla.
1556–98	Reign of Carlos's bureaucratic son, **Felipe II**.
1568	Felipe II's intolerance leads to the Second Revolt of the Alpujarras.
1580	Sevilla largest city in Spain, with population of 85,000.
1578–1621	Reign of Felipe's rapacious son, **Felipe III**.
1599	Diego Velázquez born in Sevilla (d. 1660).
1609–14	Felipe III forces half a million Muslims to move to North Africa.
1617	Murillo born in Sevilla (d. 1682).
1621–65	Reign of **Felipe IV**, chiefly remembered through Valázquez's portraits.
1627	Birth of Sevillan libertine Don Miguel de Mañara, believed to be the original Don Juan Tenorio of Tirso de Molina and the Don Giovanni of Mozart.
1630	Madrid becomes the largest city in Spain.
1649	Plague leaves one out of three people dead in Sevilla.
1665–1700	Reign of the weak and deformed **Carlos II**, last of the Spanish Habsburgs.
1700–46	Louis XIV exports his brand of Bourbon to Spain, in the form of his grandson **Felipe V**. The danger of Spain and France becoming united under a single ruler leads to the **War of the Spanish Succession**.
1704	Anglo-Dutch fleet, under the auspices of Charles of Austria, captures Gibraltar.
1713	The Spanish cede Gibraltar to Britain under the Treaty of Utrecht.

1726	Spain tries in vain to regain the Rock.
1746–59	Reign of **Fernando VI**.
1757	Completion of Sevilla's tobacco factory, where Carmen would work.
1759–88	Reign of **Carlos III**.
1779–83	The Great Seige of Gibraltar.
1783	Treaty of Versailles confirms British possession of Gibraltar.
1788–1808	Reign of the pathetic **Carlos IV**, caricatured by Goya.
1808–13	The installation by Napoleon of his brother, Joseph Bonaparte, as king leads to war with France.
1814–33	End of Peninsula War sees reinstatement of the Bourbon king, **Fernando VII**; his repeal of the Salic law and the succession of his daughter as **Isabel II** (1833–70) leads to the Carlist wars during her troubled reign.
1830	So many English winter in Málaga that they need their own cemetery.
1832	Washington Irving publishes *Tales of the Alhambra*.
1870–85	Reign of **Alfonso XII**.
1876	Manuel de Falla born in Cádiz (d. 1946).
1881	Pablo Picasso born in Málaga; Nobel-prize winning poet Juan Ramón Jiménez born in Moguer de la Frontera (d. 1958).
1886–1931	Reign of **Alfonso XIII**, who abdicated in favour of a successor who was to become king 'when Spain judges it opportune'.
1893	Andrea Segovia born near Jaén.
1898	Birth of Federico Garcia Lorca, near Granada (d. 1936).
1920	Ibero-American Exposition in Sevilla gets a disappointing turnout.
1936–9	**Civil War**.
1940	Hitler tries to get Spain to join Axis by promising to help Spain conquer Gibraltar, but **Franco** says no.
1953	First economic-military cooperation between Spain and the US.
1956	Spain ends its protectorate in Morocco, but keeps Ceuta and Mellila.
1962	Franco's Minister of Tourism gives go ahead for development of the Costa del Sol.
1966	An American bomber over Palomares collides with another plane and drops four nuclear bombs.
1975	Death of Franco; **Juan Carlos,** grandson of Alfonso XIII crowned king of Spain.
1982	Felipe González of Sevilla elected prime minister.
1983	Andalucía becomes an autonomous province.
1985	Frontier between Gibraltar and Spain opens.
1986	Spain and Portugal join the EC.
1992	International Exposition in Sevilla to commemorate the 500th anniversary of Colombus's departure from Huelva to the New World.

Topics

In Spanish newspapers, you will not find accounts of the bullfights (*corridas*) on the sports pages; look in the 'arts and culture' section, for that is how Spain has always thought of this singular spectacle. Bullfighting combines elements of ballet with the primal finality of Greek tragedy. To Spaniards it is a ritual sacrifice without a religion, and it divides the nation irreconcilably between those who find it brutal and demeaning, an echo of the old Spain best forgotten, and those who couldn't live without it. Its origins are obscure. Some claim it derives from Roman circus games, others say it started with the Moors; in the Middle Ages the bull faced a mounted knight with a lance.

There are bullrings all over Spain, and as far afield as Arles in France and Guadalajara, Mexico, but modern bullfighting is quintessentially Andalucían. It had its beginnings around the year 1800 in Ronda, when Francisco Romero developed the basic pattern of the modern *corrida*; some of his moves and passes, and those of his celebrated successor, Pedro Romero, are still in use today. The first royal *aficionado* was Fernando VII, the reactionary post-Napoleonic monarch who also brought back the Inquisition. He founded the Royal School of Bullfighting in Sevilla, and promoted the spectacle across the land as a circus for the discontented populace. Since the Civil War, bullfighting has gone through a period of troubles similar to boxing in the US. Scandals of weak bulls, doped-up bulls, and bulls with the points of their horns shaved have been frequent. Attempts at reform have been made, and all the problems seem to have decreased bullfighting's popularity only slightly.

In keeping with its ritualistic aura, the *corrida* is one of the few things in Andalucía that begins strictly on time. The show commences with the colourful entry of the *cuadrillas* (teams of bullfighters or *toreros*) and the *alguaciles*, officials dressed in 17th-century costume, who salute the 'president' of the fight. Usually three teams fight two bulls apiece, the whole taking only about two hours. Each of the six fights, however, is a self-contained drama performed in four acts. First, upon the entry of the bull, the members of the *cuadrilla* tease him a bit, and the *matador*, the team leader, plays him with the cape to test his qualities. Next comes the turn of the *picadores*, on padded horses, whose task is to slightly wound the bull in the neck with a short lance or *pica*, and the *banderilleros*, who agilely plant sharp darts in the bull's back while avoiding the sweep of its horns. The effect of these wounds is to weaken the bull physically without diminishing any of its fighting spirit, and to force it to keep its head lower for the third and most artistic stage of the fight, when the lone *matador* conducts his pas de deux with the deadly, if doomed, animal. Ideally, this is the transcendent moment, the *matador* leading the bull in deft passes and finally crushing its spirit with a tiny cape called a *muleta*. Now the defeated bull is ready for 'the moment of truth'. The kill must be clean and quick, a sword thrust to the heart. The corpse is dragged out to the waiting butchers.

More often than not the job is botched. Most bullfights, in fact, are a disappointment, especially if the *matadores* are beginners, or *novios*, but to the *aficionado* the chance to see one or all of the stages performed to perfection makes it all worthwhile. When a

matador is good, the band plays and the hats and handkerchiefs fly; an excellent performance earns as a reward from the president one of the bull's ears, or both; or rarely, for an
exceptionally brilliant performance, both ears and the tail.

You'll be lucky to see a bullfight at all; there are only about 500 each year in Spain, mostly
coinciding with holidays or a town's fiesta. During Sevilla's *feria* there is a bullfight every
afternoon at the famous Maestranza ring, while the rings in Málaga and Puerto de Santa
María near Cádiz are other major venues. Tickets can be astronomically expensive and
hard to come by, especially for a well-known *matador*; sometimes scalpers buy out the lot.
Get them in advance, if you can, and directly from the office in the *plaza de toros* to avoid
the hefty commission charges. Prices vary according to the sun—the most expensive seats
are entirely in the shade.

City Slickers

You're on the train for Córdoba, passing the hours through some of the loneliest landscapes in Europe. For a long time, there's been nothing to see but olive trees—gnarled
veterans, some of them planted in the time of Fernando and Isabel. You may see a donkey
pulling a cart. At twilight, you pull in at the central station , and walk four blocks down to
the Avenida del Gran Capitán, an utterly Parisian boulevard of chic boutiques and
pompous banks, booming with traffic. The loudspeakers from the *Galerías Preciados*
department store broadcast the latest singles of Lisa Stansfield and The Pet Shop Boys.

You don't often see Andalucíans going off on picnics in the country. The ground is dry,
vegetation usually sparse, and the sun can seem like a death-ray even in winter. Climate
has always forced people here to seek their pleasure elsewhere; it is the impetus behind
their exquisite gardens, and it has made of them the most resolutely urban people in
Europe.

In city centres the air is electric, a cocktail of motion, colour, and fragrances that goes to
your head like the best *manzanilla*. It has probably been much the same for over 2000
years; the atmosphere may be hard to recapture, but we can learn a lot by looking at decoration and design.

We know little about city life in Roman times—only that for relatively small populations,
towns like Italica had amphitheatres and other amenities comparable to any in the empire.
The cities of Moorish Spain were a revelation—libraries, public gardens and street
lighting, at a time when feudal Europe was scratching its carrot rows with a short stick.
Their design, similar to that of North African and Middle Eastern cities, can be traced
(with some difficulty) in Granada, Córdoba and Sevilla today.

It is difficult to say how many of Andalucía's Moorish cities were inherited from Roman
Bætica, and how much was introduced by the Moors themselves. Enclosure was the key
word: a great mosque and its walled courtyard at the centre, near the fortified palace
(*alcázar* or *alcazaba*) and its walled gardens. Along with the markets and baths, these
were located in the *medina*, and locked up behind its walls each night. The residential

quarters that surrounded the *medina* were islands in themselves, a maze of narrow streets where the houses, rich or poor, looked inwards into open patios while turning blank walls to the street. Some of these survive, with their original decoration, as private homes in Granada's Albaicín.

In Roman times, the patio was called a *peristyle*. The gracious habit of building a house around a colonnaded central court was perfected by the Greeks, and became common across the Mediterranean in Roman times. Today, while most of us enjoy the charms of our cramped flats and dull, squarish houses, the Andalucíans have never given up their love of the old-fashioned way. In Córdoba especially, the patios of the old quarters spill over with roses, wisteria and jasmine; each year there is a competition for the prettiest.

Besides the houses, some of the cellular quality of Moorish cities survived the Reconquista. In 16th-century Sevilla, thick with artful bandits, the silversmiths had their own walled quarter (and their own cops to guard it). The Moorish urban aesthetic evolved gracefully into the modern Andalucían: the simple, unforgettable panorama of almost any town—an oasis of brilliant white rectangularity, punctuated sharply by upright cypresses and by the warm sandstone of churches, palaces and towers. One Spanish invention, combining Italian Renaissance planning with native tradition, was the arcaded, rectangular square usually called *Plaza Mayor*. The best are in Madrid and Salamanca, but many Andalucían towns have one, and there is a huge dilapidated specimen in Córdoba. Architecturally unified—the four walls often seem like a building turned inside-out—the *Plaza Mayor* translated the essence of the patio into public space. Such a square made a perfect stage for the colourful life of a Spanish city. Not coincidentally, Spanish theatres in the great age of Lope de Vega and Calderón took the same form, with three sides of balconies, the fourth for the stage, on the narrow end, and a Shakespearean 'pit' at ground level.

FLOWERED PATIO
CORDOBA.

In the last two centuries, while the rest of Spain continued to create innovations in urban design and everyday pageantry, impoverished Andalucía contributed little—some elegant bullrings, exquisite redesigns of the old Moorish gardens, grand boulevards like the Alameda of Málaga and the *paseos* of Granada, and some eccentric decorations, such as the gigantic, sinister stone birds of prey that loom over most city centres— symbols of an insurance company. Since the 1970s and the end of Francoism, one can sense a momentum of slickness gathering steam: a touch of anonymous good design in a shop sign, new pavements and lighting, ambitious new architecture with a splash of colour and surprise. The *El Corte Inglés* department store in Málaga has been known to be entirely covered in computer-controlled electric lights at Christmas, nearly a vertical acre of permanent fireworks, flashing peacock tails and other patterns in constantly changing, brilliant colours—as spectacular and futuristic a decoration as any city has ever had. Watch out for these sharp Andalucíans—and for Spaniards in general. While we fog-bound northerners are nodding off with Auntie at twelve o'clock, they may well be plotting the delights of the future.

Dust in the Wind

The poets of al-Andalus devoted most of their attention to sensuous songs of love, nature, wine, women and boys, but amidst all the lavish beauty there would linger, like a *basso continuo*, a note of refined detachment, of melancholy and futility. Instead of forgetting death in their man-made paradises, the poets made a point of reminding their listeners of how useless it was to become attached to these worldly delights. After all, only God is forever, and why express love to something that would one day turn to dust? Why even attempt to build something perfect and eternal—the main ingredients of the lovely, delicate Alhambra are plaster and wood. The Nasrid kings, were they to return, might be appalled to find it still standing.

The Christians who led the Reconquista had no time for futility. In their architecture and art they built for eternity, plonking a soaring church right in the middle of the Great Mosque and an imperial palace intruding on the Alhambra—literal, lapidarian, emanating the power and total control of the temporal Church and State. Their oppression reduced the sophisticated songs of the Moorish courts to a baser fatalism. The harsh realities of everyday life encouraged people to live for the moment, to grab what happiness they could in an uncertain world. This uncertainty was best expressed by the 17th-century Spanish playwright Calderón de la Barca, especially in his great *La Vida es Sueño* (Life is a Dream), known as the Catholic answer to *Hamlet*.

There wasn't much poetry in Granada between 1492 and the advent of Federico García Lorca, born in 1898 in the Vega just outside of town. Lorca, a fine musician as well as a poet and playwright, found much of his inspiration in what would be called nowadays Granada's 'alternative' traditions, especially those of the gypsies. In 1922, Lorca was a chief organizer of Granada' s first *cante jondo* festival, designed to bring flamenco singing to international attention and prevent it from sliding into a hackneyed Andalucían joke. In 1927, he published the book of poems that made him the most popular poet in Spain, the *Romancero Gitano* (Gypsy Ballads); his plays, like *Bodas de sangre* (Blood Wedding) and *Yerma*, have the lyrical, disturbing force of the deepest *cante jondo*. But of post-Reconquista Granada he was sharply critical, accusing Fernando and Isabel of destroying a much more sophisticated civilization than their own—and as for the modern inhabitants of Granada, they were an imported reactionary bourgeois contingent from the north, not 'real' Andalucíans. Lorca criticized, but he kept coming back, and had dreams of bringing the city's once great culture back to life.

In Granada, a commemorative park at Víznar marks the spot where on 18 August 1936, local police or rebel soldiers took Lorca and shot him dead. No one knows who gave the orders, or the reason why; the poet had supported the Republic but was not actively political. When news of his secret execution leaked out, it was an embarrassment to Franco, who managed to hush up the affair until his own death. But most historians agree that the killing was a local vendetta for Lorca's outspoken views of his home town, a blood sacrifice to the stone god of Fernando and Isabel and Carlos V who fears all change, closing (one can only hope, once and for all) a full circle of bittersweet futility, frustration, and death.

Flamenco

For many people, flamenco is the soul of Spain—like bullfighting—an essential part of the culture that sets it apart from the rest of the world. Good flamenco, with that ineffable quality of *duende*, has a primitive, ecstatic allure that draws in its listeners until they feel as if their very hearts were pounding in time with its relentless rhythms, their guts seared by its ululating Moorish wails and the sheer drama of the dance. Few modern experiences are more cathartic.

As folklore goes, however, flamenco is a newborn. It began in the 18th century in Andalucía, where its originators, the gypsies, called one another 'flamencos'—a derogatory term dating back to the days when Carlos V's Flemish (*flamenco*) courtiers bled Spain dry. These gypsies, especially in the Guadalquivir delta cities of Sevilla, Cádiz, and Jerez, sang songs of oppression, lament, and bitter romance, a kind of blues that by the 19th century began to catch on among all the other downtrodden inhabitants of Andalucía.

Yet despite flamenco's recent origins, the Andalucían intelligentsia, especially Lorca and Manuel de Falla, found (or invented) much to root it deeply in the south's soil and soul. Its rhythms and Doric mode are as old as Andalucía's ancient Greek settlers; its spirit of improvisation and spontaneity date from the famous Córdoba school of music and poetry, founded in 820 by Abu al-Hassan Ali Ibn Nafi, better known as Ziryab, the 'Blackbird' (see History, p. 51); the half-tonal notes and lyrics of futility of the *cante jondo*, or deep song, the purest flamenco, seem to go straight back to the Arab troubadours of al-Andalus. But just how faithfully the music of al-Andalus was preserved among the gypsies and others to be reincarnated as flamenco will never be known; the Arabs knew of musical notation, but disdained it in their preference for improvisation.

By the late 19th century, flamenco had gone semi-public, performed in the back rooms of cafés in Sevilla and Málaga. Its very popularity in Spain, and the enthusiasm set off by Bizet's *Carmen* abroad, began seriously to undermine its harsh, true quality. At the same time, flamenco's influence spread into the popular and folk repertories to create a happier, less intense genre called the *sevillana* (often songs in praise of you know where). When schoolchildren at a bus stop in Cádiz burst into an impromptu dance and hand-clapping session, or when some old cronies in Málaga's train-station bar start singing and reeling, you can bet they're doing a *sevillana*. In Europe, only the Greeks dance and sing their own music as much, for the pure joy of it.

In the 1920s attempts were made to establish some kind of standards for the real thing, especially *cante jondo*, though without lasting results; the 'real, original flamenco' was never meant to be performed as such, and will only be as good as its 'audience'. This should ideally be made up of other musicians and flamenco *aficionados*, whose participation is essential in the spontaneous, invariably late-night combustion of raw emotion, alcohol, drugs and music, to create *duende*. With so many intangible factors, your chance of getting in on some genuine soul-stirring flamenco are about as rare as getting in on a genuine soul-stirring bullfight. But perhaps it is this very fleeting, hard-to-pin-down quality that makes both arts so compelling in the midst of a programmed, homogenized world.

The Founding Father

Andalucía for itself, for Spain and for Humanity

So reads the proud device on the regional escutcheon, hurriedly cooked up by the Andalucíans after the regional autonomy laws of the 1970s made them masters in their own house once again. Above the motto we see a strong fellow, mythologically under-dressed and accompanied by two lions. Though perhaps more familiar to us for his career among the Hellenes, he is also the first Andalucían—HERCULES DOMINATOR FUNDATOR.

The Greeks themselves admit that Hercules found time for two extended journeys to the distant and little-known West. In the eleventh of his Twelve Labours, the Apples of the Hesperides caper, he made it as far as the environs of Tangier, where he dispatched the giant Antaeus. The tenth Labour brought Hercules into Spain, sailing in the golden goblet of Helios and using his lion skin for a sail. In the fabled land of Tartessos, on the 'red island' of Erytheia, he slew the three-headed titan Geryon and stole his cattle. Before heading back to Greece, he founded the city of Gades, or Cádiz, on the island (Cádiz, surrounded by marshes is, in a sense, an island). He also erected his well-known Pillars, Gibraltar and Mount Abyle, across the way in Africa. His return was one of the all-time bad trips; whenever you're crazed and dying on some five-hour 'semi-direct' Andalucían bus ride (say, Granada to Córdoba *via* Rute), think of Hercules, marching Geryon's cows through Spain and over the Pyrenees, then making a wrong turn that took him halfway down the Italian peninsula before he noticed the mistake. After mortal combats with several other giants and monsters, he finally made it to Greece—but then his nemesis, Hera, sent a stinging blue-tail fly to stampede the cattle. They didn't stop until they reached the Scythian Desert.

To most people, Hercules is little more than mythology's most redoubtable Dog Warden, rounding up not only Cerberus, the Hound of Hell, but most of the other stray monsters that dug up the roses and soiled the footpaths of the Heroic Age. But there is infinitely more than this to the character of the most-travelled, hardest-working hero of them all. In antiquity, wherever Hercules had set foot the people credited him with founding nations and cities, building roads and canals, excavating lakes and draining swamps. And there is the intellectual Hercules, the master of astronomy and lord of the zodiac, the god of prophecy and eloquence who taught both the Latins and the Spaniards their letters. One version has it that the original Pillars of Hercules were not mountains at all, but columns, like those of the Temple of Jerusalem, connected with some alphabetical mysticism.

Ancient mythographers had their hands full, sorting out the endless number of deities and heroes known to the peoples of Europe, Africa and the Middle East, trying to decide whether the same figure was hiding behind different names and rites. Varro recorded no less than 44 Hercules, and modern scholars have found the essential Herculean form in myths from Celtic Ireland to Mesopotamia. Melkarth, the Phoenician Hercules, would have had his temples in southern Spain long before the first Greek ever saw Gibraltar. Not a bad fellow to have for a founding father—and a reminder that in Andalucía the roots are as strong and as deep as in any corner of Europe.

Getting Them Back

In the 1970s Robert Graves recalled overhearing two London secretaries talking about their vacations: 'I went to Majorca this year', says one. Her friend asks, 'Where's that?' and receives the answer, 'I don't know, I flew.' But the boom years of the Spanish package tour are definitely over. The drop in visitors is ringing alarm bells in Spain, and Europe's most intelligent and capable tourism bureaucracy is making a determined effort to put the country back in its former position, by means of a far-sighted and extensive change of image.

The down-market profile of resorts like Torremolinos will take a long time to change in the minds of the foreign public, who understandably but somewhat mistakenly connect it with tattooed lager louts, late-night punch-ups and raucous discos belting out music until dawn. There's a fair degree of snobbery involved in these attitudes; who in Britain, for example, boasts of having just spent a holiday on the Costa del Sol, with destinations such as Turkey, Florida and the Caribbean beckoning at affordable prices? The principal obstacle to attracting and sustaining mass tourism is the quality of holiday and destination on offer. Whilst the independent traveller is happy to pack guide book, camera and sensible shoes, and head off on a cultural pilgrimage to Granada's Alhambra, Córdoba's Mezquita, Sevilla's Giralda or the Cádiz Carnival, and along the way experience and indulge in the *real* Andalucía, the majority of visitors are interested in less ethereal pursuits, and the ingredients for their fun are beaches, hotels, food and entertainment at a reasonable price.

Spain can meet these criteria; too well, some malcontent Hispanophiles would say—those who think that the country has sacrificed its integrity to provide monstrous concrete resort playgrounds, paint them white and pass them off as Andalucían *pueblos*. So what can be done? It's too late to tear down what already exists, but it's time the government pushed the stop button on the coastal developments, on the Costa del Sol particularly, but no less so on the Costa de la Luz, where full-scale construction would mean, and in some places has already meant, the ruination of an untamed stretch of coast. Control future development, improve the existing infrastructure and abolish Spain's reputation as solely a paradise for sun-seeking tipplers, and maybe more visitors will come for the most genuine of motives—to get a balanced view of a country rich in history, culture and fun.

Hot-blooded Andalucían Women

Andalucía holds roughly a sixth of Spain's people, which means one twelfth of the population consists of the most sultry, sensuous women in Europe. Ah, señores, how they arch their supple torsos in an improvised *sevillana*, clicking their magic castanets! Dios, how provocative they are behind the iron grilles of their windows with their come-hither-burning-black-eyes over flickering fans, serenaded by their handsome guitar-strumming *caballero*, tossing him a red rose of promise and desire!

Ever since the first boatload of dancing girls from Cádiz docked at the slave-markets of ancient Rome, the women of Andalucía have had to put up with this—an extraordinary reputation for grace, beauty, and amorous dispositions. Travellers' accounts and novels elaborate on their exotic charms, spiced by the languor of the Moorish harem odalisque and the supposed promiscuity of the passionate gypsy. After all, when Leporello counts off his master's conquests in Mozart's *Don Giovanni*, which country comes out on top? Spain, of course, with 1003 victims to the arch-libertine's art of persuasion.

Nothing kept this fond male fancy afloat as much as the fact that nubile Andalucían women were tantalizingly inaccessible, thanks to a rigid Latin code of honour second to none. It took the Industrial Revolution, the Sevilla Tobacco Factory, and a French visitor, Prosper Mérimée, to bring this creature of the imagination out into the open, in the form of the beautiful gypsy tomato *Carmen* (1845), rendered immortally saucy in Bizet's opera of 1873. Step aside, Don Juan, or be stepped on! This new stereotype was as quick to light up a cheroot as to kick aside her sweetheart for a strutting matador in tight trousers. Not surprisingly, it wasn't long before the Tobacco Factory and its steamy, scantily-clad examples of feminine pulchritude (labouring for a handful of pesetas a day) attracted as many tourists as the Giralda tower.

Alas, where is the kitsch of yesteryear? Modern young Andalucían women are, like modern Andalucían men, among the most normal, mentally well-balanced people in the world. Ask them about the cloistered señoritas of the past and they'll laugh. Ask them about the unbridled Carmen, and they'll laugh. Ask them about the bizarre wind called the *solano* that troubles Cádiz in the springtime, a wind that in the old days drove the entire female population en masse to the beach, where they would fling off their clothes and dive into the sea to seek relief while the local cavalry regiment stood guard. Ask them about it, and they'll just laugh.

Roses of the Secret Garden

Western art and Islamic art are two worlds that will never agree. Even today, the sort of folk who believe in the divinity of Michelangelo or the essential greatness of the Baroque can be found in print, sniffing at the art of the Alhambra as merely 'decorative'. On the other side, you will discover a state of mind that can dismiss our familiar painting and sculpture as frivolous, an impious obsession with the appearances of the moment that ignores the transcendent realities beneath the surface. A powerful idea was in the air, in the 7–8th centuries, perhaps a reaction against the worldliness and incoherence that drowned classical civilization. It was not limited to Islam alone; the 'iconoclastic' controversy in Byzantium, following the attempt of Emperor Leo III to end the paganistic veneration of icons, was basically the same argument.

However this argument started, Islam grew up with an aversion to figurative art. At the same time, Islam was gaining access to the scientific and mathematical heritage of Greece and Rome, and finding it entirely to its liking. A new approach to art gradually took form, based on the sacred geometry of Byzantine architecture, and on a trend of mathematical mysticism that goes back to Pythagoras. Number, proportion, and symmetry were the tools God used to create the world. The same rule could be found in every aspect of creation, and could be reproduced in art, courtesy of the simple methods of Euclidean geometry. This geometry now found its place not only in the structure of a building, but also in its decoration.

Once the habit of thinking this way was established, it profoundly affected life and art in all the Islamic world, including Spain. The land itself became a careful mosaic, with neat rows of olive trees draped over the hills and the very beans and carrots in the gardens laid out in intricate patterns (Andalucían farmers still do it: you can see a remarkable example of such a landscape from the *mirador* in Úbeda). While nature was being made to imitate art, Muslim artists, consciously or not, often imitated the hidden processes of nature—as in the Córdoba mosque, growing like a crystal with the columns and aisles of each new addition. Often, they created novelties by changing scales, reducing and replicating old forms to make new, more complex ones. One example would be the Visigothic horseshoe arch. You can see it in its simplest form at Córdoba or Madinat az-Zahra; later, as in Sevilla's Alcázar, the same arch is made of smaller versions of itself. And in the Alhambra, you'll see arches made of arches made of arches, seeming to grow organically down from the patterns on the walls. A tree or a snowflake finds its form in much the same way. Fans of chaos theory, take note—the Moors had anticipated fractals and Koch curves 600 years ago.

Three dimensions is the domain of the mundane shell, the worldly illusion. The archetypes, the underlying reality, can be more fittingly expressed in two. With their straight-edge and compass, Islamic artists developed a tradition of elaborate geometrical decoration, in painted tiles, stucco, or wooden grilles and ceilings. The highest levels of subtlety reached by this art were in Isfahan, Persia, in Egypt, and in Granada. The foundation, as in all constructive geometry, is the circle— *man's heart is the centre, heaven the circumference*, as a medieval Christian mystic put it. From this, they wove the exquisite patterns that embellish the Alhambra, exotic blooms interlaced in rhythms of 3, 5, 6, 8 or 12. This is not the shabby, second-hand symbolism of our times. A 12-pointed flower does not *symbolize* the firmament and the 12 signs of the zodiac, for example; it *recalls* this, and many other things as well. For philosophers, these patterns could provide a meditation on the numerical harmony of creation; for the rest of us, they stand by themselves, lovely, measured creations, whispering a sweet invitation to look a bit more closely at the wonders around us. The patterns of the Alhambra haunt Andalucía to this day. In Granada especially, these geometric flowers are endlessly reproduced on *azulejo* tiles in bars and restaurants, and in the *taracea* work boxes and tables sold in the Alcaicería.

One of the favourite games of the Islamic artists was filling up space elegantly, in the sense a mathematician understands that word. In geometry, only three regular polygons, when repeated, can entirely fill a plane. One is the hexagon—as in a honeycomb; the others are the square—as on a chessboard— and the equilateral triangle. Some not-so-regular polygons (any triangle or parallelogram, for example) can do it too. Try and find some more complex forms; it isn't easy. One modern artist fascinated by these problems was M. C. Escher, whose tricks of two-dimensional space are beloved of computer programmers and the other Pythagoreans of our own age. The first four figures on this page can fill a plane.

The first, with a little imagination and geometrical know-how, could be made into one of Escher's space-filling birds or fish. The third doesn't quite do the job, but properly arranged it creates a secondary pattern of eight-pointed stars (fig. 5) in

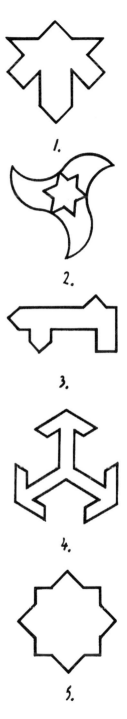

1.

2.

3.

4.

5.

between. For a puzzle, try and multiply each of the four on paper to fill a plane. Answers can be found on the walls of the Alhambra.

By now, you may suspect that these shapes were not employed without reason. In fact, according to the leading authority on such matters, Keith Critchlow (in his book *Islamic Patterns*), the patterns formed by figs 1 and 3 mirror the symmetrical arrangement of numbers in a magic square. Triangular figs 2 and 4 are based on the *tetractys*, a triangle of numbers closely related to the magic squares that was a favourite study of the Pythagoreans. But a Spanish Muslim did not need to be a mathematician to appreciate the lesson of this kind of geometry. Everyone understood the basic tenet of Islam—that creation is One: harmonious and complete. Imagine some cultured minister of a Granadan king, musing under the arcades of the Court of the Lions, reflecting perhaps on the nature that shaped the roses in the court, and how the same laws are proclaimed by the ceramic blossoms within.

Andalucía: the Guadalquivir Valley

Qui non ha vista Sevilla, non ha vista marravilla
(Who hasn't seen Sevilla, has seen no wondrous thing)

Hijo de Sevilla, uno bueno por marravilla
(You'll be lucky if you find a good *sevillano*)

Andalucían sayings

Apart from the Alhambra in Granada, the place where the lushness and sensuality of al-Andalus survives best is Andalucía's capital. Sevilla may be Spain's fourth-largest city, but it is a place where you can pick oranges from the trees, and see open countryside from the centre of town. Come in spring if you can, when the gardens are drowned in birdsong and the air becomes intoxicating with the scent of jasmine and a hundred other blooms. If you come in summer, you may melt; the lower valley of the Guadalquivir is one of the hottest places in Europe.

The pageant of Sevilla unfolds in the shadow of La Giralda, the Moorish tower that means so much to Sevilla ('the mother of artists, the mould for bullfighters' according to a *sevillano* poet). It is still the loftiest tower in Spain, and its size and the ostentatious play of its arches and arabesques make it the perfect symbol for this city, full of the romance of the south and the perfume of excess.

At times Sevilla has been a capital, and it remains Spain's eternal city; neither past reverses nor modern industry have been able to shake it from its dreams. That its past glories should return and place it alongside Venice and Florence as one of the jewels in the crown of Europe, a true metropolis with full international recognition and status, is the first dream of every *sevillano*. Crimped and prinked for Expo 92, Sevilla opened her doors to the world. The new 'Golden Gate' bridge, soaring higher than La Giralda itself, beckoned would-be suitors to the pavilions on the Isla de la Cartuja and the Age of Discoveries. Fresh romance and excess mingled with the old. New roads, a new opera house, the *Alamillo* (the harp), another new and wonderfully stringed bridge, combined with Moorish palaces and monuments, restored and repaired, in a vainglorious display. A come-on that attracted 16 million visitors. But Sevilla is a city very much in love with itself. When a *sevillano* sings in the street or in a café, which charmingly enough he often does, the subject of the song is invariably the city itself, and posters advertise concerts with the theme '*Sevilla, ¿por qué te quiero?*' ('Sevilla, why do I love you?'). Even the big celebration during Holy Week—although enjoyable to the foreigner (anyone from outside the city), with revelry in every café and on every street corner—is essentially a private one; the *sevillanos* celebrate in their own *casetas* with friends, all the time strongly aware that they are being observed by the general public, who can peek but may not enter, at least not without an *enchufe* ('the right connection').

Sevilla is like a beautiful, flirtatious woman; she'll tempt you to her doorstep and allow you a peck on the cheek—whether you get over the threshold depends entirely on your charm.

History: from Hispalis to Isbiliya to Sevilla

One of Sevilla's distinctions is its long historical continuity. Few cities in western Europe can claim to have never suffered a dark age, but Sevilla did well after the fall of Rome—and even after the coming of the Castilians. Roman Hispalis was founded on an Iberian settlement, and soon became one of the leading cities of the province of Bætica. So was Itálica, the now ruined city just to the northwest; it is difficult to say which was the more important. During the Roman twilight, Sevilla seems to have been a thriving town. Its first famous citizen, St Isidore, was one of the Doctors of the Church and the most learned man of the age, famous for his great *Encyclopedia* and his *Seven Books Against the Pagans*, an attempt to prove that the coming of Christianity was not the cause of Rome's fall. Sevilla was an important town under the Visigoths, and after the Moorish conquest it was second only to Córdoba as a political power and a centre of learning. For a while after the demise of the western caliphate in 1023, it became an independent kingdom, paying tribute to the kings of Castile. Sevilla suffered under the Almoravids after 1091, but enjoyed a revival under their successors, the Almohads.

The disaster came for Moslem Isbiliya in 1248, 18 years after the union of Castile and León. Fernando III's conquest of the city is not a well-documented event, but it seems that more than half the population found exile in Granada or Africa preferable to Castilian rule; their property was divided among settlers from the north. Despite the dislocation, the city survived, and found a new prosperity as Castile's window on the Mediterranean and South Atlantic trade routes (the Río Guadalquivir is navigable as far as Sevilla). Everywhere in the city you will see its emblem, the word NODO (knot) with a double knot between the O and D. It recalls the civil wars of the 1270s, when Sevilla was one of the few cities in Spain to remain loyal to Alfonso the Wise. '*No m'a dejado*' ('She has not forsaken me'), Alfonso is recorded as saying; *madeja* is another word for knot, and placed between the syllables NO and DO it makes a clever rebus besides a tribute to Sevilla's loyalty to medieval Castile's greatest king.

From 1503 to 1680, Sevilla enjoyed a legal monopoly of trade with the Americas. The giddy prosperity this brought, in the years when the silver fleet ran full, contributed much to the festive, incautious atmosphere that is often revealed in Sevilla's character. Sevilla never found a way to hold on to much of the American wealth, and what little it managed to grab was soon dissipated in showy excess.

It was in this period, of course, that Sevilla was perfecting its charm. Poets and composers have always favoured it as a setting. Bizet's Carmen rolled her cigars in the Royal Tobacco Factory, and for her male counterpart Sevilla contributed Don Juan Tenorio, who evolved through Spanish theatre in plays by Tirso de Molina and Zorrilla to become Mozart's Don Giovanni; the same composer also used the city as a setting for *The Marriage of Figaro*.

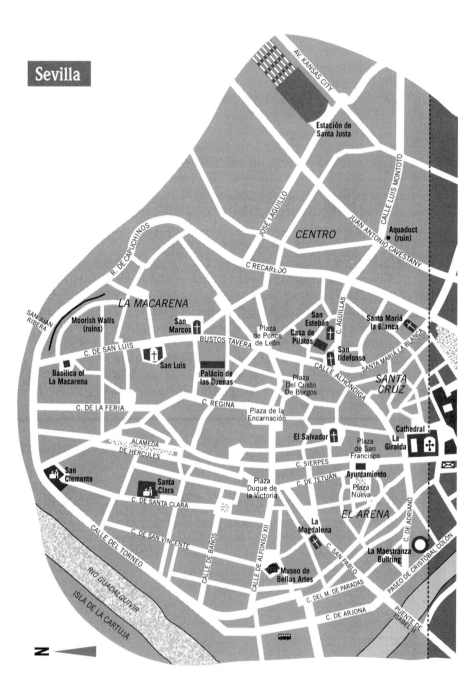

Sevilla

AV. KANSAS CITY

Estación de
Santa Justa

CENTRO

Aquaduct
(ruin)

CALLE LUIS MONTOTO

JUAN ANTONIO CAVESTANY

JOSE LAGUILLO

C RECAREDO

R. DE CAPUCHINOS

LA MACARENA

Moorish Walls
(ruins)

San
Marcos

San
Esteban

Santa Mariá
la Blanca

SAN JUAN
RIBERA

C. AGUILLAS

Plaza
de Ponce
de León

Casa de
Pilatos

BUSTOS TAVERA

C. DE SAN LUIS

San
Ildefonso

SANTA MARIA LA BLANCA

San Luis

CALLE ALHONDIGA

Basilica of
La Macarena

Palácio de
las Duenas

Plaza
Del Cristo
De Burgos

SANTA
CRUZ

C. DE LA FERIA

C, REGINA

Plaza de la
Encarnación

ALAMEDA
DE HERCULES

El Salvador

Plaza
de San
Francisco

Cathedral
La
Giralda

San
Clemente

C. SIERPES

Santa
Clara

Plaza
Duque de
la Victoria

C. DE TETUÁN

Ayuntamiento

Plaza
Nueva

C. DE SANTA CLARA

CALLE DEL TORNEO

C. DE SAN VINCENTE

EL ARENA

C. DE ADRIANO

CALLE DE BAÑOS

La
Magdalena

C. SAN PABLO

La Maestranza
Bullring

CALLE DE ALFONSO XII

PASEO DE CRISTÓBAL COLÓN

RIO GUADALQUIVIR

Museo de
Bellas Artes

ISLA DE LA CARTUJA

C. DEL M. DE PARADAS

C. DE ARJONA

PUENTE DE
ISABEL II

N

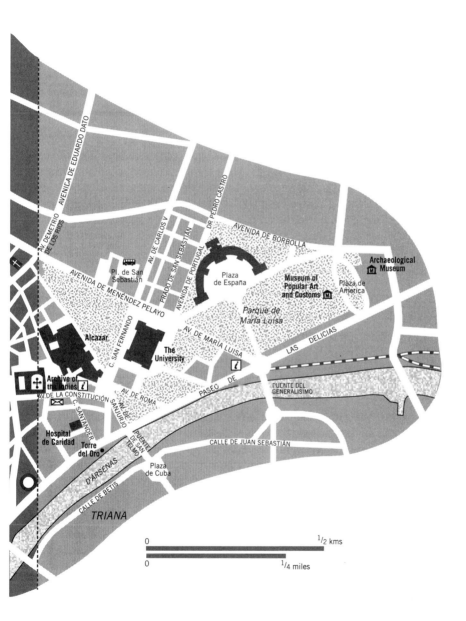

Though modern Sevilla has been loth to leave all this behind, the World Fair allowed it to show off not only the Sevilla of orange blossoms and guitars, but the Sevilla of the future.

Getting There

by air

Sevilla has regular flights from Madrid, Málaga, and Barcelona, less regularly from Lisbon, the Canary Islands and Valencia. The new San Pablo airport is 12km (7½ miles) east of the city, and the airport bus leaves from the Bar Iberia on Calle Almirante Lobos, near the southern end of Avenida de la Constitución. **Airport information**: © (95) 451 06 77.

by train

Estación de Santa Justa is the modern Expo showpiece in the northeast of town on José Laguillo and Avenida Kansas City. There are train connections—to Madrid, a daily *Talgo* to Valencia and Barcelona, and to Córdoba, Jerez and Cádiz, among the other frequent regular services to these cities; for trains to Málaga, Ronda and Algeciras, you should watch out for possible train changes at Bobadilla Junction, the black hole of Andalucían railways where all lines cross. The central RENFE office is at Calle Zaragoza 29. **Information**, © (95) 441 41 11; **reservations**, © (95) 442 15 62.

by bus

Almost all lines for Madrid, the Levante, Andalucía and Portugal, leave from the Estación de Autobuses, Plazas de Armas. Buses for Jerez and Cádiz run about every 1½ hours, and there are frequent connections to most other points in Andalucía (five daily to Granada, four to Málaga, three to Córdoba and Úbeda, two to the Costa del Sol, Aracena, Almería, La Línea, Tarifa and Algeciras, also three each to Madrid, Valencia and Barcelona.

For destinations within the province (e.g. Carmona, Écija), buses depart from outside this station, across the Avenida de Carlos V. Buses for Matalascañas, Huelva, Badajoz and Ayamonte leave from Calle Segura 18, while those for Santiponce and the ruins leave from Marqués de Parada every hour or so during the day. **Information** on routes and timetables, © (95) 441 71 11.

Tourist Information

The permanent tourist office is an especially helpful one, at Avenida de la Constitución 21 near the Cathedral, © (95) 422 14 04 (open weekdays 9.30–2.30). The municipal information centre is near the Parque de María Luisa, next to the US consulate off Avenida de María Luisa, © (95) 423 44 65. There's also an information centre at the airport, © (95) 425 50 46.

La Giralda

Open daily 10–6; adm 500 pts, including entrance to the cathedral.

A good place to start your tour of Sevilla is at one of Andalucía's most famous monuments. You can catch the 319ft tower of **La Giralda** peeking over the rooftops from almost anywhere in Sevilla; it will be your best friend when you get lost in the city's labyrinthine streets. This great minaret, with its *ajimeces* and brickwork arabesques, was also built under the Almohads, completed in 1195, just 50 years before the Christian conquest. The surprisingly harmonious spire stuck on top is a Christian addition. Whatever sort of turret originally stood on top was surmounted by four golden balls (or apples, according to one chronicler) stacked up at the very top, designed to catch the sun and be just visible to a traveller one day's ride from the city; all came down in a 13th-century earthquake. On the top of their spire, the Christians added a huge, revolving statue of Faith as a weathervane (many writers have noted the curious fancy of having a supposedly constant Faith turning with the four winds). La Giralda—the weathervane—has given its name to the tower as a whole.

THE GIRALDA TOWER SEVILLE

The climb to the top is surprisingly easy; instead of stairs, there are shallow ramps—wide enough for Fernando III to have ridden his horse up for the view after the conquest in 1248.

The Cathedral: the Biggest Gothic Building in the Whole World

For a while after the Reconquista, the Castilians who repopulated Sevilla were content to use the great Almohad mosque, built at the same time as La Giralda. At the turn of the 1400s, in a fit of pious excess, it was decided to build a new cathedral so grand that 'future ages shall call us mad for attempting it'. If they were mad, at least they were good organizers—they got it up in slightly over a century. The architects are unknown, though there has been speculation that the original master was either French or German.

The exterior, with its great rose window and double buttresses, is as fine as any of the Gothic cathedrals of northern Spain—if we could only see it. Especially on the west front, facing the Avenida de la Constitución, the buildings close in; walking around its vast bulk, past the fence of Roman columns joined by thick chains, is like passing under a steep and ragged cliff. Before it was cleaned to look pretty for the World Fair the grime contributed to the effect. Some of the best original sculptural work is on the two portals flanking the main door: the **Puerta del Bautismo** (left), and the **Puerta del Nacimiento** (right).

The groundplan of this monster, roughly 400ft by 600ft, probably covers the same area as did the mosque. On the northern side, the **Patio de los Naranjos** (Patio of the Orange Trees, and planted accordingly) preserves the outline of the mosque courtyard, now planted with orange trees. The Muslim fountain (built around a basin from the previous Visigothic cathedral) survives, along with some of the walls and arches. In the left-hand corner, the Moorish 'Gate of the Lizard' has hanging from it a stuffed crocodile, said to have been a present from an Egyptian emir asking for the hand of a Spanish infanta. Along the eastern wall is the entrance of the **Biblioteca Colombina**, an archive of the explorer's life and correspondence.

The cavernous interior overpowers the faithful with its size more than its grace or beauty. The main altarpiece is the world's biggest *retablo*, almost 120ft high and entirely covered with carved figures and golden Gothic ornament; it took 82 years to make, and takes about a minute to look at. The cathedral is dark and cold inside, and without the usual nave and transept, the enormous space is ill-defined and disorienting. Just behind the Capilla Mayor and the main altar, the **Capilla Real** contains the tombs of San Fernando, conqueror of Sevilla, and of Alfonso the Wise; Pedro the Cruel and his mistress, María de Padilla, are relegated to the crypt underneath. The art of the various chapels around the cathedral is lost in the gloom, but there are paintings by Murillo in the Capilla de San Antonio (in the north aisle), and an altarpiece by Zurbarán in the Capilla de San Pedro (to the left of the Capilla Real).

In the southern aisle, four stern pall-bearers on a high pedestal support the tomb of **Christopher Columbus**. They represent the kingdoms of Castile, León, Navarre, and Aragón. Columbus has been something of a refugee since his death. In the 16th century his remains were moved for unknown reasons from Valladolid to the island of Santo Domingo, and after Dominican independence from there to Havana Cathedral. In 1899, after Cuba became independent, he was brought to Sevilla, and this idiosyncratic monument put up to honour him. In the Dominican Republic, they'll tell you Columbus is still buried in Santo Domingo. Of course, most Spaniards are convinced Columbus was born in Spain, so it is appropriate that the life of this most elusive character should have mysteries at both ends.

The Sacristy

Most of the cathedral's collections are housed in a few chambers near the turnstiles at the main entrance. In the **Sala Capitular**, with .an *Immaculate Conception* by Murillo, Sevilla's bishop can sit on his throne and pontificate under the unusual acoustics of an elliptical Baroque ceiling. The adjacent **sacristy** contains paintings by Zurbarán, Murillo, Van Dyck and others, most in dire need of restoration. Spare a moment for the reliquaries. Juan de Arfe, maker of the world's biggest silver monstrances, is represented here with one that seems almost a small palace, complete with marble columns. Spain's most famous, and possibly most bizarre reliquary, is the **Alfonsine Tables**, filled with over 200 tiny bits of tooth and bone. They were said to have belonged to Alfonso the Wise and were made to provide extra-powerful juju for him to carry into battle.

The Archive of the Indies

Open weekdays, 10–1.

In common with most of its contemporaries, parts of Sevilla's cathedral were public ground, and the porches, the Patio de los Naranjos, and often even the naves and chapels were used to transact all sorts of business. A 16th-century bishop put an end to this practice, but prevailed upon Felipe II to construct next to the cathedral an exchange, or **Lonja**, for the merchants. Felipe sent his favourite architect, Juan de Herrera, then still busy with El Escorial, to design it. The severe, elegant façades are typically Herreran, and the stone balls and pyramids on top are practically the architect's signature. By the 1780s, little commerce was still going on in Sevilla, and what was left of the American trade passed through Cádiz, so Carlos III converted the lonely old building to hold the **Archive of the Indies**, the repository of all the reports, maps, drawings and documents the crown collected during the age of exploration. The collection, the richest in the world, has not even yet been entirely sifted through by scholars; but they are always worth a look.

The Alcázar

Open daily 9–12.45, 3–5.30; Sat and Sun 9–1.30; adm 600 pts.

It's easy to be fooled into thinking this is a Moorish palace; some of its rooms and courtyards seem to come straight from the Alhambra. Most of them, however, were built—by Moorish workmen, to be sure—for King Pedro the Cruel of Castile in the 1360s. The Alcázar and its king represent a fascinating cul-de-sac in Spanish history and culture, and allow the possibility that al-Andalus might have assimilated its conquerors rather than have been destroyed by them.

Pedro was an interesting character. In Froissart's *Chronicle*, we have him described as 'full of marveylous opinyons... rude and rebell agaynst the commandements of holy churche'. Certainly he didn't mind having his Moorish artists, lent by the kings of Granada, adorn his palace with sayings from the *Koran* in Kufic calligraphy. Pedro preferred Sevilla, still half-Moorish and more than half-decadent, to Old Castile, and he filled his court here with Moorish poets and dancers, and Moorish bodyguards—the only ones he trusted. Unfortunately, he was not the man for the job of cultural synthesis. The evidence, in so far as it is reliable, suggests he richly deserved his honorific 'the Cruel'; his brother Don Fadrique is only one of many he is said to have assassinated in this palace. One of the biggest jewels set in the British crown was a gift from Pedro to the Black Prince—he murdered an ambassador from Granada to get it off his turban.

Long before Pedro, the Alcázar was the palace of the Moorish governors. Begun under Abd ar-Rahman II in the 840s, it assumed its present form gradually over the next four centuries. Important additions were made under the Almohads; the Alcázar was their capital in al-Andalus. Almost all the decorative work you see now was done under Pedro, some by the Granadans and the rest by Muslim artists from Toledo; altogether it is the outstanding production of Mudéjar art in Spain.

The Alcázar is entered through a little gate on the Plaza del Triunfo, on the south side of the cathedral. The first courtyard, the **Patio de la Montería**, has beautiful arabesques, with lions amid castles for Castile and León mixed in; this was the public court of the palace, where visitors were received, corresponding to the Mexuar at the Alhambra. At the far end of the Patio is the lovely **façade** of the interior palace, decorated with inscriptions in Gothic and Arabic scripts.

Much of the best Mudéjar work can be seen in the adjacent halls and courts; their seemingly haphazard arrangement was in fact a principle of the art, to increase the surprise and delight in passing from one to the next. The **Patio de Yeso** (Court of Plaster) is largely a survival of the Almoravid palace of the 1170s, itself built on the site of a Roman *praetorium*. The **Patio de las Doncellas** (Court of the Maidens), entered through the gate of the palace façade, is the largest of the courtyards, a little more ornate than the rooms of the Alhambra—built at the same time and possibly by some of the same craftsmen.

The Patio de las Doncellas leads to the **Salón de los Embajadores** (Hall of the Ambassadors), a small, domed chamber that is the finest in the Alcázar despite jarring additions from the time of Carlos V. In Moorish times this was the throne room. Another small court, the **Patio de la Muñecas** (Court of the Dolls) where King Pedro's bodyguards cut down Don Fadrique, takes its name from two tiny faces on medallions at the base of one of the horseshoe arches—a little joke on the part of the Muslim stone-carvers. The columns here come from the ruins of Medinat az-Zahra.

Spanish kings after Pedro couldn't leave the Alcázar alone. Fernando and Isabel spoiled a large corner of it for their **Casa de Contratación**, a planning centre for the colonization of the Indies. There's little to see in it: a big conference table, Isabel's bedroom, a model of the *Santa María* in wood and a model of the royal family (Isabel's) in silver. Carlos V added a **palace** of his own, as he did in the Alhambra. This one isn't much, either, but it contains a spectacular set of **Flemish tapestries** showing finely detailed scenes of Carlos's campaigns in Tunisia.

Within its walls, the Alcázar has extensive and lovely **gardens**, with reflecting pools, palm trees, avenues of clipped hedges, and lemons and oranges everywhere. The park is deceptively large, but you can't get lost unless you find the little **labyrinth** near the pavilion built for Carlos V in the lower gardens. Outside the walls, there are more gardens, a formal promenade called the **Plaza Catalina de Ribera**, with two monuments to Columbus, and the **Jardines de Murillo**, small though beautifully landscaped, bordering the northern wall of the Alcázar.

West of the Cathedral

Avenida de la Constitución, passing the façade of the cathedral, is Sevilla's main street. Between it and the Guadalquivir are mostly quiet neighbourhoods, without the distinction of the Barrio Santa Cruz but still with a charm of their own.

Hospital de la Caridad

Built in 1647 behind a colourful façade on Calle Temprado is the Hospital de la Caridad. The Hospital's original benefactor was a certain Miguel de Mañara, a reformed rake who may have been the prototype for Tirso de Molina's Don Juan. Though it still serves its intended purpose as a charity home for the aged, visitors come to see the art in the hospital chapel. The best is gone, unfortunately—in the lobby they'll show you photographs of the Murillos stolen by Napoleon. Among what remains are three works of art, ghoulish even by Spanish standards. Juan de Valdés Leal (1622–90) was a competent enough painter, but warmed to the task only with such subjects as you see here: a bishop in full regalia decomposing in his coffin, and Death snuffing out your candle while bestriding paintings, church paraphernalia, and books. Even better than these is the anonymous, polychrome bloody Jesus, surrounded by smiling Baroque *putti*, who carry, instead of harps and bouquets, whips and scourges.

Torre del Oro

The Moorish tower stands on the banks of the Guadalquivir. In the days of the explorers, ships were still small enough to make this the maritime centre of the city; with a little imagination you can picture the scene when the annual silver fleet came in: the great, low-riding galleons tossing ropes to stevedores on the quay, the crowds and scrambling children, the king's officials and their battalions of guards, more than a few Indians probably, and the agents of the Flemish and Italian bankers in the background, smiling bemusedly while mentally plotting the most expeditious means of finessing the booty out of Spain. For over a century, the fleet's arrival was the event of the year, the turning point of an annual feast-or-famine cycle when all debts would be made good, and long deferred indulgences could finally be had.

The Torre del Oro, built by the Almohads in 1220, was the southernmost point of the city's fortifications, constructed on a now demolished extension of the walls to guard the river. In times of trouble a chain would be stretched from the tower and across the Guadalquivir. It took its name from the gold and *azulejo* tiles that covered its 12-sided exterior in the days of the Moors. The interior now houses a small **Maritime Museum** (*open daily except Mon, 10–2, Sun till 1*). On the Guadalquivir, however, there probably won't be a ship in sight. The water you see, in fact, isn't the Guadalquivir at all; the river has been canalized around the city to the new ports to the south, leaving the old bed a backwater.

La Maestranza Bullring

On the river just north of the tower is another citadel of Sevillan *duende*. La Maestranza bullring, built in 1760, is not as big as Madrid's, but is still a lovely building, and perhaps the most prestigious of all *plazas de toros*. It also carries the third-busiest schedule, after Madrid and Barcelona; if you like to watch as your *cola de toro* is prepared, you may be fortunate enough to see a *corrida* while in town. The bullring's name comes from the big **Maestranza arsenal** across the street.

Triana

Across the Guadalquivir from the bullring is the neighbourhood of Triana, an ancient suburb that takes its name from the Emperor Trajan. It has a reputation as the 'cradle of flamenco' and its workmen make all Sevilla's *azulejo* tiles. Queipo de Llano's troops wrecked a lot of it at the start of the civil war, but there are still picturesque, white streets overlooking the Guadalquivir, and quite a few bars and clubs.

Gypsy Eggs

 Tapas bars dominate Sevilla although the city has a reputation for *huevos a la flamenca* or gypsy eggs. The eggs are oven-baked with chorizo, ham, tomatoes, potatoes and numerous other vegetables. There are three wine-producing regions in the province of Sevilla but the favourite tipple is *manzanilla* sherry, which is matured in Sanlúcar de Barrameda in bodegas along the coast.

Northwest of the Cathedral

Back across the river, over the Puente de Triana, you'll approach the San Eloy district, full of raucous bars and hotels. On Calle San Pablo is **La Magdalena** (1704), with an eccentric Baroque façade decorated with sundials. Among the art inside are two paintings of the *Life of St Dominic* by Zurbarán, and gilded reliefs by Leonardo de Figueroa.

Museo de Bellas Artes

Open daily except Mon, 10–2 and 4–7; Sat and Sun, mornings only.

This excellent collection is housed in the **Convento de la Merced** (1612), on Calle San Roque. There are some fine medieval works—sweetly naïve-looking virgins, and an especially expressive triptych by the 'Master of Burgos' from the 13th century. The Italian sculptor Torregiani (the fellow who broke Michelangelo's nose, and who died in a Sevilla prison) has left an uncanny barbaric wooden **St Jerome**. This saint, *Jerónimo* in Spanish, is a favourite in Sevilla, always pictured with a rock and a rugged cross instead of his usual lion; as the Doctor of the Church, he helped most to define the concepts of heresy and self-mortification.

The museum has a roomful of Murillos (the painter was Sevillan and is buried in the Barrio Santa Cruz), including an *Immaculate Conception* and many other artful missal-pictures. Much more interesting are the works of Zurbarán, who could express spirituality without the simpering of Murillo or the hysteria of the others. His series of **female saints** is especially good, and the *Miracle of Saint Hugo* is perhaps his most acclaimed work. Occasionally even Zurbarán slips up; you may enjoy the *Eternal Father* with great fat toes and a triangle on his head, a *St Gregory* who looks like the scheming church executive he really was, and the wonderful *Apotheosis of St Thomas Aquinas*, where the great scholastic philosopher rises to his feet as if to say 'I've got it!'. Don't miss El Greco's portrait of his son Jorge. There are also more Valdés Leal—heads on plates, and such—and works by Jan Brueghel, Ribera, Caravaggio, and Mattia Preti.

North of the Cathedral

Sevilla's business and shopping area has been, since Moorish times, the patch of narrow streets north of La Giralda. **Calle Sierpes** ('serpent street') is its heart, a sinuous pedestrian lane lined with every sort of old shop. Just to the north, **El Salvador** is a fine Baroque church by Leonardo de Figueroa, picturesquely mouldering; the base of its tower was the minaret of an important mosque that once stood here; the plaza in front is a popular hang-out of Sevilla's youth, as well as their backpacking cousins from northern Europe.

On the **Plaza Nueva**, Sevilla's modern centre, you can see the grimy 1564 **Ayuntamiento**, with a fine, elaborate plateresque façade. From here, Avenida de la Constitución changes its name to Calle Tetuán. Sevilla has found a hundred ways to use its *azulejos*, but the best has to be in the **billboard** on this street for 1932 Studebaker cars; so pretty that no one's had the heart to take it down.

Marcarena

The north end of Sevilla contains few monuments; most of it is solid, working-class neighbourhoods clustered around Baroque parish churches. The **Alameda de Hércules**, a once fashionable promenade adorned with copies of ancient statues, is in the middle of one of the shabbier parts. **Santa Clara** and **San Clemente** are two interesting monasteries in this area: Santa Clara includes a Gothic tower built by Don Fadrique, Pedro the Cruel's brother; its pretty chapel has one of Sevilla's best *artesonado* ceilings. North of Calle San Luis, a stretch of the city's **Moorish walls** survives, near the **Basilica of La Macarena**, which gives the quarter its name. The Basilica is the home of the best-worshipped of Sevilla's idols, a delicate Virgin with glass tears on her cheeks who always steals the show in the Holy Week parades. Like a film star she makes her admirers gasp and swarm around her, crying '*¡O la hermosa! ¡O la guapa!*' ('O the beautiful! O the handsome!') The small adjacent **museum** is divided between La Macarena's trinkets and costumes of famous bullfighters.

DETAIL FROM CHURCH.

South from here, along Calle San Luis, you'll pass another Baroque extravaganza, Leonardo de Figueroa's **San Luis**, built for the Jesuits (1699–1731), with twisted columns and tons of encrusted ornament. **San Marcos**, down the street, has one of Sevilla's last surviving Mudéjar towers.

East of the Cathedral

If Spain envies Sevilla, Sevilla envies **Barrio Santa Cruz**, a tiny, exceptionally lovely quarter of narrow streets and whitewashed houses. It is the true homeland of everything *sevillana*, with flower-bedecked patios and iron-bound windows through which the occasional nostalgic young man still gets up the nerve to embarrass his sweetheart with a serenade.

Before 1492, this was the Jewish quarter of Sevilla; today it's the most aristocratic corner of town. In the old days there was a wall around the barrio; today you may enter through the Jardines de Murillo, the Calle Mateos Gago behind the cathedral apse, or from the **Patio de las Banderas**, a pretty Plaza Mayor-style square next to the Alcázar. On the eastern edge of the Barrio, **Santa María la Blanca** (on the street of the same name) was a pre-Reconquista church; some ancient details remain, but the whole was rebuilt in the 1660s, with spectacular rococo ornamentation inside and paintings by Murillo.

Casa de Pilatos

Open daily 10–1 and 3– 9 in summer, 3–7 in winter; adm 400 pts.

On the eastern fringes of the old town, the Barrio Santa Cruz fades gently into other peaceful pretty areas—less ritzy, though their old streets wear more palaces. One of these, built by the Dukes of Medinaceli (1480–1571) is the **Casa de Pilatos** on Plaza Pilatos. The dukes like to tell people that it is a replica of 'Pontius Pilate's house' in Jerusalem. (Pilate, without whom Holy Week would not be possible, is a popular figure; there's a common belief that he was a Spaniard.) It is a pleasant jumble of Mudéjar and Renaissance work, with a lovely patio and lots of *azulejos* everywhere. The entrance, a mock-Roman triumphal arch done in Carrara marble by sculptors from Genoa, leads through a small court into the **Patio Principal**, with 13th-century Granadan decoration, beautiful coloured tiles, and rows of Roman statues and portrait busts—an introduction to the dukes' excellent collections of antique sculpture in the surrounding rooms, including a Roman copy of a Greek herm (boundary marker, with the head of the god Hermes), imperial portraits, and a bust of Hadrian's boyfriend, Antinous.

Behind the Casa de Pilatos, **San Esteban**, rebuilt from a former mosque, has an altarpiece by Zurbarán; around the corner on Calle Luis Montoto are remains of an Almoravid **aqueduct**. On Calle Aguilas, **San Ildefonso** has a pretty yellow and white 18th-century façade. Another post-1492 palace with Mudéjar decoration, several streets north on Calle Busta Tavera, is the huge **Palacio de las Dueñas**.

South of the Cathedral

Sevilla has a building even larger than its cathedral—twice as large, in fact, and probably better known to the outside world. Since the 1950s it has housed parts of the city's **university** and it does have the presence of a college building, but it began its life in the 1750s as the state Fábrica de Tabacos (Tobacco Factory). In the 19th century, it employed as many as 12,000 women to roll cigars—as historians note, the biggest female urban proletariat in the world. One of its members, of course, was Bizet's Carmen. These sturdy women, with 'carnations in their hair and daggers in their garters', hung their capes on the altars of the factory chapels each morning, rocked their babies in cradles while they rolled cigars, and took no nonsense from anybody.

Parque de María Luisa

For all its old fashioned grace, Sevilla has been one of the most forward-looking and progressive cities of Spain in this century. In the 1920s, while they were redirecting the Guadalquivir and building the new port and factories that are the foundation of the city's growth today, the *sevillanos* decided to put on an exposition. In a tremendous burst of energy, they turned the entire southern end of the city into an expanse of gardens and grand boulevards. The centre of it is **Parque de María Luisa**, a paradisical half-mile of palms and orange trees, elms and Mediterranean pines, covered with flower beds and dotted with hidden bowers, ponds and pavilions. Now that the trees and shrubs have reached maturity, the genius of the landscapers can be appreciated—this is one of the loveliest parks in Europe.

Two of the largest pavilions on the **Plaza de América** have been turned into museums. The **Archaeological Museum** (*open daily except Sun and Mon, 10–2*) has one of the best collections of pre-Roman jewellery and icons, reproductions of the fine goldwork of the 'Treasure of Carambelo', and some tantalizing artefacts from mysterious Tartessos. The Romans are represented, as in every other Mediterranean archaeology museum, with copies of Greek sculpture and oversized statues of emperors, but also with a mosaic of the *Triumph of Bacchus*, another of Hercules, architectural fragments, some fine glass, and finds of all sorts from Itálica and other nearby towns. Across the plaza, the **Museum of Popular Art and Customs** (*open daily except Mon, 10–2*) is Andalucía's attic, with everything from ploughs and saucepans to *azulejo* tiles, flamenco dresses (polka dots weren't always the style), musical instruments, religious bric-à-brac and exhibits for the city's two famous celebrations, Semana Santa and the April Feria.

The Plaza de España

In the 1920s at least, excess was still a way of life in Sevilla, and to call attention to the *Exposición Iberoamericana* they put up a building even bigger than the Tobacco Factory. With its grand Baroque towers (stolen gracefully from Santiago de Compostela), fancy bridges, staircases and immense colonnade, the Plaza de España is World Fair architecture at its grandest and most outrageous. Much of the fanciful neo-Spanish architecture of 1930s Florida and California may well have been inspired by this building. *sevillanos* gravitate naturally to it at weekends, to row canoes in the Plaza's canals and nibble curious pastries. One of the things Sevilla is famous for is its painted *azulejo* tiles; they adorn nearly every building in town, but here on the colonnade a few million of them are devoted to maps and historical scenes from every province in Spain.

Cartuja

Open 7pm–2am Tues–Sun in the summer; 11am–midnight Fri–Sun in the winter; adm 2000 pts, 1500 pts for under-15s, 500 pts excluding the pavillions; © (95) 446 16 16.

The Isla de la Cartuja is slowly regaining its identity after Expo 92. The island was part of the Expo site during the world fair whose theme, the 'Age of Discoveries', marked the

500th anniversary of the discovery of the New World. Expo 92 attracted 16 million people with its 98 pavilions and more than a hundred countries took part. Today only 17 pavilions remain and Cartuja has been repackaged as the 'Park of Discoveries' with minigolf and other open air entertainments. Columbus once stayed on the island while he mulled over his ambitions and geographical theories. Now the ghost of Expo hangs over Cartuja. The entrance fees are exorbitant and it's rather like turning up for a party a day late. One of the pavilion titles says it all: 'Memories of Expo'.

Where to Stay

Not many of Sevilla's hotels are distinctive in any way, but there are plenty of rooms all over the centre. High season is March and April. During *Semana Santa* and the April *Feria* you should book even for inexpensive *hostales*, preferably a year ahead.

expensive

The ★★★★★**Alfonso XIII**, Calle San Fernando 2, ✆ (95) 422 28 50, fax 421 60 33, built for the *Exposición Iberoamericana* in 1929, this luxury hotel is named after the unfortunate monarch then reigning. Probably *the* prestige hotel of southern Spain, in a huge building in landscaped grounds next to the University, the Alfonso attracts royalty, opera stars and heads of state; Sevilla society still meets around its lobby fountain and bars (38,000–57,000 pts for a palatial double). The ★★★★★**Hotel Colón**, Calle Canalejas 1, ✆ (95) 422 29 00, fax 422 09 38, was totally refurbished for the 1992 Expo and in former times was a haunt of bullfighters and their hangers-on. It is a grand and extremely comfortable place to stay (19,000–31,000 pts for a double). By the Macarena walls, the ★★★★**Macarena**, San Juan de Rivera 2, ✆ (95) 437 57 00, fax 438 18 03, is another classy establishment although it's not exactly central; the lobby has a beautiful *azulejo* tiled fountain, and the service is excellent. The roof-top terrace has views over the city, and a swimming pool. Rates are very reasonable for this category: 19,000–29,000 pts. Near the Prado de San Sebastián, the ★★★★**Meliá Sevilla**, Doctor Pedro Castro 1, ✆ (95) 442 26 11, fax 442 16 08, is a very pleasant modern hotel within easy walking distance of the city centre, and has some lovely suites (22,500–32,000 pts for double rooms). The ★★★★**Hotel Doña María**, Calle Don Remondo 19, ✆ (95) 422 49 90, fax 421 95 46, is superbly located by the cathedral and is also utterly charming. Furniture is mostly antique with some beautifully painted headboards (10,000–24,000 pts).

moderate

The ★**Hotel Simón**, García de Vinuesa 14, ✆ (95) 422 66 60, fax 456 22 41, just off the Avenida de la Constitución by the cathedral, is in a restored 18th-century mansion, and is also quite popular (6,000–9,000 pts for a double). The ★★**Hostal Atenas**, Calle Caballerizas 1, ✆ (95) 421 80 47; quiet and very nice, in a good location between the Plaza Pilatos and the cathedral. Take a cab, it's hard to find

(7,000–10,000 pts for doubles with bath). The ***Hostal Plaza Sevilla**, Canalejas 2, ℂ (95) 421 71 49, fax 421 07 73, is the work of Aníbal González, the architect of the 1929 Expositión, and is ideal for the restaurants and bars of St Eloy (10,000–16,000 pts). The ***Pensión Toledo**, Santa Teresa 15, ℂ (95) 421 53 35, is respectable and good value (6,000–10,000 pts). The **Monreal***, Calle Rodrigo Caro 8, ℂ (95) 421 41 66, is closest to the cathedral, a lively place with almost too much character and a good cheap restaurant when they feel like opening it (5,500–10,000 pts for a double).

inexpensive

For inexpensive *hostales*, the Barrio Santa Cruz is surprisingly the best place to look. Even in July and August, you'll be able to find a place on the quiet side streets off Mateos Gago. The ***Pensión Fabiola**, Fabiola 6, ℂ (95) 421 83 46 (6,000–8,000 pts), the ***Hostal Córdoba**, Farnesio 12, ℂ (95) 422 74 98 (4,700–7,000 pts) and the ***Hostal El Buen Dormir**, Farnesio 8, ℂ (95) 421 74 92 (4,500–8,000 pts) are all officially listed, but there are many more and it's best to explore on foot and see for yourself. The biggest selection of all, however, is along Calle San Eloy just east of the now defunct Córdoba station; it's theatrically urban any hour of the day.

Eating Out

Restaurants here are more expensive than in most of Spain, but even around the cathedral and the Barrio Santa Cruz, there are few places that can simply be dismissed as tourist traps. Remember that in the evening the *sevillanos*, even more than most Andalucíans, enjoy bar-hopping for tapas, rather than sitting down to one meal; two Sevillanos in a bar is a party, three is a fiesta.

expensive

A few places have attractions beyond the cuisine: **La Albahaca**, Plaza Santa Cruz, ℂ (95) 422 07 14, has tables outside, artwork on its crockery and three dining rooms, creating a romantic and relaxing atmosphere. Specialities include scorpion fish with fennel and peanuts; mushrooms with green asparagus; partridge with endives. Prices start at around 4,000 pts per head (closed Sun). Splendidly situated on the corner of the Jardines Alcázar, opposite the university, is one of Sevilla's best-oved restaurants, the **Egaña-Oriza**, San Fernando 41, ℂ (95) 422 72 11. It serves the best of Andaluz and Basque cuisine. Among its tempting delights are: spider crab mousse, and escalope of goose in pear sauce (4,500 pts minimum with wine; closed Sun and Aug). The restaurant also has the separately run **Bar España** for good fish and salad tapas. North of La Giralda, you can dine well on French and Italian specialities at **San Marco**, Cuna 6, ℂ (95) 421 24 40, in a large, old, elegantly decorated *sevillana* house; try the ravioli stuffed with sea bass, crayfish salad in *Marie-Rose* sauce, tournedos of duck foie gras. (4,000–5,000 pts). By the cathedral, in the narrow Argote de Molina (at no. 26) is **Mesón Don Raimundo**,

© (95) 422 33 55, a restaurant in what was once a convent. No enforced abstinence here, though. You can pig out on the large selection of fish, shellfish, and game dishes amid an eclectic decor of religious artefacts and suits of armour (3,000–4,000 pts; closed Sun evening). Along the Triana side of the Guadalquivir, you can dine with a view of the Torre del Oro and La Giralda at the restaurant **Río Grande**, Calle Betis s/n, © (95) 427 39 56. The kitchen here specializes in regional cuisine (3,500 pts), and on a Sunday afternoon if there's a good *corrida*, you can join in the roars of *olé* that erupt from the bullring on the opposite bank. Along from here is **Ox's**, Calle Betis 61, © (95) 427 95 85, with Basque novelties—cod-stuffed peppers, fish and steaks (at least 3,000 pts; closed Sun and Aug).

moderate

Don Raimundo also owns two other restaurants near his Mesón: **La Barca**, Placentines 25, © (95) 456 04 91, which specializes in fish and seafood; and **Las Meninas** on Calle Manara. The **Bodegón Torre del Oro**, Calle Santander 15, © (95) 421 42 41, specializes in *urta roteña*, a hard-fleshed fish caught on the coast. There's a three course set meal with wine for 3,000 pts and the *raciones* are good (closed Sun except July and Aug).

inexpensive

The lively tapas bar **Bodega La Andana**, Argote de Molina, is where hordes of Sevilla's *caballeros* and *señoritas* spill out onto the pavement, particularly at weekends, to misspend their youth. Around the corner you can eat decently at the bar-restaurant **Gonzalo**, corner of Alemanes and Argote de Molina, with the Giralda looming overhead. There's a reasonably priced and varied menu (around 1,200 pts), but the walls could do with a lick of paint. **Bar Giralda**, Calle Mateos Gago, as its name suggests, is closer still and has a good selection of sherries. **Bar Modesto** is a short walk away from the cathedral on Calle Cano y Cueta serving breakfast, *raciones* and full meals. **Kiosko de las Flores** serves light fish lunches of *boquerones*, among other things. The place is an informal café-bar, right by the Puente de Isabel II, and part of it looks over the water. Prices are a little high—a glorified fishy snack with a drink costs 1,300 pts. A little difficult to find, but well worth the search, is the best tapas bar in Sevilla, and the most charming in all of Andalucía. North of the cathedral, between the church of San Pedro and the convent

Espíritu Santo, is **El Rinconillo**, at Gerona 42; the place dates back to 1670 and is decorated in moody brown *azulejo*; here lively *sevillana cognoscenti* gather to dabble at the tasty nibbles, but their real purpose is to model their designer clothes and spend the evening in loud animated highbrow chatter. The staff, oblivious, chalk up the bill on the bar.

cheap

Sevilla's cheapest restaurants lurk around Calle San Eloy. Some almost give meals away, and they're worth the price. It's better to stick with the tapas and *mariscos* bars here and in the little streets of Calle Tetuán and Calle Sierpes. The **Antigua Bodequita** is a find, a tiny bar opposite the church on Plaza del Salvador, but if you just fancy cakes, coffee or ice cream head for **La Campana** on Calle Sierpes. Established in 1885, it's probably the prettiest patisserie around.

Entertainment and Nightlife

Take a **river cruise** along the Guadalquivir. Two companies do it daily (3.45 and 4.30), both from around the Torre del Oro. See a **bullfight** in the famous Maestranza if you can, but don't just turn up! Get tickets as far ahead as you can; prices at the ring office, © (95) 422 45 77, will be cheaper than at the little stands on Calle Sierpes. If you've been longing to experience **flamenco**, Sevilla is probably the place to do it. The touristy flamenco factories will hit you for 1,000 pts and up per drink. Bars in Triana and other areas do it better for less, but try to find an enthusiast (it shouldn't be hard) to steer you straight. The **Puerto de Triana**, Calle Castilla 137, © (95) 434 25 07, is well known for up-and-coming performers (open 10–3am); best to get there by taxi. They do play other kinds of music in Sevilla, and a little publication called *El Giraldillo*, available around town, has listings. For mainstream **drama**, the best-known theatre is the Teatro Lope de Vega, Avenida de María Luisa, © (95) 423 18 34, though a newcomer has recently taken over as principal lead—the Teatro de Maestranza, Paseo de Cristóbal Colón, © (95) 422 3344, opened in time for Expo 92 and has quickly established itself as one of the top **opera** houses in Europe.

Shopping

All the paraphernalia associated with Spanish fantasy, like *mantillas*, *castanets*, wrought iron, gypsy dresses and Andalucían dandy suites, *azulejo* tiles and embroidery, is available in Sevilla. Most of it's made here, and if you're interested in tours or just shopping, ask the Tourist Information office what's currently available. There are two branches of *El Corte Inglés*, where the well-heeled *sevillanos* shop, and even a branch of *C&A* on Calle Sierpes and a *Marks & Spencer* on Plaza Duque de la Victoria. *Vértice* is a bookshop on Mateos Gagos near the cathedral, with a small selection of English-language literature and local guide-books and history books; but for a pleasant wander head for the pedestrianised Calle Sierpes.

Getting Around

There is no train service for the towns around Sevilla, but plenty of buses. Itálica is on the Ctra Menda and ˙ has local buses leaving every half an hour from the Plaza de Armas, near the Puento del Cachorro. The main highway east and south is the N IV.

If you're travelling south on your way to Jerez or Cádiz, stops at a few towns on the way will make an interesting alternative to the big four-lane highway. **Alcalá de Guadaira**, off the N334, is jocularly known in Sevilla as Alcalá de los Panadores ('of the bakers'), as it used to supply the city with its daily bread. Its **castle** is the best-preserved Almohad fortress in Andalucía. Just outside Utrera, the tiny village of **Palmar de Troya** received a visit in 1968 from the Virgin Mary (to little girls, as usual) that has led to the founding of a new church, the 'Orden de la Santa Faz'. They have their own Pope in Palmar and include among their saints Franco, José Antonio and Ramon Llull. In **Lebrija**, the church of **Santa María de la Oliva** is really a 12th-century Almohad mosque, with a typical Middle Eastern roof of small domes and a tower that is a miniature version of La Giralda, built by a Basque architect in the 19th century.

Take care before you start any rambles in the countryside; this area south of Sevilla contains some of the best-known ranches where fighting bulls are bred, and the bulls are always allowed to run free.

Itálica

Open Tues–Sat 9.30–6.30, Sun 9–5.

Eight kilometres (5 miles) north of the city, the only significant Roman ruins in Andalucía are at **Itálica**, a city founded in the 3rd century BC by Scipio Africanus as a home for his veterans. Itálica thrived in the imperial age. The Guadalquivir had a reputation for constantly changing its course in the old days, and this may explain the presence of two important cities so close together. Three great emperors, Trajan, Hadrian and Theodosius, were born here. The biggest ruins are an **amphitheatre**, with seating for 40,000, some remains of temples, and a street of villa foundations. Surviving mosaics portray Hercules and Bacchus, a Cretan labyrinth, and battle of pygmies and cranes.

The village of Santiponce, near the ruins, has a fine Gothic-Mudéjar monastery built for the Cistercians in 1301: **San Isidoro del Campo**, with another gruesome Saint Jerome, carved in the 1600s by Juan Montañes, on the altarpiece.

From Sevilla to Córdoba

Getting There

There are two ways to go, both of approximately equal length. The train, and most of the buses, unfortunately take the duller route through the flat lands along the

Guadalquivir. The only landmark here is the Spanish-Moorish castle of **Almodóvar del Río**, perched romantically on a height planted with olive trees, overlooking the river. The southern route (the NIV) also follows the Guadalquivir valley, though the scenery is a little more varied, and the road passes through two fine towns, Carmona and Écija. There are regular buses from Sevilla to these towns, from which you can easily find connecting buses for Córdoba.

Tourist Offices

Carmona: there is no tourist office, but basic information is available from the Casa de Cultura, Plaza de las Descalzas.

Écija: the Ayuntamiento, Plaza de España, ✆ (95) 590 02 40.

Carmona

The first town along the NIV, Carmona seems a miniature Sevilla. It is probably much older. Remains of a Neolithic settlement have been found around town; the Phoenician colony that replaced it grew into a city and prospered throughout Roman and Moorish times. Pedro the Cruel favoured it and rebuilt most of its extensive **Alcázar**. Sitting proudly on top of the town, with views over the valley, this fortress is now a national *parador*.

Carmona is well worth a day's exploration. Its walls, mostly Moorish fortifications built over Roman foundations, are still standing, including a grand gateway on the road from Sevilla, the **Alcázar de la Puerta de Sevilla** (*open Fri and Sat 11–1*). Continue through the arch and up to the palm-decked Plaza de San Fernando, where the under-16s and over-60s gather; the Ayuntamiento here has a Roman mosaic of Medusa in its courtyard. Next, take Calle Martín López up to the lofty 15th-century church of **Santa María**, built on the site of an old mosque (*open daily except Mon 10–12, 7–8 and Sun 11–12, 7–8*). The old quarters of town have an ensemble of fine palaces, and Mudéjar and Renaissance churches. On one of these, **San Pedro** (1466), you'll see another imitation of La Giralda, *La Giraldilla*—though not as fussily ornate as her big sister, she has a cleaner exterior. Carmona's prime attraction is the **Roman necropolis**, a series of rock-cut tombs off the Avenida Jorge Bonsor. Some, like the 'Tomb of Servilia', are elaborate creations with subterranean chambers and vestibules, pillars, domed ceilings and carved reliefs (*open daily except Mon, 10–2 and 4–6, Sun 10–2*). Near the entrance to the site are remains of the Roman amphitheatre, forlorn and unexcavated.

Twenty-eight kilometres (17½ miles) south of Carmona on the C339, **Marchena** still retains many of its wall defences, dating from Roman times with later Moorish and Christian additions. Of its gates, the arch of **La Rosa** is best, and in the **Torre del Oro** there is a new archeological museum. The Gothic church of **San Juan Bautista** has an altar *retablo* by Alejo Fernández and a sculpture by Pedro Roldán. There's also a small museum with a collection of paintings by Zurbarán. Nearby **El Arahal** is a bleached white town worth visiting for its Baroque monuments, notably the church of **La Victoria** of Mudéjar origin.

Écija

Écija makes much of one of its nicknames, the 'city of towers' and tries to play down the other—the 'frying pan of Andalucía', which isn't exactly fair. Any Andalucían town can overheat you thoroughly on a typical summer's day, and if Écija is a degree hotter and a little less breezy than most, only a born Andalucían could tell the difference. Ask one, and you'll soon learn that the Andalucíans are the only people yet discovered who talk about the weather more than the English.

Don't be put off by the clinical outskirts of the town, nor by the ill-concealed gasometers; all is forgiven when you reach the **Plaza de España**, one of the loveliest in Andalucía, charmingly framed by tall palms and centred on an exquisite fountain. There's a church façade on the 18th-century **Santa María** that wouldn't look out of place in a Sergio Leone movie. The atmosphere here is laid-back, and once you've finished rubber-necking the steeples, choose your favourite corner of the plaza and do what the locals do—sit and watch. Most of the **towers** are sumptuously ornate late Baroque, rebuilt after the great earthquake of 1755—the one that flattened Lisbon. Santa María has one, along with **San Juan Bautista**, gaily decorated in coloured tiles, and **San Gil**. This last is the highest of the towers, and within are paintings by Alejo Fernández and Villegas Marmolejo.

Écija also has a set of Renaissance and Baroque palaces second in Andalucía only to those in Úbeda; most of these showy façades can be seen on or near the **Calle de los Caballeros**. Worth visiting is the **Mudéjar Palace**, dating from the 14th century, where you can find some interesting archeological remains, part Mudéjar, part Baroque, some Roman mosaics, reliefs, coins and glass. There's a museum in the **Peñaflor Palace** on Calle de Castellar, with exhibits of 18th-century art and sculpture, contemporary art and local traditional costumes. The palace itself (1728), with its grandiose façade and lovely patio, is one of the outstanding works of Andalucían Baroque. The **Santa Bárbara Museum of Sacred Art**, due to open in 1994, will have a more religious theme, and will also include furniture, silverware and handicrafts from the 16th to 19th centuries.

In the evening the town buzzes. After the big city crush of Sevilla, you might find that this is the perfect place to spend a couple of days—busy enough to be interesting, but not too frantic.

Where to Stay

Carmona

The ★★★★**Parador Nacional Alcázar del Rey Don Pedro**, Calle Los Alcázares, ℂ (95) 414 10 10, fax 414 17 12, occupying a section of Cruel Pete's castle, has commanding views, a garden, pool and luxurious furnishings and is good value for 15,000–16,000 pts for a double. Or sleep just as well at any of the town's attractive little *pensiones* and *hostales*. Good ones include the ★**Casa Carmelo**, Calle San Pedro 15, ℂ (95) 414 05 72, and the ★**Pensión Comercio**, Calle Torre del Oro, ℂ (95) 414 00 18, both for 4,000–5,000 pts.

There are two *hostales*, the **★★Ponce**, Plaza de Alvarado 2, ℂ (95) 584 60 88, and **★La Rubia**, Calle San Sebastián s/n; both with rooms for 4,800–5,200 pts. The **★★Hostal Los Ángeles** is on the Ctra Sevilla–Granada, Km 67, ℂ (95) 484 70 88.

Écija

The hotels are mostly motels on the outskirts, serving traffic on the Madrid–Cádiz highway. The **★★Hotel Platería**, Calle Garcilópez, ℂ (95) 483 50 10, is probably the best in town. It's just off the main square with a lovely black and white marbled courtyard (8,500 pts). The **★★Ciudad del Sol**, Calle Cervantes 42, ℂ (95) 483 03 00, fax 483 58 79, is also good with friendly service and air-conditioned rooms (7,500 pts for a double). If that's full, try the **★★Astigi**, ℂ (95) 483 01 62, on the same road (7,300 pts). A minute's walk from the main plaza, in a little back street behind the fabulously named Gasolina Bar, will take you to the delightful little **Fonda Santa Cruz**, ℂ (95) 483 02 22. The simple rooms open out to the tiled courtyard, and were probably stables once (3,400 pts).

Eating Out

Carmona

The restaurant **San Fernando**, Plaza San Fernando, has the best reputation in town and the highest prices with a splendid five course set menu at 3,500 pts; you'll find all the local dishes here. Fish features largely on the menu at the **Parador**, but prices are more reasonable, and at **El Ancla**, Bonifacio 4, ℂ (95) 414 15 18 (closed Mon and Sun nights), where a full fish meal with wine will set you back a moderate 2,500–3,000 pts. **Mesón de la Reja** is on the main street as you enter from Sevilla. With a cool *azulejo* interior, it's a good place to try *cola de toro* and down a beer (about 1,000 pts), while keeping an eye on the bus departures opposite. (Incidentally, if you need bus information, don't ask the drivers— the only person who knows for sure is the man behind the bar at the bus stop.)

Marchena

You can find the local specialities in the two restaurants on Travesía de San Ignacio: **Los Muleros**, ℂ (95) 484 31 99, and **El Fogón**, both for around 1,500 pts.

Écija

The best place in town is the stylish **Bodegón del Gallego**, Calle A. Aparicio 3, ℂ (95) 483 26 18, which concentrates on Andaluz dishes (3,500 pts). Also in the heart of town, the **Pasareli**, Pasaje Virgen del Rocío, ℂ (95) 483 20 24, looks like any modern cafeteria, but there's a surprisingly efficient little restaurant tucked away in the corner, where you can eat well from a large selection of meat and fish for under 2,000 pts.

Córdoba

There are a few spots around the Mediterranean where the presence of past glories becomes almost tangible, a mixture of mythic antiquity, lost power and dissipated energy that broods over a place like a ghost. In Istanbul you can find it, in Rome, or among the monuments of Egypt, and also here on the banks of the Guadalquivir at Córdoba's southern gate. Looking around, you can see reminders of three defunct empires: a Roman bridge, a triumphal arch built for Felipe II and Córdoba's Great Mosque, more than a thousand years old. The first reminds us of the city's beginnings, the second of its decline; the last one scarcely seems credible, as it speaks of an age when Córdoba was the brilliant metropolis of all Europe, city of half-a-million souls, a place faraway storytellers would use to enthral audiences in the rude halls of the Saxons and Franks.

The little plaza by the bridge concentrates melancholy like a magnet; there isn't much left for the rest of the town. Unlike Rome or Istanbul, Córdoba seems largely free of the burden of the past. Its recent growth has allowed it a chance to renovate its sparkling old quarters and monuments. With the new prosperity has come a contentment the city probably hasn't known since the Reconquista.

Everyone who visits Andalucía comes for the Great Mosque, but you should spare some time to explore the city itself. Old Córdoba is one of the largest medieval quarters of any European city, and certainly the biggest in Spain. More than Sevilla, it retains its Moorish character, in a maze of whitewashed alleys opening into the loveliest patios in all Andalucía.

History

Roman *Corduba*, built on the site of an Iberian town, was almost from the start the leading city of interior Spain, capital of the province of *Hispania Ulterior*, and later of the reorganized province of Bætica. Córdoba had a reputation as the garden spot of Hispania; it gave Roman letters Lucan and both Senecas among others, testimony to its prominence as a city of learning.

Córdoba became Christianized at an early date. Ironically, the True Faith got its come-uppance here in 572, when the Arian Visigoths under Leovigild captured the city from Byzantine rule. When the Arabs arrived, they found it an important town still, and it became the capital of al-Andalus when Abd ar-Rahman established the Ummayyad emirate in 756. For 300 years, Córdoba enjoyed the position of unqualified leader of al-Andalus. It is hard to take the chroniclers at face value—3,000 mosques

MAIMONIDES STATUE
CÓRDOBA

and 80,000 shops, a library of 400,000 volumes, in a city stretching for 16km (10 miles) along the banks of the Guadalquivir. We can settle for half that, and still be impressed. Beyond doubt, Córdoba was a city without equal in the West as a centre of learning; it would be enough to mention two 12th-century contemporaries, **Averroës**, the Muslim scientist and Aristotelian philosopher who contributed so much to the rebirth of classical learning in Europe, and **Moses Maimonides**, the Jewish philosopher (and later personal physician to Saladin in Palestine) whose reconciliation of faith and reason were assumed into Christianity by Thomas Aquinas.

Medieval Córdoba was a great trading centre, and its luxury goods were coveted throughout western Europe; the old word *cordwainer* is a memory of Córdoba's skill in leather goods. At its height, picture Córdoba as a city of bustling international markets, great palaces, schools, baths and mosques, with 28 suburbs and the first street lighting in Europe. Its population, largely Spanish, Moorish and Arab, included students and merchants from all over Europe, Africa and Asia, and an army and palace secretariat made up largely of Slavs and black Africans. In it Muslims, Christians, and Jews lived in harmony, at least until the coming of the fanatical Almoravids and Almohads. We can sense a certain amount of decadence; street riots in Córdoba were an immediate cause of the breaking-up of the caliphate in 1031, but here, as in Sevilla, the coming of the Reconquista was an unparalleled catastrophe. When Fernando III captured the city in 1236, much of the population chose flight over putting themselves at the mercy of the priests. Three centuries of Castilian rule sufficed to rob Córdoba of all its glories and turn it into a shrunken and depressed backwater. Only in the last hundred years has it begun to recover; today Córdoba is an industrial city, though you wouldn't guess it from its immaculately restored centre. It is the third city of Andalucía, and the first and only big town since Franco's death to have elected a communist mayor and council.

History down the Hatch

 Córdoban cuisine reflects its history—many local dishes maintain Arabic and Jewish traditions. There are casseroles with chick peas, chards and spinach, and *rabos de toro* (oxtail stew) is popular. So is *picadillo*—the finely chopped peppers, tomatoes and onions often used as an accompaniment. The surrounding olive groves provide oil for the basis of Córdoban cooking such as an orange salad with oil, cod and green peppers. El Valle de los Pedroches used to be known as 'the valley of granite' by the Moors and its Iberian pig hams are as renowned as those from Huelva. Ham occasionally finds its way into Córdoba's famous desserts, such as *pastel cordobés*, which is otherwise made of puff pastry and angel's hair.

Getting Around

by train

Córdoba is on the major Madrid–Sevilla rail line, so there are always plenty of trains in both directions, besides two daily *Talgos* to each of Madrid and Málaga,

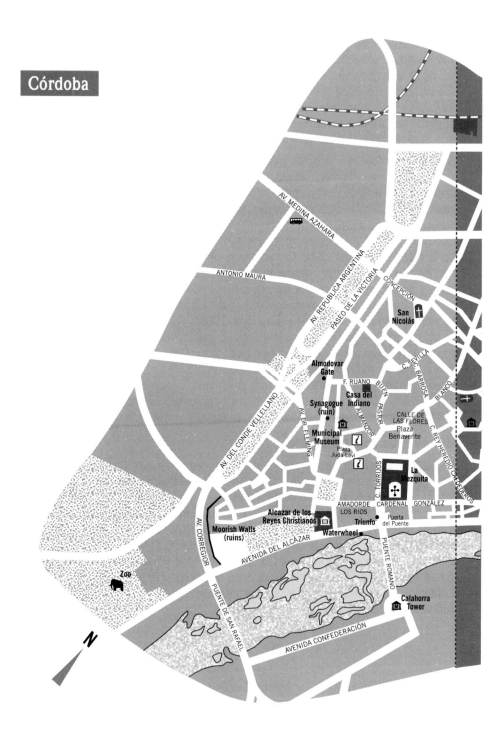

Córdoba

AV. MEDINA AZAHARA

ANTONIO MAURA

AV. REPÚBLICA ARGENTINA

PASEO DE LA VICTORIA

CONCEPCIÓN

San
Nicolás

C. SEVILLA

C. C. BARROSA

BLANCO

Almodovar
Gate

F. RUANO

BUEN

PASTOR

Casa del
Indiano

Synagogue
(ruin)

ALMANZOR

CALLE DE
LAS FLORES

Plaza
Benavente

C. REY HEREDIO

CALDEREROS

Municipal
Museum

Plaza
Judá Leví

AV. DEL CONDE VELLELLANO

AV. DR. FLEMING

C. TORRIJOS

La
Mezquita

AMADORDE
LOS RIOS

CARDENAL GONZÁLEZ

Alcazar de los
Reyes Christianos

Triunfo

Puerta
del Puente

AV. CORREGIOR

Moorish Walls
(ruins)

Waterwheel

AVENIDA DEL ALCÁZAR

PUENTE ROMANO

Zoo

PUENTE DE SAN RAFAEL

Calahorra
Tower

AVENIDA CONFEDERACIÓN

N

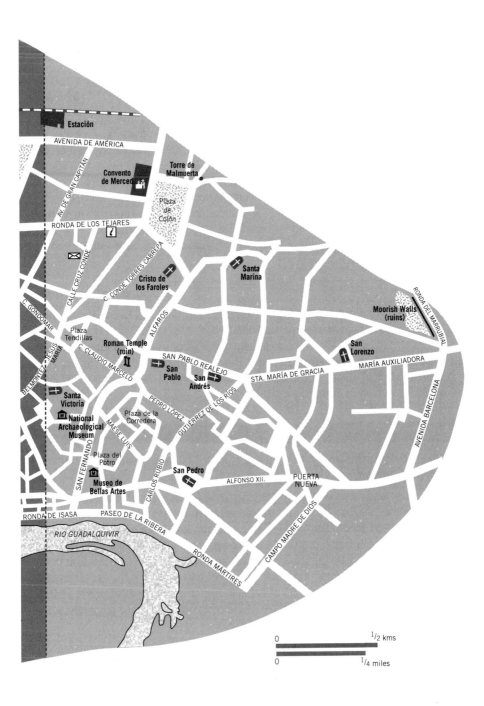

Estación

AVENIDA DE AMÉRICA

AV DE GRAN CAPITÁN

Convento de Merced

Torre de Malmuerta

Plaza de Colón

RONDA DE LOS TEJARES

CALLE CRUZ CONDE

C. CONDE TORRES CABRERA

Cristo de los Faroles

Santa Marina

C. GONDOMAR

ALFAROS

RONDA DEL MARRUBIAL

Moorish Walls (ruins)

BELMONTE Z-JESÚS MARÍA

Plaza Tendillas

Roman Temple (ruin)

C. CLAUDIO MARCELO

SAN PABLO REALEJO

San Pablo

San Andrés

STA. MARÍA DE GRACIA

San Lorenzo

MARÍA AUXILIADORA

Santa Victoria

PEDRO LÓPEZ

GUTIÉRREZ DE LOS RÍOS

AVENIDA BARCELONA

National Archaeological Museum

SAN FERNANDO

MAESE LUIS

Plaza de la Corredera

Plaza del Potro

CARLOS RUBIO

San Pedro

ALFONSO XII.

PUERTA NUEVA

Museo de Bellas Artes

RONDA DE ISASA

PASEO DE LA RIBERA

CAMPO MADRE DE DIOS

RIO GUADALQUIVIR

RONDA MÁRTIRES

| 0 | 1/2 kms |
| 0 | 1/4 miles |

one *Talgo* daily to Cádiz, Valencia and Barcelona, and regular trains to Huelva, Algeciras and Alicante. Trains for Granada, Málaga and Algeciras pass through Bobadilla Junction, and may require a change. Córdoba's station is on the Avenida de América, 1.6km (1 mile) north of La Mezquita, ✆ (957) 49 02 02.

by bus

Buses for Sevilla (three daily), Granada, Cádiz and Málaga and most nearby towns leave from the Alsina Graells terminal on Avenida Medina Azahara 29, ✆ (957) 23 64 74. Buses for Madrid (one daily), Valencia (three daily) and Barcelona (two a day), leave from the Ureña office on Avenida de Cervantes 22, ✆ (957) 47 23 52. Other firms do go to Sevilla—but the train's a better bet for that city and for Málaga. The Córdoba bus network is complicated and it's always best to check with tourist information as to times and departure points. If you want to go to Medinat az-Zahra, take any bus for Lora del Rio (from San Sebastián) or Palma del Río (from Calle La Bodega); it will drop you off short of the site, and you will have to walk about 2km (1.3 miles).

Tourist Information

The regional tourist office is on Calle Torrijos 10, ✆ (957) 47 12 35. The municipal office is in the Judería on Plaza Judá Levi, ✆ (957) 47 20 00 ext 209, and should reopen by January 94. It's definitely worth a stop at either to get a detailed map, for Córdoba has the biggest and most labyrinthine old quarter in Spain. To arrange personal guides to the mosque and other sights, ✆ (957) 48 69 97 or 41 06 29, or turn up at the mosque itself.

La Mezquita

Open 10–7 in summer; 10.30–1.30 and 3.30–5.30 in winter; adm 600 pts, free before 10 am and Sun.

La Mezquita is the local name for Abd ar-Rahman's Great Mosque. It means 'mosque' and even though the building has officially been a cathedral for 750 years, no one could ever mistake its origins. Abd ar-Rahman, founder of a new state, felt it necessary to construct a great religious monument for his capital. As part of his plan, he also wished to make it a centre of pilgrimage to increase the sense of divorce from eastern Islam; Mecca was at the time held by his Abbasid enemies. Islam was never entirely immune to the exaltation of holy relics, and there is a story that Abd ar-Rahman had an arm of Mohammed to legitimize his mosque as a pilgrimage site. The site, at the centre of the city, had originally held a Roman temple of Janus, and later a Visigothic church.

Only about one-third of the mosque belongs to the original. Successive enlargements were made by Abd ar-Rahman II, al-Hakam, and al-Mansur. Expansion was easy: the plan of the mosque is a simple rectangle divided into aisles by rows of columns, and its size was increased to serve a growing population simply by adding more aisles. The result was the second-largest of all mosques, exceeded only by the one in Mecca. After 1236, it was converted to use as a cathedral without any major changes. In the 1520s, however, the city's clerics succeeded in convincing the Royal Council, over the opposition of the Córdoba city government, to allow the construction of a choir and high altar, enclosed structures as is typical in Spanish cathedrals. Carlos V, who had also opposed the project, strongly reproached them for the desecration when he saw the finished work—though he himself had done even worse to the Alhambra and Sevilla's Alcázar.

Most people come away from a visit to La Mezquita somewhat confused. The endless rows of columns and red-and-white striped arches make a picture familiar to most of us, but actually to see them in this gloomy old hall may not increase one's understanding of the work. They make a pretty pattern, but what does it mean? It's worth going into some detail, for learning to see La Mezquita the way its builders did is the best key we have to understanding the refined world of al-Andalus.

Before entering, take a few minutes to circumnavigate this massive and somewhat forbidding pile of bricks. Spaced around its 685m of wall are the original entrances and windows, excellent examples of Moorish art. Those on the western side are the best, from the time of al-Mansur: interlaced Visigothic horseshoe arches, floral decorations in the Roman tradition, and Islamic calligraphy and patterns, a lesson in the varied sources of this art.

The only entrance to the mosque today is the **Puerta del Perdón**, a fine Mudéjar gateway added in 1377, opening to the **Patio de los Naranjos**, the original mosque courtyard, planted with orange trees, where the old Moorish fountain can still be seen. Built into the wall of the courtyard, over the gate, the original minaret—a legendary tower said to be the model for all the others in al-Andalus—has been replaced by an ill-proportioned 16th-century bell tower which is currently being restored. From the courtyard, the mosque is entered through a little door, the **Puerta de las Palmas**, where they'll sell you a ticket and tell you to take off your hat. Inside, it's as chilly and old as Sevilla Cathedral.

Now here is the first surprise. The building is gloomy only because the Spanish clerics wanted it that way. Originally there was no wall separating the mosque from the courtyard, and that side of the mosque was entirely open. In the courtyard, trees were planted to continue the rows of columns, translating inside to outside in a remarkable tour-de-force that has never been equalled in architecture. To add to the effect, the entrances along the other three walls would have been open to the surrounding busy markets and streets. It isn't just a trick of architecture, but a way of relating a holy building to the life of the city around it. In the Middle East, there are many medieval mosques built on the same plan as this one; the pattern originated with the first Arabian mosques, and later in the Ummayyad Mosque of Damascus, one of the first great shrines of Islam. In Turkey they call them 'forest' mosques, and the townspeople use them like indoor parks, places to sit and reflect or talk over everyday affairs. In medieval Christian cathedrals, whose doors were always open, it was much the same. The sacred and the secular become blurred, or rather the latter is elevated to a higher plane. In Córdoba, this principle is perfected.

In the aesthetics of this mosque, too, there is more than meets the eye. Many European writers have seen it as devoid of spirituality, a plain prayer-hall with pretty arches. To the

Christian mind it is difficult to comprehend. Christian churches are modelled after the Roman basilica, a government hall, a seat of authority with a long central aisle designed to humble the suppliant as he approaches the praetor's throne—or altar. Mosques are designed with great care to free the mind from such behaviour patterns. In this one, the guiding principle is a rarefied abstraction—the same kind of abstraction that governs Islamic geometric decoration. The repetition of columns is like a meditation in stone, a mirror of Creation where unity and harmony radiate from innumerable centres.

Another contrast with Christian churches can be found in an obscure matter—the distribution of weight. The Gothic masters of the Middle Ages learned to pile stone upwards from great piers and buttresses to amazing heights, to build an edifice that seems to aspire upwards to heaven. Córdoba's architects amplified the height of their mosque only modestly by a daring invention—adding a second tier of arches on top of the first. They had to, constrained as they were by the short columns they were recycling from Roman buildings, but the result was to make an 'upside-down' building, where weight increases the higher it goes, a play of balance and equilibrium that adds much to the mosque's effect.

There are about 580 of these columns, mostly from Roman ruins and Visigothic churches the Muslims pulled down; originally, legend credits there being an even thousand. Some came from as far as Constantinople, a present from the emperors. The same variety can be seen in the capitals—Roman, Visigothic, Moorish and a few mysteries. The surviving jewel of the mosque is its **mihrab**, added in the 10th century under al-Hakam II, an octagonal chamber set into the wall and covered by a beautiful dome of interlocking arches. A Byzantine emperor, Nicephoras Phocas, sent artists to help with its mosaic decoration, and a few tons of enamel chips and coloured glass cubes for them to work with. That these two states should have had such warm relations isn't that surprising: in those days, any enemy of the Pope and the western Christian states was a friend of Constantinople. Though the *mihrab* is no longer at the centre of La Mezquita, it was at the time of al-Hakam II; the aisle extending from it was the axis of the original mosque.

Looking back from the *mihrab*, you will see what once was the exterior wall, built in Abd ar-Rahman II's extension, from the year 848. Its gates, protected indoors, are as good as those on the west façade, and better preserved. Near the *mihrab* is the **Capilla de Villaviciosa**, a Christian addition of 1377 with fancy convoluted Mudéjar arches that almost succeed in upstaging the Moorish work. Behind it is a small chapel usually closed off. Fortunately, you can see most of the **Capilla Real** above the barriers; its exuberant stucco and *azulejo* decoration are among the greatest works of Mudéjar art. Built in the 14th century as a funeral chapel for Fernando IV and Alfonso XI of Castile, it is contemporary with the Alhambra and shows some influence of the styles developing in Granada.

Far more serious intrusions are the 16th-century **Coro** (choir) and **Capilla Mayor** (high altar). Not unlovely in themselves, they would not offend anywhere else but here. Fortunately, La Mezquita is so large that from many parts of it you won't even notice them. Begun in 1523, the plateresque Coro was substantially altered in the 18th century, with additional stucco decoration, as well as a set of Baroque choir stalls by Pedro Duque

Cornejo. Between the Coro and Capilla Mayor is the tomb of Leopold of Austria, Bishop of Córdoba at the time the works were completed (and, interestingly, Carlos V's uncle). For the rest of the Christian contribution, dozens of locked, mouldering chapels line the outer walls of the mosque. Never comfortable as a Christian building, today the cathedral seems to be hardly used at all, and regular Sunday masses are generally relegated to a small corner of the building.

Around La Mezquita

The masses of souvenir stands, cafés and tourists that surround La Mezquita on its busiest days do their best to re-create the atmosphere of the Moorish *souks* that once thrived here, but walk a block in any direction and you'll enter the essential Córdoba—whitewashed lanes with glimpses into dreamily beautiful patios, each one a floral extravaganza. One of the best is a famous little alley called **Calle de los Flores** ('street of the flowers') just a block north of La Mezquita.

Below La Mezquita, along the Guadalquivir, the melancholic plaza called **Puerta del Puente** marks the site of Córdoba's southern gate with a decorative **arch** put up in 1571, celebrating the reign of Felipe II. The very curious churrigueresque monument next to it is called the **Triunfo** (1651) with a statue of San Rafael (the angel Raphael). Wild Baroque confections such as this are common in Naples and south Italy (under Spanish rule at the time); there they are called *guglie*. Behind the plaza, standing across from La Mezquita, is the **Archbishop's Palace**, built on the site of the original Alcázar, the palace of Abd ar-Rahman.

The **Roman bridge** over the Guadalquivir probably isn't Roman at all any more; it has been patched and repaired so often that practically nothing remains of the Roman work. Another statue of Raphael can be seen in the middle—probably replacing an old Roman image of Jupiter or Mercury. The stern-looking **Calahorra Tower** (1369), built over Moorish foundations, once guarded the southern approaches of the bridge; now it contains a small **museum** of Córdoba's history, with old views and plans of the city, and the armour of Gonzalo Fernández de Córdoba, the 'Gran Capitán' who won much of Italy for Fernando and Isabel. It also has an historical multivision extravaganza, which is expensive and for the dedicated tourist.

Just to the west, along the river, Córdoba's **Alcázar de los Reyes Cristianos** was rebuilt in the 14th century and used for 300 years by the officers of the Inquisition. There's little to see, but a good view of La Mezquita and the town from the belvedere atop the walls. The **gardens** are peaceful and lovely, an Andalucían amenity much like those in Sevilla's Alcázar. On the river's edge you'll see an ancient **waterwheel**. At least some of the Moors' talent for putting water to good use was retained for a while after the Reconquista. This is the mill that disturbed Isabel's dreams when she stayed at the Alcázar; it was rebuilt only in the early 1900s. If you continue walking along the Guadalquivir, after about a kilometre you'll come to Parque Cruz Conde and the new **Córdoba zoo**, where you can see a rare black lion, who probably doesn't enjoy being called 'Chico' (*open daily 10am to sunset*).

The Judería

As in Sevilla, Córdoba's ancient Jewish quarter has recently become a fashionable area, a nest of tiny streets between La Mezquita and Avenida Dr Fleming. Part of the Moorish walls can be seen along this street, and the northern entrance of the Judería is the old **Almodóvar gate**. The streets are tricky, and it will take some effort to find Calle Maimonides and the 14th-century **synagogue**, of which little remains but a wall of Alhambra-style arabesques and Hebrew inscriptions. On Calle Ruano Torres, the 15th-century **Casa del Indiano** is a palace with an eccentric façade.

On Plaza Maimonides is the misleadingly named **Municipal Museum**—it's mostly about bullfights. Manolete and El Cordobés are the city's two recent contributions to Spanish culture; here you can see a replica of Manolete's sarcophagus, the furniture from his home (!) and the hide of Islero, the bull that did him in, along with more bullfight memorabilia than you ever thought existed. The turn-of-the-century Art-Nouveau posters are beautiful, and among the old prints you can pay homage to the memory of the famous taurine malcontent Moñudo, who ignored the *toreros* and went up into the stands after the audience (*open daily 9–1.30 and 4–7 in summer, 5.30–8.30 in winter*).

White Neighbourhoods

From the mosque you can walk eastwards through well over a mile of twisting white alleys, a place where the best map in the world wouldn't keep you from getting lost and staying lost. Though it all looks much the same, it's never monotonous. Every little square, fountain or church stands out boldly, and forces you to look at it in a different way than you would a modern city—another lesson in the Moorish aesthetic.

These streets have probably changed little since 1236, but their best buildings are a series of **Gothic churches** built soon after the Reconquista. Though small and plain, most are exquisite in a quiet way. Few have any of the usual Gothic sculptural work on their façades, to avoid offending a people accustomed to Islam's prohibition of images. The lack of decoration somehow adds to their charm. There are a score of these around Córdoba, and nothing like them elsewhere in the south of Spain. **San Lorenzo**, on Calle María Auxiliadora, is perhaps the best, with a rose window designed in a common Moorish motif of interlocking circles. Some 15th-century frescoes survive around the altar and on the apse. **San Pablo** (1241), on the street of the same name, is early Gothic (5 years after the Christian conquest) but contains a fine Mudéjar dome and ceiling. **San Andrés**, on Calle Varela, two streets east of San Pablo, **Santa Marina** on Calle Morales, and the **Cristo de los Faroles** on Calle Alfaros are some of the others. Have a look inside any you find open; most have some Moorish or work in their interiors, and many of their towers (like San Lorenzo's) were originally minarets. **San Pedro**, off Calle Alfonso XII, was the Christian cathedral under Moorish rule, though largely rebuilt in the 1500s.

The neighbourhoods have other surprises, if you have the persistence to find them. **Santa Victoria** is a huge austere Baroque church on Calle Juan Valera, modelled after the Roman Pantheon. Nearby on Plaza Jerónimo Páez, a fine 16th-century palace houses the

National Archaeological Museum, the largest in Andalucía, with Roman mosaics, a two-faced idol of Janus that probably came from the temple under La Mezquita, and an unusual icon of the Persian *torero-god* Mithras, also some Moorish-looking early Christian art, and early funeral steles with odd hieroglyphs. The large collection of Moorish art includes some of the best work from the age of the caliphate, including finds from Medinat az-Zahra (*open daily 10–2 and 3.30–5.30, Sunday 10– 2*).

East of Calle San Fernando, the wide street that bisects the old quarter, the houses are not as pristinely whitewashed as those around La Mezquita. Many parts are a bit run down, which does not detract from their charm. In the approximate centre of the city is the **Plaza de la Corredera**, an enclosed 'Plaza Mayor', like the famous ones in Madrid and Salamanca. This ambitious project, surrounded by uniform blank façades (an echo of the *estilo desornamentado*) was never completed. Now neglected and a bit eerie, the city is trying to rehabilitate it a little at a time.

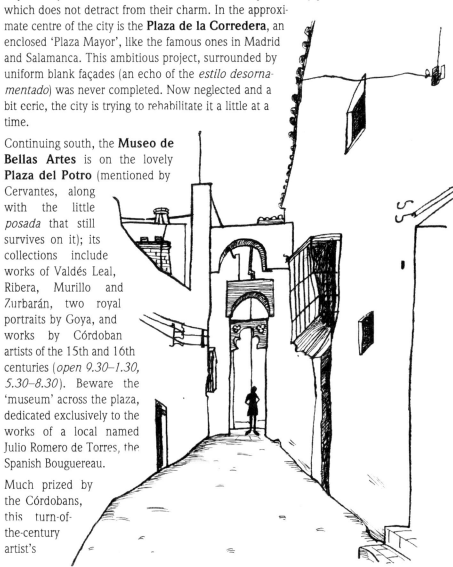

Continuing south, the **Museo de Bellas Artes** is on the lovely **Plaza del Potro** (mentioned by Cervantes, along with the little *posada* that still survives on it); its collections include works of Valdés Leal, Ribera, Murillo and Zurbarán, two royal portraits by Goya, and works by Córdoban artists of the 15th and 16th centuries (*open 9.30–1.30, 5.30–8.30*). Beware the 'museum' across the plaza, dedicated exclusively to the works of a local named Julio Romero de Torres, the Spanish Bouguereau.

Much prized by the Córdobans, this turn-of-the-century artist's *œuvre* consists almost entirely of naked ladies. Eastwards from here, the crooked white-washed alleys continue for almost a mile, as far as the surviving stretch of **Moorish walls** along Ronda del Marrubial.

Plaza de las Tendillas

The centre of Roman Corduba, by chance, has become the centre of the modern city. Córdoba is probably the slickest and most up-to-date city in Andalucía (Sevilla would beg to differ), and it shows in this busy district of crowded pavements, modern shops, cafés and wayward youth. The contrast with the old neighbourhoods is startling, but just a block off the plaza on Calle Gondomar, the beautiful 15th-century **San Nicolás Church** will remind you that you're still in Córdoba. And in the other direction, well-preserved remains of a collapsed **Roman temple**, one of the most complete Roman monuments in Spain, have been discovered on the Calle Nueva near the Ayuntamiento. The city has been at work reassembling the walls and columns; already the front pediment is largely complete.

Next to the **Plaza de Colón**, a park a few blocks north of the Plaza de las Tendillas, the **Torre de Malmuerta** ('Bad Death') takes its name from a commander of this part of the old fortifications who murdered his wife in a fit of passion; it became the subject of a well-known play by Lope de Vega, *Los Comendadores de Córdoba*. Across the plaza is a real surprise, the rococo **Convento de Merced** (1745), an enormous building that has recently been restored to house the provincial government and often hosts cultural exhibitions on various subjects. Don't miss it. The façade has been redone in its original painted *esgrafiado*, almost decadently colourful in pink and green, and the courtyards and grand staircases inside are incredible—more a palace than a monastery.

Medinat az-Zahra

Open 10–2, and 6.30–8.30.

Eight kilometres (5miles) northwest of the centre of Córdoba, Caliph Abd ar-Rahman III began to build a palace in the year 936. The undertaking soon got out of hand, and with the almost infinite resources of the caliphate to play with, he and his successors turned Medinat az-Zahra ('city of the Flower', so named after one of Abd ar-Rahman's wives) into a city in itself, with a market, mosques, schools and gardens, a place where the last caliphs could live in isolation from the world, safe from the turbulent street politics of their capital. Hisham II was kept a virtual prisoner here by his able vizier, al-Mansur.

The scale of it is pure Arabian Nights. One chronicler records an ambassador, being taken from Córdoba to the palace, finding his path carpeted the entire 8km (5 mile) route and lined from end to end with maidens to hold parasols and refreshments for him. Stories were told of the palace's African menageries, its interior pillars and domes of crystal, and curtains of falling water for walls; another fountain was filled with flowing mercury. Such carrying-on must have aroused a good deal of resentment; in the disturbances that put an end to the caliphate, Medinat az-Zahra was sacked and razed by Berber troops in 1013.

After serving as a quarry for 900 years it's surprising anything is left at all; even under Muslim rule, columns from the palace were being carted away as far as Marrakesh. But in 1944 the royal apartments were discovered, with enough fragments to permit a restoration of a few arches with floral decorations. One hall has a roof on, and more work is under way, but as yet the rest is only foundations.

Where to Stay

Near La Mezquita, of course. Even during big tourist assaults the advantages outweigh the liabilities. However, if this area is full, or if you have a car and do not care to brave the old town's narrow streets and lack of parking, there are a few hotels in the new town and on the periphery worth trying.

moderate

The ★★★★**Meliá Córdoba**, ℂ (957) 29 80 66, fax 29 81 47, is a big modern hotel right in the middle of the Jardines de la Victoria, on the edge of the Judería. It has every conceivable luxury the chain is known for, including a pool and TV—but a double room will set you back 16,750 pts—rather overpriced, considering the service. The ★★★★**Adarve**, Mag. González Francés 15, ℂ (957) 48 11 02, has rooms that look out onto the floodlit walls of La Mezquita, literally just a few metres from your balcony. The breakfasts are somewhat meagre, though, and service could do with a polish; there's an underground car park, something to consider in this part of town (16,000 pts). Also next to the mosque is the ★★★**Maimonides**, Torrijos 4, ℂ (957) 47 15 00, fax 48 38 03, again with underground parking, but prices are not much lower (12,000–15,000 pts). Five minutes north of the train station is ★★★★**Las Adelfas**, Avenida de la Arruzafa s/n, ℂ (957) 27 74 20, fax 27 27 94, a modern hotel set in spacious gardens with a pool and beautiful views over Córdoba, elegant rooms and excellent service, and a bargain at present for its rates in this category at 13,500–16,600 pts. On the outskirts of town, the ★★★★**Parador Nacional La Arruzafa**, Avenida de la Arruzafa, ℂ (957) 27 59 00, fax 28 04 09, isn't in an historic building (it was built in the 1960s), but offers a pool, tennis courts and air-conditioned rooms and a view (doubles 15,000 pts).

inexpensive

In the Judería, 200m or so from La Mezquita is the attractive, affordable and immaculate ★★**Albucasis**, Calle Buen Pastor 11, ℂ (957) 47 86 25, fax 47 41 44, a former silversmith's with a charming flower-filled courtyard; it's one of the prettiest hotels in Córdoba (8,500 pts). The ★★**Marisa**, Calle Cardinal Herrero 6, ℂ (957) 47 31 42, is a simple but well-run establishment opposite the Patio de los Naranjos. The location is the only real amenity, but it will do for the price (7,500–8,200 pts for a double with bath). The ★★**Hotel González** is on the edge of the Judería, ℂ (957) 47 98 19, fax 48 61 87 (7,000–8,500 pts). Rooms contain family antiques and the arabesque patio houses a popular restaurant.

The **★Hostal Seneca**, Calle Conde y Luque 5, © 47 32 34, just north of La Mezquita, is the real find among the inexpensive *hostales*, with a beautiful patio full of flowers, nice rooms and sympathetic management. Not surprisingly, it's hard to get a room (3,450–4,100 pts a double without bath). Plenty of other inexpensive *fondas* can be found in the area east of La Mezquita, especially on and around Calle Rey Heredia—which is also known as the street with five names so don't be thrown by the number of different calle signs. The **Fonda Agustina** on nearby Calle Zapatería Vieja, © 47 08 72, is clean and central (2,500 pts for a double). Off the Plaza de Tendillas, the **★Boston**, Calle Málaga 2, © 47 41 76, has modern clean rooms that are air-conditioned at night and popular with a young American crowd (4,300 pts). The **★★Hostal Las Tendillas**, Calle Jesús y María 1, © 22 30 29, has simple and unpretentious doubles for 2,600 pts while the **Hostal La Magdalena**, © 48 37 53, is perfect for those who don't mind a 10-minute walk through the picturesque backstreets into town. It's in a quiet location, there's no trouble parking, and doubles range between 3,500–4,000 pts.

Eating Out

Don't forget that Córdoba is the heart of a wine-growing region; there are a few bodegas in town that appreciate visitors, including **Bodega Campos**, Calle Colonel Cascajo; and **Bodega Doña Antonia**, Avenida Virgen Milagrosa 5, really a small restaurant serving its own wines.

expensive

Sitting in the heart of the old Jewish quarter, **El Churrasco**, Calle Romero 16, © (957) 29 08 19, is Córdoba's best-loved restaurant, located in an old town house. Before eating in one of the lovely rooms or on the elegant patio, see if you can first have a glass of *montilla* and some tapas in the bodega just up the street from the restaurant. It's not officially open to the public, but if you get there when it's not busy, the owner may open it up for you, especially if you are in a party. Painstakingly restored by the owner, the house and courtyard (complete with well) are decorated with local handicrafts and antiques, and the wine cellar is vast. Upstairs is a salon where the top gourmets of the city meet once a month, including the rogue El Cordobés. The restaurant itself specializes in grilled meats but try also the excellent *dorada*, covered in salt and oven-baked, sole with garlic from the oven, salmon and swordfish steaks. In winter, braziers are put under tables making it possible to dine on the patio all year round, and there's a personal parking service. Relatively speaking, it's not expensive—count on 3,000–4,000 pts (closed Thur, Aug and Christmas). Rival to El Churrasco is one of the best-known restaurants in Andalucía, **El Caballo Rojo**, Cardenal Herrero 28, © (957) 47 53 75. Its menu is based on traditional Andaluz cooking and old Arab recipes—*samorejo* with cured ham, artichokes in Montilla wine, Mozarabic angler fish, lamb with honey and *cola de toro*—oxtail with onions and tomatoes (4,000 pts). The

Almudaina, Campo Santo de los Mártires 1, © (957) 47 43 42, is in an attractive old house dating from the 16th century, and is a cool and sophisticated spot to eat. Its menu varies from day to day, depending on market availability, and special attention is paid to local produce. Look out for *ensalada de pimientos, alcachofas a la Cordobés, verduras a la crema de espinacas* and *lomo relleno a la Pedrocheña* (*menú del día* 2,500 pts, à la carte 3,500 pts and up; closed Sun evening). More quality surroundings and fare are at **Oscar's**, Plaza de Chirinos 6, © (957) 47 75 17, where the emphasis is on fish—*ensalada de salmón marinado, lubina al vino oloroso de Montilla, lomos de merluza con langostinos en salsa de ajo* (3,500–4,500 pts; closed Sun and Aug).

moderate

Adjoining El Caballo Rojo is the pleasant little **El Burlaero**, Calle La Hoguera 5, © (957) 47 27 19, where you can eat out in the courtyard or in the room upstairs. Specialities include *rabo de toro, Paloma Torcaz, perdiz, jabalí* (full meal for around 3,000 pts).

cheap

Just around the corner from the Mezquita, **El Tablón**, Cardenal González 75, © (957) 47 60 61, is a restaurant with character, offering one of the best bargains in the city, with a choice of *menús del día* (700 pts) or *platos combinados* at around 1,000 pts, glass of wine included. There's also the tiny **Bar Mezquita** on Calle Cardenal Herrero, which is famed locally for its *boquerones en vinagre*. On the corner of Calle Deanes and Buen Pastor is the take-it-or-leave-it **Bodegón Rafaé**, with true bodega atmosphere and food. Sausages drape from barrels, religious figurines hang next to fake bulls' heads, the radio and TV are on simultaneously; *cola de toro* with a glass of wine at one of the vinyl-topped tables will cost you an exorbitant 700 pts. Some other inexpensive choices are around Plaza de las Tendillas. For the young, or young at heart, a lively spot is **El Campeón**, Munda 8, © (957) 47 02 07, near Plaza de las Tendillas in one of those narrow streets. Here students gather amid the dotty decor to order enormous glass tankards of beer and sangría, and enjoy the loud music and snack food in one of the half-dozen tiny rooms with wooden benches. **Bar Sociedad de Plateros**, San Francisco 6, is another popular place with good tapas and cheap wine.

Shopping

Córdoba is famous for its silverwork—try the shops in José Cruz Grande, where you'll get better quality than in the old quarter round the mosque. Handmade **crafts** are made on the premises at *Meryan*, Calle de los Flores 2, © (957) 47 59 02, where they specialize in exquisitely embossed wood and leather furniture. For **antiques**, there's one shop with a very good selection of Spanish art and furniture in Plaza San Nicolás, and they'll arrange packing and shipment. High-quality ladies' and gents' suede and **leather goods** are sold at *Sera*, on the corner of Rondo de los Teares and Cruz Conde. The mainstream shopping areas are along Calle Conde de Gondomar and Calle Claudio Marcelo on either side of the Plaza de las Tendillas.

North of Córdoba

The N432 out of Córdoba leads north to the Sierra Morena, the string of hills that curtain the western part of Andalucía from Extremadura, Castilla and La Mancha. This area is the **Valle de los Pedroches**, fertile grazing lands for the pigs, sheep and goats and an important hunting area for deer and wild boar. Thousands of these animals are stalked and shot in the numerous annual hunts, or *monterías*. It's also healthy hiking territory, but keep yourself visible at all times—you don't want to be mistaken for someone's supper.

Getting Around

Although **buses** do run from Córdoba up into the Sierra and villages of Los Pedroches, they are infrequent and very time-consuming. To explore the best parts, you really need a **car**.

A road winds 80km (50 miles) up to Belmez, with its Moorish castle perilously perched on a rock, from which there are panoramic views over the surrounding arid countryside. **Peñarroya-Pueblonuevo** is a dull industrial town that has fallen into decline, but is useful here as a reference point. Sixteen kilometres (10 miles) west on the N432, the village of **Fuente Obejuna** is best remembered for the 1476 uprising of its villagers, who dragged their tyrannical lord from his palace and treated him to a spectacularly brutal and bloody end. The event is the subject of the drama *Fuenteovejuna* by Lope de Vega.

Forty-four kilometres (27½ miles) east of Peñarroya (take the C421, then the C420) is the village of **Pozoblanco**, famous for the last *corrida* of the renowned bullfighter Francisco Rivera, better known as Paquirri. Gored, he died in the ambulance on the way to Córdoba; presumably, bouncing around on those roads didn't help. Paquirri's widow, the singer Pantoja, soared to even greater heights of popularity on his death, the Spanish public obsessed as ever by the drama of life and the proximity of death. **Pedroche**, 10km (6 miles) away, is a sleepy little village with a fine 16th-century Gothic church, with a proud, lofty spire. This place too has had its fair share of drama—in 1936 communist forces shot nearly a hundred of the menfolk. Beyond the villages of **Villanueva de Córdoba** and **Cardeña** to the east is the **Parque Natural de Sierra Cardeña**—rolling hills forested in oak, more stag-hunting grounds and ideal rambling terrain.

Where to Stay and Eat

North of Córdoba there's nothing in the way of de luxe accommodation, but the area has a small selection of one- and two-star hotels. Two and a half kilometres (1½miles) out of Pozoblanco (Ctra Villanueva de la Serena–Andújar, Km 129), in a listed historic building, is the quiet **★★San Francisco**, © (957) 10 14 35, with

tennis courts and rooms with bath for 8,500 pts. Villanueva de Córdoba has the
★Demetrius, Ctra de Cardeña s/n, © (957) 12 02 94, a place that offers no frills
for its 3,200 pts rooms. Though there's no reason to stay in Peñarroya-
Pueblonuevo, you may like to use it as a base for your day trip. The **★Sevilla**,
Miguel Vigara 15, © (957) 56 01 00, fax 56 23 07, is the most comfortable place
to stay, rooms with bath go for 4,400 pts, while **★El Sol**, El Sol 24, © (957) 56 20
50, has basic rooms for around 3,800 pts.

This area is famed throughout Andalucía for its supreme quality *jamón ibérico*
(locally cured ham) and sucking pig, the excellent *salchichón* from Pozoblanco,
and the strong, spicy cheese made from ewes' milk. There are no oustanding
restaurants around; drop in on a family *venta* and see what the day's special is, or
head for the tapas bars in the villages. Better still, grab some goodies from a supermarket and have a picnic out on the slopes.

From Córdoba to Úbeda

In this section of the Guadalquivir valley the river rises into the heights of the Sierra
Morena; endless rolling hills covered with neat rows of olive trees and small farms make a
memorable Andalucían landscape. The three large towns along the way, **Andújar, Bailén**
and **Linares**, are much alike, amiable industrial towns still painted a gleaming white.

The Gateway to Andalucía

GOATHERD
SIERRA MORENA

This area is Andalucía's front door. The roads and railways from
Madrid branch off here for Sevilla and Granada. Many important battles were fought nearby, including Navas de Tolosa
near La Carolina, in 1212, which opened the way for the
conquest of al-Andalus; and Bailén, in 1808, where a Spanish-
English force gave Napoleon's boys a sound thrashing and built
up Spanish morale for what they call their War of Independence.

The NIV snakes along the Guadalquivir valley,
and 42km (26 miles) east of Córdoba it
brings you to the delightfully placed town of
Montoro, sitting on a bend in the river.
The facetious-looking tower that rises
above the whitewashed houses belongs to
the Gothic-ss church of **San Bartolomé**
in Plaza de España. Also in the square is the
16th-century **Ducal Palace**, with a plateresque
façade. The beautiful 15th-century bridge that
connects Montoro to its suburb, Retamar, is known
as the Puente de Las Doñadas, a tribute to the
women   of   the   village   who

sacrificed their jewellery to help finance its construction. Seek out the kitsch **Casa de las Conchas**, a house and courtyard done out in sea shells.

Approaching **Andújar**, a further 35km (22 miles) down the NIV, you'll find the countryside dominated by huge, blue sunflower-oil refineries like fallen space stations. Sunflowers, like olives, are a big crop in the region and much in evidence in late summer. Nothing remains of Andújar's Moorish castle, but there are a couple of surprises in this town which might tempt you to linger a while. The church of **Santa María**, in the plaza of the same name, has in one chapel the *Immaculate Conception* by Pacheco, Velázquez's teacher, and in another chapel the magnificent *Christ in the Garden of Olives*, by El Greco.

A possible diversion, 30km (19 miles) north of Andújar on the J501, is the **Santuario de la Virgen de la Cabeza**. Although very little is left of the 13th-century sanctuary, and the present one is disappointing, it's worth packing a picnic and enjoying the drive; when you get there you'll be rewarded with panoramic *SUNFLOWER FIELDS, WHITE VILLAGE ROUTE* views of the whole area. One of southern Spain's biggest fiestas is the annual *romería* to the sanctuary on the last Sunday in April, when a quarter of a million pilgrims trek up on foot, horseback, carts and donkeys. The day before there's a competition for the best-decorated carriage.

Twenty-seven kilometres (17 miles) further east on the NIV is the modern, unprepossessing town of **Bailén**. The tomb of the Spanish general Castaños, who so cleverly whipped the French troops and sent Napoleon back to the drawing board, is in the Gothic parish church of the **Encarnación**, which also has a sculpture by Alonso Cano. But don't dally here—the real treat is to be found 11km (7 miles) to the north on the NIV at **Baños de la Encina**, where the 10th-century Moorish castle is one of the best preserved in all Andalucía, and evokes the glory of a bygone age. Dominating the town, the castle has 14 sturdy towers, scarcely touched by time, and from the walls you get a sweeping vista of the olive groves and distant peaks beyond Úbeda.

Twenty kilometres (12½ miles) north of here on the NIV is **La Carolina**, a model of 18th-century grid planning. The village owes its existence to forward-thinking Carlos III, who imported a few thousand German artesans in the late 1700s and set them to work excavating the lead and copper mines, tilling the fields and herding sheep. A side effect of this colonization was supposed to be the decline of banditry in the then wild and unpopulated hills. But within two generations almost all the Germans had died off or fled. The town and surrounding area are best known now as a big game-hunting reserve, particularly for partridge.

From Bailén the N322 heads eastward to the mining town of **Linares**, birthplace of the guitarist Andrés Segovia, who later moved on; others weren't so lucky—in 1947 the great bullfighter Manolete had an off day and met his end on the horns of a bull in the ring here. If things had gone well for him, he might have gone to view the finds from the Roman settlement of nearby Castulo, housed in the town's **archaeology museum**, but unfortunately the last thing he probably saw was the ornate Baroque portal of the hospital **San Juan de Dios**. From Linares it's a 27km (17 mile) run to Úbeda; a little more than halfway you'll pass an elegant castle at **Canena**.

Where to Stay and Eat

On the main Madrid–Cádiz road is the ★★**Montoro**, at Km 358, ✆ (953) 16 07 92, with doubles at 3,500 pts. Andújar has a bigger selection, but less reason to stay. The best here is the ★★**Don Pedro**, Gabriel Zamora 5, ✆ (953) 50 12 74, fax 50 47 85, in the centre of town, with pleasant rooms for 5,500–7,250 pts, and a tavern-style restaurant that specializes in game dishes; meal with wine about 3,000 pts. There's a modern ★★★**Parador**, Ctra NIV, Km 296, ✆ (953) 67 01 00, fax 67 25 30, just outside Bailén, with pleasant gardens, air-conditioning and pool –rates are a reasonable 8,500 pts. It also houses a restaurant and average tapas bar. In Linares the ★★★**Aníbal**, Cid Campeador 11, ✆ (953) 65 04 00, is the jumbo in town (7,400–9,000 pts for double with bath); and for dining **Mesón Castellano**, Puente 5, ✆ (953) 69 00 09, is the place to go (3,000 pts; closed Sun, July and Aug). In La Carolina the hotel ★★★★**Perdiz**, Ctra NIV, Km 268, ✆ (953) 66 03 00, has a pretty good restaurant and as its name ('partridge') implies, has seasonal game dishes (2,500 pts). Rates for the hotel, which has a pool, are 9,500 pts a double.

Baeza

Campo de Baeza, soñaré contigo cuando no te vea

(Fields of Baeza, I will dream of you when I can no longer see you)

Antonio Machado, 19th/20th century

Sometimes history offers its recompense. The 13th-century Reconquista was especially brutal here; nearly the entire population fled, many of them moving to Granada, where they settled the Albaicín. The 16th century, however, when the wool trade was booming in this corner of Andalucía, was good to Baeza, leaving it a distinguished little town of neatly clipped trees and tan stone buildings, with a beautiful ensemble of monuments in styles from Romanesque to Renaissance. It seems a happy place, serene and quiet as the olive groves that surround it.

Getting Around

Come to Baeza by **train** at your own risk. The nearest station, officially named Linares-Baeza, is far off in the open countryside, 14km away. A bus to Baeza usually meets the train, but if you turn up at night or on a Sunday you may be stranded. Baeza's **bus** station, in a residential area without many street signs, is incredibly difficult to find—keep asking. Baeza is a stop on the Úbeda–Córdoba bus route.

Plaza del Pópulo (also known as the Plaza de los Leones), © (953) 74 04 44. (open 8.30–2.30 weekdays).

First among the 16th-century monuments is the **cathedral**, on Plaza Santa María, a work of Andrés de Vandelvira. This replaced a 13th-century Gothic church (surviving chancel and portal), which in turn took the place of a mosque; a colonnade from this can be seen in the cloister. For the best show in town, drop a coin in the box marked *custodia* in one of the side chapels; this will reveal, with a noisy dose of mechanical *duende*, a rich and ornate 18th-century silver tabernacle. The fountain in front of the cathedral, the **Fuente de Santa María**, with a little triumphal arch at its centre (1564), is Baeza's landmark and symbol. Behind it is the Isabelline Gothic **Casas Consistoriales**, formerly the town hall.

Heading north on the Cuesta de San Felipe, you pass the 15th-century **Palacio de Jabalquinto**, with an eccentric façade covered with coats of arms and pyramidal stone studs (a Spanish fancy of that age; you can see others like it in Guadalajara and Salamanca). The prettiest corner of the town is a small square, the **Plaza del Pópulo**, enclosed by decorative pointed arches, containing a fountain with four half-effaced lions; the fountain was patched together with the help of pieces taken from the Roman remains at Castulo, and the centrepiece, the fearless lady on the pedestal, is traditionally considered to be Imilce, the wife of Hannibal. In Plaza Cardenal Benavides, the façade of the **Ayuntamiento** (1599) is a classic example of Andalucían plateresque, and one of the last.

Where to Stay and Eat

The best place to stay is the ★★★**Hotel Baeza**, Calle Concepción 3, © (953) 74 81 30, fax 74 25 19, which lies behind the *Iglesia del Hospital de la Purísima Concepción,* near the Plaza de España. This monasterial building, once part of the hospital, used to be a religious school and rooms open on to a peaceful arched quadrangle. The ★★★**Juanito**, Avenida Arca del Agua s/n, © (953) 74 00 40, fax 74 23 24, has rooms with bath for 4,200–5,200 pts plus its own pool, and the *pensión* ★★**Comercio**, Calle San Pablo 21, © (953) 74 01 00, is a reasonably comfortable lodging where Machado stayed and penned a few poems (2,900 pts).

The restaurant of the Juanito is in the Michelin guide; try the *pastel de perdiz* (partridge in a pastry crust), pheasant with mushrooms, artichokes, *merluza a la Baeza*; dinners average 2,500–3,500 pts. For a real treat try the regional specialities at **Andrés de Vandelvira**, Calle San Francisco 14, © (953) 74 43 61. The restaurant is inside the San Francisco convent with tables filling the arched quadrangle; for more intimacy, dine upstairs (around 4,000 pts; closed Sun afternoons).

Úbeda

Even with Baeza for an introduction, the presence of this nearly perfect little city comes as a surprise. If the 16th century did well by Baeza, it was a golden age here, leaving Úbeda a 'town built for gentlemen' as the Spanish used to say, endowed with one of the finest collections of Renaissance architecture in all of Spain. Two men can take much of the credit: Andrés de Vandelvira, an Andalucían architect who created most of Úbeda's best buildings, and Francisco de los Cobos, imperial secretary to Carlos V, who paid for them. Cobos is a forgotten hero of Spanish history. While Carlos was off campaigning in Germany, Cobos had the job of running Castile. By the most delicate management, he kept the kingdom afloat while meeting Carlos's ever more exorbitant demands for money and men. He could postpone the inevitable disaster, but not prevent it. Like most public officials in the Spanish Age of Rapacity, though, he also managed to salt away a few hundred thousand ducats for himself, and he spent most of them embellishing his hometown. Like Baeza, Úbeda is a peaceful and happy place; it wears its Renaissance heritage gracefully, and is always glad to have visitors. Tourism is still something of a novelty here but it's easy to understand the Spanish expression '*irse por los cerros de Úbeda*' ('take the Úbeda hill routes'). It basically equates to getting off the subject or wasting time and arose many years ago after Úbeda gradually lost traffic to more commercial routes. Legend has it that a Christian knight fell in love with a Moorish girl and was reproached for his absence by King Fernando III. When questioned about his whereabouts during the battle the knight idly replied, 'Lost in those hills, sire.'

Getting Around

Úbeda's **bus** station is on Calle San José, © (953) 75 21 57, at the western end of town, and various lines connect the city directly to Madrid, Valencia and Barcelona, at least once daily, and more frequently to Baeza, Córdoba, Sevilla, Jaén and Granada. Cazorla and other villages in the region can easily be reached from Úbeda.

Tourist Office

Plaza Ayuntamiento, © (953) 75 08 97 (open 8.15–3).

Úbeda today leaves no doubt how its local politics are going. In the **Plaza de Andalucía**, joining the old and new districts, there is an old metal statue of a fascist civil war general named Sero, glaring down from his pedestal. The townspeople have put so many bullets into it, it looks like a Swiss cheese. They've left it here as a joke, and have merrily renamed another square from Plaza del Generalísimo to Plaza 1 de Mayo. The **Torre de Reloj**, in the Plaza de Andalucía, is a 14th-century defensive tower now adorned with a clock. The plaque near the base, under a painting of the Virgin, records a visit of Carlos V.

From here, Calle Real takes you into the heart of the old town. Nearly every corner has at least one lovely palace or church on it. Two of the best can be seen on this street: the early 17th-century **Palacio de Condé Guadiana**, with an ornate tower and distinctive windows cut out of the corners of the building, a common conceit in Úbeda's palaces.

Two blocks down, the **Palacio Vela de los Cobos** (*open 10–2 and 6–8*) is in the same style, with a loggia on the top storey.

The home of Francisco de los Cobos's nephew, another royal counsellor, was the **Palacio de las Cadenas**, now serving as Úbeda's Ayuntamiento, on a quiet plaza at the end of Calle Real. The side facing the plaza is simple and dignified (the tourist office is here) but the main façade, facing the **Plaza Vázquez de Molina**, is a stately Renaissance creation, the work of Vandelvira.

Plaza Vázquez de Molina

This is the only place in Andalucía where you can look around and not regret the passing of the Moors, for it is the only truly beautiful thing in all this great region that was not built either by the Moors or under their influence. The Renaissance buildings around the Palacio de las Cadenas make a wonderful ensemble, and the austere landscaping, old cobbles, and a plain six-sided fountain create the same effect of contemplative serendipity as any chamber of the Alhambra. Buildings on the plaza include the church of **Santa María de los Reales Alcázares** (which is currently being restored), a Renaissance façade on an older building with a fine Gothic cloister around the back; the *parador*; two sedate palaces, both from the 16th century; and Vandelvira's **Sacra Capilla del Salvador**, begun in 1540, the finest of Úbeda's churches, where Cobos is buried.

From The Façade of the church El Salvador ÚBEDA

All the sculpture on the façades of Úbeda is first class work, and the west front of the Salvador is especially good. This is a monument of the time when Spain was in the mainstream of Renaissance ideas, and humanist classicism was still respectable. Note the mythological subjects on the west front and elsewhere in the church, and be sure to look under the arch of the main door. Instead of Biblical scenes, it has beautifully carved panels of the ancient gods representing the five planets; Phoebus and Diana with the sun and moon; and Hercules, Aeolus, Vulcan and Neptune to represent the four elements. The interior, with its great dome, is worth a look despite a thorough sacking in 1936 (the sacristan lives on the first door on the left of Calle Francisco Cobos, on the north side of the church). Behind El Salvador, the **Hospital de los Honrados** has a delightful open patio—but only because the other half of the building was never completed. South of the plaza, the end of town is only a few blocks away, encompassed by a street called the **Redonda de Miradores**, a quiet spot favoured by small children and goats, with remnants of Úbeda's wall and exceptional views over the Sierra de Cazorla to the east.

Beyond Plaza Vázquez de Molina

Calle Montiel, north of El Salvador, has a few more fine palaces. At the foot of the street, on Plaza 1 de Mayo, is the 13th-century **San Pablo** church, much renovated in the 16th-century; inside is an elegant chapel of 1536, the Capilla del Camarero Vago. **San Nicolás de Bari,** further north, was originally a synagogue, and confiscated in 1492, which has left it with one Gothic door and the other by Vandelvira, who oversaw the reconstruction. On the western outskirts of town, near the bus station on Calle Nueva is Vandelvira's most remarkable building, the **Hospital de Santiago** (*open 9–3, 4–9*). This huge edifice, recently restored, has been called the 'Escorial of Andalucía'. Both have the same plan, a grid of quadrangles with a church inside. Oddly, both were begun at about the same time, though this one seems to have been started a year earlier, in 1568. Both are supreme examples of the *estilo desornamentado*. The façade here is not as plain as Herrera's; its quirky decoration and clean, angular lines are unique, more like a product of the 20th century than the 16th.

Around Úbeda: the Sierra de Cazorla

If you go east out of Úbeda, you'll be entering a zone few visitors ever reach. The Sierra de Cazorla, a jumble of ragged peaks, pine forests and olive-covered lowlands, offers some memorable mountain scenery, especially around **Cazorla**, a lovely, undiscovered white village of narrow alleys hung at alarming angles down the hillsides. Cazorla's landmarks are a ruined Renaissance church (again, by Vandelvira) half-open to the sky, and its castle. But there's an even better castle, possibly built by the Templars, just east of town. **La Iruela** is a romantic ruin even by Spanish standards, with a Homage tower on a dizzying height behind. Beyond La Iruela is the pass into the Sierra, the wild territory of hiking, hunting and fishing. The mountain ranges of Cazorla and Segura make up one of the 10 national parks in Spain. Gun-toting hunters stalk wild boar, deer, mountain goat, buck and *muflón,* and rainbow trout do their best to outwit the patient but determined anglers. Not all visitors are in for the kill, however, and those interested in flora and fauna find the area one of the richest in Europe, with a variety of birdlife that's hard to match.

Where to Stay

Úbeda

The ★★★★**Parador Condestable Dávalos,** Plaza Vázquez de Molina, © (953) 75 03 45, fax 75 12 59, an old palace with a glassed-in courtyard, is one of the loveliest and most popular of the chain (14,000 pts for a big double room). All the beamed ceilings and fireplaces have been preserved and the restaurant is the best in town, featuring local specialities for around 3,000 pts a full dinner. Ask to see the ancient wine cellar . The rest of Úbeda's hotels are all good bargains; you'll find a large selection on Calle Ramón y Cajal, just east of the bus station. The ★**Hostal Los Cerros,** Peñarroya, 1, © (953) 75 16 21, is spotless (3,500 pts) and at the *pensión* ★★**Sevilla,** Calle Ramón y Cajal 9, © (953) 75 06 12, you can get a clean and pleasant double with bath for 3,200–3,400 pts; the ★**San Miguel,** Avenida Libertad 69, © (953) 75 20 49, is another cheapie, 2,800 pts for a double without bath; while at the ★★**Hotel Consuelo,** Calle Ramón y Cajal 12, © (953) 75 08 40, the rooms are a bit fancier for 5,000–5,500 pts.

Cazorla has a surprising number of hotels, both in town and up in the mountains on the road to the dam and reservoir at El Tranco, 20km (12½ miles) north in a beautiful mountain setting. One of these is the ★**Mirasierra**, Santiago de la Espada, Ctra del Tranco, Km 20, ℂ (953) 72 15 44, with a restaurant (doubles with bath 2,800 pts). The ★★★**Parador El Adelantado**, ℂ (953) 72 10 75, fax 72 15 44, is a small mountain chalet—only 20 rooms—in another pretty setting in the mountains outside Cazorla, a base for hunting, fishing and walking in the Sierra (doubles 10,500 pts). The ★**Don Diego**, Calle Hilario Marcos 163, ℂ (953) 72 05 45, is a comfortable little hotel with doubles for 4,200–4,700 pts.

Eating Out

Apart from the Parador, there aren't any really good restaurants in Úbeda. The best is **Cuzco**, Parque Vandelvira 8, ℂ (953) 75 34 13, which has local dishes and standard Andaluz fish and meat menus. It has a 750 pts day menu which includes two courses and wine. There are plenty of characters at the bar in **El Gallorojo**, Calle Estrella at the top of Calle Trinidad, during the day and it's a lively place in the evening with excellent tapas and restaurant (1,000–2,000 pts). A smattering of unremarkable places are around Calle Ramón y Cajal. **El Olivo**, Avenida Ramón y Cajal 6, ℂ (953) 75 20 92, has average fare at average prices (1,500–2,000 pts). The restaurant at the **Hostal Sevilla**, Avenida Ramón y Cajal, 20, ℂ (953) 75 06 12, is good value, and for pre-dinner drinks try the **Bar Palacio** in the courtyard of the Palacio de los Bussianos on Calle Trinidad.

Jaén

In the middle of the vast tracts of olive groves on which it depends is Jaén, the most provincial of all the Andalucían capitals. Jaén lacks the Renaissance charms of Úbeda or Baeza, but it is a decent, modern town, not as unattractive as many books claim; easily

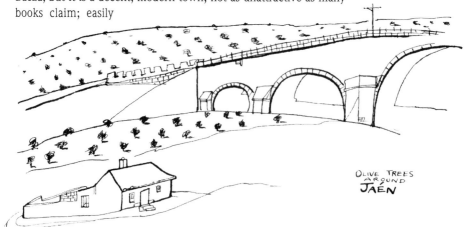

OLIVE TREES
AROUND
JAÉN

explored on foot in one day, along pleasant pedestrian walkways.

Getting Around

Jaén has direct **rail** links only with Córdoba (three trains daily) and Madrid (about six). The RENFE station is on the Paseo de la Estación, the main street, at the northern edge of town, by the Plaza de la Concordia. **Buses** are the best bet for Úbeda or Granada. The bus station is on the Avenida de Madrid, near the tourist office.

Tourist Office

Arquitecto Berges 1, © (953) 22 27 37.

Olive Oil

Olive oil is an important part of Jaén cuisine and contributes to dishes such as *espinacas jiennenses* (spinach Jaén-style) and *ajilimójili* (potatoes, red peppers, oil and vinegar). There's even a dessert called *ochío*—oil cakes covered by a layer of salt and paprika. *Pipirrana* is considered a local speciality with peppers, tomatoes, onions, hard-boiled egg and tuna fish. It's especially popular in the summer. During the winter try *migas de pan* or bread crumbs, usually served with pieces of pork. Wherever you eat, look out for Jaén black pudding, a concoction of pork, beef, garlic, paprika, nutmeg and sherry, *cabrito asado* (roast baby kid with garlic), *chorizo* and the famous salad, *pipirrana*. In Úbeda, ask for the convent cakes, *tocinos de cielo*. The clay *cazuela* bowl gives its name to a savoury cake made from chickpeas, aubergine, marrow and sausage, topped with sesame seeds.

Jaén was the first capital of the kingdom of Granada and the old Arab quarter is a part of the town well worth a visit. Its weaving, narrow, paved lanes are at the foot of the hill crowned by the 13th-century Moorish castle of **Santa Catalina**, built by ibn-Nasr (*open Sun 10–2*). Towering above the town, it's an ideal place to take in the views of the wild countryside and the mountains beyond.

The city's pride is its monumental **cathedral** on Plaza Santa María, begun in 1548 by Andrés de Vandelvira. His work inside has suffered many changes, and the façade isn't his at all; not begun until 1667, Eufrásio López de Rojas's design was the first genuine attempt at Baroque in Andalucía, decorated with extravagant statuary by Pedro Roldán (*open 8.30–1, 4.30–9*). Adjacent to the cathedral is the **Iglesia del Sagrario**, with a neoclassical interior designed by Ventura Rodríguez. On Calle Martínez Molina, west of the cathedral, an old hospital has been restored to hold a small **museum** of crafts and naïve art but the real attraction is the **Baño Arabes**, well-preserved 11th-century ruins of Moorish baths, discovered underneath (*10–2, 5–8 weekdays, 10.30–2 weekends, closed Mon; adm free with an EU passport*).

Jaén's modern quarters can be a bit dreary, and peculiar at the same time. The centre, Plaza de las Batallas, has an extremely silly winged statue atop a pedestal, commemorating

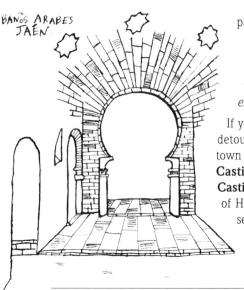

BAÑOS ARABES
JAÉN.

past victories over the Moors. Nearby, on the broad Plaza de la Estación, there is a good archaeological collection in the **Museo Provincial**, with some exceptional Iberian sculptures (*open daily except Mon, 9–2*).

If you're on the way to Granada, a possible detour is **Alcalá La Real**, with an unusual town square and another picturesque castle, the **Castillo de la Mota** on top of a hill. The **Castillo de Solera**, in that tiny village just east of Huelma, is an even finer sight; the castle seems to grow out of its narrow crag. Like Cazorla, the views are breathtaking but it will be some trouble to get up to them on foot.

Where to Stay

The ★★★★**Parador Castillo de Santa Catalina** is in the castle overlooking Jaén, ✆ (953) 26 44 11, fax 22 39 30 (12,000–13,000 pts for a double), and is where General de Gaulle spent time on his memoirs. If you are suffering from writer's block, you might do better at the ★★★**Condestable Iranzo**, Paseo de la Estación 32, ✆ (953) 22 28 00, fax 26 38 07, near the tourist office. It doesn't have the view, but more luxuries at a better price (9,000–11,000 pts a double, for an air-conditioned double room with TV). Another conveniently placed major hotel is the ★★★**Xauen**, Plaza Deán Mazas 3, ✆ (953) 26 40 11, further down the Paseo near Plaza Constitución (7,000–8,500 pts). A couple of acceptable budget hotels are ★**La Española**, Bernardo López 9, ✆ (953) 25 84 34 (around 3,000–4,000 pts) and the ★**Carlos V**, Avenida de Madrid 4, ✆ (953) 22 20 91 (2,700–2,900 pts).

Eating Out

For dining, the acknowledged best place in the city is **Restaurant Nelson**, Paseo de la Estación 33, ✆ (953) 22 92 01, decorated very much in the style of an English pub, but that's as far as it goes—you won't find bangers and mash here, but some excellent Spanish and international dishes (2,500–3,500 pts; closed Sun and Aug). For local specialities at their best, try **Casa Vicente**, Maestra Madre, 8 ✆ (953) 23 28 16, where a wide-ranging menu concentrates on meat and fish (3,000 pts; closed Sun). During the summer try and get a table in the courtyard. The *parador's* restaurant has a good reputation and has wonderful views towards the Sierra Morena (3,000–4,000 pts).

Andalucían Coasts

Everyone has heard of the Costa del Sol, but there is a good deal more to Andalucía's coasts than just that narrow strip of salty Babylon—about 640km (400 miles) of it, from the empty spaces of Huelva to the empty spaces of Almería.

Andalucía's Atlantic coast, from Portugal to the Straits of Gibraltar, is not at all scenic, but it has plenty of long golden beaches that haven't yet become too crowded. The image-makers of the Spanish Tourism Ministry have bestowed upon it the name **Costa de la Luz**. The piquant, sea-washed town of **Cádiz** is its major attraction. After Cádiz the mountains close in, until **Algeciras**, a port town with the promise of a side-trip to Morocco, or to **Ceuta**, a tiny remnant of Spain's colonial empire in Africa. Next we stop for fish and chips in **Gibraltar**; there the endless *urbanizaciones* of the **Costa del Sol** begin, reaching their greatest intensity around **Marbella** and **Torremolinos**. **Málaga** comes next, a busy city not without charm, and after it the only section of the coast with any pretensions to scenery, around **Nerja**. After **Motril**, and the road to Granada, there's more solitude on the **Costa de Almería**, which is in parts pretty, in others nearly a desert.

Altogether, these coasts have only one real purpose—for planting yourself on a beach and dozing off. There are the inevitable peripheral attractions (mini-golf, seafood dinners, funfairs, English beer on tap, etcetera), but little else. Pack a potent sunscreen and have a good time.

Huelva

A Huelva una vez y nunca vuelvas.
(One trip to Huelva and you don't go back.)

This Andalucían saying does seem a little unkind, but the provincial capital *is* full of factories and freshly laid cement; from the outskirts it looks like some dilapidated Slovak town. Hit the centre however and, small as it is, it boasts an incongruously large number of fur shops and amusement arcades. (History will probably prove that Las Vegas was actually founded by a Huelvan.) Another surprise is to be found on its streets, a species now extinct in northern Europe but which can occasionally be spotted here after nightfall—the crêpe-soled teddy boy.

Getting Around

The **railway** station is on the Avenida de Italia, a 5-minute walk from the centre of Huelva; daily *Talgo* to Sevilla and Madrid (change at Linares for Granada and Almería), apart from the regular services to Sevilla, from where there are connections to Cádiz, Jerez, Códoba, other points in Andalucía and Barcelona; also regular trains to Ayamonte, on the Portuguese border. The Damas **bus** company has its station at Avenida de Portugal 9, with services to Sevilla, Granada, Cádiz and Algeciras, and other destinations within the province: Ayamonte, Isla Cristina, Punta Umbría, Mazagón and Matalascañas on the coast, less frequently to Nerva and the mountain villages to the north. The nearest **airport** is in Sevilla.

Tourist Office

Avenida Alemania 14, ✆ (955) 25 74 03. Open weekdays 9–2, 4.30–7.30; Sat 9–2.

The town's tourist brochure, in a unique and disarmingly modest display of candour, states that Huelva 'has no particular historic interest'. The town was severely damaged by the earthquake of 1755, explaining the near-absence of anything older than that; exceptions include the 16th-century Baroque church of **San Pedro**, built on the site of an old mosque, and the **Museo Provincial**, Alameda Sundheim 13 (*open Mon–Fri, 8.30–2.30*). The town's theatre is an Art Deco aberration that resembles an Italian ice-cream parlour, but the real curiosity of Huelva is the **Barrio Reina Victoria**, a neighbourhood constructed by, and for, the employees of the English Río Tinto mining company in the 19th century. The houses, now in a state of disrepair, sport gable ends and chimney pots in true English suburban style. Just out of town, where the Odiel and Tinto rivers meet, is the 36m-high hooded statue of Christopher Columbus, sculpted by Gertrude Whitney and presented to Spain by the US in 1929.

Chocos and choqueros

Huelvan cuisine is based on fish and mountain sausages—white, horse-shoe, smoke-cured, salami and blood. The Huelva hills house the Iberian pig, which has a justifiably high reputation for the quality of its pork: the local ham's reputation is of a fine aromatic meat. Huelvans are also known as *choqueros*, because of their love for *chocos*—small cuttlefish; but just as popular as is *mojama*, an expensive, usually salty fish delicacy of raw wind-dried tuna. Although Condado de Huelva is near to Jerez, it is still within Huelva province and provides decent white table wine and *finos* such as Condado Pálido and Condado Viejo.

Huelvans are an isolated bunch, flanked and maybe intimidated by the presence of haughty Sevilla on one side and the expanse of Portugal on the other. They are nonetheless friendly and welcoming, and hoping to put aside centuries of stagnation, are optimistic and fervent in their desire to play a more important role in the future of the new Spain and Europe.

Where to Stay

To be honest, there's little to detain you in Huelva for longer than one night, but there's a reasonable selection. The ★★★★**Luz Huelva**, ✆ (955) 25 00 11, fax 25 81 10, is out on the Alameda Sundheim near the Columbus monument, with pool, tennis courts and air-conditioned rooms (15,300 pts). The ★★★**Tartessos**, Martín

The Costa de la Luz: Huelva   123

Alonso Pinzón 13, ✆ (955) 28 27 11, fax 25 06 17, is comfortable and central (10,000 pts). The ★★**San Miguel**, Santa María 6, ✆ (955) 24 52 03, has decent rooms for around 4,500 pts, and at the bottom of the scale the ★**París**, Rico 6, ✆ (955) 24 88 16, and **La Vega**, Plaza Independencia, 15 ✆ (955) 24 15 63, both have rooms for 3,500 pts, but don't expect any home comforts.

Eating Out

Huelva packs some surprises in the culinary department; its markets keep the restaurants well supplied with gleaming fresh seafood and Huelvans like to eat out. For perfectly prepared seafood at affordable prices, head out to **Las Candelas**, Ctra Punta Umbria at the Aljaraque crossing, ✆ (955) 31 83 01 (2,000 pts; closed Sun). Traditionally the best place in town is **Los Gordos**, Carmen 14, ✆ (955) 24 62 66, where they concentrate on simple dishes such as shellfish soup and grilled red mullet, but there's also a good selection of meats (2,500 pts; closed Sat eve and Sun). In the busy pedestrian heart of the town **El Timón**, Arq. Peréz Carasa 18, ✆ (955) 24 66 28, may be a bit shabby on the outside but inside it's as a good little Spanish restaurant should be, typical both in its decor and menu. A full dinner with starter, mixed fried fish and wine costs 2,000 pts and there's a set menu for 1,000 pts. The real find in Huelva has to be the plain, family-run bar **Los Gallegos** on the same street, where delicious tapas cost a measly 100–150 pts, *raciones* from 400 pts; *pinchitos, gambas ajillo, merluza frita* or *a la plancha, pulpo a la gallega, calamares*—they're all scrumptious.

Around Huelva

Twenty-seven kilometres (17 miles) east of Huelva on the N431 you may visit the once-important town of **Niebla**, now forgotten behind its decayed Romano-Moorish walls. There's a Roman bridge and some interesting old churches and Moorish buildings. Christopher Columbus set out on his epic voyage from **Palos de la Frontera**, 5km (3 miles) southeast of Huelva. Some 4km (2½ miles) to the west, the **Convento de la Rábida** was Columbus's home while he planned the trip, and the rooms he used are maintained as they were then.

West of Huelva

Coming from Huelva by bus to **Ayamonte**, you'll be deposited next to the pretty square behind the harbour filled with small boats, which you can eye from the comfort of one of the *azulejo* benches. If you're on your way to Portugal, walk through the square and follow the signs for about 500m, where a flat-bottomed boat will be waiting to take you and 40 cars across the narrow stretch of the Guadiana river to the Portuguese town of Vila

Real de Santo António. The back streets of Ayamonte are not without character and there are plenty of little cafés where you can sit and muse, or bring your diary up to date. Just across the water, the beaches of the resort **Isla Cristina** are more popular with Spaniards than foreigners.

Heading back east to Huelva, along the N431, you'll pass the sleepy town of **Lepe**; the butt of Andalucían jokes, in the same way as the Irish, Polacks and Newfies are elsewhere. Rather sportingly, every May the *leperos* hold a festival of humour—and even if they mind the abuse, they're laughing all the way to the bank, for the ever-abundant strawberry, orange and asparagus crops in this area have made the town very wealthy. (Those silver lakes you see along the road are actually sun-tinted plastic sheets protecting the strawberries.)

This stretch of road between Huelva and Ayamonte has no real attraction for the tourist—orange groves interspersed with derelict buildings, scrapyards and mudflats. South of Lepe on the coast are two spots worth a visit—**La Antilla**, with its fine white sandy beach, and **El Rompido**, a pleasant little place that is now being developed for tourism. Further east, the peninsula of **Punta Umbria** is one of the main tourist resorts of the area; its long sandy beaches offer all types of water sports.

Where to Stay

Ayamonte

The ****Parador Costa de la Luz**, El Castillito, ✆ (955) 32 07 00, fax 32 07 00, may not be on the beach but it has fine views over the sea and a big swimming pool. Although it occupies the site of a long-gone Moorish castle, the *parador* was built more recently, in 1966 (doubles 10,000–12,000 pts). Ayamonte has a number of inexpensive places, like the *****Hostal La Ribera**, at Paseo de la Ribera 1, ✆ (955) 32 02 89 (doubles 2,500–3,000 pts), or the *****Europa**, Avenida de la Playa 45, ✆ (955) 32 01 91 (2,500–4,000 pts).

Isla Cristina

On the beach you have a choice between ****Los Geranios**, Ctra Isla Cristina–Playa, ✆ (955) 33 18 00 (doubles 4,000–4,800 pts) and *****El Paraíso**, Camino de la Playa, ✆ (955) 33 18 73 (doubles 3,600–5,500 pts).

Punta Umbria

The choice is wider at Punta Umbria. ****El Ayamontino**, Avenida Andalucía, ✆ (955) 31 14 50, fax 31 03 16, has the advantage of a good restaurant although it's a fair walk from the beach (6,000–7,500 pts). Its sister hotel, the **Ayamontino Ría**, is better located on Plaza Pérez Pastor 25, ✆ (955) 31 14 58. ****La Playa**, Avenida Océano 95, ✆ (955) 31 01 12, is one of the cheapest hotels on the beach (doubles 5,500–6,000 pts). All these little resorts have cheaper hotels within reasonable distances of the beaches. In the busy season, phone ahead.

Ayamonte

There's a line of fine little restaurants behind the plaza, on the Paseo de la Ribera, all offering the day's special for around 900 pts; a seafood meal will cost 1,500–2,000 pts. For shellfish and *paella*, try the **Casino España** with its cool arches and terrace. At the **Casa Barberi**, Paseo de la Ribera, 13 © (955) 47 02 89, you can peep through the palm trees at Portugal.

Isla Cristina

The local favourite is the restaurant **Acosta**, Plaza Caudillo 13, © (955) 33 14 20, for fresh fish and traditional Andalucían stews (1,500 pts; closed Mon in winter).

Punta Umbria

You'll raise a few eyebrows if you don't order fish. Long popular is **La Esperanza**, Plaza Pérez Pastor 7, © (955) 31 10 45, with satisfying well-cooked dishes at reasonable prices—dogfish with tomato 1,500 pts; the rest are under 1,000 pts. Another established restaurant is the **El Ayamontino**, Avenida Andalucía 13, © (955) 31 14 50, serving tasty fish soup, oven-cooked bream and sirloin steaks (2,000 pts).

North of Huelva to the Sierra de Aracena

If you have a car you can comfortably explore the little-visited mountain villages in the Sierra de Aracena, less than a 2-hour drive from the capital. The N435 takes you to the heart of this area, passing through beautiful forests of holm oaks and cork trees, as the countryside gets more mountainous and the views more scenic.

Tourist Office

Aracena: Plaza San Pedro, © (955) 11 03 55.

Aracena has the big attraction, the **Gruta de las Maravillas**, a spectacular cave of stalagmites and stalactites, underground lakes and cavernous natural chambers. On the hill above the cave stand the ruins of a **Moorish castle**, once occupied by the Knights Templars, and the church of **Nuestra Señora de los Dolores**, a fine medieval church with a Mudéjar tower. Twelve kilometres (7½ miles) away to the west on the bumpy H521 is the extremely pretty village of **Alájar**, worth a visit for its natural caves, the *Sillita del Rey* and the *Salón de los Machos*; and also for the **Hermitage of Nuestra Señora de los Ángeles**, with a 13th-century Gothic carving, and wonderful views. From this point you can look down on the mining lands of **Río Tinto**, excavated as early as Phoenician and Roman times, and bought by a British company in the late 19th century.

Perhaps the best of these villages is the white village of **Almonaster la Real**, in an attractive rural setting, with the remains of a 1,000-year-old **mosque**. Nearby **Cortegana** has the 16th-century church of **Divino Salvador**, with three handsome wrought-iron pulpits, and the inevitable ruins of a medieval castle. In **Aroche**, further west, the white houses bask in the sun under the remains of an Almoravid fortress, containing a bullring. There's a small municipal **archaeological museum** and the tiny, unbelievable **Museo del Rosario**—yes, a rosary bead museum. On your way back to Huelva from here, you can stop in **Jabugo** to try the best known and best tasting cured ham in Spain , and don't dare say otherwise. Heading back to Huelva on the N435, **Valverde del Camino** is notable only for its furniture and shoe industries.

Where to Stay

In the middle of the Sierra Morena on the road to Portugal, 6km (3½ miles) from Aracena, is the **★Finca Buen Vino**, Los Marines, Huelva, ✆ (955) 12 40 34, fax 12 40 34, a grand guesthouse run by a charming English family; lunch is served beside the spring-fed pool (12,000 pts per person including dinner; ring in advance). Otherwise, accommodation north of Huelva is limited to simple *hostales*. Aracena has the most comfortable rooms at the modern **★★Sierra de Aracena**, Gran Vía 21, ✆ (955) 12 61 75 (5,500 pts doubles with bath) and the **★Sierpes**, Mesones 19, ✆ (955) 11 01 47 (3,200 pts with bath). In Almonaster la Real, **★La Cruz**, Los Llanos 8, ✆ (955) 13 04 35, has doubles for 3,500 pts. Jabugo has only two pensiones: **★La Aurora**, Barco 9, ✆ (955) 12 11 46 (2,800 pts) and the **★Casa García**, San Martín 2, ✆ (955) 13 04 09 (3,500–4,500 pts).

Eating Out

In the villages to the north there are no real outstanding restaurants, with the exception of Aracena. At the entrance to the caves, **Casas**, Plaza de San Pedro, ✆ (955) 11 00 44, is a small rustic place that serves mostly Sierra pork and game dishes (2,000 pts).

The Coast South of Huelva

Tourist Offices

Mazagón: Edificio Mancomunidad Moguer–Palos, ✆ (955) 37 60 44 (in the same building as the police station).

Matalascañas: Urb. Playa de Matalascañas, ✆ (955) 43 00 86.

Twenty-three kilometres (14½ miles) south of Huelva, along the coastal route, is **Mazagón**, a get-away-from-it-all family resort, surrounded by pine trees and lovely beaches. From here it's a straight shot to Torre de la Higuera, and the big hotel developments around the endless **Matalascañas Beach**, the most international of Huelva's resorts. This is the dead end of the coastal highway; the only place you can go is the tiny inland village of **El Rocío**, which would not even be on the map were it not for the annual *romería* at Pentecost, the biggest and perhaps the oldest in Spain. Every year hundreds of thousands of pilgrims bring their families for a few days of music and merry making in the fields; it is traditional to arrive in a horse-drawn, covered wagon, decorated with flowers and streamers. Campfires burn all night, and the atmosphere is pure electricity.

Las Marismas

LYNX – LAS MARISMAS

Add the water of the broad Guadalquivir to this flat coastal plain, and the result is southern Europe's greatest marshland wildlife preserve. Las Marismas is another world, a bit of the Everglades in a country better known for dry heated mountains. Hundreds of species of migratory birds pass through in the spring and autumn—storks among them—but Las Marismas has a fantastically varied population of its own: rare golden eagles, snowy egrets, flamingoes, griffin vultures, tortoises, red deer, foxes and European lynx.

As in the Everglades, wildlife congregates around 'islands' among the wetlands; here they're called *corrales*, built of patches of dune anchored by surrounding shrubs and stands of low pines. Also like the Everglades, Las Marismas is threatened by development, from the growing resorts like Matalascañas. This has become Spain's top environmental concern, and the government has limited coastal development and also set aside a large slice of the area as the **Parque Nacional del Coto de Doñana**.

For visitors, the park conducts tours by Land Rover from a station about half-way between El Rocío and Matalascañas; check with the tourist offices in Huelva or Sevilla for details before you go. Keep in mind that the wetlands are largely dried up in the summer. Whenever you come, bring a few gallons of mosquito repellent and watch out for quicksand.

Where to Stay

In an attractive pine-tree setting and looking down onto Mazagón beach, the ★★★★**Parador Cristóbal Colón**, Ctra Huelva–Matalascañas, © (955) 53 63 00, fax 53 62 28, is the best option, with pleasant gardens, pool and air-conditioned rooms (12,500–15,000 pts). There are a number of resort hotels at Matalascañas, predictably packed in high season. ★★**El Cortijo**, Sector E-P 15/49, © (955) 43 02 59, fax 44 85 70, is a pleasant alternative next to Coto de Doñana; it's a 5-minute walk from the beach and there are facilities for horse-riding (doubles 7,500–10,000 pts).

Eating Out

Mazagón has a number of restaurants and cafés around Avenida Fuente Piña. There's not much to distinguish between them but at least they're lively. Many people eat in their hotels down on Matalascañas Beach. **Da Pino**, Avenida

Adelfas 1, © (955) 43 02 03, is a pricey Italian restaurant but the food is good, with pastas, excellent salads and good steaks (2,500 pts; closed Mon and Christmas). **Los Galanes**, in the Edificio Las Begoñas, has a lovely terrace where you can enjoy your seafood at leisure (1,500 pts).

Cádiz

If Cádiz were a tiny village, the government would immediately declare it a National Monument and put up a sign. It's a big, busy seaport, though, and the tourist business generally leaves it alone. It's a pity, for Cádiz (if you pronounce it any other way but 'Caddy' no one will understand you) is one of the most distinctive Spanish cities, worth spending a few days in even if there are few 'sights'. The city is a small peninsula, resembling a sturdy galleon patiently waiting to put to sea, packed tightly and pounded by the rough Atlantic breakers on all sides. It comes in colours—a hundred shades of off-white, bleached and faded by sun and spray into a soft patina, broken only by the golden dome of a rambling Baroque cathedral that would be a civic misfortune anywhere else, but seems inexplicably beautiful here.

History

Cádiz modestly claims to be the oldest city in western Europe. It's hard to argue; the Phoenician city of *Gadir* has a documented foundation of 1100 BC, and while other cities have traces of older settlements, it would be difficult to find another city west of Greece with a continuous urban life of 3,000 years. Gadir served as the port for shipping Spanish copper and tin, and was undoubtedly the station for the now-forgotten Phoenician trade routes with west Africa and England—and possibly even for explorations to America. Cádiz, however, prefers to consider Hercules its founder, and he appears on the arms of the city between his famous pillars.

Under Roman rule, *Gades* as it was called, was a favoured city, especially under Julius Caesar who held his first public office here. The city was out of the spotlight until the 16th century, when the American trade and Spain's growth as a naval power made a major

CÁDIZ

port of it once again. Sir Francis Drake came here to 'singe the king of Spain's beard' in 1587, and later British admirals followed the custom for a century, calling every decade or so for a fish dinner and an afternoon's sacking and burning. The years after 1720, when Cádiz controlled the American market, shaped its present character. Street names like Calle Conde O'Reilly (an Irish-born royal governor who did a lot for Cádiz) and a statue of one José MacPherson y Hemas testify to the contacts the city enjoyed with the outside world—uniquely so for Spain in those dark years—and it became the most liberal and tolerant corner of Spain. Its shining hour came in 1812, when the constitution was declared here, and the city became the capital of free Spain.

The Best Carnival in Spain

This took its present form in the 19th century; some claim there is a strong Cuban influence behind its masquerades and crazy music. It says something about Cádiz that under the dictatorship, theirs was the only carnival Franco failed to suppress, and if you ever experience it you'll know why. In the second week of February, if there were an instrument to measure atmosphere, it would glow red here; everyone, young or old, native or stranger, is roaming the streets, singing and dancing. Small food stalls spring up on every corner, and the bars, cafés and restaurants have a hard time keeping up with the constant flow of revellers.

Getting Around

by ferry

Cádiz isn't the big passenger port it used to be, but you can still take the weekly ferries to Almería, Genoa, Italy, Tenerife–Las Palmas–Arrecife in the Canary Islands, or to Palma de Mallorca with various stops along the way. They run a little more frequently in the summer. There's also a regular ferry ride from the port to El Puerto de Santa María. **Tickets**: Transmediterránea office, Avenida Ramón de Carranza 26, © (956) 28 41 62 or 28 41 63.

by train

You can go only to Jerez (20 daily, stopping at El Puerto de Santa María) and Sevilla (8 directly). The station is at the narrow landward end of the old city; just a few blocks from the Plaza San Juan de Dios, © (956) 25 43 01.

by bus

Cádiz is served by two bus companies: Los Amarillos, Avenida Ramón de Carranza 31 (by the port), © (956) 28 58 52, takes the route west to Rota and Sanlúcar de Barrameda; Comes, Plaza de España, takes the route east to Tarifa and Algeciras. City bus 1 will take you from the Plaza de España to Cádiz's suburban beaches and to new Cadiz, © (956) 21 17 63.

Tourist Office

On the corner of Plaza de Mina and Calle Calderón de la Barca 1, © (956) 21 13 13. Open weekdays 9–2, 5–7 and Sat 10–1.

The approach to Cádiz is a dismal one, through marshes and saltpans cluttered with power lines and industrial junk. After this, you must pass through a long, narrow strip of land full of modern suburbs before arriving at the **Puerta de Tierra**, entrance to the old city on the peninsula. Almost everything about warfare in the 18th century had a certain decorum to it, and Cádiz's gates and formidable **land walls** (1757), all well preserved, are among the most aesthetically pleasing structures in town.

It's a great city for exploring—streets as narrow as those of Toledo, neither decaying nor prettified for the tourists. The old city is a maze of lanes bathed in soft lamplight after dusk, when the numerous cafés fill up with young, exuberant *gaditanos*. A walk through the myriad of cobbled streets, past solid doors carved from the trees of South American forests, and balconies spilling over with flowers, will take you back in history to the time when mighty Cádiz bustled with industry as the gateway to the Americas. Keep an eye out for the little plaques—marking the birthplaces, amongst others, of Manuel de Falla, and of Miranda, the first president of Venezuela—reminders of what an important role this little city has often played. Note the houses, too, in a style unique to Cádiz, with roof-terraces and little Moorish-looking turrets, from which the *gaditanos* watch for ships coming in. In an hour or so you can walk entirely around Cádiz, on the coast road past parks like the pretty **Alameda de Apodaca**, and forts and bastions of the 18th century.

LANTERN
CÁDIZ

Plaza San Juan de Dios and Around

From the Puerta de Tierra, the Cuesta de las Calesas leads down to the port and rail station, then around the corner to **Plaza San Juan de Dios**, the lively, palm-shaded centre of Cádiz, with most of the restaurants and hotels on the surrounding streets. Two blocks away is the **cathedral**, on a small plaza. A recent, thorough restoration of this ungainly bulk has not destroyed its ingratiating charm. It was begun in 1722, at the height of Cádiz's prosperity. Funds soon started running short, sadly enough; if original architect Vicente Acero had had his way, he might have made this as fanciful a work as his cathedral in Guadix. Of the paintings within, Zurbarán's *Santa Ursula* stands out. The composer Manuel de Falla has his tomb in the cathedral crypt (*open weekdays 5.30–7.30, Sat 9.30–10.30 and 5.30–8, Sun 11–1*). The **Museo de la Catedral** has a lot of religious gold and silverware, paintings by Murillo, Zurbarán, and Alejo Fernández, and painted panels and an ivory crucifix by Alonso Cano (*open daily except Sun and Mon, 10–1; adm 250 pts*).

Continuing eastwards, the Plaza Topete was named after a *tophet*, the Phoenician temple dedicated to that nasty habit of theirs—sacrificing first-born babies; remains of one were found here. Now this is Cádiz's almost excessively colourful **market district**, spread around a wonderful, dilapidated old market building.

A few more blocks east, the little church of **San Felipe Neri** on Calle Sacramento is an unprepossessing shrine to the beginnings of Spanish liberty. On 29 March 1812, an assemblage of refugees from Napoleon's occupation of the rest of Spain gathered here and declared Spain an independent republic, guaranteeing full political and religious freedom. Though their **constitution**, and their revolution, proved stillborn, it was a notable beginning for Spain's struggle towards democracy. Big marble plaques, sent as tributes, cover the church's façade. Inside is a beautiful *Immaculate Conception* by Murillo (*open daily 8.30–10 and 7.30–9.45*).

Around the corner, Cádiz's very good **Municipal Museum** has a huge Romantic-era mural depicting the 1812 event. In front of it, in the main hall, is the museum's star exhibit, a 15.4m (50ft) **scale model of Cádiz**, made entirely of mahogany and ivory by an unknown obsessive in 1779. Nearly every building is detailed—Cádiz hasn't changed much since. Among a collection of portraits of Spanish heroes is the Duke of Wellington, who in Spain carried the title of Duke of Ciudad Rodrigo. The best picture, though, also from that era, shows Hercules about to give Napoleon a good bashing with his club (*open daily except Mon, 9–1 and 5–8, Sat and Sun 9–1*).

Goat Cuisine

One of Cadiz's most well-known dishes is *berza*—a cabbage-based stew. Goat's cheese is called Cádiz cheese, produced in the mountains where it is semi-cured and develops a yellow colour. Cheese from Grazalema is only made in the spring and must be consumed within two months. For desserts try an almond pastry (*torta de almendra*) from the convent of the Augustinian Reverend Mothers.

Plaza de Mina and Around

On this lovely square, in the northwestern corner of the peninsula, you'll find the Tourist Information Office and the **Museum of Fine Arts and Archaeology**. The archaeology section contains a Phoenician sarcophagus, Phoenician jewellery, Roman pottery and Greek ceramics; among the statues there's a dumb-looking Emperor Trajan with a big Roman nose. But best in the museum are the paintings: some Murillos and very good portraits of the *Four Evangelists* and *John the Baptist* by Zurbarán. On the top floor are unaffectedly charming puppets and stage sets from a Cádiz genre of marionette show called *Tía Norica*, still performed in these parts (*open daily except Mon, 10–2; adm 275 pts, free with an EU passport*).

Around the corner, on Calle Rosario Ponce, the **Oratorio de la Santa Cueva**, with its three Goya frescoes (the only ones in Andalucía) has irregular opening times, but generally is safe to visit 10–1.

Where to Stay

moderate

There is a good *parador* in Cádiz—the ★★★★**Atlántico**, Avenida Duque de Nájera 9, ✆ (956) 22 69 05, fax 21 45 82. It is a modern building with wonderful views over the Atlantic and a large outdoor swimming pool (13,000 pts for a double).

inexpensive

The ★★★**Francia y París**, Plaza San Francisco 2, ✆ (956) 22 23 48, fax 22 24 31, is a quiet, elegant, well-run hotel around the corner from Plaza Mina at a very reasonable 7,500–8,500 pts for a double. Nearby, the ★**Imares**, San Francisco 9, ✆ (956) 21 22 57, has comfortable rooms for 3,000–4,500 pts, depending on the plumbing.

On the other side of the Puerta de Tierra, in the new part of Cádiz, there's just as much choice. The Paseo Marítimo is lively, so don't feel you're missing out if you stay here. The ★★**San Remo**, Paseo Marítimo 3, ✆ (956) 25 22 02, fax 25 22 03, has doubles for 6,500–8,500 pts with bath, and the rooms are adequately comfortable and overlook the beach.

cheap

There will be no problem finding cheaper—lots of sailors pass through here. The ★**Hostal Manolita**, Benjumeda 2, ✆ (956) 21 15 77, is clean and family-run and has doubles for around 2,500 pts. For even cheaper establishments just look for the *camas* signs and take your pick. Don't hesitate to turn down anything that appears too run down; some places appear as if they haven't had visitors for decades.

In a side street off the Paseo Marítimo is the reasonable ★**La Playa**, Dr Herrera Quevedo 1, ✆ (956) 25 84 00, with rooms going for 3,600–4,600 pts without.

expensive

Dining, of course, means more fish. **El Faro**, Calle San Felix 15, © (956) 21 25 01, is a place that takes it seriously, where you can get to know all of the amazingly wide range of seafood—things that we don't even have names for in English like *mojarras* and *urtas*—that come out of this part of the Atlantic; but apart from these outlandish creatures you'll have no problem ordering the more recognizable varieties—steamed hake with asparagus, clams with spinach, fried fish *a la Gaditana*, as well as a selection of meat dishes (full-course dinners 3,000–4,000 pts and a *menú del día* at 2,100 pts). **El Anteojo**, Alameda Apodaca 22, © (956) 22 57 02, is by the Alameda Apodaca walls, and its rustically decorated upstairs dining room looks over to Puerto de Santa María. The menu is a mix of Cádiz, Galician and Basque kitchens (3,000–4,000 pts).

moderate

El Sardinero, Plaza San Juan de Dios 4, © (956) 28 25 05, is one of the oldest restaurants in the city, with a variety of Basque and Andaluz dishes, which you can enjoy at the outside tables (about 2,500 pts).

In newer Cádiz, along the Paseo Marítimo, there's a wide choice of restaurants, nearly all with terraces or outside seating. **Curro el Cojo**, Paseo Marítimo 2, © (956) 25 31 86, specializes in meats from the Sierra, pork and game in particular (full dinner 2,500 pts). **La Costera**, further along on Calle Dr Fleming 8, © (956) 27 34 08, specializes in fish and also has a good wine list, and dining on the terrace (around 3,000pts). Behind the sea front, at Avenida José León de Carranza 4, **El Brocal**, © (956) 25 77 59, is a small restaurant serving meat with a North African and Greek bias (2,000–2,500 pts; closed Sun, Mon lunch and Nov).

inexpensive

A little further along, on the corner of Honduras and San Germán, the family-run **La Piconera**, Calle San Germán 5, © (956) 22 18 84, is a less expensive choice with a simpler, yet nonetheless wholesome menu (around 1,500 pts)—but you don't get the view.

Two smaller restaurants near La Costera in new Cádiz are **El Noray** and **Baro**, both predictably specializing in shellfish (2,000 pts).

Around Cádiz

Like those to the east, the beaches around Cádiz are popular mostly with Spaniards—more crowded, though, at least in July and August. Just the same, the beaches are lovely and huge, the towns behind them relatively unspoiled; there may be few better places in Spain to baste yourself, with plenty of opportunities for exploring *bodegas*.

Sanlúcar de Barrameda: Calzada del Ejército s/n, ✆ (956) 36 61 10

Rota: Plaza de Andalucía 3, ✆ (956) 81 01 00.

Puerto de Santa María: Calle Guadalete, ✆ (956) 54 24 13.

Sanlúcar and Rota

Sanlúcar de Barrameda makes *manzanilla*, most ethereal of sherries. It is known as the port that launched Magellan on his way around the world, and Columbus on his second voyage to the Indies; and is the birthplace of the artist Pacheco, Velázquez's teacher. The town has a certain crumbling colonial charm and an exceptionally pretty main plaza. Worth a visit are the church of **Nuestra Señora de la O**, with its fine Mudéjar portal and 16th-century coffered ceiling (although it may still be being restored), and the 19th-century **Montpensier Palace**, with an extensive library and paintings by Murillo, El Greco, Rubens and Goya (*open 8–2.30*). Although its beaches are not major league, this town has always been a popular summer destination with Spanish holidaymakers for its excellent cheap seafood. The Bajo de Guía is a particularly charming and run-down fishing district, and from here you can take the motor boat over to Coto de Doñana. If you have an afternoon to spare, amuse yourself by visiting the public fish auction in **Bonanza**, 4km away. **Chipiona** is a family resort, full of small *pensiones* and *hostales*, with a good beach at **Playa de Regla** near the lighthouse.

Next, on the edge of the bay of Cádiz, comes **Rota**, a bigger, flashier resort taking advantage of the best and longest beach on the coast; the town is pretty, though it's a bit overbuilt. It's also full of unpicturesque Americans from the largest naval base in the region, just outside town. This was the key base Franco gave up in the 1953 deal with President Eisenhower; in the recent dealings over the future of Spain's role in NATO, the Americans made it unpleasantly clear this base is not a subject for negotiation, although in the 1986 NATO referendum this region turned out the highest 'yes' vote in Spain.

El Puerto de Santa María and Puerto Sherry

Across the bay from Cádiz lies **El Puerto de Santa María**, the traditional port of the sherry houses in Jerez, which has quite a few *bodegas* of its own—Osborne, Terry and Duff Gordon among other famous names. The town has some interesting churches, mansions of the Anglo-Spanish sherry aristocracy, and the fine, restored 13th-century Mudéjar **Castillo de San Marcos**. The century-old **bullring** ranks with those of Sevilla and Ronda in prestige. El Puerto itself isn't a big resort, but it's a typical town of Cádiz province, with bright bustling streets, excellent restaurants and some good beaches (**Puntilla** especially) on the edges of town.

Puerto Sherry is a modern marina, built in the late 1980s, and a pleasant place to spend an afternoon or evening. It has yet to reach its potential (or occupancy) so it's a little lacking in character.

Where to Stay

It's no problem finding a place in any of the coastal resorts: especially in the high season, little old ladies meet the buses to drag you off to their *hostales*.

Sanlúcar, Chipiona and Rota

In Sanlúcar, try the modern ★★★**Doñana**, Avenida Cabo Noval, ℂ (956) 36 50 00, fax 36 71 41 (6,000–10,000 pts), or the neo-classical ★★★**Tartaneros**, Tartaneros 8, ℂ (956) 36 20 44, fax 36 00 45 (8,000–10,000 pts). In Chipiona, the ★**Paquita**, Francisco Lara 26, ℂ (956) 37 02 06, is a decent *hostal* near the beach—and really typical of what you'll find in these modest resorts (doubles 3,000–4,000 pts—no bath). The ★★**Del Sur**, Avenida Sevilla 2, ℂ (956) 37 03 50, is fancier, with a pool and garden, and still a bargain at the price (doubles 7,000 pts). Rota is more of the same, but has a few classy modern resort hotels including the ★★★**Playa de la Luz**, on the beach at Arroyo Hondo, ℂ (956) 81 05 00, fax 81 06 06, a sports-oriented hotel with a lovely pool and gardens (doubles 9,500 pts).

El Puerto de Santa María

The loveliest place to stay in El Puerto de Santa María is the ★★★★**Hotel Monasterio San Miguel**, Calle Larga 27, ℂ (956) 54 04 40, fax 54 26 04, an 18th century former monastery. It's marvellously soothing with tranquil cloisters, religious artefacts and a swimming pool discreetly placed where the vegetable garden used to be. The games room (once the refectory) and the restaurant are particularly interesting (12,500–15,000 pts). Another place many people like is the ★★★**Puertobahía**, Avenida de La Paz 38, Urb. Valdelagrana, ℂ (956) 86 27 21, fax 86 27 21, also on the beach (doubles 7,200–10,000 pts).

Eating Out

Sanlúcar and Rota

Most of the restaurants in this area are open only during the summer; informal cafés where you can pick out the fish that catches your fancy. Famous throughout Andalucía, and rightly so, is **Casa Bigote**, Bajo de Guía, ℂ (956) 36 26 9 6; it serves delicious appetizers, classic dishes of the region, and the best and freshest of seafood in all its varieties; the crayfish are a must, and you can try the local *manzanilla* with the day's catch. You may find you'll need more than one visit, though, as the tapas selection in the bar opposite is extensive and truly excellent. Get there early or you won't find a table (3,000–4,000 pts; closed Sun). Down on the beach front, Casa Bigote's main rival is the attractive **Mirador de Doñana**, Bajo de Guía, ℂ (956) 36 42 05, another popular bar and restaurant on three levels with a panoramic view across to the bird reserve. Particularly delicious are: *cigalas* (crayfish), *angulas* (baby eels) and *nido de rapé a la Sanluqueña*, a nest of straw potato chips, deep-fried with monkfish and parsley (2,000–2,500 pts). In

Rota the cuisine is heavily influenced by the presence of the naval base—pizza and Chinese restaurants alongside the usual seafood.

El Puerto de Santa María

Apart from the excellent *bodegas* and simple beach cafés, El Puerto has some deservedly popular restaurants. The most successful is **La Goleta**, Ctra Rota, © (956) 85 42 32, with simple but well-prepared seafood dishes, especially the fish cooked in salt, the *tosta de salmón* and the *porgy* in brandy (3,000 pts; closed Mon and first two weeks in Nov). **El Faro**, © (956) 87 09 52, near the round-about on Ctra de Roma Km 0.5 just outside town also has an excellent reputation for its regional cuisine (3,000 pts). Down on the riverside quay, the **Guadalete**, Avenida Bajamar 14, © (956) 87 02 98, attracts the crowds for its shrimps, sole and clams (2,000 pts). The liveliest place to dine, however, is **Romerijo's** on the Ribera del Marisco, © (956) 54 33 53. The freshest of fish and seafood is either ordered sitting down on the tables outside or bought as a take-away and wrapped in a paper funnel. Everyone throws discarded shells or crab claws into one of the red buckets on each table and munches their way through one of five kinds of prawns on offer. A kilo of shellfish is enough for four people. Noisy and fantastic value, you can be fully sated for around 1,000 pts.

If you're in Puerto Sherry, try and get a table at **Curro del Cojo**, Plaza Marqués Real Tesoro 7, © (956) 54 16 91. It's small, intimate and like the inside of a ship's cabin (2,000–2,500 pts).

Jerez de la Frontera

The name is synonymous with wine—by the English corruption of Jerez into sherry—but besides the *finos, amontillados, olorosos* and other varieties of that noble sauce, Jerez also ships out much of Spain's equally good brandy. Most of the well-known companies, whose advertising is plastered all over Spain, have their headquarters here, and they're quite accustomed to taking visitors—especially English ones—through the *bodegas*. Don't be shy. Most are open to visitors between 9am and 1pm on Mondays to Fridays, though not in August, or when they're busy with the *vendimia* (harvest) in September. Admission prices are around 300 pts upwards and usually include tasting sessions.

One of the most interesting *bodegas* to visit is that belonging to González Byass, Calle Manuel Maria González 12, © (956) 34 00 00. The tour includes the old sawdust-strewn *bodegas* that have held the sherry *soleras* for two centuries; the casks have been signed by many famous visitors over the years from Orson Welles to the Hollywood swimming star Esther Williams! The tour ends at the *degustacíon*, where the motto is, 'If you don't have a *copa* at eleven o'clock, you should have eleven at one', and cellarmen demonstrate their skill at pouring sherry from distances of a metre or more into the small *copitas*, in order to aerate the wine.

Just desserts

 If you like desserts then you'll understand why *tocino de cielo* is called heaven's bacon. This delicious sunshine-coloured sweet originated from the yolks left over from wine cellars as egg whites were once used to clarify wine. Wines from Jerez are full bodied and the climate is ideal for producing the dry *fino* and *manzanilla* sherries. *Olorosos* are medium dry while the *moscatel* and *Pedro Ximénez* sherries are darker and sweeter.

The *Semana Santa* festival in Jerez is more intimate, but just as splendid as that in Sevilla. The nightly processions escorting the Saint and Madonna images create a city-wide pageant. Late in the night, as they return home through the backstreets, they are sere-naded by impromptu solo voices; for the finest singers, the whole procession halts in appreciation.

Getting Around

Cádiz is the base for visiting Jerez and the coasts. The Amarillo company provides a regular **bus** service from Cádiz to all the coastal towns, and at least five daily to Jerez. Infrequent buses connect Jerez with Rota, Sanlúcar and El Puerto. Almost all the Sevilla–Cádiz buses stop in Jerez and El Puerto as do the trains. Frequent connections for Arcos de la Frontera and Ronda. One bus a day to Córdoba and Granada. Jerez stations for buses and trains are together on the eastern edge of town, © (956) 33 66 82. There's a regular **ferry** service from El Puerto to Cádiz (200 pts)—more fun than the bus. Parking can be hard to find if you're in a **car** but it is sometimes best to be based in Jerez for the surrounding area to avoid the queues on the roads into Cádiz.

Tourist Office

Alameda Cristina s/n, © (956) 33 11 50/33 11 62. Check here for information on visiting the sherry *bodegas*.

Business is good, and Jerez is growing. Though not an attractive town, it has a few lovely buildings for you to squint at after you've done the rounds of the *bodegas*. Its landmark is **La Colegiata** (also called San Salvador), a curious pseudo-Gothic church with a separate bell tower and Baroque staircase; though begun in the 13th century, its façade, largely the work of Vicente Acero, was not completed until 1750. Works inside include a *Madonna* by Zurbarán and sculptures by Juan de Mesa. Nearby, on the central Plaza de los Reyes Católicos, **San Miguel** (begun 1482) changes the scene to Isabelline Gothic—a fine example of that style, with a florid *retablo* inside (*open daily 8–9.45, 7–9; Sun 9–1*). The

Ayuntamiento (1575) is a lovely building that also houses a small archaeology museum. There is a Moorish **Alcázar** at the end of Calle Pérez Galdós, with a tower and some remains of the baths. **La Atalaya**, at Calle Cervantes, © (956) 18 21 00, is an interesting clock museum. Go before midday to hear them all chime (*open Mon–Sat 10–1*). There's also a new archaeology museum on Plaza de San Mateo.

Outside town, on the road to Medina Sidonia, is the **Cartuja de la Defensión**, a 15th-century monastery with the best Baroque façade (added in 1667) in Andalucía—a sort of giant *retablo* with sculptures by Alonso Cano and others. This is still a working monastery, and you'll need special permission to go inside. There is little reason to; the main attraction, a great altarpiece by Zurbarán, is scattered to the four winds—you can see panels in the museums of Sevilla and Cádiz. You can, however, visit the gardens and patio (*open Tue, Thur, and Sat 5–6.30*).

Horses and Flamenco

While in Jerez, look out for exhibitions scheduled at the **Escuela Andaluz del Arte Ecuestre** (School of Equestrian Art, Avenida Duque de Abrantes, © (956) 31 11 11). Jerez's snooty wine aristocracy takes horsemanship very seriously; they have some of the finest horses you're likely to see anywhere, and they know how to use them. You can see them, proud as Tío Pepe bottles, at the annual **Horse Fair** during the first half of May. The origin of this fair can be traced back to the 13th century, and its events include jumping, classical riding, harness and Andalucían country riding. Being Andalucían, it is also the best excuse for attending the *corrida*, drinking plenty of sherry and of course joining in the flamenco extravaganza. Every Thursday there is a 'horse ballet' at 12 noon (*adm 1,750 pts*) and there are tours between 11am and 1pm weekdays except Thursdays (*adm 425 pts*). Check with the tourist information for details of any special shows.

Housed in one of the most beautiful buildings of the old part of the city is the **Flamenco Centre**, Palacio Penmartín, Plaza de San Juan, © (956) 34 92 65, which presents different activities throughout the year—concerts, exhibitions, seminars and video shows—in an effort to promote and prolong the art (*open Mon–Fri 9–1; usually closed for two weeks during Aug*).

Where to Stay

In Jerez, there are many unremarkable hotels. The two top hotels are close to the centre of town and provide convenient access to the fair and the Spanish Riding School.

expensive/moderate

The luxury ★★★★**Jerez**, Avenida Álvaro Domecq 35, © (956) 33 06 00, fax 30 50 01, with a pool and tennis courts, is set in lovely tropical gardens, but is no bargain (19,000–23,000 pts). On the same avenue, but closer to town, the modern ★★★★**Royal Sherry Park**, Avenida Álvaro Domecq 11, © (956) 30 30 11, fax 31 13 00, is surrounded by a park, and also has a pool (13,500–16,500 pts).

Almost opposite is the more affordable ★★★**Avenida Jerez**, Avenida Álvaro Domecq 10, ✆ (956) 34 74 11, fax 33 72 96, a rather characterless modern place (9,000–14,000 pts). The ★★**Virt**, Higueras 20, ✆ (956) 32 28 11, is a middle-range bargain with decent air-conditioned rooms with bath for 7,000–9,800 pts.

inexpensive/cheap

In the centre of town, with underground parking, the ★★**Serit**, Higueras 7, ✆ (956) 34 07 00, fax 34 07 16, has comfy rooms for 5,500–9,000 pts. There's a decent selection down the lower end of the price scale. The ★**Las Palomas**, Higueras 17, ✆ (956) 34 37 73, at 2800–3400 pts; and the ★**San Andrés**, Morenos 12, ✆ (956) 34 09 83, and the ★**Sanvi**, Morenos 10, ✆ (956) 34 56 24, both with basic rooms for about 2,500 pts.

Eating Out

expensive

Jerez boasts one of Andalucía's loveliest restaurants, **El Bosque**, Avenida Álvaro Domecq 26, ✆ (956) 30 33 33 or 30 70 30, beautifully situated in the woods near the Parque de González Montoria, yet only a short distance from the centre of town. The seafood is top-class; try *langostinos de Sanlúcar, gambas de Huelva*, hake cooked in salt, angler fish in shellfish sauce (3,500 pts; closed Sun).

moderate

Closer to town, by the bullring, the **Tendido 6**, Circo 10, ✆ (956) 34 48 35, has a covered patio with adjoining dining room, decorated on a *feria* theme, with bull-fight memorabilia on the walls. Here the emphasis is on robust helpings of traditional food, and you can gorge to the full for 3,000 pts (closed Sun eve). A couple of streets behind the tourist office is one of the favourite dining places in town, **Gaitan**, Gaitan 3, ✆ (956) 34 58 59, proud bearer of a gastronomy award in the 1980s (3,000 pts; closed Sun eve). Near the Avenida Jerez hotel, **La Mesa Redonda**, Manuel de la Quintana 3, ✆ (956) 34 00 69, is beautifully decorated with antique furniture and paintings, giving the impression of an old aristocratic Jerez home. It's home cooking here—sole with mushrooms, game dishes and fresh salads (2,000–2,500 pts; closed Sun and Aug, reservations essential).

inexpensive

Close by Gaitan, there's a great tapas bar tucked away in a passage off the Plaza del Arenal. **Bar Juanito** is the best among a clutch of tiny places on Pescadería Vieja. Try the *alcachofas en salsa* or the *costillas en adobo* (marinaded grilled pork chops). Crushed at lunchtime; arrive early in the evening (opens at 8pm) if you want a table. Two or three tapas plus wine for around 1,000 pts. There are many street *bodegas* where you can try the whole spectrum of the area's produce. Try the **Alcazaba**, Medina 19, or **La Tasca**, Calle Matadero s/n, both near the centre.

The green, hilly countryside of this region looks a lot like the parts of Morocco just across the straits. The hills force the main road away from the sea, leaving a few villages with fine beaches relatively unspoilt, and good places to take time out from your overactive holiday; the problem is they're hard to reach unless you have a car.

Getting Around

by bus

Buses to Algeciras from the Comes station in Cádiz are frequent enough, but services to the nascent resorts along the coast like Conil, Barbate and Zahara are less frequent (two per day during the week). Algeciras's bus station is in the Hotel Octavio complex, Calle San Bernardo; there are buses to La Línea (for Gibraltar) about every half-hour, and also connections to the Costa del Sol and Málaga.

by train

Trains go to Ronda, and from there to all points in eastern Andalucía; there is a daily *Talgo* to Madrid and points north. The station is across from the bus station.

Tourist Office

Algeciras: Juan de la Cierva s/n, by the port, © (956) 60 09 11.

Beyond the marshland around Cádiz, you'll see the turn-offs first for **Sancti Petri**, a deserted town with a castle by the beach, then **Conil**. The main attraction of this stretch of road is **Vejer de la Frontera**, whitest of the 'white villages' of Andalucía, strangely moulded around its hilltop site like a Greek island town. The village is dominated by its Moorish castle and Gothic church built over the site of a mosque. The town's spanking clean, narrow whitewashed streets are evocative of its Arab origins. In the upper part of town there are still the original Moorish gates. From Vejer the C343 goes down to the modern town of **Barbate de Franco**, whose income comes not from tourists but tuna. Twice a year large shoals of tuna pass here, to be thwarted in a bloody ambush similar to the *matanza* (slaughter) off the coast of Sicily.

A small road leads west out of Barbate to the summer resort of **Los Caños de Meca**. Traditionally busy in the height of summer with tourists from Sevilla and Cádiz, recent years have seen hordes of Germans adopt the place as their escape haven. Half-an-hour's walk west of here takes you to **Cape Trafalgar**, where Nelson breathed his last in 1805. Spaniards remember this well; it was mostly their ships that were getting smashed, under incompetent French leadership. Every Spaniard did his duty, though, and with their unflappable sense of personal honour the Spanish have always looked on Trafalgar as a sort of victory.

Ten kilometres (6 miles) south of here is another developing resort, **Zahara de los Atunes** ('of the tunas'). This is one of the most unspoilt coastlines in southern Spain, with miles of fine sandy beach that will be all yours in spring and autumn. The town was the birthplace of Francisco Rivera, or Paquirri, the famous bullfighter.

Tarifa

Tarifa, at the tip of Spain and of Europe, has the quality of looking either exotic and evocative, or merely dusty and dreary, depending on the mood you're in and the hour of the day. You might even think you've arrived in Africa, it's so bleached by sun and salt. The town is one of the top destinations in Europe for the masters of the art of windsurfing; the *levante* and *poniente* winds are relentless in their attack on this coast. There are miles of beaches around to choose from. The town has a 10th-century Moorish **castle**, much rebuilt since. As every Spanish schoolboy knows, this is the site of the legend of Guzmán el Bueno. In 1292, this Spanish knight was defending Tarifa against a force of Moors. Among them was the renegade Infante Don Juan, brother of King Sancho IV, who had Guzmán's young son as a prisoner, and threatened to kill him if Guzmán did not surrender. Guzmán's response was to toss him a dagger. His son was killed, but Tarifa did not fall. Fascist propaganda recycled this legend for the 1936 siege of the Alcázar in Toledo, with the Republicans in the villain's role.

Outside Tarifa, along the beaches east of the town, there are **ruins** of a once sizeable Roman town, Bolonia, parts of which are currently undergoing restoration (visit by guided tour).

Algeciras

Ask at the tourist office what there is to see and you'll be told, 'Nothing. Nobody ever stays here'. Once you've seen the town you'll understand why: it's a dump. Nevertheless, Algeciras has an interesting history, and an attractive setting opposite the Rock of Gibraltar if you can see through the pollution. It played a significant role in the colonization of the eastern Mediterranean, becoming an important port in the Roman era. From AD 713 on, it was occupied by the Moors, and its name derives from the Arabic *Al Djezirah al Hadra* (Green Island). Today, apart from its importance as a port with regular connections to Ceuta, Tangier and the Canary Islands, Algeciras is a sizeable industrial and fishing centre.

The bustling, seedy port area has little attraction for the visitor, although the small bazaars in the side streets, selling Moroccan leather goods, may whet your appetite for a trip across the straits—you can see Morocco's jagged, surreal peaks all along the coastal highway. It is also the centre of one of the busiest drug-smuggling routes in the world, and every stevedore and cab driver will be whispering little propositions in your ear if you look the type.

Inland, lying in a pleasantly wooded area is **Los Barrios**, settled by refugees when Gibraltar was lost to the British; archaeological finds indicate that it was inhabited from earliest times. The parish church of **San Isidro** dates from the 18th century. There are two fairly decent beaches nearby—Guadarranque and Palmones.

On the N340 heading north, the road passes **San Roque**, with exceptional views over the bay of Algeciras and Gibraltar. Here are the ruins of *Carteya*, the first Roman settlement in the south of the peninsula. The 18th-century parish church of **Santa María Coronada** was built above the ancient hermitage of San Roque, and is worth a visit. This pretty little town is a welcome relief after the more sordid quarters of Algeciras, and an added bonus are the nearby clean beaches of Puente Mayorga, Los Portichuelos and Carteya.

Where to Stay

Tarifa

As the recently 'discovered' resort along this coast, rooms are surprisingly and unnecessarily expensive; the same is true of Conil. The ★★★★**Balcón de España**, Ctra Cádiz–Málaga, Km 77, © (956) 68 43 26, is one of the better options, situated in a pretty spot by the Playa de los Lances between Tarifa and Punta Palomas to the west of town. It has a pool, tennis courts and horse-riding facilities (7,000–10,000 pts; closed Nov–Mar). Further along the coast, windsurfers stay (where else?) at the ★★**Hurricane**, Ctra N340, Km 94, © (956) 68 49 19, but they pay for the privilege (9,000–15,000 pts; closed Jan). Near Zahara de los Atunes, at the Bahía de la Plata, the big resort complex the ★★★★**Sol Atlanterra**, Urb. Cabo de Plata, © (956) 43 90 00, fax 43 90 51, is German-owned and offers a variety of sports and recreational activities (11,000–19,000 pts, depending on the season; closed Nov–April). Alternatively, there are two very popular *hostales*, the ★**Castro**, Dres. Sánchez Rodríguez s/n, © (956) 43 02 48, on the boulevard near the beach (2,500–4,800 pts) and the ★★**Nicholas**, María Luisa 13, © (956) 43 11 74 (4,000–5,000 pts), but both are packed throughout August.

Algeciras

The hotel of the town's bygone elegance is the ★★★★**Reina Cristina**, on Paseo Conferencia, © (956) 60 26 22, fax 60 33 23 (all the luxuries for 12,000–15,000 pts), where W. B. Yeats rested one winter. The convenient ★★★★**Octavio**, Calle San Bernardo 1, © (956) 65 27 00, borders the bus station and is within a few metres of the train station (10,000–12,000 pts). Right on the seafront, above the busy arcades filled with cafés and ticket offices, and looking out over the port area is ★★★**Al Mar**, Avenida de la Marina 2, © (956) 65 46 61, fax 65 45 01, (8,400–9,000 pts). Clustered in the back streets of the area behind the Avenida de la Marina are a host of convenient little *hostales* in the 2,500 pts range.

Tarifa, Zahara and Los Caños de Meca

In Tarifa, near the Hurricane hotel is one of the best restaurants in the area, in the hotel **Mesón de Sancho,** Ctra N340, Km 94, © (956) 68 49 00, fax 68 47 21, specializing in home-cooked dishes—favourites are the garlic soup, bream *provençal, rabo de toro* (2,500 pts). There's also a set menu for 1,700 pts, which includes wine or water. In Zahara, tourists flock to the beach restaurant **Antonio,** Ctra Atlanterra, Km 1, © (956) 43 12 41, for high-quality fish and seafood (2,000 pts). During the season, the **Bar Marisquería Porfirio** on Plaza Tamrón serves excellent seafood. Inevitably, in Los Caños de Meca there had to be a **Trafalgar;** on the seafront with a pleasant terrace, the menu concentrates on international fare (1,600–2,200 pts; closed in winter).

Algeciras

Just back from the Avenida Virgen del Carmen (on the corner of Gómez Ortega and Trafalgar) is the **Marea Baja,** Trafalgar 2, © (956) 66 36 54, a fashionable restaurant specializing in seafood; try their *lubina* (3,500 pts for a full meal with wine). For a break from salty marine life, you may care to drive out on to the N340 and try some of the grilled meats on offer at **El Bosque,** charmingly situated in the woods at Pelayo 5, Bda. Pelayo, © (956) 67 91 1 3 (2,000–2,500 pts; closed Mondays). Back in town, a popular place with working people is **Casa Montes,** San Juan 16, where *urta* surfaces again, along with roast kid and poultry (1,000 pts). If you want to splurge, **El Copo,** Palmones (near Los Barrios) © (956) 67 77 10, is a good place for it. The restaurant is draped with fishermen's nets and takes pride in its enormous tanks of lobsters, sea urchins, spider crabs and mussels so that any fish or seafood dishes are supremely fresh. It serves a wide range of dishes, from fried sea nettles to *rabo de toro* and *solomillo* (3,500–4,000 pts; reservations essential). If you get a chance take a look upstairs at the bullfighters' room and the room with a painted panorama of views from Palmones several hundred years ago. The most famous restaurant in the area is **Los Remos,** © (956) 76 08 12, in an old house surrounded by lovely gardens, on the road out of San Roque to La Línea, at Villa Victoria, but carnivores beware—it serves mostly fish (3,000–4,000 pts).

An Excursion to North Africa

The main reason for making the crossing will be to take a look at the limited attractions of Tangier. Unfortunately, the real treasures are all far to the south, in Rabat, Fez and Meknes. But even an admittedly international city like Tangier will give you the chance to explore a fascinating society—and perhaps see a little reflection of the lost culture of al-Andalus. On the other hand, you could shop at Ceuta, one of Spain's last remaining *presidios* on the North African coast.

Algeciras's *raison d'être* is its port, and there's no trouble getting a **ferry** either to Ceuta (at least six boats a day, nine in the summer) or to Tangier (two at least, as many as seven daily in summer). Ceuta is 1½ hours away by ferry (2,000 pts each way) and Tangier is 2 hours away (3,000 pts each way). The **hydrofoil** is the faster, slightly more expensive option, but takes passengers only. Ceuta is half an hour away by hydrofoil (every hour; 3,200 pts each way) and Tangier an hour away (every half-hour; 3,000 pts each way). There are plenty of official Transmediterránea agents at the port. You'll need your passport, and you are advised not to do anything foolish on these well-policed borders. There's also a summer hydrofoil service from Tarifa to Tangier.

Ceuta

Every time the Spanish make self-righteous noises about getting Gibraltar back, someone reminds them about their two colonial leftovers on the North African coast, Melilla (*see* p. 164) and Ceuta. Morocco's King Hussein (a good friend of Juan Carlos) mentions them every year in his New Year's speech. Lately Colonel Qaddafi has also been heard from on the issue. Ceuta has a mainly Spanish population; that is why it was excluded from the 1955 withdrawal from the Spanish Moroccan protectorate. They are the stumbling block, and some way will have to be found to accommodate them before the inevitable transfer of sovereignty. Ceuta is a pleasant enough town, but there's little reason to go there, perhaps only the impressive 16th-century **walls** and moat. There's a **museum** dedicated to Spain's Foreign Legion (a band of cut-throats who became notorious during the civil war under a one-armed, one-eyed commander named Millán Astray; their slogan: 'Long live Death'). Like Andorra at the other end of Spain, Ceuta is a big duty-free supermarket. You can easily cross into Morocco from here, though it's better to take the ferry to Tangier.

Tourist Office

Muelle Cañonero Dato 1, © (956) 51 13 79.

Where to Stay and Eating Out

Finding a place to sleep can be a problem as there are only a few hotels. Within the walls, ★★★★**La Muralla**, Plaza Virgen de África 15, © (956) 51 49 40, offers the most comfort and luxury, with a pool and gardens (9,000–11,000 pts). The ★★**Atlante**, Paseo de las Palmeras 1, © (956) 51 35 48, is a good bargain in the middle of town (3,600–5,500 pts double with bath, 3,000–3,500 pts without).

The best restaurant in Ceuta is **La Kasba**, General Yagüe 12, © (956) 52 10 13, serving the requisite North African speciality, couscous, besides Spanish dishes (3,000 pts). One place to meet the locals (and a strange bunch they are) is the **Restaurante Mar Chica**, Paseo Colón 9, © (956) 51 39 57, with decent fish dinners from 800 pts up.

Getting There

The most direct way of getting to Morocco is by **ferry** or **hydrofoil** from Algeciras. If you're travelling from Ceuta, you'll have to take a **cab** or **city bus** (the one marked 'frontera') to the border; after some cacophanous border confusion, you wait for the infrequent bus or carefully negotiate a taxi trip to **Tetuán**, 30km (18.8 miles) away. There's no train from Tetuán to Tangier, but **buses** are cheap and regular, run by a number of companies from the central bus station. They'll take you right to Tangier's port.

Tourist Offices

Tetuán: 30 Avenue Mohammed V, ✆ (9) 96 44 07 or (9) 96 70 09.

Tangier: 29 Boulevard Pasteur, ✆ (9) 93 82 39/40.

Some Moroccan Practicalities

money

Wait until you get into Morocco to change money. Spanish travel agents will do it, often at a dishonestly low rate, and the rates at the border crossings aren't much better. The currency is the *dirham*, lately averaging about 14 to the pound, 9 to the dollar.

dealers and dealing

This corner of Morocco, being the fullest of tourists, is also full of English-speaking hustlers and creeps. We do not exaggerate: around the bus stations and ports they're thick as flies and 10 times as persistent, sometimes weaseling, sometimes menacing. Entertain no offers, especially of drugs or guided tours, and do your best to totally ignore the scum. The Moroccans don't like them either. Beyond that, you'll need your wits to bargain, with merchants, taxi drivers, and even hotel-keepers. There's no reason why you can't do this firmly and gracefully. Also, crime is a problem after dark in these two cities.

Tetuán and Tangier

Tetuán is a decent town, full of gleaming white, Spanish colonial architecture; it has a famous market in its *medina*, a historical museum, and it's a good place to purchase Moroccan crafts. On the way into **Tangier**, note how the Moroccans have turned the old *plaza de toros* into flats. Once in the big square outside the port entrance, you may take your chances with the inexpensive hotels in the surrounding streets, or take a cab to fancier spots in the newer, Europeanized districts. Tangier may not be as romantic as you expect; the wares in the markets of the *medina* are fun to look at, but the quarter itself is down-at heel and dusty. You may not enter mosques in Morocco, but in the old governor's palace are two fine **museums** of archaeology and Moroccan art.

Hotels, restaurants, and everything else will be almost half as expensive as in Spain. The food has an international reputation; national dishes like couscous and *harira* are superb. Don't judge Morocco by Tangier and Tetuán, and don't even judge these places by first impressions. A little side-trip to Morocco may not be an epiphany, but think how much you'll regret it if you pass up the chance.

The Costa del Sol

At first glance, it doesn't seem the speculators and developers could have picked a more unlikely place to conjure up the Mediterranean's biggest holiday playground. The stretch of coast between Gibraltar and Málaga is devoid of beautiful or even attractive scenery, and its long beaches come in a uniformly dismal shade of grey. Spain's low prices are one explanation, and the greatest number of guaranteed sunny days in Europe another. The reason it happened here, though, is breathtakingly simple—cheap land. Forty years ago, all this coast had was fantastically poor fishing villages and malaria, and it was one of the forgotten backwaters of Spain.

After a few decades of holiday intensity, though, this unlikely strip, all concrete and garish signboards, is beginning to develop a personality of its own. Any hype you hear or read about the Costa, anything that employs flowery prose and superlatives, is utter nonsense; on the other hand, it has become almost fashionable to mock the Costa for its brash *turismo* exuberance, and that is uncalled for. The Costa does attract people who don't expect much from their holiday (or retirement) except good weather, like-minded companions, and places to play. Their presence, in such large numbers and from so many nations, has created a unique international community of everyday folks. It's easy to forget you're in Spain, but if you ever get homesick you can always take a break from Andalucía and have a noisy good time by the beach.

La Línea

Not a resort at all, but the town on the Spanish side of the border with Gibraltar. La Línea ('the line'), named after Gibraltar's old land walls is a lively, fun town that has built up dramatically since the reopening of the Gibraltar border in 1985.

Getting Around

Two **bus** companies serve La Línea: Transportes Comes runs the service to Algeciras (every half-hour) and points west; and the Portillo company to the Costa del Sol, Málaga and Madrid. Both have offices on Avenida de España, just off La Línea's central square. From here it's a 5-minute walk to the border with Gibraltar. There are no **trains** to La Línea. The nearest railway station, 8km (5 miles) away at San Roque, has services to Ronda and all destinations in Andalucía.

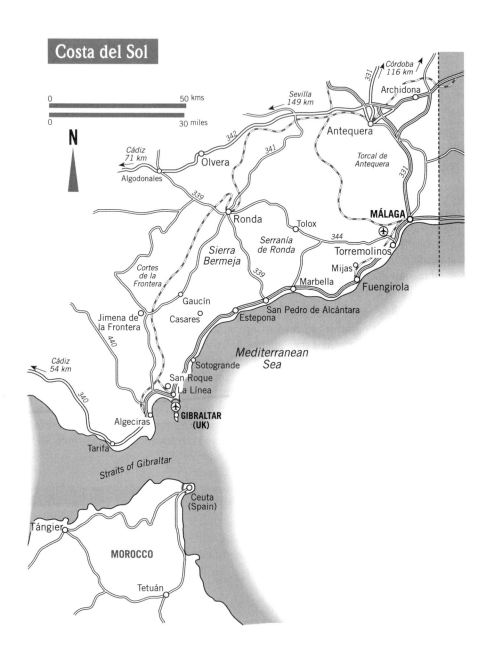

Costa del Sol

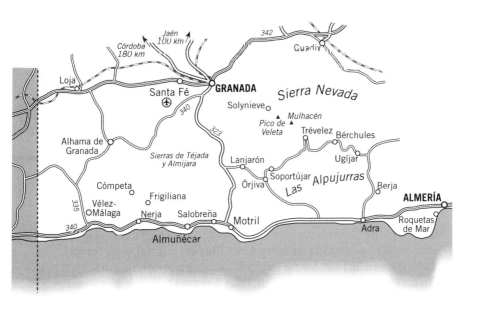

Tourist Office

Avenida 20 de Abril, © (956) 76 99 50.

Given its unique status as the only Spanish town to border with British territory, La Línea has almost taken on a split personality. Whilst retaining its Spanish essence, it takes in its stride the daily invasion of soldiers, day-trippers and smugglers (of tobacco especially), who have descended on the town since the barrier came down. Not that the people of La Línea are unhappy about the situation—the open frontier means they can scoot over in their coffee breaks to buy up tax-free goods and off-the-peg clothing, and hope that the Spanish customs officers aren't too rigorous in their searches on the way back.

But the *linenses* are still guarded about their colonial neighbours, and not for reasons of politics. They have in the past had to suffer the jolly old British tradition of street brawls involving servicemen, although this practice is admittedly now in decline due to its lack of novelty and vigilant military police. La Línea's reputation is not exactly unblemished either —stray too far from the centre of town or the waterfront after dark, and there are some exceedingly unpleasant seedy people skulking in dark doorways and hungry for your money, whether by selling you drugs or just stealing your wallet.

The centre of La Línea, however, is safe and tame, and worth an overnight stay for its sparkling, hybrid nightlife, if not for its monuments. There's only the 19th-century church of **La Inmaculada**, with its Baroque-style altar; and the **Cruz Herrera Museum**, tucked away in a modern dilapidated building 100m from the main square, Plaza de la Constitución, on Calle Carboneros.

The ★★★**Rocamar**, Avenida de España 170, ✆ (956) 76 79 23, fax 70 30 19, has the most comforts (8,000–11,000 pts), but the best bargain in town is the *pensión* ★**La Campana**, Carboneros 3, ✆ (956) 10 30 59, just off the main plaza. In the high season doubles with bath are 4,500 pts, low season 3,500 pts, and there's a good little restaurant downstairs with *menú del día* for 950 pts. There are cheaper *hostales*, recommended only if you are on a budget. Heading the list is the ★**Sevilla**, Duque de Tetuán 4, ✆ (956) 76 47 96, for no other reason than its flamboyant, crumbling glass-and-stone building, and the cranky old folks who run it (2,000 pts for a double, no bath).

Eating out in La Línea is a lot cheaper than in Gibraltar, particularly if you want to spoil yourself on fish. At **La Marina** on Paseo Marítimo the speciality is the favourite of the southern coast: grilled sardines on a spit (2,500 pts). In an unfortunate position opposite the cemetery, **Casa Manuel** is nevertheless thriving. The menu is varied, but best are the *solomillo* and *entrecôte* steaks (1,500–2,000 pts). On the central pedestrian thoroughfare, the **Jerez** is a bar more than a restaurant, serving simple, cheap *raciones* for 650 pts.

La Línea to Málaga

Thirty years ago Gibraltarians who had money bought villas in Algeciras. Nowadays it's **Sotogrande**, a recently built, up and coming marina complex with restaurants, shops and apartments. It's worth a stop for lunch to break the drive along the Costa.

The Portillo **bus** company has the franchise for this stretch of coast; and with the growth of tourism its service has become almost like a city bus-line, stopping every few hundred yards in the developed areas between Algeciras and Málaga. There's never too long a wait in either direction. San Pedro is where the buses branch off for Ronda, an easy destination from any town on the coast. You can also go directly to Sevilla or Madrid at least once daily from the bus station in Marbella, Avenida Ricardo Soriano 21, ✆ (95) 277 21 92.

The N340 connects all the towns and villages along the coast, and at Fuengirola you can pick up a suburban **train**, which runs a regular service to Málaga. It stops at Torremolinos and most other points in between.

To discover what's on, take a quick look through the local publications—*Lookout*, a slick monthly magazine for the British on the Costa; a weekly English edition of Málaga's newspaper, *Sur*; and various local entertainment guides will show you all sorts of chances.

There are bullrings in Marbella, Fuengirola, Estepona, Mijas (a square one!) and Benalmádena Costa, though *corridas* are infrequent and the really serious action occurs in the big ring in Málaga. There are **concerts** at the Casa de Cultura and Salon Varietés in Fuengirola and the Mijas Arts Centre, among others; art exhibitions and guitar and dance courses; and, occasionally, movies in English at the Cine Puerto Banús.

For sports, there are over 50 **golf courses** on the Costa, though green fees are a little dear (3,000 pts and up); **tennis** at many of the hotels, most open to the public; even **snooker clubs** (in Fuengirola). Of course all the **water sports** are popular; you can always make arrangements for equipment or instruction through your hotel. There are **casinos** at Benalmádena Costa (the Torrequebrada, on the coastal highway) and quite a bit higher stakes, at Puerto Banús (the Casino de Marbella, at Torre del Duque).

For kids there's a Disneyland-style amusement park at Benalmádena Costa called **Tivoli World** with a Wild West, Chinese pagodas, Cinerama and flamenco can-can shows. Also, a small **zoo** in Fuengirola, Super Bonanza cruise boats for leisurely excursions between Torremolinos and Puerto Banús, and horse-riding from the El Castillo Salvador stables outside Fuengirola (1,000 pts per hour). The **Aquapark** in Fuengirola has slides and rides to keep the little ones amused for an afternoon. For something out of the ordinary, get in touch with the Viajes CHAT travel agency in Torremolinos, © (95) 238 71 86, and they'll make arrangements for a hot-air balloon ride over the Costa, champagne included.

Estepona and San Pedro

Tourist Offices

Estepona: Paseo Marítimo, © (95) 280 09 13. Open 9.30–1.30, 5–7, closed Sun.

San Pedro: Arco de San Pedro, © (95) 278 13 60.

Estepona, the first of the resort towns east of Gibraltar, is also the quietest. Unfortunately the big developers have moved in, concrete blocks are sprouting all over and the town is losing its appeal. Its biggest attraction is a nudist beach although there's still a touch of fishing village simplicity, despite the highway which slices its way through. The old town remains a pleasant, quiet place, with narrow streets and whitewashed houses, a heritage of its Arab occupation. It has a marina, where you can grab a beer and a bite to eat while you study the classy yachts. If you're staying here, a worthwhile side-trip would be **Casares**, 20km (12½ miles) northwest, up in the Sierra Bermeja, a typical white Andalucían village perched on a steep hill under the ruins of its castle. Nearby, outside the village of Manilva, there are ruins of a **Roman spa**. The old spring still pours out strange, sulphurous water, and the locals drop in to bathe for what ails them.

San Pedro de Alcántara along the coast, is a little fancier, and probably the most attractive resort on the Costa del Sol—its developers get credit for learning at least a little from past mistakes. Most of the town is a good walk from the beaches. From here the only good road through the mountains will take you to Ronda and its surrounding villages—the best excursion you can make from the Costa. Also, if you're short of reading matter, there's Bookworld España on Las Palmeras 25, © (95) 278 63 66. It's run by James Ross, an ex-army captain, and has an extensive range of English language books (including Cadogan guides) with little or no mark-up.

Where to Stay and Eating Out

Estepona

There are more real bargains to be found here than elsewhere on the coast. For a modicum of concrete splendour near the beach, the **Buenavista**, Paseo Marítimo, © (95) 280 01 37, is the best bet (doubles 3,500–5,000 pts). Estepona isn't a place to spend money, though; there are plenty of inexpensive *hostales* (like **El Pilar**, Plaza de las Flores 22, © (95) 280 00 18; 3,600–4,000 pts a double, in a pretty setting), both in the town and on the beach.

The best bet when you're tired of seafood is to try the Moroccan couscous at the **Restaurante del Paseo** on the coastal highway (1,500–2,000 pts). **El Vagabundo**, Urb. Monte Biarritz, Ctra Cádiz, Km 168.5, © (95) 78 66 98, a converted outpost tower on the N340, offers a choice of international dishes, including seafood pancakes and roast duck (2,500 pts).

San Pedro

San Pedro doesn't yet have a wide choice. **El Pueblo Andaluz**, on the coastal highway, Km 172, © (95) 272 06 39, is one of the outstanding bargains on the coast, a pretty place near the beach built around an old Andalucían home with a pool, playground, restaurant and garden (6,000 pts for a double). There are some *hostales* in the town: the **Bamar**, San Antonio 3, © (95) 278 41 92, the **Marta**, Lagasca 24, © (95) 278 33 36, and the **Casa Armand**, 19 de Octubre 53, © (95) 278 11 90, all have rooms in the 2,400–3,000 pts range.

There are a few restaurants, but none is outstanding. Most people prefer to dine in nearby Marbella instead.

Marbella

Tourist Offices

Marbella: Calle Miguel Cano 1, © (95) 277 14 42. Open weekdays 9.30–8.30 (9.30–9.30 in the summer) and Sat 10–4 (10–2 summer). There's also a small office on Plaza Los Naranjos, © (95) 282 35 50.

Puerto Banús: Avenida Principal, © (95) 281 74 74.

Marbella is the poshest and most expensive resort in Spain. When you arrive, you'll find yourself asking why—Marbella has no visible attraction whatsoever. Its recently trendy old village, with a square full of orange trees, has been swallowed up by lookalike developments; it's nothing more than a high-rise suburb by the sea. The answer is simple: rich people come here because other rich people do, and it's really *people* who make Marbella; a heady mixture of adventurers, celebrities, executives, tycoons and the ordinary man, coming from every corner of the globe.

This is said to be the fastest-growing area in Europe, but it is not without its growing pains. Until recently, zoning laws were permissive to the point of being totally ineffective, and developers, eager to make a quick profit, threw up one unattractive building after another. But for every ugly development there is a stunningly beautiful one, carefully preserving Andalucían tradition and delightfully landscaped with trees, lawns and flowering shrubs. So, despite her limited charm, Marbella continues to thrive, and the fun-loving teenager she was is now slowly but surely turning into a respectable matron. Wild parties, eccentric ways and a live-for-today attitude have given way to serious business, fuelled by the property boom on the Costa del Sol in the 1980s.

Nonetheless, for the earnest tourist there is not a great deal of point in spending time in the town. You'll pay jet-set prices without getting in on the action, which takes place in a score of private clubs, private villas and very private yachts. The top crust have already forsaken Marbella for **Puerto Banús**, a new development 6km (4 miles) to the west, with a yacht harbour full of crystal chandelier gin palaces, though you shouldn't pass up the chance of spending an afternoon here in one of the many waterside cafés, sipping chilled rosé and observing how the other half live.

Where to Stay

Don't count on finding a room at any price during the season; package tours have taken over here just as they have in the resorts to the east, and most places are booked pretty solid.

expensive

If you want to brush shoulders with gossip-mag personalities, eastern princes or western tycoons, check into Marbella's most expensive hotel, ★★★★★**Los Monteros**, Ctra Cádiz, Km 187, © (95) 277 17 00, fax 282 58 46, and enjoy all the luxuries that 36,000 pts will buy. The ★★★★★**Meliá Don Pepe**, Finca Las Merinas, © (95) 277 03 00, is another mega-luxury hotel facing out over the sea. It has a large tourist and sports complex, including an 18-hole golf course, 11 tennis courts, 5 squash clubs, a riding school, heated pool, gym and sauna (20,500–32,000 pts) but these are not the only top-price luxury hotels here. The ★★★★★**Puente Romano**, Ctra Cádiz, Km 178, © (95) 277 01 00, fax 277 57 66, is one of the most beautiful, if not the most expensive, and its name comes from the genuine Roman bridge incorporated into its lovely surroundings (20,000–33,000 pts).

Ideally placed next to the Marbella shopping centre, at the end of the promenade overlooking the sea, is ★★★★**El Fuerte**, Avenida El Fuerte s/n, ✆ (95) 277 15 00, fax 282 44 11, at a more affordable 11,000–13,000 pts for a double. If you do want to splurge here, the best buys among the luxury hotels will be found on the less-crowded beaches outside the town, like ★★★**Las Chapas**, Ctra Cádiz, Km 192, ✆ (95) 283 13 75, a nearly self-sufficient holiday complex with opportunities for tennis, golf and water sports—it's right on the beach on the coastal highway, 8km (5 miles) to the east (12,000–13,000 pts for a double).

On Marbella's main street is the reasonably priced ★★**Alfil**, Avenida Ricardo Soriano 19, ✆ (95) 277 23 50, fax 277 29 58, with rooms for 4,200 pts. Surprisingly, there is a wide selection of *hostales* in the 3,000–5,000 pts range, most of them in the old town, like the pleasant ★★**Hotel Paco**, Calle Peral 16, ✆ (95) 277 12 00 (doubles 3,800 pts with bath), and a dozen other places in the 4,000 pts range around Calle Peral, Calle San Francisco and other streets nearby. The ★★**Hostal Enriqueta**, Los Caballeros 18, ✆ (95) 282 75 52, is particularly well placed near the Plaza Los Naranjos (3,500–4,400 pts).

Eating Out

Dining in Marbella can empty your pockets quickly enough, and there's a wealth of places to choose from. **Hostería del Mar**, Avenida Cánovas del Castillo 1A, ✆ (95) 277 55 81, has summer dining on the patio looking onto the swimming pool, and in winter is cosy inside. Specialities include: chicken and shrimp Catalan style, stuffed quail, roast duck in a sauce of *cassis* and candied figs (4,000 pts; open evenings only). The Marbella Hill Club has now been transformed into the restaurant **La Camargue**, Ctra Cádiz, Km 178.5, ✆ (95) 282 40 85, but still attracts the same, select clientele. Its setting in beautiful gardens with lovely views and a flexible, interesting menu, assure its continued popularity. The menu includes a medley of shrimp and lobster in a delicate sauce, poached salmon with fresh basil sauce, *solomillo* with two pepper sauces, and a selection of desserts, mostly based on fresh fruit (4,000–5,000 pts; open every evening in summer). Next to the Marbella Club, **Villa Tiberio**, ✆ (95) 277 17 99, is a palatial restaurant with affordable prices, soft music and luxurious surroundings. Superb antipasto dishes—*bresola con aguacate* (thinly sliced cured beef with avocado), delicious pasta. Main courses are good too, although less adventurous (4,000–5,000 pts for dinner with wine). A favourite, even in competitive Marbella, **La Meridiana**, situated just behind the mosque, on Camino de la Cruz s/n, ✆ (95) 277 61 90, offers international cuisine and unusual dishes such as salad of angler fish marinated in dill, or braised veal sweetbreads with grapefruit (5,000–6,000 pts; open evenings only in summer). For a treat go to **Francis Butler's Rustic Farmhouse**, Finca Besaya, Río Verde Alto, ☎ (95) 286 13 86. Butler is a charming host and the baroque farmhouse interior is a magnificently tasteful testament to his background as a former West End theatre designer. There's a terrace overlooking the avocado trees and there are several rooms indoors warmed by open fires during the winter and littered with antiques. He serves an international cuisine which includes duck breast in mango sauce and an exquisite chocolate sorbet (4,000 pts; open evenings Wed–Sat, reservations essential—if only to ask for directions!) Another special outing in Marbella is to the restaurant **Toni Dalli**, The Oasis Club, Ctra Cádiz, Km 176, ☎ (95) 277 00 35, housed in a Moorish mansion with a central courtyard and a magnificent view of the beach. Dalli, a retired Italian opera singer, often entertains his customers personally with the odd aria; otherwise there's the regular lively showbiz band to tap your toes to. Italian food is obviously the order of the day (4,000 pts). In town, on the Plaza de los Naranjos, there are plenty of places to eat in this picturesque square. **Restaurante Mena**, ☎ (95) 277 15 97, has the best reputation, serving superb paella, fish and seafood plus roast leg of yearling lamb and Châteaubriand (3,000 pts upwards). East of Marbella on the N340 in Las Chapas, **La Hacienda**, Ctra Cádiz, Km 193, Urbanización Las Chapas, ☎ (95) 283 11 16, is frequently described as the best restaurant on the Costa del Sol. It prides itself on its super-fresh ingredients. Try the hake in wine sauce, river crab and mushroom salad, fresh pasta, home-made ice cream. Dining out on the terrace, among the statues and stone arches, will set you back around 6,500 pts. **Club Miraflores**, on the Urbanización Miraflores, Ctra Cádiz, Km 199, ☎ (95) 283 01 02, serves consistently good food: fresh spinach with onions and cream, *croquettes de crevettes*, fresh grilled salmon with hollandaise sauce, beef stroganoff, or baby chicken casseroled in white wine (3,500 pts); it would be hard to imagine a more agreeable spot to spend an evening, complete with live music and dancing.

moderate

Toni Dalli seems to building an empire around Marbella. His three sons each run a pasta or pizza restaurant. The **Dalli Pasta Factory**, in the centre of Marbella, ☎ (95) 277 67 76, serves fresh pasta, delicious antipasto and a spicy *tagliolini rabiaha* (pasta with prawns and chillis). You can easily eat well with wine for under 1,500 pts. In Puerto Banús the Dalli brothers' Pasta and Pizza factories stand next door on Calle Rivera (1,500–2,000 pts). There's plenty of French cuisine, including **Michel**, ☎ (95) 281 55 19, who serves terrific *bouillabaisse* in modern, plush surroundings (3,000 pts).

inexpensive

Plenty of inexpensive places, mostly specializing in seafood, can be found in the area around Calle Aduar. **Casa La Vieja** at number 18, ☎ (95) 282 13 12, does a good plate of mixed fish for 900 pts.

Silhouette, First floor, Cristamar Centre, © (95) 281 56 02, in Puerto Banús commands an attractive panorama over the town itself and the Mediterranean, and is a good place for cabaret and flamenco dancing.

Fuengirola

You really should come on a package tour if you find Fuengirola and Torremolinos to your taste. That's what these places are for, and you would get a better deal. If you're just passing through and want to rest in anonymity by the beach, there are some possibilities.

Tourist Office

Avenida Jesús Santos Rein 6, in an old railway station, © (95) 246 74 57. Open daily 9.30–1.30, 4–8; Sat mornings only.

Thirty years ago, Fuengirola was a typical whitewashed, Spanish fishing village. It's still white, but hardly typical, and even less Spanish. With the miles of speculative *urbanizaciones* that surround it, it would be easy to be unkind to Fuengirola except that everyone there seems to be having such a good time. The town, and its adjacent community of **Los Boliches** may be the only place in Spain where you'll see a sign in a shop-window reading '*Se habla español*'; the laid-back international community appreciates a good joke. The shops of the old village have been transformed into pubs, English bookshops, travel agencies and Swiss, Chinese, Belgian, Italian, Moroccan, and even Spanish restaurants, but there's something genuine in the atmosphere of this casual European village—now grown into a fair-sized city. Today the Spaniards live mostly in town, picnicking and sunbathing on their flat roofs or balconies; the foreigners drive in from the *ubanizaciones* for pub-hopping or to shop in the vast hypermarkets. The centre is becoming ever more determinedly multinational and multilingual, while upwardly mobile Spaniards are buying their way into the *urbanizaciones*. Try to imagine Fuengirola in another 20 years—it should be quite an interesting place.

Fuengirola's weekly event is the Tuesday outdoor **market**, the best place to observe this curious community. Unlike other resorts on the Costa, there are some things to see—the Moorish **Castillo de Sohail** above town, a bullring, even the brand new façade of a **Roman temple**. In Roman times there were important marble quarries in the mountains here, and recently divers discovered a wreck off the coast with these stones, bound for somewhere else; they've been salvaged and assembled on a spot near the beach.

Mijas

Visitors from Fuengirola totally overwhelm the village of Mijas, 3km (2 miles) up in the hills above town but at dusk it returns to the hands of the foreign residents, who count for 90% of the village's population. To escape the coastal sprawl, visitors drive up here by the coachload to find *real* Spain, and a typical Andalucían village. Yet it's still a pretty place with a promenade offering a view out to sea, a votive shrine to the Virgin, lots of pine woods, dozens of photogenic souvenir shops and 'officially licensed burro taxis' to take you around. The munchkin-sized whitewashed **bullring** sees its fair share of action throughout the year, but the town's museum of miniature curiosities is hard to take, even as a joke.

Where to Stay

moderate

It's difficult to tell one new holiday hotel from the next, but for the best deals two places do stand out. The ★★★**Florida**, Paseo Marítimo, © (95) 247 61 00, fax 258 15 29, has a pool and gardens, and though not luxurious is still a comfortable enough place (5,800–8,000 pts for a double). The ★★**Cendrillon**, Ctra Cádiz, Km 213, © (95) 247 53 16, just outside town on the coastal highway is much the same as the Florida, only with tennis courts (4,700–7,200 pts a double). Both are on the beach and popular with families.

inexpensive

There are plenty of inexpensive *hostales* around the centre of Fuengirola, and especially in its suburb of Los Boliches on the northern end.

Eating Out

Dining in Fuengirola is an experience; you can choose from any sort of restaurant from Indonesian to Belgian without going broke. There's plenty to choose from along Calle del Hambre, known locally as 'hungry street', and Calle Moncayo known as 'fish alley'.

expensive

Portofino, Edificio Perla 1, Paseo Marítimo, © (95) 247 06 42, is a popular restaurant where Italian specialities head the list (3,000 pts; closed Mon, Jun–Aug dinner only). Just outside Fuengirola, on the mountain road to Mijas, **Valparaíso**, Ctra de Mijas, Km 4, © (95) 248 59 75, is one of the most attractive and popular restaurants in the area, with bars, terrace, swimming pool and an extensive international menu. Starters are labelled 'temptations' and women are given menus without the prices, but it's a favourite haunt, of the foreign communities in particular (3,000 pts; closed Sun, but open Sun eve July–Oct). If you are bursting at the seams with superfluous cash and want to lighten the load, head a few kilometres north to Hotel Torrequebrada, with its casino, nightclub and **Café Royal** restaurant, Ctra Cádiz, Km 220, Benalmádena Costa, © (95) 244 60 00. In attractive surroundings, and with a fine view over the curve of the coastline, it offers mouthwatering international cuisine: pheasant with sour oranges, sea scallops in cider, smoked salmon between veal scallops with truffles. Once you've paid around 5,000 pts for the meal, you can join the high rollers and spend some real money.

The **Raj**, Calle Asturias 3, © (95) 246 94 70, is an attractive Indian restaurant and a welcome addition to Fuengirola's already cosmopolitan culinary scene. Decorated with charming *objets d'art* brought back from India, the cuisine is from the north of the subcontinent (2,500 pts). If you've ever tried an Indonesian rijsttafel in the Netherlands, you'll be glad to know there are plenty of such places on the Costa; the Dutch wouldn't live without it. Long famous for these delectable dishes is **Bali Mas**, Sol Playa, Calle Martínez Catena, © (95) 247 19 94 (2,000 pts; closed Wed). **Mesón El Castellano**, Camino de Coín 5, © (95) 246 27 36, serves authentic Castilian food: roast meats, especially pork and lamb, and the service is fast and friendly (2,000 pts). **Don Pé**, Calle de la Cruz, is also worth a visit (2,000 pts). Near Valparaíso on the road to Mijas **Casa Navarra**, Ctra de Mijas, Km 4, © (95) 258 04 39, serves Spanish cuisine, unsurprisingly, from Navarra, including huge steaks and delicious fish that you can choose yourself. Try the *merluza* in shrimp and parsley sauce (2,000 pts; closed Tues). In Mijas itself there's a fair selection of eating places, **Blanco**, Plaza de la Constitución 13, © (95) 248 57 00, is a family-run restaurant with reasonably priced Basque fish specialities (2,500 pts).

If you miss pub grub then drop into **La Cepa**, the English bar on Plaza Constitución in Fuengirola, run by Diane and her brother-in-law, Manolo. It's a good place to observe the plaza if you like chilli con carne or steak and kidney pie tapas.

Torremolinos

Tourist Office

Bajos de la Nogalera, Local 517, © (95) 238 15 78.

All sources agree about Torremolinos, one of the oldest and biggest resort towns on the Costa: it is a ghastly, hyperactive, unsightly holiday inferno. In other words, it has character. Torremolinos isn't at all interested in our opinion, though, or in yours either; it's doing quite well with its endless screaming blocks of bars, shopping centres and concrete hotels. For those who want to spend their holiday in the fast lane, in a raucous, international, entirely synthetic environment, this is the place.

In the summer, the tourists, hustlers, gypsies, drug-pushers, sailors and an assortment of others mingle in the streets and the movement is fast and frantic between the bars. The predominant language is English, but a dozen others can be heard in the space of a few steps. To escape this Babylonian horde, step down to one of the beach cafés, popular day and night; if your luck is in, you'll be treated to some of the local street performers sharing their talents: an anís-soaked troubadour mangling an aria, cigarette dangling from his

lower lip, or a transvestite flamenco dancer, whirling between the passing cars, his grim-looking mother handing round the hat. This is all treated with good humour by the Spaniards, even if some of the tourists look a bit nonplussed.

Part of Torremolinos's character arises from its status as capital of what the newspapers like to call the 'Costa del Crime'. Literally thousands of clever bank-heisters, cons and embezzlers, mostly from Britain, add to the local colour, courtesy of Spain's traditional unwillingness to conclude extradition treaties with other nations. However, an agreement with Britain has finally been reached, and the crooks will have to move along when their visas run out. There will still be plenty of other types left—smooth operators of uncertain nationality, religious cult agents, hedonists of all shapes and sizes, and other European detritus. They're only the surface, though, the most noticeable segment of an enormous permanent and transient population made up of gawking sun-seekers from every corner of Europe. The welcome signs on the outskirts of town proclaim 'City of Tourists'.

Where to Stay

In Torremolinos and its neighbouring stretch of tourist sprawl at Benalmádena Costa, the possibilities are endless, though these, too, will probably be packed with package tours. They come in all price ranges, from about 10,000 pts to rock-bottom *hostales.*

expensive

There are several golfers' hotels on the Costa, but the one that stands out is the ★★★★**Parador del Golf** on the road to Málaga, © (95) 238 12 55, fax 238 21 41, with tennis courts and a pool, right on the beach, attracting an active crowd to some of the best rooms in Torremolinos. The price is average for a *parador*, at 12,500–14,000 pts.

One of the finest of the beach hotels (though it's hard to tell from the outside) is the ★★★★**Don Pablo**, Paseo Marítimo, ✆ (95) 238 38 88, fax 238 37 83, in the centre of the action, with nice beds, fancy salons, even a billiard room (8,400–13,000 pts). In a quiet corner of the Playamar area, 2km (1¼ miles) from the centre, the ★★★**Príncipe Sol**, Paseo Colorado 26, ✆ (95) 238 41 00, is a comfortable hotel with three pools and a good restaurant (9,000 pts).

inexpensive

Some of the good bargains can be found out towards Carihuela, along Avenida Carlota Alessandri. Whether staying a few days or just passing through, the *hostal* **Victoria**, Los Naranjos 103 (opposite the bus station), ✆ (95) 238 10 47, is pleasant, conveniently placed and reasonably priced (3,500–5,250 pts for double with bath). The ★★**Miami**, Calle Aladino 14 in Carihuela, ✆ (95) 238 52 55, is special, built around an old mansion and beautifully furnished (doubles 3,500–5,200 pts; you'll need to book). Carihuela is also the place to look for inexpensive accommodation, such as the spartan but acceptable ★★**Hostal Pedro**, Calle Bulto 1, ✆ (95) 238 05 36 (3,000–4,000 pts a double).

Eating Out

expensive

Dining in Torremolinos is much like Fuengirola—a lot of choice. **Dana's**, Avenida Carlota Alessandri 25, ✆ (95) 238 22 88, on the main Fuengirola road, has long been one of the best restaurants, both for international cuisine and some classy Spanish dishes (4,000 pts). On the main Carretera, next to Los Álamos petrol station, **Frutos**, Ctra Cádiz, Km 235, ✆ (95) 238 14 50, is a popular restaurant, with high-quality food at reasonable prices, and the portions are generous: leg of lamb, sucking pig, Málaga fry, *tocino de cielo*—not a hint of *nouvelle cuisine*! (3,000 pts; closed Sun eve July–Sept).

moderate

For fine Moroccan cuisine and charmingly garish decor, try the **Restaurant Marrakesh**, Avenida Joan Miró 7, ✆ (95) 238 21 69, which serves a big full-course dinner with a choice of couscous, kebabs and stuffed pastries (2,500–3,000 pts). The best seafood restaurants are in Carihuela, along the beach from Torremolinos, and the **Casa Guaquín**, Calle Carmen 37, ✆ (95) 238 45 30, is very good indeed; try such specialities of the Costa as 'fish baked in salt'—it's better than it sounds (2,500 pts). Another good place on the beach here is **La Jabega**, Mar 15, ✆ (95) 238 63 75, with fish, of course, and a wide variety of starters and shellfish (2,500 pts). In Torremolinos's Eurosol complex the **María de Valladolid**, ✆ (95) 238 95 25, presents an alternative to Andaluz cuisine. Its dishes are mainly Castilian; especially good are the stews, rabbit with rice, sucking lamb and, for more wholesome appetites, tripe with chickpeas (2,500 pts; closed Sun). If you want to escape the bedlam of Torremolinos, head up into the hills to the rambling, ranch-type restaurant run by a Hispano-German couple, **Venta los Pinos del Coto**, Cañada de Ceuta s/n, Churriana, © (95) 243 58 00, a 10-minute drive from town behind the airport. The spacious, attractive interior has stained-wood ceilings and a log fire for cold winter evenings. The menu is devoted to meat in large quantities (2,500 pts; closed Sun eve and Mon).

inexpensive

A short walk from the Torremolinos bus station, and on the main road, **Mesón Gallego Antoxo** is a typical Spanish restaurant with a beautiful interior and charming little courtyard. There's a wide choice of fish, many dishes cooked to Galician recipes. Your wine will be served in the traditional Galician ceramic jug, and the drinking vessels resemble large finger bowls (1,500–2,000 pts). If you've never had the Vietnamese variations on Chinese cuisine so popular in France, try **El Vietnam del Sur**, Paseo del Colorado, Urbanización Playamar, Bloque 9, © (95) 238 67 37, where they serve delicious food at affordable prices (2,000 pts; closed Jan/Feb). Back in town, for a cheap aperitif, sit out at the **Bodega Quitapeñas** on the central steps down to the beach—everybody passes this way.

Málaga

Much-maligned Málaga, capital not only of the Costa del Sol, but also of crime and sleaze in southern Spain, is making a determined effort to improve her reputation and attract more tourists. In the past, a visit to the swish department store, El Corte Inglés, may have been the only reason a tourist considered spending any time here at all.

To miss Málaga, however, means to miss the most Spanish of cities, certainly on the Costa del Sol. Whatever you may think of the place, it is alive and real: ungainly cranes and elegant palm trees compete for dominance of the skyline; police helicopters roar over the Plaza de la Constitución as pretty Spanish girls toss their skirts and stamp their heels to flamenco music, to a private audience in a public square; elegant old Spanish ladies, scented with *Maja* soap, sit and reminisce, and dark-eyed tattooed gypsy boys flash their double-edged smiles to lure you into a shoeshine. From its tattered billboards and walls splashed with political slogans, to its public gardens overflowing with exotic fauna, Málaga is a jamboree bag of colours, aromas and sounds. Admittedly she cannot compete with Sevilla or Granada for sheer wealth of cultural distractions, but the *malagueños* are proud of their fun-loving metropolis. To experience real local *juerga*, treat yourself to an after-noon ramble through her many and famous tapas bars, where you will encounter more Spaniards in one afternoon than in a week in Torremolinos.

Unfortunately, the old quarters of Málaga have been treated ruthlessly by town planners, and *El Perchel*, once the heart of Málaga's flamenco district, has lost a lot of its personality and charm. The Avenida de Andalucía cuts through this old district and then becomes the

Alameda Principal and the Paseo del Parque. The essence of Málaga is within this limited area, from the elegant Avenida de Andalucía to the seedy, teeming neo-Moorish market on the Calle Atarazanas.

You will find it difficult to decide whether you love or loathe this city—will you notice the two snarling drivers impatient for the green light; or the two old gentlemen sipping sherry in the doorway of a cool, dark bodega, hung with Serrano hams and lined with wine casks?

Getting Around

As the main port of entry to the Costa del Sol and southern Andalucía, you'll probably pass through Málaga either coming or going.

by air

Málaga's often frenetic airport connects the city to Madrid, Valencia, Almería, Sevilla, Melilla and Tangier, besides being the charter-flight gateway to the Costa. A new terminal has also relieved some of the summer congestion and baggage delays. The easiest way to get into the city, or to Torremolinos or Fuengirola, is the suburban railway line (separate stops at the airport for the regular and charter terminals). These trains and local buses stop running before midnight. After that you'll have to get a taxi (about 1,500 pts to Málaga centre or Torremolinos). **Airport information,** © (95) 224 00 00.

by train

There's a daily *Talgo* to Madrid (7 hours), plus four normal trains (7½–9½ hours), two trains a day to Valencia and Barcelona. Direct connections also to Sevilla and Córdoba; for all other destinations in Andalucía you'll have to make a change at that inescapable Bobadilla Junction. The station is on Calle Cuarteles. **Information**: Calle Strachen 2, © (95) 231 25 00.

by bus

The main bus station is by the train station at Paseo de los Tilos, south of the Avenida de Andalucía, © (95) 235 00 61. Connections for local destinations run hourly; for provincial destinations, generally every 1–2 hours. Portillo, © (95) 238 24 19, operate buses for the Costa, Sevilla, Granada, Ronda, Algeciras and towns and villages in the interior; Bacoma, © (95) 232 12 62, buses to Alora and Ronda; Los Amarillos, © (95) 231 59 78, for Antequera, Carratraca; Alsina Graells, © (95) 231 04 00 for Granada, Nerja and Almería, and also for Alicante and Barcelona.

Málaga: Pasaje Chinitas 4, just north of the Alameda, *℃* (95) 221 34 45, and also at the airport, *℃* (95) 224 00 00. Open 9–2 except Sun.

Melilla: Edificio Correos, Pablo Vallesca, *℃* (95) 268 43 05.

As the Avenida de Andalucía, the main road from the west, crosses the dry rocky bed of the Guadalmedina river, it becomes the **Alameda Principal**, a majestic 19th-century boulevard. North of the Alameda is the **Plaza de la Constitución**, in the heart of the commercial centre, and the Pasaje Chinitas, an all-and-sundry shopping arcade. One of the clothes shops bears a commemorative plaque—it's the original site of the Café Chinitas, where bullfighters and flamenco singers would gather in the old days; the spirit of it was captured by García Lorca.

The Alameda continues into the Paseo del Parque, a tree-lined promenade that runs along the port area, and leads to the city's **bullring**, built in 1874 with a capacity for 14,000, and very much in use today. Nearby is the **English cemetery**. William Mark, the 19th century consul, so loved Málaga that he described it as a 'second paradise', and encouraged his fellow countrymen to join him here. In 1830 he founded this cemetery, allowing a decent burial to Protestants who had previously been buried on the beach. Hans Christian Andersen declared he could 'well understand how a splenetic Englishman might take his own life in order to be buried in this place'. Its sea views, however, have long since been blocked by concrete buildings.

Just off the Paseo del Parque, the steps lead up to the Moorish **Alcazaba,** *℃* (95) 216 00 55. Under the Moors, Málaga was the most important port of al-Andalus, and from contemporary references it seems also to have been one of its most beautiful cities. King Fernando thoroughly ruined it in the conquest of 1487, and after the expulsion of the Moors in 1568, little remained of its ancient distinction. Little too remains of the Alcazaba, except a few Moorish gates, but the site has been restored to a lovely series of terraced gardens. At the top is an **Archaeological Museum**, containing relics from the Phoenician necropolis found on the site, and lists of Moorish architectural decoration salvaged from the ruins. The top of the Alcazaba also affords fine views over Málaga (*open 9.30–1.30 and 5–8 summer, 10–1 and 4–7 winter, mornings only on Sat and Sun*). There is a half-ruined **Roman theatre**, recently excavated, on the lower slopes of the hill, and from the Alcazaba you may climb a little more to the **Gibralfaro**, the ruined Moorish castle that dominates the city (*open 9–9*).

Back on the Paseo, note the chunky Art-Nouveau **Ayuntamiento**, one of the more unusual buildings in Málaga. On the opposite side of the Alcazaba, is the **Museo de Bellas Artes**, Calle San Agustín 8, in a restored 16th-century palace. It's worth a look for some good medieval polychrome icons, two strange paintings by Luis de Morales (*c.* 1580) and a small collection of Picassos on the first floor. Picasso was a native of Málaga, though once he left it at the age of 14, he never returned. Much of the museum is given over to the works of other late 19th-century *malagueño* painters who made up in eccentricity what they lacked in genius; one of them, Muñoz Degrain, was Picasso's first teacher. Also present are works of Zurbarán, Murillo and Ribera (*open summer 10–1.30 and 5–8; winter 10–1, 4–7; closed Mon and weekends*).

Málaga's **cathedral** is a few blocks away on Calle Molina Lario. It's an ugly, unfinished 16th-century work, immense and mouldering. Known as *La Manquita* (the one-armed lady), the only interesting feature is the faded, gaudy façade of the **sacristy**, left over from the earlier Isabelline Gothic church that once stood here. The **Museo de Arte Sacro**, also on the cathedral square, is currently closed for renovations. Next to the dry river bed, the **Museo de Artes Populares,** Pasillo de Santa Isabel 10, occupies a restored 17th-century inn with a collection of household bric-à-brac from days gone by (*open 10–1 and 5–8 in summer, 4–7 in winter; closed Sat afternoon and Sun*). Picasso's birthplace, **Casa Natal Picasso**, Plaza de la Merced, © (95) 221 50 05, is now open for visits and holds occasional exhibitions. An old farm, the **Finca de la Concepción**, 7km (4½ miles) north of Málaga on the new road to Granada, is now owned by the municipality, and has been turned into botanical gardens, with occasional summer shows of folklore and Andalucían dance; there are also some Roman remains on the site (*inquire at tourist office for details*).

Melilla

Nobody ever goes to Melilla, the more obscure of Spain's two remaining *presidios* on the North African coast. It's a long boat ride from Málaga, or a slightly shorter one from Almería, and onward destinations are severely limited. Morocco's big towns are far away, though you may consider Melilla as a quieter, less exasperating way to slip into Morocco than Tangier or Tetuán, with their hustlers and aggravations. The town itself is prettier than Ceuta, hiding behind stern-looking fortifications over the water's edge, and a 1.6km (1 mile) beach spreads awkwardly from the walls. Melilla has had its problems lately; the Spanish papers regularly report the local police bullying the Moroccan minority during protests over discrimination and citizenship.

Where to Stay

moderate

Málaga looks deceptively good from the ★★★**Parador de Gibralfaro**, Apdo. de Correos 274, © (95) 222 19 02, fax 222 19 04, up in the old Moorish castle above the city; the small hotel offers few luxuries (there are only 12 rooms), but the quality and the view make it a better bet than the more expensive modern hotels around the port (doubles 11,500 pts). For a slightly higher price you can stay at ★★★**Los Naranjos**, Paseo de Sancha 35, © (95) 222 43 17, fax 222 59 75, (12,900 pts) out at the eastern end of Málaga, 1km (½ mile) from the beach, such as it is.

inexpensive

Try the ★**Avenida**, Alameda Principal 5, © (95) 221 77 29 (3,000–3,400 pts, double with bath). South of here is the small ★★**Alameda**, Casa de Campos 3,

© (95) 222 20 99 (3,400–4,300 pts). Also south, the ★**Castilla** and the ★**Guerrero**, both Calle Córdoba 5, © (95) 221 86 35, are well-run establishments in the same building. The **Casa Huéspedes Bolivia**, Casa de Campos 24, © (95) 221 88 26, is spotlessly clean, central and inexpensive (2,000–3,000 pts, shared bath). Any place on or around the Alameda will be decent, but avoid the cheap dives around the train station.

In Melilla, the ★★**Anfora**, Calle Vallesca 8, © (95) 268 33 40, is a reliable, unremarkable hotel (5,000–5,500 pts), and there are quite a few modest *hostales* scattered all over.

Eating Out

Start your day with breakfast at the **Café Cosmopolita** on Marqués de Larios. Tables spill onto the pavement and surround the wooden horseshoe bar inside. Service is outrageously slow but allows you to relax over an international paper from the kiosk next door, or watch the shoeshine boys at work on the customers' footwear.

If you've exhausted yourself shopping at the department store **El Corte Inglés**, Avenida de Andalucía, © (95) 230 00 00, stroll up to the top floor for their buffet lunch: meat and fish dishes, pastas and salads (2,200 pts). North of Picasso's house is the **Café de la Ópera**, Calle Ramos Martín 3, © (95) 221 48 56, a popular place to people-watch and especially interesting on theatre nights (Andaluz specialities, imaginative decor, 2,000 pts). In the Cervantes Edificio Horizonte, **El Figón de Bonilla**, © (95) 260 10 28, attracts a trendy crowd for its excellent fish and pork dishes; particularly good are the fish soup, lobster, swordfish and *cola de toro* (2,000 pts; closed Sun). Next door, the **Cafetería Horizonte**, © (95) 222 56 23, serves good tapas, cakes and ice creams. Popular with young people and reasonably priced is **La Taberna del Pintor**, Maestranza 6, © (95) 221 53 15, by the bullring, deserving its reputation as one of the best places to eat meat in Málaga; soups, salads and steaks done to your liking (1,600–2,000 pts). For sherry, shrimps and a marvellous atmosphere go to **Antigua Casa de Guardia**, Alameda 18; choose a drink from one of the 20 or so barrels lining the bar with names like *Pajarete 1908* and *Guinda*; a glass of sherry and a dozen mussels costs around 400 pts. For tapas head for the **Bar Lo Güeno**, Marín García 9; it's literally a hole in the wall serving imaginative *raciones* and a decent selection of wines. *Malagueños* flock to the Paseo Marítimo and the El Palo district east of town on Sunday especially, to fill up the many restaurants that line the beaches in what was once a simple fishing community. A favourite is **Antonio Martín**, out on the Paseo Marítimo, © (95) 222 21 13, right next to the sea; fish and rice dishes are the basis of the menu; try scrambled eggs with baby eel and salmon, or gilthead cooked in salt (3,000 pts; open 1–4, 8–12; closed in winter). Other restaurants in the area include **El Cabra**, Calle Copo 21, Pedregalejo, © (95) 229 15 95, which has a more expensive range of seafood; and **Casa Pedro**, Quitapenas 4, El Palo,

© (95) 229 00 13, where you may well be deafened by the din while you tuck into skewered sardines or Sierra-style angler fish (2,500 pts; closed Mon eve). At **Tintero II**, Playa del Dedo, © (95) 229 00 01, you don't order your food—fish are 'auctioned off' at 600 pts per portion as they appear from the kitchen. If heading south from Málaga, pop into **Casa Pepe** on the Carretera de Cádiz. It's an honest-to-goodness family-run place with local goodies on the menu (1,500 pts).

Málaga to Motril

For some reason the tourist industry has neglected the areas east of the city. There are a few resorts strung out along the coastal highway, notably **Torre del Mar**, but they are all grim-looking places, little bits of Málaga that escaped to the beach. Nearby are some scanty remains of a Graeco-Phoenician settlement called **Mainake**.

Getting Around

The Portillo and Alsina Graells **buses** from Málaga or Motril serve Nerja, Almuñécar and Salobreña, and connections can be made from these towns to the interior villages. Note that long-distance buses along the coast do not usually stop at these towns.

Tourist Offices

Nerja: Puerto de Mar 2, © (95) 252 15 31. Open weekdays 10–4, 5–9, Sat 10–1.

Almuñécar: Avenida de Europa (in the small Moorish palace), © (958) 63 11 25.

Salobreña: Plaza Goya, © (958) 82 83 45.

Vélez-Málaga and Alhama de Granada

From Torre del Mar you can make a short detour inland to **Vélez-Málaga**, lying in a fertile valley at the foot of the Axarquía mountain area. The new town holds no particular charm, but the old part tells of its Moorish past; above the town, the castle (of which a restored tower remains) was one of the last Moorish outposts to fall to Christian forces during the purge by Isabel and Fernando. Below it, the church of **Nuestra Señora de la Encarnación** has had a chequered career—first as a Visigothic church, then a mosque, then a church again when the town was recaptured by Christian forces in 1487.

For a further detour into the mountains, you can tackle the 50km (31 mile) drive up on the C335 (becoming the C340 at Ventas) over the Sierra to **Alhama de Granada**. The road winds its way up through the serene surroundings of olive trees, trickling streams and rocky gulches; but pay close attention—the road has some helter-skelter turns. Alhama balances precariously on a rocky lip and looks down to the deep grassy-banked gorge, through which runs the river bed of the Alhama. Up here you're away from it all. 'Oh for my Alhama' was the lament of Boabdil el Chico, who had to abandon this beauty spot to the Christians in 1482. The town's 17th- to18th-century church of **El Carmen** has a terrace from which you can enjoy the panorama. No prizes for guessing the town's other attractions—the remains of a Moorish castle, in the main square, and a 15th-century parish church, a gift to the town from Fernando and Isabel. The Catholic Kings' Granada architects, Enrique de Egas and Diego de Siloé, both worked on it. Alhama has been famous since Roman times for its spa waters; ask at the modern spa, the Hotel Balneario, to see the Roman and Moorish baths below.

Another detour, one that will eventually bring you back to the coast, is to take the twisting MA117 to Archez, and continue on to **Cómpeta**, a truly lovely old village known principally for its sweet wines; the grapes are sun-dried to sweeten and fortify them. The big wine fiesta is held on 15 August in the main square. Like many Andalucían villages near the coast, new northern invaders have discovered its charm, Brits and Danes particularly. Beyond Cómpeta begin the wilds of the **Reserva Nacional de Sierra de Tejeda**; you'll have to leave your car to explore it, though, and strong comfortable shoes are recommended. To get back to the coast, take the MA137 through beautiful vine-clad slopes to **Torrox**, another Nordic enclave, and continue down to **Torrox-Costa**, an expanding resort, 8km (5 miles) from Nerja.

Málaga Virgen and Moorish Tarts

Two grapes, muscatel and Pedro Ximénez, define Málaga province wines and sherries. All are sweet, enjoyed with gusto in bars and the best known are the Málaga Virgen. Fish and seafood dominates cuisine in Málaga but there are plenty of *gazpachos*, particularly *ajo blanco con uvas*—a creamy white garlic soup with grapes. Prawns and mussels are plump, served simply with lemon and are divine. All fish is fresh from the coast and virually every tapas bar serves Victorian anchovies or *boquerones*. Forget British fried fish: in Málaga *fritura mixta* is one of Spain's culinary art forms. Nearly every village in the province has its own dessert, usually influenced by the Moors. Try the almond tarts in Ardales, the honey-coated pancakes in Archidona and the mixture of syrup of white roses, oil and eggs called *tocino de cielo* in Vélez. There again you can always substitute a sweet Málaga dessert wine for pudding—delicious sipped with dry biscuits.

Nerja

Approaching this town, the scenery becomes impressive as the mountains grow closer to the sea. Sitting at the base of the Sierra de Tejeda, Nerja itself is pleasant and quiet for a Costa resort. In Moorish times the town was a major producer of silk and sugar, an industry that fell into rapid decline after their departure. An earthquake in 1884 partially destroyed Nerja, and from then to the early 1960s it had to eke a living from fishing and farming.

Its attractions are the **Balcón de Europa**, a promenade with a fountain overlooking the sea, and a series of secluded beaches under the cliffs—the best are a good walk away on either side of the town. A few kilometres east, the **Cueva de Nerja** is one of Spain's fabled grottos, full of Gaudiesque formations and needle-thin stalactites—one, they claim, is the longest in the world. The caves were discovered in 1959, just in time for the tourist boom, and they have been fitted out with lights and music, with photographers lurking in the shadow who'll try to sell you a picture of yourself when you leave. The caves were popular with Cro-Magnon man (first found in a cave of that name in France), and there are some Paleolithic artworks. Occasionally, this perfect setting is used for ballet and concerts.

A scenic 7km (4½-mile) drive north of Nerja on the MA105 finds pretty **Frigiliana**, a pristine whitewashed village of neat houses and cobbled streets, with great views down to the eastern coast, especially from the ruins of the Moorish fort. This was the site of one of the last battles between Christians and Moriscos in 1569; the story of the battle is retold on ceramic plates around the village's old quarter. Nowadays, Frigiliana is like an English colony, rather than an inland Andalucían village.

Almuñécar and Salobreña

The coastal road east of Nerja, bobbing in and out of the hills and cliffs, is the best part of the Costa, where avocado pears and sugar cane keep the farming community busy; the next resort, however, **Almuñécar**, is better left alone; a nest of dreary high-rises around a beleaguered village. Its only interesting feature is the **Moorish castle**, which houses the local cemetery. Outside the town are the remains of a Roman aqueduct. **Salobreña** is much better, though it may not stay that way. The village's dramatic setting, slung down a steep, lone peak overlooking the sea, is the most stunning of any on the coast, and helps to insulate it just a little from the tourist industry. The beaches, just starting to become built up, are about 2km (1¼ miles) away.

From here, the next town is **Motril**, a large settlement set back from the sea with little to attract visitors; it's the centre of the coastal sugar-cane production, thanks to the gin family, Larios. There isn't much Costa left further east, and the only real choice for a destination is the spectacular mountain road through the Sierra Nevada towards Granada.

Where to Stay

Nerja

Nerja has two fine hotels: the ★★★★**Parador Nacional de Nerja**, Almuñécar 8, © (95) 252 00 50, fax 252 19 97, just outside town at El Tablazo (12,000–13,000 pts a double) and the ★★★**Balcón de Europa**, 1 Paseo Balcón de Europa, © (95) 252 08 00, fax 252 44 90 (7,000–10,500 pts, doubles with suites from 10,000–13,000 pts). The latter is probably the better bet, though not quite as luxurious as the *parador*; the beautiful location on the 'balcony of Europe' in the town centre and the reasonable rates make the difference. Both hotels have lifts down to the beaches under Nerja's cliffs. Another good bargain on the beach is the ★**Portofino**, Puerta del Mar 4, © (95) 252 01 50 (around 6,500 pts a double with bath). There are a few more inexpensive places about town, notably the ★**Florida**, Calle San Miguel 35, © (95) 252 07 43 (2,800 pts a double with bath, 2,600 pts without), but Nerja is notoriously tight during the high season. You will have serious trouble finding a place without a reservation.

Almuñécar and Salobreña

There are plenty of hotels to be found in Almuñécar along the narrow tiled streets of the old town. In Salobreña, you have a choice between the ★★★**Salobreña**, outside the town on the coastal highway, ✆ (95) 261 02 61, fax 261 01 01, with pool, garden and close to the beach (6,000–7,650 pts for doubles) and a number of *hostales* on the beach and in the alleys. Of these, the ★**Mari Tere**, Ctra de la Playa 7, ✆ (95) 261 01 26, has doubles with bath for 3,300–4,200 pts.

Eating Out

Nerja

A popular restaurant is the **Rey Alfonso**—nothing special about the cuisine but the view is superb, on cliffs directly under the Balcón de Europa (3,000 pts). You can dine in genuine old Spanish surroundings in the restaurant at the hotel **Cala Bella**, Puerta del Mar 10, ✆ (95) 252 07 00, complete with wrought ironwork, ceramics and cool tiled floors, and views of Calahonda Bay and the Balcón; *salmón con salsa de anchoa* (salmon in anchovy sauce), *perdiz a la almijara* (partridge with local herbs), plus a selection of meats (3,000 pts). Reservations are essential at **Miguel's**, Calle Pintada 2, ✆ (95) 252 29 96, for its international meat and fish dishes, not least for the flambéd strawberries. **Jiménez** on the Plaza de la Marina serves a wide range of fish and seafood tapas for under 1,000 pts.

Almuñécar

Los Geranios, Plaza Rosa 4a, ✆ (95) 263 07 24, is a cheerful place, full of geraniums; owned by a Hispano-Belgian couple, the menu is international with a Spanish bias (about 2,500 pts; closed Sun). The **Bodega Francisco**, Calle Real 15, ✆ (95) 263 01 68, is a wonderful watering hole serving inexpensive tapas and the usual Andaluz staples (1,000–1,500 pts).

Salobreña

Salobreña has one good restaurant, the **Mesón Durán**, N340, Km 323, specializing in meat and some Andaluz dishes (2,500 pts; closed Mon). If you're in the Motril area and hungry, head for Gualchos, 17km (10½ miles) to the east. There you'll find **La Posada**, Plaza Constitución 9, ✆ (95) 264 60 34, where they serve spinach rolls with fish mousse, red mullet with Andaluz mayonnaise, swordfish with garlic, cream and wine, duck in Jerez vinegar and raisins (2,000–3,000 pts; closed Mon).

Motril to Mojácar

The coastal road cuts between the sea and the plastic—not coastal development, but agricultural plastic, covering a good percentage of Europe's winter vegetables. At **Adra** you enter the province of Almería, the sunniest, driest and hottest little corner of all Europe. What they call winter here lasts from the end of November to March; scores of films (most famously *Lawrence of Arabia*) have been shot here, taking advantage of the light and the scenery. Until the 1970s, the **Costa de Almería**, difficult of access and bereft of utilities and water, was untouched by tourism. Now, charter flights drop in from northern Europe, and hotels are sprouting up here and there—but compared to the region further west, it's pleasantly underwhelming.

Adra was an ancient Phoenician town, and the last spot in Spain surrendered by the Moors, at the moment Boabdil sailed from here to Africa. Though it's still basically a fishing and agricultural village, it has spawned **Almerimar**, a large new development of mostly villas and flats, with a new marina and one of Spain's best golf courses. From here you can dip into the eastern Alpujarras to the pretty 'city' of **Berja**, with its palatial country homes or *canjáyar*; this area supplies most of northern Europe's Christmas grapes. The resorts at **Roquetas de Mar** (more golfing) and **Aguadulce** (oldest and biggest course on the Almería coast) are easily reached from Almería capital by bus.

Almería

Getting Around

by air

Almería's airport is 8km (5 miles) from the city on the road to Níjar, © (950) 22 19 54. Besides charters from London, Iberia has regular connections with Madrid, Barcelona and Melilla.

by boat

Transmediterránea runs car ferries from Almería to Melilla on the North African coast at 2pm every Tuesday, Thursday, and Saturday; the voyage takes 6½ hours. Ticket office is at Parque Nicolás Salmerón 28, © (950) 23 63 56.

by train

Almería's RENFE station is a block from the bus station, on Ctra Ronda, easy walking distance from the centre, © (950) 25 11 35—the city office is at Calle Alcalde Muñoz 1, © (950) 23 12 07. There are daily trains and *Talgos* to Madrid, Barcelona and Valencia; you can go to Granada twice a day; or make an all-night journey across Andalucía, departures daily at 11pm arriving in Córdoba at 7am, or Sevilla at 8.30am.

by bus

The bus station, in the new part of town on the Plaza Barcelona, © (950) 21 00 20, has a daily service to the major cities of the Levante up to Barcelona; also to Madrid, Granada, Sevilla, Cádiz, Málaga and Algeciras. There are two buses daily to Adra; hourly connections to Aguadulce and Roquetas; five buses daily to Berja; three to Cabo de Gata, four to Mojácar, one each to Níjar and Tabernas, and weekday connections to Jaén and Guadix.

Tourist Office

Calle Hermanos Machado 4, in the big ministries building, © (950) 23 08 58; open 9–2, 3–7.30.

Almería has been a genial, dusty little port since its founding by the Phoenicians, though for a short time in the 11th century, after the fall of the caliphate, it dominated this end of al-Andalus, rivalling Córdoba and Sevilla. The upper city, with its narrow streets, tiny pastel houses and whitewashed cave dwellings hugging the looming walls of the **Alcazaba**, has retained a fine Moorish feel to this day. Built by Caliph Abd ar-Rahman II in the 10th century, the Alcazaba was the most powerful Moorish fortress in Spain; today its great curtain walls and towers defend mostly market- and flower-gardens—nothing remains of the once splendid palace (*open 10–2 and 4–9*). Behind the fortress, by the wall of Jayrán, you can visit the **Centre for the Rescue of Animals of the Sahara**: before going up, get permission from the centre's headquarters near the tourist office—they'll give you a note letting you wander through the cages and enclosures of a wide variety of endangered animals, in an environment that must feel just like home.

Almería's **cathedral**, begun in 1524, was seemingly built for defence with its four mighty towers. Prettier, and boasting a fine carving of St James Matamoros and a minaret-like tower, is **Santiago El Viejo**, just off the Puerta Purchena near the top of the Paseo de Almería. It's a bit unusual to find a pilgrimage church, complete with St James's cockle-shells, so far off the main routes.

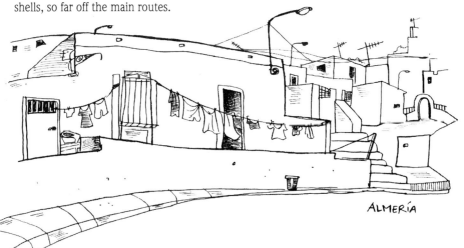

ALMERÍA

Almería has a small **archaeological museum** on Calle Javier Sanz, with remains from the remarkable Neolithic culture of Los Millares that flourished here about 3500–3000 BC (*adm free with an EU passport*). You'll learn more about it here than at the sites themselves, but determined Neolithic fans will want to see Los Millares itself, in stark, barren mountains about 25km (15½ miles) north on the N324 at Santa Fe de Mondújar. Five thousand years ago this was rich farmland, and the people who lived here had the leisure to create one of the most advanced prehistoric civilizations in Spain. The burial mounds here are almost true temples, with interior passages and surrounding concentric stone circles, broken by concave semicircular entrances. Five millennia of erosion have made these difficult to make out, and you'll have an even harder time distinguishing the remains of the walled town that once stood nearby.

East of Almería

The **Sierra Alhamilla**—one of the driest, most rugged and lunar of Spanish sierras—occupies this most southeastern corner of Spain. The coastal road struggles out to the **Cabo de Gata**, with a pretty beach, solitary lighthouse and crystal-clear waters, popular with divers. Inland, the white village of **Níjar** is a charming oasis in an arid setting where potters actively carry on a craft introduced by the Phoenicians. Lorca's play *Blood Wedding* was based on incidents that occurred here around the turn of the century.

The main road east winds through the northern flanks of the sierra, passing through a lush *huerta* of country estates before rising into a weirdly beautiful but perfectly desolate region, where even in the springtime green is a foreign colour. Here in **Tabernas** are a couple of spaghetti-western sets. At

Mini Hollywood, the town built by Sergio Leone for such classics as Clint Eastwood's first vehicle, *A Fistful of Dollars*, cowboy shoot-ups and bank robberies are staged at weekends for the benefit of visitors (*open July–Sept; adm 595 pts*).

Sorbas, with its hanging houses, is most impressively seen from the highway; between the two, the government has decided to exploit the province's greatest natural resource—sunlight—with the country's largest solar energy installation.

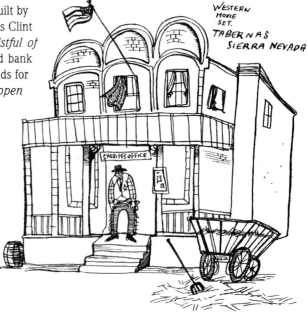

Mojácar

Isolated amidst the rugged mountains, on a hill 2km (1¼ miles) from the beach, trendy Mojácar has often been compared to a pile of sugar cubes. No town in Spain wears such a Moorish face—its little, flat-roofed, white houses stacked almost on top of one another. Before the equally white hotels were added to the scene a couple of decades ago, the women covered their faces with their veils when passing a stranger; a plaque by the fountain tells how the townspeople valiantly defended themselves against the army of the Catholic Kings. Most unusually, it was the practice of the old women in the village to paint a symbol known as the *indalo* (a stick figure with outstretched arms, holding up an arc) on their doors as a charm against the evil eye and thunderbolts. No one knows when the practice originated, though in the nearby caves of Vélez-Blanco, Neolithic drawings of *indalos* dating from 3000 BC have led anthropologists to the conclusion that this is one of the few, if only, cases of a prehistoric symbol being handed down in one place for thousands of years.

Northeast of Mojácar, there's nothing but empty spaces as far as the Andalucía-Murcia border (and well beyond it, for that matter). The nondescript village of **Palomares** may ring a bell; it occupied all the world's headlines for a while in 1966, when an American B-52 crashed nearby and littered the countryside and sea with live hydrogen bombs.

Where to Stay

Adra, El Ejido and Níjar

In Adra you can spend an economy beach holiday at the ★**Delfín**, Natalio Rivas 106, © (950) 40 00 50, (2,800–3,000 pts for doubles with bath); or splurge and golf nearby at El Ejido in the ★★★★**Gran Hotel Almerimar**, © (950) 49 70 50, fax 40 70 19, a plush 38-room refuge, with tennis courts, pool, recreational activities in an attractive setting (9,000–11,000 pts for doubles; open all year). If you'd prefer peace and quiet to comfort and facilities, try the little ★**Isleta del Moro**, © (950) 36 63 13, a *hostal* near Níjar, with a simple restaurant and rooms with bath for 2,000 pts (open all year).

Almería

When on location in Almería, Hollywood denizens have traditionally checked into the ★★★★**Gran Hotel Almería**, in town at Avenida Reina Regente 8, © (950) 23 80 11, fax 27 06 91. Rooms are plush and air-conditioned, and among the available diversions are a pool and bingo hall; breakfast only (15,300–16,800 pts for doubles). On the beach similar smart lodgings are available at the ★★★★**Playalúz**, Playa del Palmer, © (950) 34 05 04, located in a lovely setting, and offering golf, tennis, sauna, indoor and outdooor pools, and children's facilities (8,000–12,500 pts for doubles; open all year). Another comfortable and air-conditioned choice in town is the ★★★**Torreluz**, Plaza de Flores 1, © (950) 23 47 99 (7,500–8,200 pts for doubles). There are a number of inexpensive *hostales*. The

*Maribel, Avenida Lorca 153, ✆ (950) 23 51 73, is within easy walking distance of the bus and train stations, offering simple but adequate doubles for around 3,000 pts with bath.

Mojácar

The modern beach-side ******Parador Reyes Católicos**, ✆ (950) 47 82 50, fax 47 81 83, has a pool and air-conditioning (8,500–10,500 pts for doubles). In the village there are a couple of new, trendy hotels at lovely Mirador de la Puntica; *****El Moresco**, Avenida Horizón; ✆ (950) 47 80 25, fax 47 81 76, has the advantage of being open all year, and indoor, outdoor and children's swimming pools (6,500–8,000 pts). There's little in the budget category; you'll spend less at **El Puntazo** on the beach, ✆ (950) 47 82 29, where a nondescript double will set you back 3,800–4,250 pts with bath (open all year).

Eating Out

Almería

The best restaurant is the **Anfora**, G. Garbín 25 (off the Plaza San Sebastián), ✆ (950) 23 13 74, specializing in the freshest of local ingredients—vegetables and seafood (2,500–3,000 pts; closed Sun). Nearby is another good seafood restaurant, the **Imperial**, Puerta de Purchena 13, ✆ (950) 23 17 40, with a decent three course house menu for 1,500 pts, and good seafood soups and mixed fish platters for 2,000 pts (closed Wed). On the seafront, facing the gardens, are a couple of inexpensive choices, **La Cartuja** and the **Canoe**, the latter with a 850 pts set menu.

Mojácar

Seafood and couscous to order on Fridays are served at **Mamabel's** on Embajadores, along with onion tart and chicory salad with roquefort and nuts (2,000 pts); less expensive and overlooking the sea, **Mediterráneo** at Cueva del Lobo has more seafood for 1,200–1,500 pts. **Palacio** in Plaza del Caño is the best restaurant in town, with excellent chocolate truffles (2,500 pts).

ALGATOCÍN,
MALAGA.

Andalucían Interior

For some, the mountainous area between the Guadalquivir and the coast will be the best of Andalucía. It doesn't have beaches, and it doesn't have famous buildings or museums. Tourists are in short supply too—mostly young Germans and Britons with backpacks, along with day-trippers from the Costa and a few examples of that beloved but endangered species, the serious British traveller, with nose in a Latin chronicle or a bird-watcher's guide. What this region does have is a chain of peaceful white villages, draped along hillsides under their castles, their steep streets lined with pots of geraniums. Some are prosperous, some quite poor; some have a reputation for friendliness, others can seem silent and introverted. None of them is really different from the others—except to their natives, of course—and they all share some of southern Spain's most delightful scenery. It is a region of rolling hills broken by patches of grey mountains, well-tended lands devoted to the traditional Mediterranean staples of wheat, vines and olives, coloured in the spring by orange and almond blossom in the lower areas. The big town of Ronda and the curiosities around Antequera are the main attractions, but if you're like many of the travellers who come here, you won't worry too much about destinations, but lazily pick your way from one pretty village to the next, get to know the land and its people, and look for the little surprises that make the trip worthwhile.

Arcos de la Frontera to Ronda

Getting Around

In this region, you'll be depending on **buses**. Arcos de la Frontera has regular connections to Jerez, Cádiz and Ronda; less frequently to Sevilla. From Ronda you can go directly to Jerez, Cádiz, Málaga, and most of the towns along the Costa del Sol; there are also four daily buses to and from Sevilla. Arcos and Ronda have connections to the villages in their hinterlands—usually only once a day, so if you're day-tripping, make sure there's a return. Ronda's bus station is in the new town, on the Paseo de Andalucía.

Ronda has **trains**, too; there are at least three a day for Algeciras and Málaga, with connections at Bobadilla Junction for Madrid and the other cities of Andalucía. Some trains stop at Gaucín and Setenil. The station is just a few blocks down Paseo de Andalucía, © (95) 287 16 73.

When you are travelling by **car**, be warned that the streets of the Sierra towns and villages can be very narrow, and difficult for a large vehicle to negotiate.

Tourist Office

Ronda: Plaza de España, by the bridge, © (95) 287 12 72. Open weekdays 10–2.

Arcos de la Frontera

Starting from the west, near Jerez, **Arcos de la Frontera** is the first and one of the most spectacular of the towns, hung on a steep rock with wonderful views over the valley of the Guadalete from the *mirador* near the Plaza del Ayuntamiento. The narrow streets twist and turn like an oriental maze, an inheritance from its Moorish past. Follow the long street up to the castle and you'll be rewarded with panoramic views in all directions. The older sections of town under the castle contain some ancient palaces and the Isabelline Gothic **Santa María de la Asunción**, next to which is a rectangular esplanade hanging over the cliff above the Guadalete. Way below stretches the river and its fertile valley. Arcos was an important fortress for the Moors, a seemingly impregnable eyrie that Alfonso the Wise was smart enough to take in 1264.

Further east, **Grazalema** is a lovely village, full of flowers and surrounded by pine woods. It is considered by many to be the most representative of the Sierra towns, and its peaceful beauty is in perfect accord with its surroundings. It has been famous for hand-woven blankets since Moorish times, and they still make them here on big, old, wooden looms. The surrounding area is a national park; details of walks, horse-trekking, etcetera, can be found at the campsite office just above the village. To the south is **Benaocaz**, which has a small museum of local archaeology. Nearby, **Ubrique** hangs dramatically over the Río Majaceite; though a growing industrial town, best known for its leather-craft work, it still manages to retain some of its medieval charm. **Zahara** and **Olvera** have memorable silhouettes, their castles and churches sticking bravely up over the whitewashed houses. Zahara ('desert' or 'flower' in Arabic) is a quiet town, perfumed by orange groves, at the foot of a hill crowned by a medieval castle which the Christians captured from the Moors towards the end of the 15th century. Once a famous bandits' hideout, Olvera has the ruins of a 12th-century Moorish castle, from which there is a heady view down to the village; and a very dignified 17th-century church, **La Encarnación**. Halfway between Olvera and Ronda is **Setenil**, an odd village with some of its few streets lining the walls of a gorge. The houses are tucked under the overhanging rock, and their front doors overlook a stream.

Ronda

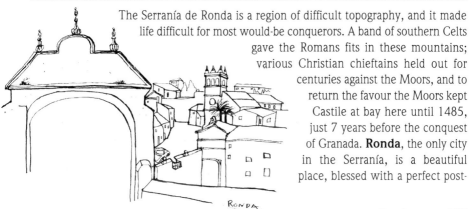

The Serranía de Ronda is a region of difficult topography, and it made life difficult for most would-be conquerors. A band of southern Celts gave the Romans fits in these mountains; various Christian chieftains held out for centuries against the Moors, and to return the favour the Moors kept Castile at bay here until 1485, just 7 years before the conquest of Granada. **Ronda**, the only city in the Serranía, is a beautiful place, blessed with a perfect postcard shot of its lofty bridge over the steep gorge that divides the old and new towns. Because of its proximity to the Costa del Sol, it has lately become the only really tourist-ridden corner of the interior. The town's monuments are few; what Fernando the Catholic didn't wreck in 1485, the French finished off in 1809. Ronda saw plenty of trouble in the civil war, with hundreds of bodies being tossed into the gorge (the exact numbers and who was doing the tossing, depend on who is telling you the story).

Don't be discouraged, though; the views alone are worth the trip. One of the best places to enjoy them is the **Alameda del Tajo**, a park on the edge of the **Mercadillo**, as the new town is called. Next to it, Ronda has one of Spain's oldest and most picturesque bullrings. The 1785 **Plaza de Toros**, the 'cathedral of bullfighting', gets only about three *corridas* a year, but it still has great prestige: the art of bullfighting was developed here; there's a small museum inside. The **Puente Nuevo** was built on the second try in 1740—the first one immediately collapsed. The bridge's two thick piers descend almost 92m (300ft) to the bottom of the narrow gorge. Crossing the bridge into the **Ciudad** (old town), a steep path heads downwards to two 18th-century palaces: the **Palacio de Salvatierra** and the **Casa del Rey Moro**, built over Moorish foundations. From its garden there is a stairway—365 steps cut out of the rock, called the **Mina**—that takes you down to the bottom of the gorge. Here there's a Moorish bridge and well-preserved remains of a **Moorish bath**. Back on top, if you survive the climb back up, there is the town's main church, **Santa María La Mayor**, still retaining the mihrab and minaret of the mosque it replaced, and the ruins of the **Alcázar**, blown up by the French.

White Beans and Black Pudding

Regional dishes usually include white beans, haricot beans, sausage and black pudding. Ronda's blood sausage, *morcilla rondense*, is seasoned with cloves, oregano, cumin and coriander, while the local goats' milk cheese is yellow with small holes and is preserved in olive oil.

Around Ronda

Besides the opportunities for walks in and around the valleys under Ronda, an interesting excursion can be made to an area of curiosities 15–20km (9–12 miles) west of town. The hills around the hamlet of Montejaque are full of caves. Two, the Cueva del Gato and Cueva del Hundidero, both full of stalactites and odd formations, are connected. The little stream called the Gaduares disappears in one and comes out in the other. Five kilometres (3 miles) south, past the village of Benaoján, the Cueva de la Pileta has some 25,000-year-old art—simple drawings in black of animals and magic symbols (*open 9–1, 4–6*; the care-taker lives in the farmhouse near the entrance if no one's around). Twelve kilometres (7½ miles) west of Ronda, off the road to Grazalema, are the Roman ruins of **Acinipo** known locally as 'Ronda la Vieja', with a theatre and stage building like Mérida's. And finally, from the ancient isolated village of **Gaucín**, 25km (15½ miles) southwest of Ronda, you can see Gibraltar and the African coast over the peaks of the Serranía.

Where to Stay

Arcos

The ★★★★**Parador Nacional Casa del Corregidor**, Plaza de España, ✆ (956) 70 05 00, fax 70 11 16, has recently been reopened after a thorough restoration of the old palace that houses it; it's a lovely place, and quite popular, so book ahead (doubles 13,000 pts). More reasonable is ★★★**Los Olivos**, San Miguel 2, ✆ (956) 70 08 11, fax 70 20 18, where rooms with bath go for 6,650–8,500 pts. Apart from these, the 'white villages' offer only the simplest of places to stay and eat.

Ronda

Ronda has a wider choice. The ★★★★**Reina Victoria**, Calle Jerez 25, ✆ (95) 287 12 40, fax 287 10 75, is a fine old hotel, built by the British around the turn of the century, with lovely views over the cliffs. The German poet Rainer Maria Rilke stayed here for a season and wrote some of his best-known works (9,200–12,000 pts for doubles). Less expensive, near the old town, is the ★★**Royal**, Calle Virgen de la Paz 42, ✆ (95) 287 11 41, near the bullring (4,200 pts for doubles). There are dozens of small *hostales* and *camas* over bars—most of them quite agreeable—on all the side streets of Calle Jerez in the Mercadillo.

Benaoján

The ★★★**Molino del Santo**, Bda de la Estacíon, ✆ (95) 216 71 51, is a converted water mill beside a mountain stream, close to the Pileta caves. It's friendly and intimate (10 rooms, all with bath), and offers excursions each week—hiking, cycling and mini-bus nature tours in the Grazalema National Park. There's a spring-fed swimming pool, and the kitchen serves Andaluz cuisine (6,500–7,900 pts).

Eating Out

Arcos

Arcos has a couple of reputable restaurants, namely **Mesón del Brigadier**, Presa de Arcos, ✆ (956) 70 10 03, serving mostly pork and game dishes (2,500 pts) and **Curro el Cojo**, ✆ (956) 70 10 03. Curro's is also known as Mesón del Brigadier and is found just off the El Bosque road a couple of kilometres outside Arcos towards Ronda. Once you've crossed the bridge, take a right up the hill and you'll see the restaurant on high overlooking the lake. It's an eccentric place containing stuffed foxes, an old horsedrawn carriage and a biro collection (!) but the game and meat dishes are excellent (2,500).

Ronda

The best meals Ronda can offer, with a view to match, are at the **Don Miguel**, Villanueva 4, ✆ (95) 287 10 90, overlooking the gorge next to the famous bridge; they also have a bar built into the bridge itself (3,000–4,000 pts for a full-course dinner). Otherwise, stick to the restaurants in the Mercadillo like the **Mesón Santiago**, Calle Marina 3, ✆ (95) 287 15 59, or the **Doña Pepa** overlooking the square on Plaza del Socorro, ✆ (95) 287 47 77 (2,000–3,000 pts), with its quail sautéd in garlic, and partridge. Quite a few really inferior tourist restaurants have been opening in conspicuous places to take advantage of day-trippers from the Costa. Watch out.

Antequera and Around

Getting Around

Antequera is on the **rail** line from Algeciras to Granada, and there are easy connections to all points from nearby Bobadilla Junction. The station is on Avenida de la Estación, ✆ (95) 284 23 30. There are lots of **buses** to Málaga and Sevilla, less frequently to Granada and Córdoba, as well as to Olvera, Osuna and the other villages of the region. The bus station is on Calle Alameda.

Tourist Offices

Antequera: Calle Infante de Don Fernandos, ✆ (95) 270 04 05. Open 10–2, 5–8.

Alora: Avenida de la Constitución (next to municipal swimming pool), ✆ (95) 249 83 80. Open weekdays 9–2, Sat 10–2.

Antequera

Known in Roman times as *Antikaria*, later history saw it as the first of the Granadan border fortresses to fall to the Reconquista, in 1410, although subsequently it was retaken by the Moors and lost again. The centre of a leather-tanning industry, it is not an especially interesting city, though it's as large as Ronda. There is, however, quite an impressive ensemble of 16th- to 18th-century buildings. The 17th-century Nerja Palace houses the **Municipal Museum**, with many religious works including a wonderful *St Francis* by Alonso Cano and a Roman bronze of a boy that dates back nearly 2,000 years (*open Tues–Sat 10–1.30*).

Up the Cuesta Zapateros, at the top of the hill, is the 16th-century **Arco de los Gigantes**, meant as a sort of triumphal arch for the seldom-victorious Philip II, and incorporating ancient fragments; next to it, the ruins of a Moorish fortress offer views over the town.

Nearby is the plateresque church of **Santa María La Mayor**, attached to which is an art restoration centre, teaching stonemasonry, woodwork and ironwork.

East of Antequera

The Romans may have given Antequera its name—'old town', and there was probably a settlement here some centuries before the arrival of the Phoenicians. Another possibility is that the name is related to *anta*, the local word for dolmen. Just out of town are the Neolithic monuments known as the **Cueva de Menga**, the 'first real architecture in Spain'. They are hardly as impressive as the *talayots* and *taulas* of the island of Menorca, but there's nothing like them in mainland Spain. Le Corbusier came here in the 1950s, as he said 'to pay homage to my predecessors'. There are three, dating from anything between 4500 BC and 2500 BC. The two largest, the Menga and Viera dolmens, are covered chambers about 21.5m (70ft) long, roughly elliptical and lined with huge, flat stones; other monoliths support the roof-like pillars (*open 10–1.30 and 5–7*). At El Romeral nearby, under a mound and in the grounds of a sugar factory, the third of these temples has two chambers with domed ceilings. Originally the mound would have been about 100m in diameter, as big as Newgrange in County Meath, Ireland. All three have etchings of figures and symbols around their walls.

Fifteen kilometres (9 miles) east of Antequera on the N342 is **Archidona**. The town overlooks acres of olive trees, but its main feauture is the unique, octagonal Plaza Mayor, the **Ochavada**. Built between 1780–86 by Francisco Astorga and Antonio González, it is one of the loveliest plazas in Andalucía. Nearby **Loja** had a 9th-century **alcazaba** and the 16th-century church of **San Gabriel** has a cupola attributed to Diego de Siloé.

South of Antequera

The sierras between Antequera and Málaga contain some of the remote villages of the region and offer some spectacular scenery—almond trees, cactus, olive groves and mountains that drop steeply away to the silver ribbon of a stream down below. A natural park has been laid out around the rock formations at **El Torcal,** a tall but hikeable mountain with unusual, eroded red limestone crags around it. Several paths are marked out. The nearest town is **Villanueva de la Concepción**. Here you should take the MA424 and travel south for about 17km (10½ miles). You will be rewarded with **Almogía**, presenting a dramatic spectacle overlooking a high ridge. From 15–18 August this place comes to life with dancing in the streets in celebration of San Roque and San Sebastián. The best views are from the ruined tower.

A more roundabout route south from Antequera will take you to the town of **Alora**. Originally a Roman settlement and one of the last towns to be held by the Moors, it is mainly of interest now as the point where you should turn northwest towards one of Andalucía's natural wonders. **El Chorro Gorge**, in the deep rugged canyon of the Río Guadalhorce, has sheer walls of limestone tossed about at crazy angles. Thrill-seekers can circumnavigate it on an old concrete catwalk called **El Camino del Rey**, gradually crumbling into a ruin; amazingly they still keep it open. It's definitely worth the walk if you're nimble and don't suffer from vertigo, and it's easy to reach without a car. El Chorro has a train station on the Antequera–Málaga line. If you're not up to stopping, the views from the train, as it weaves in and out of the tunnels around the gorge, are great too.

If you have time to explore this region, seek out the church of **Bobastro**. Just west of El Chorro, it's a twisty drive for a couple of kilometres after turning off the little Alora–Ardales road. Bobastro is a 9th-century basilica cut out of bare rock that supposedly contains the tomb of ibn-Hafsun, the (possibly) Christian emir who founded a short-lived independent state in the mountains around 880. Some remains of the city and fortress he built can be seen on the heights nearby. The nearby lakes were created as part of a big government hydroelectric scheme, but their shores, surrounded by gentle hills, make an ideal place to have a lazy picnic.

From Bobastro follow the road to **Ardales** and **Carratraca**. Carratraca has been a spa town from Greek and Roman times, but its heyday was in the 19th and early 20th centuries. Visitors included Byron, Dumas, Rilke and Napoleon II's wife, the Empress Eugénie, who gadded about everywhere else in Europe, and lived to the ripe old age of 94. The baths have been restored and can be visited by would-be cure-seekers from June to October. The town is famous for its Passion play. As part of their *Semana Santa* celebrations, 140 of the villagers perform *El Paso* in the bullring. From here the road twists its way back to Alora.

Where to Stay and Eating Out

Archidona

Archidona only has small one-star *hostales*. Of them, ★**Las Palomas**, Ctra Jerez–Granada, Km 177, ℂ (95) 271 43 26, is the best bet (3,000 pts without bath). If you're not on a budget, then *the* hotel in the area is ★★★★★**La Bobadilla**, Finca La Bobadilla, ℂ (958) 32 18 61, fax 32 18 10, on the same road, halfway to Loja. It's an honest attempt at reconstructing the typical Andalucían *pueblo*, complete with Moorish touches, and covers a large area of land on a hilltop. Luxuries like this don't come cheaply, though (from 19,200–24,000 pts). Andaluz and international dishes are on the menu of **La Finca**, the hotel's restaurant (6,000–7,000 pts for a full dinner).

Antequera

The ★★★**Parador de Antequera**, García del Olmo s/n, ℂ (95) 284 00 61, fax 284 13 12, is a plain, modern building but has the most comforts here, and is reasonably priced at 10,000 pts for air-conditioned doubles. In the town centre, the best choice is the ★**Manzanito**, Plaza San Sebastián, ℂ (95) 284 10 23 (3,500–4,200 pts for doubles with bath). The management also runs a good restaurant underneath (1,000 pts). **Bar Madrona**, Calzada 25, ℂ (95) 284 00 14, is clean and basic (2,900 pts) and does good *churros* and breakfasts.

Alora's only hotel is the **★Durán**, Calle La Parra 9, © (95) 249 66 42, (3,500 pts).
The place to stay in Carratraca is **★El Príncipe**, Antonio Riobo 9, © (95) 245 80 20,
but in season it's always advisable to book beforehand (4,000 pts).

Away from the hotels, the roadside *ventas* are probably the best bet for eating out.

North of Antequera

This is the heart of Andalucía, a vast tract of bountiful hills covered in olive groves and
vines. The area is more densely populated, and a bit more prosperous than most of the
region's rural districts. The towns are closer together, all white, and all punctuated by the
warm sandstone of their palaces and towers. Some did well even in Andalucía's grim 18th
century: Osuna under its haughty dukes, and Priego de Córdoba with its once-famous
textiles; others haven't had a break since the passing of the Moors. Some towns inspired
poets and novelists, others are famous for leather or barrels. Along the way, on what we
hope will be a properly Spanish picaresque journey through a region few tourists enter,
there will be flamingos, dolmens, rococo frippery, memorabilia of Julius Caesar, a cask of
amontillado, a pretty fair canyon, and 139 gargoyles.

Tourist Offices

Osuna: Casa Cultura, near Plaza Mayor, © (95) 481 22 11.

Estepa: Plaza del Carmen 1, © (95) 482 10 00.

Priego de Córdoba: in the Ayuntamiento,
Plaza de la Constitución 3, © (957) 54 01 34.

Lucena: Plaza Nueva 1, © (957) 50 03 27.

Cabra: Plaza de España 11, © (957) 52 21 11.

Heading northwest out of Antequera into the gentler hills flanking
the southern slopes of the Guadalquivir valley, there are
a few more towns worth seeing. But before you reach
the first of these, turn off the N334 at Fuente de
Piedra and you'll come to the **Laguna de Fuente
de Piedra**, one of Europe's largest breeding
grounds for flamingos. They're here from March to
September; the rest of the year you'll have to look
them up in Senegal. Back on the N334, you'll come to
Estepa, known for its Christmas biscuits (*polvorones* and
mantecado), and the mass suicide of its inhabitants who
preferred not to surrender to the Roman enemy in 208 BC.
Above the town are the remains of a castle with a well-
preserved Almohad keep; the two Baroque showpieces

are the churches of **El Carmen**, in the main square, with a spectacular façade, and the 18th-century **Virgen de los Remedios**.

Further west, **Osuna** is a larger, neater version of Estepa. Founded by a busy, go-ahead governor named Julius Caesar, it was an important Roman military centre for the south of Spain, and survives as an attractive little city of white houses with characteristic *rejas* over every window. Osuna was an aristocratic town after the Reconquista, home of the objectionable Dukes of Osuna who lorded it over much of Andalucía. Their 'pantheon' of tombs may be seen in the fine Renaissance **Colegiata** church on a hill on the west side of town. Inside is a memorable *Crucifixion* by José Ribera, and four other of his works in the high altar *retablo*. Behind the church is the old university building, founded in 1548 and now serving as a school. Several decorative façades of 16th-century mansions can be seen along the **Calle San Pedro**. Osuna has a little **archaeology museum** in the **Torre del Agua**, part of the old fortifications, and a museum of dubious art in **La Encarnación** convent, a Baroque work of the late 18th century; the cloister is done out in ceramic tiles (*both open daily except Mon, 10–1.30 and 4–7.30*).

The Cordobés Subbética and La Campiña

Here in the heartland of Andalucía lies the grandly titled **Parque Natural de las Sierras Subbéticas de Córdoba**—a succession of wooded hills that dip into the valleys of the rivers Zagrillo, Salado and Caicena. The landscape of oak trees, olive groves and much shrubland is home to eagles, falcons and vultures, rabbit and partridge, the odd adder, field mice, bats and badgers; the rivers and small lakes dotted around brim with bass, perch and trout. Most tourists miss these corners of Andalucía that seem untouched by the passing of time, where the people are god-fearing and industrious, and where the visitor is welcomed but watched carefully.

Twenty kilometres (12½ miles) north of Estepa on the C338 at **Puente Genil,** an old Moorish-style mill still turns in a pretty setting along the Río Genil. In the town is the 15th-century church of **La Concepción**, but the town's latter-day claim to fame is its local importance as a food manufacturing centre. *Semana Santa* here is a big affair, and people come from all over the province to see the very colourful procession in Roman costume and biblical dress.

Further east on the C338, **Lucena** is one of the centres of a great wine-growing region. The town is not known for its beauty, but for making the biggest wine barrels in Andalucía, and as the birthplace of the Baroque architect Hurtado Izquierdo. He produced the incredible Cartuja chapel in Granada, though he is not responsible for Lucena's wonderful Baroque *sagrario* chapel in the church of **San Mateo**. Before the Reconquista, Lucena seems to have been for a time an autonomous Jewish republic, and a major trading centre. Its small industries still thrive today, notably furniture-making, the manufacture of brass and copperware, and barrels. Nearby are the remains of the **Tower of Moral**, where Granada's last king, Boabdil el Chico was imprisoned by Ferdinand in 1483. Twenty kilometres (12½ miles) south of here, the town of **Rute** produces the potent elixir *anís*. Right at the centre of Andalucía, fittingly set in a sea of olive groves and vineyards, is

Cabra, 10km (6 miles) north of Lucena on the C327. From here you get a sweeping view of the Sierra Nevada to the southeast and the Guadalquivir valley to the north.

Priego de Córdoba lies at the foot of the highest mountain in the province, **La Tiñosa**, and has a famous ensemble of Baroque churches, monasteries and fountains; the best is the **Asunción** church with a beautiful dome over its *sagrario* chapel and a sumptuous stucco interior. The town's other pride is the Baroque **Fuente del Rey**: three connecting fountain pools lined with 139 gargoyles, and a centrepiece of Neptune and Aphrodite on a horse-drawn carriage—it wouldn't look out of place in a *piazza* in Rome. In the church of **San Pedro** is an image of the *Inmaculada*, a work attributed to Alonso Cano. The town is typified by its fancy window grillwork and ornate front doors, as on display in the Calle Río.

From Cabra the C327 heads northeast to **Baena**, a town of major importance in Moorish times, now squeezing out olive oil in remarkable quantities. A clean, tightly packed town with narrow, whitewashed streets and the ruins of a Moorish castle, Baena sees most of its visitors arrive for the Holy Week celebrations, when a deafening drum-rolling competition is held to see who can play the longest and the loudest; it lasts *two days*. Twenty-two kilometres (14 miles) northwest from Cabra is **Aguilar de la Frontera**, another attractive wine town (producing *solera fina*, mostly). It has an unusual octagonal plaza, a copy of the one in Antequera, and the Renaissance church of **Santa María del Sorerraño.**

From Aguilar it's a short hop up the road to the prince of the wine producing towns, **Montilla**, sitting on a rise amidst endless acres of vines. Although the name for pale dry sherry *amontillado* takes its name from this town, the wine produced here is not a sherry, in that no extra alcohol is added to fortify it, unlike in Jerez. The town is refreshingly short of Baroque churches, but its bodegas can be visited to sample the good stuff. A small **museum** is dedicated to Garcilaso de la Vega, Hispano-Inca son of a *conquistador* and chronicler of the Inca civilization in the 16th century. The 1512 Gothic convent of **Santa Clara** is worth a visit for its Mudéjar roof and Baroque altarpiece. The town is believed to be the site of the Battle of Munda, where former governor Caesar's men finally put paid to the Spanish followers of Pompey.

Where to Stay and Eating Out

Osuna and Estepa

In Osuna, the best is the ****Hostal Caballo Blanco**, Calle Granada 1, on the corner with Calle Franco, © (95) 481 12 43 (4,900–6,950 pts). Opposite there's the ***Cinco Puertas** (2,650 pts). In Estepa, ****Los Angeles**, Avenida Andalucía 21, © (95) 482 09 84, is adequate (4,000 pts, or 2,200 pts without bath).

the Sierra Subbética

Puente Genil has only one *hostal*, the ****Xenil**, García Lorca 3, © (957) 60 02 00, fax 60 04 43, where doubles with bath are 4,000–4,800 pts. In Priego de Córdoba, the ****Río-Piscina**, Ctra Monturque–Alcalá la Real, Km 44, © (957) 70 01 86, fax 54 09 77, has a small pool and tennis court, and reasonable rates for its doubles with bath (4,000 pts). Aguilar has a number of places, but none offering any luxury; the **San José**, Pescadería 6, © (957) 66 02 22, is the best (2,300–2,800 pts for basic room). Montilla is the only place with sophisticated accommodation; the ★★★**Don Gonzalo**, Ctra Madrid–Málaga, Km 447, © (957) 65 06 58, on the main road outside Montilla, has gardens, swimming pool and tennis court (8,000 pts). Montilla also has a decent restaurant, **Las Camachas**, again on the main road, (no phone) where you can wash down the tasty fish dishes with a glass or two of the local brew (2,000 pts).

Granada

Dale limosna mujer que no hay en la vida noda. Como la pena de ser ciego y en Granada.

(Give him alms, woman, for there is nothing in life so cruel as being blind in Granada.)

Francisco de Icaza

The first thing to do upon arrival is to pick up a copy of Washington Irving's *Tales of the Alhambra*. Every bookshop in town can sell you one in just about any language. It was Irving who put Granada on the map, and established the Alhambra as the necessary romantic pilgrimage of Spain. Granada, in fact, might seem a disappointment without Irving. The modern city underneath the Alhambra is a stolid, remarkably unmagical place, with little to show for the 500 years since the Catholic Kings put an end to its ancient glory. As the Moors were expelled, the Spanish Crown replaced them with Castilians and Galicians from up north, and even today *granadinos* are thought of as a bit foreign by other Andalucíans. Their Granada has never been a happy place. Particularly in the last hundred years it has been full of political troubles. Around the turn of the century even the Holy Week processions had to be called off for a few years because of disruptions from the leftists, and at the start of the civil war the reactionaries who always controlled Granada made one of the first big massacres of Republicans.

One of their victims was Federico García Lorca, the *granadino* who, in the decades since his death, has come to be recognized as one of the greatest Spanish dramatists and poets since the 'golden age'. If Irving's fairy tales aren't to your taste, consider the works of Lorca, in which Granada and its sweet melancholy are recurring themes. Lorca once wrote that he remembered Granada 'as one should remember a sweetheart who has died'.

History: the Nasrid Kingdom of Karnattah

First Iberian *Elibyrge*, then Roman *Illiberis*, the town did not make a name for itself until the era of the *taifas* in the early 11th century, when it emerged as the centre of a very minor state. In the 1230s, while the Castilians were seizing Córdoba and preparing to polish off the rest of the Almoravid states of al-Andalus, an Arab chieftain named Mohammed ibn-Yusuf ibn-Nasr established himself around Jaén. When that town fell to the Castilians in 1235, he moved his capital to the town the Moors called *Karnattah*. Ibn Nasr (or Mohammed I, as he is generally known) and his descendants in the Nasrid dynasty enjoyed great success at first in extending their domains. By 1300 this last Moorish state of Spain extended from Gibraltar to Almería, but this accomplishment came entirely at the expense of other Moors. Mohammed and his successors were in fact vassals of the kings of Castile, and aided them in campaigns more often than they fought them.

Karnattah at this time is said to have had a population of some 200,000—almost as many as it has now—and both its arts and industries were strengthened by refugees from the fallen towns of al-Andalus. Thousands came from Córdoba, especially, and the Albaicín quarter was largely settled by the former inhabitants of Baeza. Although a significant Jewish population remained, there were very few Christians. In the comparatively peaceful 14th century, Granada's conservative, introspective civilization reached its height, with the last flowering of Arabic-Andaluz lyric poetry and the architecture and decorative arts of the Alhambra.

This state of affairs lasted until the coming of the Catholic Kings. Isabel's religious fanaticism made the completion of the Reconquista the supreme goal of her reign; she sent Fernando out in 1484 to do the job, which he accomplished in 8 years by a breathtakingly brilliant combination of force and diplomacy. Karnattah at the time was suffering the usual curse of al-Andalus states—disunity founded on the egotism of princes. In this fatal feud, the main actors were Abu al-Hasan Ali (Mulay Hassan in Irving's tales), king of Karnattah, his brother El Zagal ('the valiant') and the king's rebellious son, Abu abd-Allah, better known to posterity as Boabdil el Chico. His seizure of the throne in 1482 started a period of civil war at the worst possible time. Fernando was clever enough to take advantage of the divisions; he captured Boabdil twice, and turned him into a tool of Castilian designs. Playing one side against the other, Fernando snatched away one Nasrid province after another with few losses. When the unfortunate Boabdil, after renouncing his kingship in favour of the Castilians, finally changed his mind and decided to fight for the remnants of Karnattah (by then little more than the city itself and the Sierra Nevada), Fernando had the excuse he needed to mount his final attack. Karnattah was besieged, and after 2 years, Boabdil agreed to surrender under terms that guaranteed his people the use of their religion and customs. When the keys of the city were handed over on 2 January 1492, the Reconquista was complete.

Under a gentlemanly military governor, the Conde de Tendilla, the agreement was kept until the arrival in 1499 of Cardinal Cisneros, the most influential cleric in Spain and a man who made it his personal business to destroy the last vestiges of Islam and Moorish culture. The new Spanish policy—planned, gradual genocide (*see* History, p. 53)—was as successful in the former lands of Granada as it was among those other troublesome heathens of the same period, the Indians of Central and South America. The famous revolt in Las Alpujarras (1568) was followed by a rising in the city itself, in the Albaicín. Between 1609 and 1614, the last of the Muslims were expelled, including most of those who had converted to Christianity, and their property confiscated. It is said that even today, there are old families in Morocco who sentimentally keep the keys to their long-lost homes in Granada.

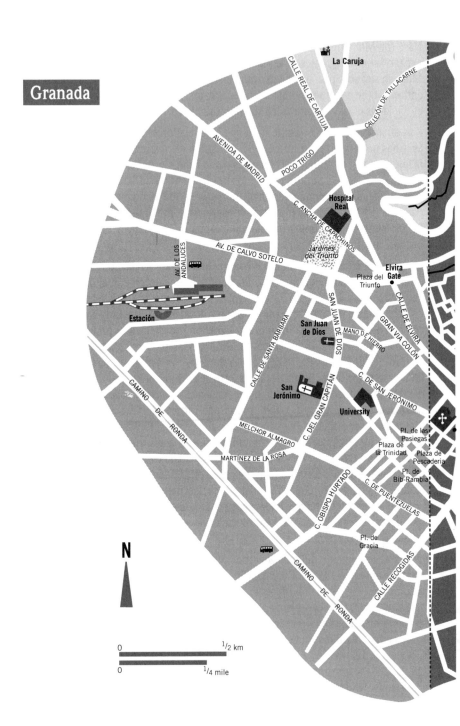

Granada

La Caruja

CALLE REAL DE CARTUJA

CALLEJÓN DE TALLACARNE

AVENIDA DE MADRID

POCO TRIGO

Hospital Real

C. ANCHA DE CAPACHINOS

AV. DE CALVO SOTELO

AV. DE LOS ANDALUCES

Jardines del Triunfo

Elvira Gate

Plaza del Triunfo

Estación

CALLE DE SANTA BARBARA

San Juan de Dios

SAN JUAN DE DIOS

MANO DE HIERRO

CALLE DE ELVIRA

GRAN VÍA COLÓN

CAMINO DE RONDA

San Jerónimo

C. DEL GRAN CAPITÁN

C. DE SAN JERÓNIMO

University

MELCHOR ALMAGRO

MARTÍNEZ DE LA ROSA

Pl. de las Pasiegas

Plaza de la Trinidad

Plaza de Pescadería

Pl. de Bib-Rambla

C. OBISPO HURTADO

C. DE PUENTEZUELAS

Pl. de Gracia

CALLE RECOGIDAS

N

CAMINO DE RONDA

0   1/2 km
0   1/4 mile

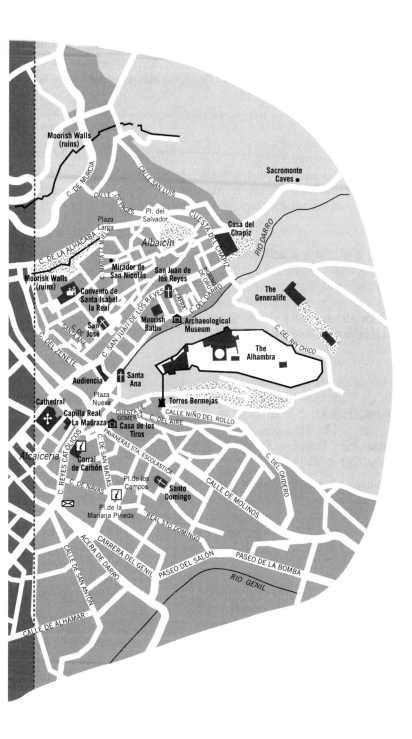

Moorish Walls
(ruins)

Sacromonte
Caves

C. DE MURCIA

CALLE SAN LUIS

CALLE DE PAGES

Pl. del
Salvador

Plaza
Larga

Casa del
Chapiz

CUESTA DEL CHAPIZ

C. DE LA ALHACABA

Albaicín

RIO DARRO

C. MARIA LA MIEL

Mirador de
San Nicolás

San Juan de
los Reyes

Moorish Walls
(ruins)

Convento de
Santa Isabel
la Real

C. SAN JUAN DE LOS REYES

HORNO DE ORO

C. DEL DARRO

C. ZAFRA

The
Generalife

C. DE
SANTA ANA

San
José

Moorish
Baths

Archaeological
Museum

The
Alhambra

C. DEL REY CHICO

C. DEL ZENETE

Audiencia

Santa
Ana

Plaza
Nueva

Torres Bermejas

CALLE NIÑO DEL ROLLO

Cathedral

Capilla Real
La Madraza

CUESTA DE GOMEREL

C. DEL AIRE

Casa de los
Tiros

PAVANERAS STA. ESCOLASTICA

C. DE SAN MATIAS

Alcaiceria

C. REYES CATÓLICOS

Corral
de Carbón

C. DE NAVAS

Pl.de los
Campos

Santo
Domingo

CALLE DE MOLINOS

C. DEL CALDERO

Pl.de la
Mariana Pineda

REAL STO. DOMINGO

CARRERA DEL GENIL

ACERA DE DARRO

PASEO DEL SALÓN

PASEO DE LA BOMBA

CALLE DE SAN ANTÓN

RIO GENIL

CALLE DE ALHAMAR

189

Such a history does not easily wear away, even after so many centuries. The Castilians corrupted Karnattah to *Granada*; just by coincidence that means 'pomegranate' in Spanish, and the pomegranate has come to be the symbol of the city. With its associations with the myth of Persephone, with the mysteries of death and loss, no symbol could be more suitable for this capital of melancholy.

Getting Around

by air

There are two flights daily to Madrid (Mon–Sat), twice daily to Barcelona (Mon–Fri) and three times a week to the Balearics and Canaries. The airport is 16km (10 miles) west of Granada, near Santa Fé; **information**: © (958) 22 75 92.

by train

Granada has connections to Guadix and Almería (three daily), to Algeciras, Sevilla, and Córdoba by way of Bobadilla Junction (they are sometimes complicated) and two daily to Madrid and Barcelona; three daily to Alicante, one a day to Valencia. The station is at the northern end of town, about a mile from the centre, on Avenida de los Andaluces; the city ticket office is on Calle Reyes Católicos, off Plaza Nueva; **information**: © (958) 22 34 97.

by bus

The main bus station, run by the Alsina Graells company, is equally inconveniently located on the Camino de Ronda with services to Madrid, and all points in Andalucía; **information**: © (958) 25 12 58. For other buses to Madrid, Murcia, Alicante, Valencia and Barcelona, the services are run by the Bacoma and Nevamar lines, from in front of the train station at Avenida de los Andaluces; **information**: © (958) 23 18 83.

In the city, one very useful bus to know is the no. 11, a route that passes the train and bus stations, the Gran Vía and Calle Reyes Católicos (catch it in either direction since it's a circular route). A good way to see the Albaicín is to take the no. 7 bus from Calle Reyes Católicos to the top of the hill (get off at Calle Pages) and walk down. The no. 2 from the Plaza Nueva will save you the trouble of climbing up to the Alhambra.

by car

Parking is a problem, so if you plan staying overnight make sure that your hotel has parking facilities and check whether there is a charge or not—it can cost as much as the accommodation in some places. Traffic police are everywhere and extremely vigilant. Fines of 10,000 pts (£50/US$75) are payable on the spot if you are a tourist. Ignore people at the bottom of the Alhambra trying to persuade you to park before you reach the top; there's plenty of parking space by the entrance and it's a steep walk to get there.

Provincial Tourist Office, Plaza Mariana Pineda 10, © (958) 22 66 88, open Mon–Fri 10–1.30, 4.30–7, Sat 10–1.

There's a smaller office inside the Corral del Carbón, © (958) 22 59 90; open 9.30–8 weekdays, 9.30–2.30 Sat.

A Sentimental Orientation

In spite of everything, more of the lost world of al-Andalus can be seen in Granada than even in Córdoba. Granada stands where the foothills of the Sierra Nevada meet the fertile 'Vega de Granada', the greenest and best stretch of farmland in Andalucía. Two of those hills extend into the city itself. One bears the **Alhambra**, the fortified palace of the Nasrid kings, and the other the **Albaicín**, the most evocative of the 'Moorish' neighbourhoods of Andalucían cities. Parts of old Karnattah extended down into the plain, but they have been largely submerged into the new city. How much you enjoy Granada will depend largely on how successful you are in ignoring the new districts, in particular three barbarically ugly streets that form the main automobile route through Granada: the **Gran Vía Colón** chopped through the centre of town in the 19th century, the **Calle Reyes Católicos** and the **Acera del Darro**. The last two are paved over the course of the Río Darro, the little stream that ran picturesquely through the city until the 1880s.

Before these streets were built, the centre of Granada was the **Plaza Nueva**, a square that is also partly built over the Darro. The handsome building that defines its character is the **Audiencia** (1584), built by Felipe II for the royal officials and judges. **Santa Ana** church, across the plaza, was built in 1537 by Diego de Siloé, one of the architects of Granada's cathedral. From this plaza the ascent to the Alhambra begins, up a narrow street called the **Cuesta de Gomerez**, past guitar-makers' shops, gypsies and vast displays of tourist trinkets, ending abruptly at the **Puerta de las Granadas**, a monumental gateway erected by Carlos V.

The Alhambra

Open Mon–Sat 9–7.45, Sun 9–5.45; also open Tue, Thur and Sat eve 10–11.45pm (summer), 8–10pm (mid season); adm 600 pts (museums excluded), free on Sun after 3pm. Due to demand arrive early to buy ticket direct or reserve one the day before on © (958) 22 09 12.

The grounds of the Alhambra begin here with a bit of the unexpected. Instead of the walls and towers, not yet even in view, there is a lovely grove of great elms, the **Alameda**; even more unexpectedly, they are the contribution of the Duke of Wellington, who took time off from chasing the French to plant them during the Peninsular War. Take the path to the left—it's a stiff climb—and in a few minutes you'll arrive at the **Puerta de Justicia**, entrance of the Alhambra. The orange tint of the fortress walls explains the name *al-hamra* (the vermilion), and the unusual style of the carving on the gate is the first clue that here is something very different. The two devices, a hand and a key, carved on the inner and outer arches, are famous. According to one of Irving's tales, the hand will one day reach down and grasp the key; then the Alhambra will fall into ruins, the earth will open, and the hidden treasures of the Moors will be revealed.

From the gate, a path leads up to a broad square. Here are the ticket booth and the **Puerta del Vino**, so called from a long-ago Spanish custom of doling out free wine from this spot to the inhabitants of the Alhambra. To the left you'll see the walls of the **Alcazaba**, the fort at the tip of the Alhambra's narrow promontory, and to the right the huge **Palacio de Carlos V**; signs point your way to the entrance of the **Casa Real** (Royal Palace), with its splendidly decorated rooms that are the Alhambra's main attraction. Try and go after dark; seeing it under the stars is the treat of a lifetime.

THE PUERTA DEL VINO, EAST SIDE, ALHAMBRA.

The Alcazaba

Not much remains of the oldest part of the Alhambra. This citadel probably dates back to the first of the Nasrid kings. Its walls and towers are still intact, but only the foundations of the buildings that once stood within it have survived. The **Torre de la Vela** at the tip of the promontory has the best views over Granada and the Vega. Its big bell was rung in the old days to signal the daily opening and closing of the water gates of the Vega's irrigation system; the Moors also used the tower as a signal post for sending messages. The Albaicín, visible on the opposite hill, is a revelation: its rows of white, flat-roofed houses on the hillside, punctuated by palm trees and cypresses, provide one of Europe's most exotic urban landscapes.

Casa Real (Royal Palace)

Palace visits are limited to ½hr and the time must be specified at time of ticket purchase, otherwise it will be arranged for approximately 1½hrs later.

Words will not do, nor will exhaustive descriptions help, to communicate the experience of this greatest treasure of al-Andalus. This is what people come to Granada to see, and it is the surest, most accessible window into the refinement and subtlety of the culture of Moorish Spain—a building that can achieve in its handful of rooms what a work like Madrid's Royal Palace cannot even approach with its 2,800.

It probably never occurs to most visitors, but one of the most unusual features of this palace is its modesty. What you see is what the Nasrid kings saw, and your imagination need add only a few carpets and tapestries, some well-crafted furniture of wood inlaid with ivory, wooden screens and grilles, and big round braziers of brass for heat or incense, to make the picture complete. Most of the actual building is wood and plaster, cheap and perishable, like a World Fair pavilion; no good Muslim monarch would offend Allah's sense of propriety by pretending that these worldly splendours were anything more than the pleasures of a moment (much of the plaster, wood, and all of the tiles, are the products of careful restorations over the last 100 years). The Alhambra, in fact, is the only substantially intact medieval Muslim palace—anywhere.

Like so many old royal palaces (those of the Hittites, the Byzantines or the Ottoman Turks, for example), this one is divided into three sections: one for everyday business of the palace and government; the next, more secluded, for the state rooms and official entertainments of the kings; and the third, where few outsiders ever reached, for the private apartments of the king and his household.

The Mexuar

Of the first, the small Mexuar, where the kings would hold their public audiences, survives near the present-day entrance to the palace complex. The adjacent **Patio del Mexuar**, though much restored, is one of the finest rooms of the Alhambra. Nowhere is the meditative serenity of the palace more apparent (unless you arrive when all the tour groups do) and the small fountain in the centre provides an introduction to an important element of the architecture—water. Present everywhere, in pools, fountains and channels, water is as much a part of the design as the wood, tile, and stone.

Patio de los Arrayanes

If you have trouble finding your way around, remember the elaborately decorated portals never really lead anywhere; the door you want will always be tucked unobtrusively to the side; here, as in Sevilla's Alcázar, the principle is to heighten the sense of surprise. The entrance to the grand Patio de los Arrayanes (Court of the Myrtles), with its long goldfish pond and lovely arcades, is one of these. This was the centre of the second, state section of the palace; directly off it, you pass through the **Sala de la Barca** (Hall of the Boat), so called from its hull-shaped wooden ceiling, and into the **Salón de Embajadores** (Hall of the Ambassadors), where the kings presided over all important state business. The views and the decoration are some of the Alhambra's best, with a cedarwood ceiling and plaster panels (many were originally painted) carved with floral arabesques or Arabic calligraphy. These inscriptions, some Koranic scripture (often the phrase 'Allah alone conquers', the motto of the Nasrids), some eulogies of the kings, and some poetry, recur throughout the palace. The more conspicuous are in a flowing script developed by the Granadan artists; look closely and you will see others, in the angular Kufic script, forming frames for the floral designs.

In some of the chambers off the Patio de los Arrayanes, you can peek out over the domed roofs of the baths below; opposite the Salón de Embajadores is a small entrance (often closed) into the dark, empty **crypt** of the Palacio de Carlos V, with curious echo effects.

Patio de los Leones

Another half-hidden doorway leads you into the third and most spectacular section, the king's residence, built around the Patio de los Leones (Court of the Lions). Here the plaster and stucco work is at its most ornate, the columns and arches at their most delicate, with little pretence of any structural purpose; balanced on their slender shafts, the façades of the court seem to hang in the air. As in much of Moorish architecture, the almost overripe

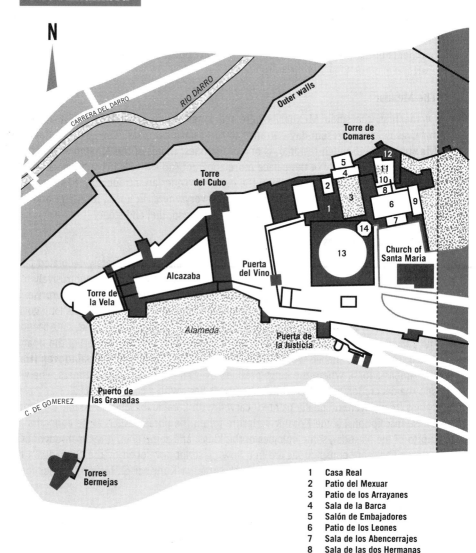

The Alhambra

N

RIO DARRO

CARRERA DEL DARRO

Outer walls

Torre de Comares

Torre del Cubo

5
4
2
1
3
12
11
10
8
6
9
7
14
13

Church of Santa Maria

Puerta del Vino

Alcazaba

Torre de la Vela

Alameda

Puerta de la Justicia

Puerto de las Granadas

C. DE GOMEREZ

Torres Bermejas

1   Casa Real
2   Patio del Mexuar
3   Patio de los Arrayanes
4   Sala de la Barca
5   Salón de Embajadores
6   Patio de los Leones
7   Sala de los Abencerrajes
8   Sala de las dos Hermanas

arabesques of this patio conceal a subtle symbolism. The 'enclosed garden' that can stand for the attainment of truth, or paradise, or for the cosmos, is a recurring theme in Islamic mystical poetry. Here you may take the 12 endearingly preposterous lions who support the fountain in the centre as the months, or signs of the zodiac, and the four channels that flow out from the fountains as the four corners of the cosmos, the cardinal points, or on a different level, the four rivers of paradise.

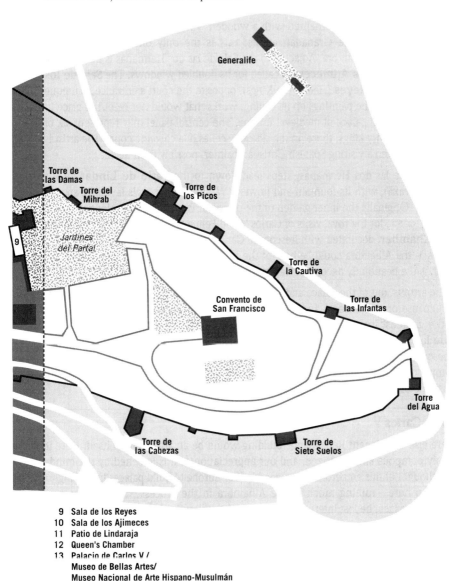

9   Sala de los Reyes
10   Sala de los Ajimeces
11   Patio de Lindaraja
12   Queen's Chamber
13   Palacio de Carlos V /
      Museo de Bellas Artes/
      Museo Nacional de Arte Hispano-Musulmán
14   Chapel and Crypt

The rooms around the patio have exquisite decorations: to the right, from the entrance, the **Sala de los Abencerrajes,** named after the legend of the noble family that Boabdil supposedly had massacred at a banquet here during the civil wars just before the fall of Granada; to the left, the **Sala de las dos Hermanas** (Hall of the Two Sisters). Both of these have extravagant domed *muqarnas* ceilings. The latter chamber is also ornamented with a wooden window grille, another speciality of the Granadan artists; this is the only one surviving in the Alhambra. Adjacent to the Sala de las dos Hermanas is the **Sala de los Ajimeces,** so called for its doubled windows. The **Sala de los Reyes** (Hall of the Kings), opposite the court's entrance, is unique for the paintings on its ceiling, works that would not be out of place in any Christian palace of medieval Europe. The central panel may represent six of Granada's 14th-century kings; those on the side are scenes of a chivalric court. The artist is believed to have been a visiting Spanish Christian painter, possibly from Sevilla.

THE
FOUNTAIN
oF LIoNS,
ALHAMBRA,

From the Sala de las dos Hermanas, steps lead down to the **Patio de Lindaraja** (or Mirador de Daraxa), with its fountain and flowers, Washington Irving's favourite spot in the Alhambra. Originally the inner garden of the palace, it was remodeled, along with the surrounding rooms, for the royal visits of Carlos V and Felipe V. Irving actually lived in the **Queen's Chamber,** decorated with frescoes of Carlos V's expedition to Tunis—in 1829, apartments in the Alhambra could be had for the asking! Just off this chamber, at ground-floor level, is the beautifully decorated **hammam,** the palace baths.

Follow the arrows, out of the palace and into the outer gardens, the **Jardines del Partal,** a broad expanse of rose terraces and flowing water. The northern walls of the Alhambra border the gardens, including a number of well-preserved towers: from the west, the **Torre de las Damas,** entered by a small porch, the **Torre del Mihrab,** near which is a small mosque, now a chapel; the **Torre de los Picos;** the **Torre de la Cautiva** (Tower of the Imprisoned Lady), one of the most elaborately decorated; and the **Torre de las Infantas,** one of the last projects in the Alhambra (*c.* 1400).

Palacio de Carlos V

Anywhere else this elegant Renaissance building would be an attraction in itself. Here it seems only pompous and oversized, and our appreciation of it is lessened by the mind-numbing thought of this emperor, with a good half of Europe to build palaces in, having to plop it down here—ruining much of the Alhambra in the process. Once Carlos had smashed up the place, he lost interest, and most of the still unfinished palace was not built until 1616.

The original architect, Pedro Machuco, had studied in Italy, and he took the opportunity to introduce into Spain the chilly, Olympian High Renaissance style of Rome. At the entrances are intricately detailed sculptural **reliefs** showing scenes from Carlos's campaigns and military 'triumphs' in the antique manner: armoured torsos on sticks amidst heaps of weapons. This is a very particular sort of art, arrogant and weird, and wherever it appears around the Mediterranean, it will usually be associated with the grisly reign of the man who dreamt of being Emperor of the World. Inside, Machuco added a pristinely classical circular courtyard, based perhaps on a design by Raphael. For all its Doric gravity, the patio was used almost from its completion for bullfights and mock tournaments.

The Museums

Open Tues–Fri 10–2, Sat 10–1; adm for each museum 250 pts; Museo de Bellas Artes © (958) 22 48 43; Museo Nacional de Arte Hispano-Musulmán © (958) 22 62 79.

On the top floor of the Palace is the **Museo de Bellas Artes**, a largely forgettable collection of religious paintings and polychromes from Granada churches. Downstairs, the **Museo Nacional de Arte Hispano-Musulmán** contains perhaps Spain's best collection of Moorish art, including some paintings, similar to those in the Moorish palace's Sala de los Reyes. Also present are original *azulejo* tiles and plaster arabesques from the palace, and some exceedingly fine wooden panels and screens. There is a collection of ceramic ware with fanciful figurative decoration—elephants and lady musicians—and some lovely astronomical instruments. Tucked in a corner of the museum are four big copper balls stacked on a pole, an ornament that once stood atop a Granada minaret. These were a typical feature of Andalucían minarets (as on La Giralda in Sevilla) and similar ones can be seen in Morocco today.

Behind Carlos's palace a street leads into the remnants of the town that once filled much of the space within the Alhambra's walls, now reduced to a small collection of restaurants and souvenir stands. In Moorish times the Alhambra held a large permanent population, and even under the Spaniards it long retained the status of a separate municipality. At one end of the street, the church of **Santa María** (1581), designed by Juan de Herrera, architect of El Escorial, occupies the site of the Alhambra's mosque; at the other, the first Christian building on the Alhambra, the **Convento de San Francisco** (1495) has been converted into a *parador.*

Around the Alhambra

The Generalife

Opening hours are the same as for the Alhambra; adm included in Alhambra ticket.

The Generalife (*Djinat al-Arif*: high garden) was the summer palace of the Nasrid kings, built on the height the Moors called the Mountain of the Sun. Many of the trillions of visitors the Alhambra receives each year have never heard of it, and pass up a chance to see the finest garden in Spain. To get there, it's about a 5-minute walk from the Alhambra along a lovely avenue of tall cypresses.

The buildings hold few surprises if you've just come from the Alhambra. They are in fact older than most of the Casa Real, probably begun around 1260. The gardens and the view over the Alhambra and Albaicín are transcendent. They are built on terraces, on several levels along the hillside; in the centre, a long pool under a vista of water sprays passes through beds of roses and an infinite variety of other blooms. A lower level, with a promenade on the hill's edge, is broken up into secluded bowers by cypress bushes cut into angular shapes of walls and gateways. There is no evidence that the original Moorish gardens looked anything like this; everything here was done in the last 200 years.

If you're walking down from the Alhambra, you might consider a different route, across the Alameda and down through the picturesque streets below the **Torres Bermejas**, an outwork of the Alhambra's fortifications built on foundations that may be as old as the Romans. The winding lanes and stairways around Calle del Aire and Calle Niño del Rollo, one of the most beautiful quarters of Granada, will eventually lead you back down near the Plaza Nueva.

Albaicín

Even more than the old quarters of Córdoba, this hillside neighbourhood of whitewashed houses and tall cypresses has successfully preserved some of the atmosphere of al-Andalus. Its difficult site and the fact that it was long the district of Granada's poor explain the lack of change, but today the Albaicín looks as if it is becoming fashionable again.

From the Plaza Nueva, a narrow street called the **Carrera del Darro** leads up the valley of the Darro between the Alhambra and Albaicín hills; here the little stream has not been covered over, and you can get an idea of how the centre of Granada looked in the old days. On the Alhambra side, old stone bridges lead up to a few half-forgotten streets hidden among the forested slopes; here you'll see some 17th-century Spanish houses with curious painted *esgrafiado* façades. Nearby, traces of a horseshoe arch can be seen where a Moorish wall once crossed the river; in the corner of Calle Baruelo there are well-preserved **Moorish baths** (*open Tues–Sat 10–2*). Even more curious is the façade of the **Casa Castril** on the Darro, a flamboyant 16th-century mansion with a portal carved with a phoenix, winged scallop shells and other odd devices that have been interpreted as elements in a complex mystical symbolism. Over the big corner window is an inscription 'Waiting for her from the heavens'. The house's owner, Bernardo de Zafra, was once a secretary to Fernando and Isabel, and seems to have got into trouble with the Inquisition.

Casa Castril has been restored as Granada's **archaeological museum** with a small collection of artefacts from the huge number of caves in Granada province, many inhabited since Paleolithic times, and a few Iberian settlements. There is a Moorish room, with some lovely works of art, and finally, an even greater oddity than Casa Castril itself. One room of the museum holds a collection of beautiful alabaster burial urns, made in Egypt, but found in a Phoenician-style necropolis near Almuñécar. Nothing else like them has ever been discovered in Spain, and the Egyptian hieroglyphic inscriptions on them are provocative in the extreme (translations given in Spanish), telling how the deceased travelled here in search of some mysterious primordial deity (*open daily except Mon, 10–2*).

Further up the Darro, there's a small park with a view up to the Alhambra; after that you'll have to do some climbing, but the higher you go the prettier the Albaicín is, and the better the views. Among the white houses and white walls are some of the oldest Christian churches in Granada. As in Córdoba, they are tidy and extremely plain, built to avoid alienating a recently converted population unused to religious imagery. **San Juan de los Reyes** (1520) on Calle Zafra and **San José** (1525) are the oldest; both retain the plain minarets of the mosques they replaced. Quite a few Moorish houses survive in the Albaicín, and some can be seen on **Calle Horno de Oro**, just off the Darro; on **Calle Daralhorra,** at the top of the Albaicín, are the remains of a Nasrid palace that was largely destroyed for Isabel's **Convento de Santa Isabel la Real** (1501).

Here, running parallel to Cuesta de la Alhacaba is a long-surviving stretch of Moorish wall. There are probably a few miles of walls left, visible around the hillsides over Granada; the location of the city made a very complex set of fortifications necessary. In this one, about halfway up, you may pass through at **Puerta de las Pesas**, with its horseshoe arches. The heart of the Albaicín is here, around the pretty, animated **Plaza Larga**; only a few blocks away the **Mirador de San Nicolás** in front of the church of that name, offers the most romantic view imaginable of the Alhambra with the snow-capped peaks of the Sierra Nevada behind it. Note the brick, barrel-vaulted fountain on the mirador, a typical Moorish survival; fountains like this can be seen throughout the Albaicín and most are still in use. Granada today has a small but growing Muslim community, and they have cleared the ground just off the mirador to build a mosque. Construction hasn't started yet; apparently they are facing some difficulties with the city government.

On your way back from the Albaicín you might take a different route, down a maze of back streets to the **Puerta de Elvira**; this area is one of the most picturesque corners of the neighbourhood.

Sacromonte

For something completely different, you might strike out beyond the Albaicín hill to the **gypsy caves of Sacromonte**. Granada has had a substantial gypsy population for several centuries now. Some have become settled and respectable, others live in trailers on vacant land around town. The most visible are those who prey on the tourists around the Alhambra and the Capilla Real, handing out carnations with a smile and then attempting to extort huge sums out of anyone dumb enough to take one (of course, they'll tell your fortune, too). The biggest part of the gypsy community, however, still lives around Sacromonte in streets of some quite well-appointed cave homes, where they wait to lure you in for a little display of flamenco. For a hundred years or so, the consensus of opinion has been that the music and dancing are usually indifferent, and the gypsies' eventually successful attempts to shake out your last peseta can make it an unpleasantly unforgettable affair. Hotels sell tours for around 2,000 pts. Nevertheless, if you care to match wits with the experts, proceed up the Cuesta del Chapiz from the Río Darro, turn right at the **Casa del Chapiz,** a big 16th-century palace that now houses a school of Arab studies, and keep going until some gypsy child drags you home with him. The bad reputation has been keeping tourists away lately so it's now much safer and friendlier as the gypsies are worried about the loss of income. Serious flamenco fans will probably not fare better elsewhere in Granada except during the festivals, though there are some touristy flamenco nightspots—the **Reina Mora** by Mirador San Cristóbal is the best of them. On the third Sunday of each month, though, you can hear a **flamenco mass** performed in the San Pedro Church on the Carrera del Darro at 9am.

Tortilla al Sacromonte

Regional dishes include cod rissole pottage, chick peas and onions plus, of course, the famous *tortilla al Sacromonte* made from a delightful concoction of brains, lamb's testicles, vegetables and eggs. The name originates from the Sacromonte gypsies. Broad beans Grenadine, cooked with fresh artichokes, tomatoes, onions, garlic, breadcrumbs and a smattering of saffron and cumin may seem less adventurous compared to *Sacromonte* but it's just as typical of Granadinas dishes. If you're in Las Alpujarras, try the fresh goats' cheese and in Trevélez you'll be hard pushed to avoid its famous ham. But if you're west of Granada near Santafé, make a detour to sample its sumptious *piononos—* babas with cream.

Central Granada

The old city wall swung in a broad arc from Puerto de Elvira to the Puerta Real, now a small plaza full of traffic where Calle Reyes Católicos meets the Acera del Darro. Just a few blocks north of here, in a web of narrow pedestrian streets that make up modern Granada's shopping district, is the pretty **Plaza de Bib-**

Rambla, full of flower stands and toy shops, with an unusual fountain supported by leering giants at its centre. This was an important square in Moorish times, used for public gatherings and tournaments of arms. The narrow streets leading off to the east are the **Alcaicería**. This was the Moorish silk exchange, but the buildings you see now, full of tourist souvenir shops, are not original; the Alcaicería burned down in the 1840s and was rebuilt in more or less the same fashion with Moorish arches and columns.

The Cathedral

Plaza de Pasiegas, © (958) 22 29 59; open Mon–Sat 10.30–1 and 4–7, Sun 4–7; adm 200 pts.

The best way to see Granada's **cathedral** is to approach it from Calle Marqués, just north of the Plaza Bib-Rambla. The unique façade, with its three tall, recessed arches, is a striking sight, designed by the painter Alonso Cano (1667). On the central arch, the big plaque bearing the words 'Ave María' commemorates the exploit of the Spanish captain who sneaked into the city one night in 1490 and nailed this message up on the door of the great mosque this cathedral has replaced. The other conspicuous feature is the name 'José Antonio Primo de Rivera' carved on the façade. Son of the 1920s dictator, Miguel Primo de Rivera, José Antonio was a mystic fascist who founded the Phalangist Party. His thugs provoked many of the disorders that started the civil war, and at the beginning of the conflict he was captured by the loyalists and executed. Afterwards his followers treated him as a sort of holy martyr, and chiselled his name on every cathedral in Spain. That you can still see it here says a lot about Granada today.

The rest of the cathedral isn't up to the standard of its façade, and there is little reason to go in and explore its cavernous interior or dreary museum. Work was begun in 1521, after the Spaniards broke their promise not to harm the great mosque. As in many Spanish cathedrals, the failure of this one stems from artistic indecision. Two very talented architects were in charge: Enrique de Egas, who wanted it Gothic, like his adjacent Capilla Real, and 5 years later Diego de Siloé, who decided Renaissance would look much nicer. A score of other architects got their fingers in the pie before the completion in 1703. Some features of the interior: the grandiose **Capilla Mayor**, with statues of the apostles, and of Fernando and Isabel, by Alonso de Mena, and enormous heads of Adam and Eve by Alonso Cano, whose sculptures and paintings can be seen all over the cathedral; the **Retablo de Jesús Nazareno** in the right aisle, with paintings by Cano and Ribera, and a *St Francis* by El Greco; the Gothic **portal** leading into the Capilla Real (now closed) by de Egas. At the foot of the bell tower is a **museum**; its only memorable work is a subject common to the degenerate art of the 1700s—a painted wooden head of John the Baptist.

Capilla Real

Gran Vía de Colón, © (958) 22 92 34; open daily 10.30–1 and 4–7; adm 200 pts.

Leaving the cathedral and turning left, you pass the outsized **sacristy**, begun in 1705 and incorporated in the cathedral façade. Turn left again at the first street, Calle de los Oficios, a narrow lane paved in charming patterns of coloured pebbles—a Granada speciality; on the left, you can pay your respects to *Los Reyes Católicos* in the Capilla Real. The royal couple had already built a mausoleum in Toledo, but after the capture of Granada they decided to plant themselves here. Even in the shadow of the bulky cathedral, Enrique de Egas's chapel (1507) reveals itself as the outstanding work of the Isabelline Gothic style, with its delicate roofline of traceries and pinnacles. Carlos V thought it not nearly monumental enough for his grandparents, and only the distraction of his foreign wars kept him from wrecking it in favour of some elephantine replacement.

Inside, the Catholic Kings are buried under a pair of Carrara marble sarcophagi with their recumbent figures, elegantly carved though not necessarily flattering to either of them. The little staircase behind them leads down to the crypt, where you can peek in at their plain, lead coffins and those of their unfortunate daughter, Juana the Mad, and her husband, Felipe the Handsome, whose effigies lie next to the older couple above. Juana was Carlos V's mother, and the rightful heir to the Spanish throne. There is considerable doubt as to whether she was mad at all; when Carlos arrived from Flanders in 1517, he forced her to sign papers of abdication, and then locked her up in a windowless cell for the last 40 years of her life, never permitting any visitors. The interior of the chapel is sumptuously decorated—it should be, considering the huge proportion of the crown revenues that were expended on it. The iron *reja* by Master Bartolomé de Jaén and the *retablo* are especially fine; the latter is largely the work of a French artist, Phillipe de Bourgogne. In the chapel's sacristy you can see most of Isabel's personal art collection—works by Van der Weyden, Memling, Pedro Berruguete, Botticelli (attributed), Perugino and others, mostly in need of some restoration—as well as her crown and sceptre, her illuminated missal, some captured Moorish banners, and Fernando's sword.

Across the narrow street from the Capilla Real, an endearingly garish, painted Baroque façade hides **La Madraza**, a domed hall of the Moorish *medrese* (university); though one of the best Moorish works surviving in Granada, it is hardly ever open to visitors (just walk in if the building is open). The Christians converted it into a town hall, whence its other name, the Casa del Cabildo.

Across Calle Reyes Católicos

Even though this part of the city centre is as old as the Albaicín, most of it was rebuilt after 1492, and its age doesn't show. The only Moorish building remaining is also the only example left in Spain of a *khan* or *caravanserai*, the type of merchants' hotel common throughout the Muslim world. The 14th-century **Corral del Carbón**, just off Reyes Católicos, takes its name from the time, a century ago, when it was used as a coal warehouse. Under the Spaniards it also served time as a theatre; its interior courtyard with balconies lends itself admirably to the purpose, being about the same size and shape as a Spanish theatre of the classic age, like the one in Almagro (La Mancha). Today it houses a government handicrafts outlet, and much of the building is under restoration.

The neighbourhood of quiet streets and squares behind it is the best part of Spanish Granada and worth a walk if you have the time. Here you'll see the Mudéjar **Casa de los Tiros**, a restored mansion built in 1505 on Calle Pavaneras, with strange figures carved on its façade; it presently houses a **museum** of the city's history. **Santo Domingo** (1512), the finest of Granada's early churches, is just a few blocks to the south. Fernando and Isabel endowed it, and their monograms figure prominently on the lovely façade. This neighbourhood is bounded on the west by the Acera del Darro, the noisy heart of modern Granada, with most of the big hotels. It's a little discouraging, but as compensation, just a block away the city has adorned itself with a beautiful string of wide boulevards very like the Ramblas of Barcelona, a wonderful spot for a stroll. The **Carrera del Genil** usually has some sort of open-air market on it, and further down, the **Paseo del Salón** and **Paseo de la Bomba** are quieter and more park-like, joining the pretty banks of the Río Genil.

Northern Granada

From the little street on the north side of the cathedral, the Calle de la Cárce, Calle de San Jerónimo skirts the edge of Granada's markets and leads you towards the old **university** district. Even though much of the university has relocated to a new campus a half-mile to the north, this is still one of the livelier spots of town, and the colleges themselves occupy some fine, well-restored Baroque structures. The long yellow College of Law is one of the best, occupying a building put up in 1769 for the Jesuits; a small botanical garden is adjacent. Calle de San Jerónimo ends at the Calle del Gran Capitán, where the landmark is the church of **San Juan de Dios**, with a Baroque façade and a big green-and-white tiled dome. **San Jerónimo**, a block west, is another of the oldest and largest Granada churches (1520); it contains the tomb of Gonzalvo de Córdoba, the 'Gran Capitán' who won so many victories in Italy for the Catholic Kings; adjacent are two Gothic cloisters.

Here you're not far from the Puerta de Elvira, in an area where old Granada fades into anonymous suburbs to the north. The big park at the end of the Gran Vía is the **Jardines del Triunfo**, with coloured, illuminated fountains the city hardly ever turns on. Behind them is the Renaissance **Hospital Real**, designed by Enrique de Egas (1504–22). A few blocks southwest, climbing up towards the Albaicín, your senses will be assaulted by the gaudiest Baroque chapel in Spain, in the **Cartuja**, or Carthusian monastery on Calle Real de Cartuja. Gonzalvo de Córdoba endowed this Charterhouse, though little of the original works remain. The 18th-century chapel and its sacristy, done in the richest marble, gold and silver, and painted plaster, fairly oozes with a froth of twisted spiral columns, rosettes and curlicues. It has often been described as a Christian attempt to upstage the Alhambra, but the inspiration more likely comes from the Aztecs, via the extravagant Mexican Baroque (*open daily except Mon, 10–1 and 4–7; © (958) 20 19 32*).

Lorca

Outside Spain Federico García Lorca is popularly regarded as Spain's greatest modern dramatist and poet (*see* Topics, pp. 65–6). The Spanish literati would acknowledge others from the so-called generation of '25 and from the previous generation of '98 to have at least equal stature. The Galician dramatist and poet Valle-Inclán springs to mind. But Lorca's murder certainly enhanced his reputation outside Spain. Under Franco, any mention of him was forbidden (understandably so, since it was Franco's men who shot him). Today the *granadinos* are coming to terms with Lorca, and seem determined to make up for the past. Lorca fans may pay their respects at two country houses, now both museums, where the poet spent much of his early years: the **Huerta de San Vicente**, on the outskirts of town at Virgen Blanca, and the **Museo Lorca** at Fuente Vaqueros, the village where he was born, 17km (10½ miles) away to the west near the Córdoba road (*both open for guided tours every hour, 10–1 and 6–8, daily except Mon*).

Where to Stay

The city centre, around the Acera del Darro, is full of hotels, and there are lots of inexpensive *hostales* around the Gran Vía—but the less you see of these areas the better. Fortunately, you can choose from a wide range around the Alhambra and in the older parts of town if you spend the time to look.

expensive

Right in the Alhambra itself, the ★★★★**Parador Nacional San Francisco**, © (958) 22 14 40, fax 22 22 64, is perhaps the most famous of all *paradors*, housed in a convent where Queen Isabel was originally interred. It's beautiful, expensive, and small—you'll always need to book well in advance (doubles 22,000 pts). Alternative choices very near the Alhambra would be the outrageously florid, neo-Moorish ★★★★**Alhambra Palace**, Calle Peña Portida 2, © (958) 22 14 68, fax 22 64 04, where most rooms have terrific views over the city (doubles with TV, air conditioning 17,600 pts). The ★★★★**Hotel Triunfo–Granada**, © (958) 20 74 44, fax 27 90 17, stands by the Moorish Puerta de Elvira at the foot of the Albaicín. It's a quiet place with a restaurant that's popular with locals (17,760 pts).

moderate

The old ★★★**Washington Irving**, Paseo del Generalife 2, © (958) 22 75 50, fax 22 88 40, is a little faded but still classy (doubles 9,900 pts). On the slopes below the Alhambra you can get a pool and air conditioning at ★★★**Los Ángeles**, Cuesta Escoriaza 17, © (958) 22 14 24, fax 22 21 25 (doubles 9,000 pts). There's one other hotel in the Alhambra, the ★**Hotel América**, Real de la Alhambra 53, © (958) 22 74 71, fax 22 74 70, with simple, pretty rooms for 8,600 pts and a delightful garden and patio, but as for the *parador*, book well in advance.

inexpensive

For inexpensive *hostales*, the first place to look is the Cuesta de Gomerez, the street leading up to the Alhambra from Plaza Nueva. Besides the ★★**Britz**, at no. 1, © (958) 22 36 52 (4,000 pts with bath, 2,400 pts without) and the ★**Gomerez**, at no. 10, © (958) 22 44 37 (2,000 pts no bath), both nice, there are plenty of other spots nearby. Off Calle San Juan de Dios, in the university area, there are dozens of small *hostales* used to accommodating students. The ★**San Joaquín**, Calle Mano de Hierro, © (958) 28 28 79, is one, with a pretty patio (3,000 pts double with bath). Centrally placed is the immaculate *hostal* ★★**Lisboa**, Plaza del Carmen 29, © (958) 22 14 13 (4,500 pts).

Eating Out

Granada isn't known for its cuisine. There are too many touristy places around the Plaza Nueva, with little to distinguish between them.

expensive

Best known and best loved is the famous **Sevilla**, Calle Oficios 12, © (958) 22 12 23, where García Lorca often met fellow poets and intellectuals. The character of the restaurant has been preserved and the specialities remain the local dishes of Granada and Andalucía (3,000–4,000 pts; closed Sun eve). Both are near the cathedral. Some of the finest cooking in Granada can be found at the **Ruta del Veleta** on the Ctra de la Sierra, Km 50, 5km (3 miles) away from the city towards the Sierra Nevada. Dishes include partridge with onion ragout and salad of angler fish with vegetable stuffing (5,000 pts).

moderate

The *granadinos* trust dining out at **Cunini**, Plaza de Pescadería 14, © (958) 25 07 77, where the menu depends on availability (2,500–3,500 pts; closed Mon). For agreeable dining in an intimate family-run restaurant, there is none better in Granada than **Mesón Antonio**, Ecce Homo 6, © (958) 22 95 99, serving international dishes of meat and fish (2,500 pts; closed Sun, July and Aug). You should try to get up to the Albaicín for dinner on at least one night. The **Mirador de Morayma**, Callejón de las Vacas 2, Albaicín, © (958) 22 82 90, is in a charming 16th-century house with views over the Alhambra from the top-floor dining room; *la sopa de espárragos verdes de Huétor* (asparagus soup) is particularly good and leave room for an Andaluz pudding (3,000 pts; closed Sun eve).

inexpensive

Everyone's favourite rock-bottom, filling 650 pts menu is served up at the tiny **Cepillo** on Calle Pescadería. It's a few doors away from the Cunini and is one of the few places where you can get paella for one—order fish or squid. For *bocadillos* (hot and cold sandwiches) try **Bar Aliatar** in a small street between Plaza de Bib-Rambla and Calle Reyes Católicos. If you like ice creams, head for **Los Italianos** at Gran Vía 4. Delicious.

The Sierra Nevada and Las Alpujarras

From everywhere in Granada, the mountains peer over the tops of buildings. Fortunately, Spain's loftiest peaks are also its most accessible; from the city centre you can be riding on Europe's highest mountain road in a little more than an hour. Even if you're without a car, there's a daily bus from town that makes the Sierra Nevada an easy day trip.

Dress warmly, though. As the name implies, the Sierra Nevada is snow-bound nearly all year, and even in late July and August, when the road is clear and you can travel right over the mountains to the valley of Las Alpujarras, it's as chilly and windy as you would expect it to be, some 3,300m (10,800ft) above sea level. These mountains, a geological curiosity of sorts, are just an over-sized chunk of the Penibetic System, the chain that stretches from Arcos de la Frontera almost to Murcia. Their highest peak, **Mulhacén**

ROCK FLOWERS
SIERRA NEVADA.

(3,481m), is less than 40km (25 miles) from the coast. From Granada you can see nearly all of the Sierra: a jagged snowy wall without really distinctive peaks. The highest expanses are barren and frosty, but on a clear day they offer a view to Morocco. Mulhacén and especially its sister peak **Veleta** (3,392m) can be climbed without too much exertion; the road goes right by Veleta, and in August you can even drive to the top.

Getting Around

For the Sierra Nevada, there is a daily **bus** from the Bar El Ventorrillo, in Granada's Paseo del Violón, to the Albergue Universitario some 12km (7½ miles) from the peak of Veleta. Departures are at 9am, returning at 5. Bus **tours** are run by Ecomar, © (958) 22 30 24, and Gran A Visión, © (958) 20 98 34; check at the Granada tourist office for other companies. Most of them cost around 3,000 pts and only run at weekends, provided there are enough passengers. If you're going by **car**, the road is open in August; it's a rough trip but worth it for the views. **Road snow reports**: in English and Spanish, © (958) 48 01 53. Some 20km (12½ miles) before you reach Veleta, you'll enter the **Solynieve** ski area, beginning at its main resort, **Pradollano**, and continuing up to Veleta. From Pradollano there are cable cars up to the peak itself.

For Las Alpujarras: some **buses** on the Granada–Motril route stop in Lanjarón, but to penetrate the more isolated sections of the valley, you'll have to take a bus from Granada to Orjiva, the base for connecting buses to the other villages.

For destinations further east, the Bacoma line (from Avenida de los Andaluces in front of Granada's train station) runs daily **buses** to Murcia and Alicante which stop in Guadix.

Tourist Information

For skiing information contact the tourist office in Granada or the Federación Andaluza de Esquí, Paseo de Ronda 78, © (958) 25 07 06.

If you're adventurous and the road is clear, you can continue onwards from Veleta down into **Las Alpujarras**, a string of white villages along the valley of the Río Guadalfeo, between the Sierra Nevada and the little Contraviesa chain along the sea coast. In Moorish times this was a densely populated region, full of vines and orchards. Much of its population was made up of refugees from the Reconquista, coming mainly from Sevilla. Under the conditions for Granada's surrender in 1492, the region was granted as a fief to Boabdil el Chico, but with forced Christianization and the resulting revolts, the entire population was expelled and replaced by settlers from the north.

RANUNCULUS
ACETOSELLIFOLIUS
RARE BUTTERCUP
OF SIERRA NEVADA

Though often described as one of the most inaccessible corners of Spain, this region has attracted growing numbers of visitors since Gerald Brenan wrote *South from Granada*. The roads wind past stepped fields, cascades of water, high pastures and sudden drops, and when the almond trees are in blossom it is at its most appealing. Unlike the rest of Andalucían villages with their red-tiled roofs, the *pueblos* of Las Alpujarras are flat-roofed. Far from the beaten track, you won't be alone if you visit Las Alpujarras. Nevertheless, they're hardly spoiled; and with the villages relatively close to each other, and plenty of wild country on either side, it's a great spot for hiking or just finding some well-decorated peace and quiet.

Most visitors don't chance the Sierra Nevada route to Capileira, but use the front door to Las Alpujarras, off the main road from Granada to Motril. On the way, just outside the city, you'll pass the spot called **Suspiro de Moro**, where poor Boabdil sighed as he took his last look back over Granada. His mother was less than sympathetic—'Weep like a woman for what you were incapable of defending like a man,' she told him. The last 33km (20½ miles) of this route, where the road joins the Guadalfeo valley down to Motril, is one of the most scenic in Spain, but if you want to seeLas Alpujarras, you'll have to take the turn-off for **Lanjarón**, the only real tourist centre of the region. Lanjarón has long attracted visitors as a spa, and today it ships out most of the mineral water drunk in Spain. At **Orjiva**, the biggest town of Las Alpujarras, is the **castle** of the Counts of Sástago, and a Renaissance church with a carving by Martínez Montañés. One other feature is the **Benizalte mill**, just outside the town.

From here you'll have a choice of keeping to the main road for **Ugíjar**, or heading north through the highest and loveliest part of the region, with typical white villages climbing the hillsides under terraced fields. **Soportújar**, the first, has one of Las Alpujarras' surviving primeval oak groves behind it. Next comes **Pampaneira**, a pretty little town of cobbled streets and flowers. In the Plaza Mayor there's a **museum** dedicated to the customs and costumes of Las Alpujarras. **Bubión** is a Berber-style village with an old textile mill.

All these villages are within sight of each other on a short detour along the edge of the beautiful (but walkable) ravine called **Barranco de Poqueira**. **Capileira**, the last village on the mountain-pass route over Mulhacén and Veleta, sees more tourists than most. North from here the road takes you up across the Sierra Nevada and eventually to Granada. In winter this pass is snowbound, and even in summer you need to take extra care—it's steep and dangerous with precipitous drops down the ravines. However, the beautiful scenery makes the risks worthwhile. Alternatively, continue on the GR421 to **Pitres**, centre of a Hispano-Japanese joint venture that produces and exports handcrafted ballet shoes—of all things.

The road carries on through the villages of **Pórtugos** and **Busquistar** before arriving in **Trevélez**, on the slopes of Mulhacén. Trevélez likes to claim it's the highest village in Europe. It's also famous in Andalucía for its snow-cured hams. From there the road slopes back downwards to Juviles and **Bérchules**, one of the villages where the traditional art of carpet weaving has been maintained since Moorish times. **Yegen**, some 10km (6¼ miles) further, became temporarily famous as the long-time home of British writer Gerald Brenan. After that come more intensively farmed areas on the lower slopes, with oranges, vineyards and almonds; you can either hit Ugíjar and the main roads to the coast and Almería, or detour to the seldom-visited villages of **Laroles** and **Mairena** on the slopes of

La Ragua, one of the last high peaks of the Sierra Nevada. Further east, through countryside that rapidly changes from healthy green to dry brown, the village of **Fondón** is of particular interest; an Australian architect, Donald Grey, and his Spanish partner, José Antonio Garvayo, have set up a school to teach the traditional crafts of ironwork, carpentry, tile- and brick-making, so most of the buildings have been restored, and Fondón is now a model village.

Around the Sierra Nevada

It's a better road entering Granada from the west than that leaving it to the east. Between the city and Murcia are some of the emptiest, bleakest landscapes in Spain. The first village you pass through is **Purullena**, long famous for its pretty ceramic ware; the entire stretch of highway through it is lined with enormous stands and displays. The poverty of this region has long forced many of its inhabitants to live in caves, and nowhere more so than in **Guadix**. Several thousand of this city's population, most of them gypsies, have homes complete with whitewashed façades built into the hillsides, and chimneys and television aerials sticking out of the top. The cave dwellings have their advantages: they're warmer in the winter and cooler in summer than most Andalucían homes, relatively spacious and well ventilated—and when the time comes to build a new room, all you need is a pick and shovel.

The centre of Guadix is dominated by a Moorish **Alcazaba**, largely rebuilt in the 16th century; near the arcaded central **Plaza Mayor** stands the huge **cathedral**, begun by Diego de Siloé, builder of Granada's cathedral, and given its magnificent façade in the 1700s by Andalucía's great rococo eccentric, Vicente Acero. The ornate traceries of the church, and the imposing castle, appearing together out of the empty, queerly eroded hills make a striking sight.

There's not much else to distract you in this corner of Spain. If you're headed for Almería and the coast (N324), you'll pass near **La Calahorra**, with an unusual Renaissance castle with domed turrets, and **Gérgal**, whose equally singular, perfectly preserved castle was built by the Moors. They claim you can see the stars more clearly here than anywhere in Europe, and Spain has built its national observatory outside town. The N342 from Guadix west to Murcia is even lonelier; here the surprisingly elegant, little whitewashed villages of

LA CALAHORRA
SIERRA NEVADA

Vélez Blanco and Vélez Rubio will provide a pleasant break in your travels. There are several caves in the neighbourhood where a wealth of 4,000-year-old rock paintings of abstract patterns and symbols have been found.

Where to Stay

Sierra Nevada

Most of the ski hotels close from June to December. Ask at the tourist office in Granada for what's available, or contact the Cetursa Reservation Centre in Pradollano, © (958) 24 91 11. An exception, staying open all year round, is the ★★★**Parador Nacional Sierra Nevada**, on the main highway, © (958) 48 02 00, fax 48 02 12 (doubles 9,000 pts), one of the smaller and newer *paradores*. Among the five modern hotels in the ski resort of Pradollano, none particularly stands out; in the skiing season accommodation at these places means a week's stay on half board for 80,000–110,000 pts per person (instruction extra). In summer months the very pleasant hotel ★**Telecabina**, Plaza de Pradollano, © (958) 24 91 20, fax 24 91 22, has doubles for 8,200 pts. The alpine style ★★★**Kenia Nevada**, © (958) 48 09 11, fax 48 08 07, has a jacuzzi, pool, gymnasium and sauna for those stiff days on the slopes (7,400–14,500 pts). Cheaper accommodation can be had at Peñones de San Francisco, at the end of the bus route, where the **Albergue Universitario**, © (958) 48 01 22, has rooms for 3,000 pts half-board.

Las Alpujarras

Lanjarón has most of the rooms; a score of good bargains in the 2,000–3,000 pts range on or near the central Calle Generalísimo Franco. Elsewhere, you'll find minimal though acceptable accommodation and food in Orjiva, Pampaneira, Capileira and Ugíjar. In Pórtugos is the ★**Mirador de Portugos**, © (958) 76 60 14 (5,500 pts, doubles with bath). The **Hostal Mulhacén**, Ctra Ugíjar, © (958) 85 85 87, in Trevélez is well situated for hill walks and the annual all-night pilgrimage up Spain's highest mountain at midnight on August 4th. The *hostal* is also beside the river, where locals swim during the summer (5,000 pts).

Eating Out

Sierra Nevada

Most restaurants are open only in the skiing season, and most are a little preten-tious. **Rincón de Pepe Reyes** in Pradollano has good Andaluz cooking for 2,000–3,000 pts. You can take the cable car up to the **Borreguiles** café/restau-rant, © (958) 48 00 79, half-way up Veleta, and sit out on the terrace to take in the view. In Solynieve, there is **Cunini** (sister restaurant to the Cunini in Granada), Edificio Bulgaria, Prado Largo, © (958) 48 01 70, serving fish and some Castilian meat dishes (3,500 pts; closed May–Nov). Also in Edificio Bulgaria is **Ruta de Veleta**, © (958) 48 12 28 (4,000 pts).

In Trevélez, **Mesón Haraiçel**, © (958) 85 85 30, serves delicious Arabic-influenced food with plenty of almond sauces and meat dishes. Try a *soplillo* for dessert (a honey and almond meringue for 80 pts). A three-course meal will cost around 1,500 pts.

Gibraltar

At first sight it looks like a sphynx, crouching at the water's edge, her hindquarters resting in Europe, her head gazing over the sea and her forepaws stretching in front of her to form the most southerly part of our continent.

Alexandre Dumas, 1846

In under two hours, you can experience the ultimate culture shock: sailing from the smoky souks of Tangier to Algeciras, Spain, with time for *churros* and chocolate before the bus takes you off to a mysterious enclave of red phone booths, warm beer and policemen in silly hats.

The Spanish bus will really take you only as far as **La Línea** ('the Line', named after Gibraltar's old land walls), a lively, fun town that has built up dramatically since the reopening of the Gibraltar border in 1985. Prices in Gibraltar are outrageous by Spanish standards, and La Línea may be the best place to stay while you visit. It's just a short walk through the **neutral zone** into Gibraltar, where immediately you'll be confronted with one of the Rock's curiosities: as you enter British territory you find yourself looking down the noses of 737s and Tridents. Where else has a busy street crossing an airport runway? The airport, built on landfill at right angles to the narrow peninsula, symbolizes British determination to hold on during the years Franco was putting the squeeze on Gibraltar, and also points up the enclave's biggest problem— lack of space.

As well as large numbers of cigarette smugglers who cross the border with regularity, British residents living on Spanish soil cross in droves to stock up with life's comforts—items either unobtainable in Spain, or just too expensive—baked beans and Christmas crackers, cheddar cheese and headache pills, pickled onions, liver salts. Smugglers are even known to drive into Gibraltar with an empty tank, fill up with petrol (which is much cheaper than in Spain) only to recross the border, syphon off the petrol for resale, and return to Gibraltar. This often adds to the border queues, known as 'the loop', which can vary from a couple of vehicles to a three-hour tailback, depending on how thorough customs decide to be. Other more discreet visitors come over to bank their 'black' (undeclared) money made in Spain, and take advantage of the no-questions-asked, tax-free, offshore banking. Needless to say, this gets the goat of the Spanish tax man.

The other gripe is the political status of the Rock itself. Spain is like the little boy who kicks his ball in to next door's garden; Britain, the grouchy old bachelor who says, 'I'm keeping it.' The question of the Rock's sovereignty comes up annually; Spain asks for concessions, Whitehall merely smiles and says, 'Sorry, old chap.'

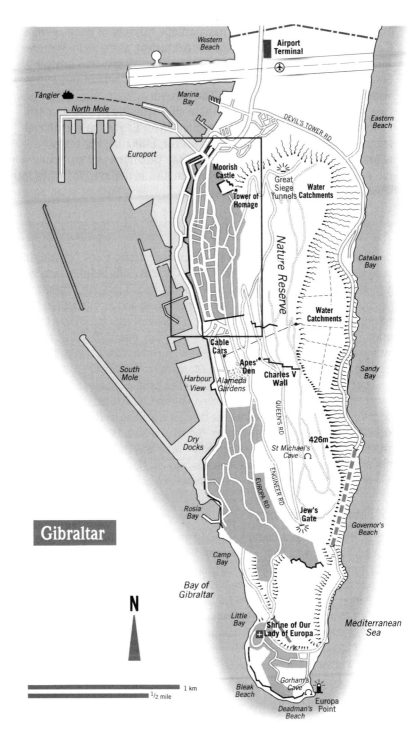

Gibraltar

You'll soon find that Gibraltar has a unique mixture of people—mostly Genoese (who have been around for centuries), along with Maltese, Indians, Spaniards, Jews and Moroccans, all as British as Trafalgar Square; when a referendum on joining Spain was held in the 1960s, they voted it down by 99.6 per cent. The dissenters were tagged *Las Palomas* (the White Doves), and some of these subsequently flew to Spanish climes; they are not missed in Gibraltar. With English as the official language, most Gibraltarians are, however, bilingual. For many Gibraltarians, Spanish is used in everyday situations and particularly in moments of high emotion and anger; English is reserved for more formal situations.

History

Some 50,000 years ago, when Spain was a cooler, more forested place, Neanderthal man was minding his own business in the caves around Gibraltar, long before Palaeo-Spaniards found the rest of Andalucía to be of any interest . The Rock's location, where the continents of Europe and Africa rub noses and the Atlantic Ocean and Mediterranean Sea meet, is one of the world's most important crossroads; as a consequence it has been fought over for centuries. *Calpe*, as the Greeks knew it, was, of course, one of the Pillars of Hercules, beyond which the jealous Phoenicians would permit no other nation's ships to trade. The other, less dramatic, pillar is Mount Abyla in Morocco (visible across the straits on clear days). The Phoenicians could well have been the first people to pass through the straits into the Atlantic and it is believed they reached England. They used the Rock solely as a naval base and never seriously entertained the thought of settling there, preferring the more hospitable land near the Bay. Similarly, under Roman rule from 190 BC onwards there was no permanent settlement on the Rock. Six hundred years later the Vandal and Gothic tribes surged through the Iberian Peninsula on their way to North Africa, followed by the Visigoths, who remained as the most powerful local force until the late 7th century AD.

711–1462: Muslim Ascendancy

By the beginning of the 8th century the Moors were poised to invade the Iberian Peninsula, under the new and forceful banner of Islam. Having swept westward through North Africa from Arabia, forcibly converting the subjugated population, the Moors landed a small expeditionary force at what is now Tarifa in 710. The following year, Tariq ibn-Ziyad led a Berber army of 7,000 men to the Rock that came to bear his name—*Jebel Tarik* (Tariq's Mountain). For the following six centuries Gibraltar remained under Moorish rule. As the Moors moved further north, Gibraltar remained a vital camp, but it was not until 1160 that any sort of permanent settlement was established, under the orders of Abdul Mamen, caliph of Morocco.

Throughout the Moorish occupation of Andalucía, Gibraltar faced a number of sieges at the hands of Moorish caliphs fighting amongst themselves over its control and Christian

Spaniards trying to win it back. Guzmán el Bueno seized it for Castile in 1309, and in the centuries that followed it was one of the major battlegrounds of the Mediterranean. It was not until 1462 that the Rock was finally wrested from the Moorish grasp by Enrico IV, king of Castile.

1462–1704: The Key of Spain

In 1469 a royal decree proclaimed the son of the Duke of Messina as the rightful owner. (The day of liberation was 29 August, the feast day of St Bernard, the patron saint of Gibraltar.) Grateful Queen Isabel granted the Rock a coat of arms, still used today, with the inscription 'Seal of the Noble City of Gibraltar, the Key of Spain'.

During this time of Spanish occupation the town was divided into three districts: *Villavieja* (the old town), *Barcina* ('wicker basket'— one was used to display the remains of the captured Count of Niebla) and *Turba*, which can be translated as 'mob'; but these names have now disappeared. This was a fairly tranquil period by Gibraltarian standards, until one fine autumn day in 1540 when, as the townsfolk were going about their daily business, a tremendous fleet of 16 galleys, manned by 2,000 men, took them by surprise. These were the hordes of the infamous Barbarossa, who operated out of North African bases, raiding ships for goods and slaves; the pirates had decided to break with tradition and sack Gibraltar, having heard of the great booty to be gained.

The horror of that day stands out in Gibraltar's chequered history—a day of slaughter, rape and looting. Some were lucky enough to escape the carnage in the safety of the castle, but most were either killed or taken into slavery. The pirates headed straight for the Shrine of Our Lady of Europa at Europa Point and the Franciscan convent in the town (both well stocked with gold, jewels and precious coins) and stripped them bare, before making off across the Bay for further pillaging and merrymaking. Over-confidence proved to be their undoing, for the Christian fleet anchored in Tarifa had time to sail along the coast and cut off their escape route. A bloody battle ensued, and what was left of Barbarossa's mob fled back to the sanctuary of its North African ports with just 75 captives in tow. But Gibraltar was left in ruins. From this time on, the Rock was heavily fortified and became an important naval base for Spain's explorations to the Americas, but life was far from peaceful, as a pirate of a different ilk, Sir Francis Drake, would drop in occasionally to 'singe the king of Spain's beard'.

The beginning of the 18th century brings us to the War of the Spanish Succession, with Britain on the side of Spain against the French. Admiral Sir George Rooke, commanding the Anglo-Dutch fleet, tried to take Toulon and Barcelona, and having failed on both counts took Gibraltar instead. At the time (1704), it was held by forces loyal to the French claimant to the Spanish throne. Rooke offered the inhabitants two choices—to pack their bags and leave, or swear allegiance to the Hapsburg claimant. Most opted for the former, probably hoping that the tide of war would change; they may also have heard of the Royal Navy's reputation—'valiant at sea, horrendous on shore'.

1704 to the present: British Colonial Rule

With Gibraltar in British hands, the grateful Hapsburgs handed it over 'in perpetuity' as a reward, under the 1713 Treaty of Utrecht. It was a crucial acquisition; Britain's imperial expansion across the Mediterranean would have been inconceivable without it. Peace did not last long, however, and the Spanish, regretting their impulsive generosity, laid siege to the Rock with the aid of French forces in 1727. Great destruction was again suffered by the town, and the area around what is today Casemates Square was completely flattened.

It is from this point that we can trace the mixed heritage of the present population, for after the disappearance of the original Spanish inhabitants it became necessary to import a workforce from various parts of the Mediterranean, especially Genoa. The British made great use of this force to strengthen the city's defences. Ragged Staff Wharf was constructed, new barracks were built and a number of Spanish churches were turned into accommodation for the troops. New batteries were put up—Montague, Orange and King's Bastion, Devil's Tongue on the Old Mole, Grand Battery north of Grand Casemates with the adjacent Couvreport and King's Lines above, Willis's, Catalan and Green's Lodge Batteries on the Upper Rock, and the Advance Batteries at Europa Point.

The Great Siege 1779–83

The preparations proved justified. In 1779 a combined Spanish and French force began the worst siege ever experienced by the population. Yet both fortifications and people endured under the command of Lord Heathfield, and the phrase 'safe as the Rock of Gibraltar' came into common use as a result. Gibraltar's rock tunnels and galleries also date from this time. Their construction allowed the gun batteries to take up defensive positions at more commanding heights. The tunnelling continued after the Great Siege, opening up what is known as St George's Hall, a large chamber under 'the Notch'. Now there are about 48km (30 miles) of tunnels; Gibraltar is still very well defended.

The Napoleonic Wars 1799–1815

After a decade of uneasy peace the Gibraltarians were once again in the thick of things—this time at the outbreak of the Napoleonic Wars between Britain and France. For once, Spain was an ally, and it can even be assumed that the people of the Rock actively welcomed the hostilities. Business perked up remarkably—repairing ships, supplying the Royal Navy with food and ammunition, and auctioning off contents of ships captured by the British fleet. On 21 October 1805, Nelson and his 27 'Wild Geese' triumphed at Trafalgar, an event still celebrated in Gibraltar. The admiral was killed during the engagement and his body, as every schoolboy knows, was borne back to Rosia Bay in a cask of brandy (whence the naval term 'Nelson's Blood'). Ten years later, the end of the war heralded the start of a long period of peace and prosperity for Gibraltar, by which time the population was firmly established in occupations that relied not only on the military presence, but also on external trade.

1814 saw the appointment of Sir George Don to lieutenant governor, a man of considerable calibre. By this time the population had swelled to 10,000, and was badly in need of an efficient civil administration. The new governor embarked on an ambitious programme of improvements: hospitals were built, public gardens laid out, opportunities created for business and trade. Life became peaceful and prosperous.

The World Wars 1914–45

During the two world wars, Gibraltar provided a safe harbour where the Allies could repair ships and replenish stocks. In the second world war many of the civilians were evacuated to safer spots, notably the UK, Madeira, Jamaica and Morocco. (Those who ended up in Morocco were forced to move on again when the Vichy government in France made it clear they were not welcome.) The airstrip was built at this time, which meant the disappearance of the cricket and football pitches, together with the racecourse. The miles of tunnels under the Rock were developed further, and used for food storage, hospitals and miltary headquarters. The invasion of Africa, *Operation Torch*, was spearheaded through Gibraltar, where General Eisenhower and his advisors completed much of the planning.

The Question of Sovereignty

By the time the war ended, the Gibraltarians had developed an even deeper sense of identity, partly through being separated from El Peñón, their homeland. In 1950 the Duke of Edinburgh inaugurated the first elected Legislative Council, and in 1964 Gibraltar was granted domestic autonomy, with the UK retaining responsibility for foreign affairs and defence. The 1968 referendum on sovereignty led to the intro-

RED TELEPHONE BOXES IN GIBRALTAR

duction of a new constitution the following year, which entrenched the British promise never to surrender the sovereignty of Gibraltar against the wishes of her people. As a direct consequence, General Franco closed the border, and it did not open again until 1985. This had a profound effect on the population and served only to strengthen its resolve, and deepen the rift with Spain. Far from being dismayed at the closure of the frontier, many older Gibraltarians were actually disappointed when it was reopened, feeling that they had lost their safe little haven, their isolated 'English village'. They now face the future with some trepidation, always suspicious of their next-door neighbour; they insist on the retention of the wire fence between the two states.

The Future

Space is at a premium in Gibraltar. Most of the prime areas in Gibraltar are owned by the Ministry of Defence (MOD), which has now agreed to confine its operational needs to smaller areas. Since 1990 the scale of the British military presence has been drastically scaled down and the three services amalgamated under one command. To give an indication of the severity of the cuts, in 1983 MOD spending was equal to 78% of Gibraltar's GDP; in 1993 it was equal to 10% and falling. This retrenchment has released a certain amount of land and housing for civilian use.

Nevertheless, existing space was never likely to accommodate the level of growth planned by the socialist GSLP government since it took office in 1988, and the circle is being squared by an ambitious and extensive programme of land reclamation. A large expanse of water south of North Mole has already been reclaimed; a part is earmarked for low-cost state housing, but its main feature is a large complex of commercial offices called Europort. The runway itself is destined for expansion, and the EU has agreed to fund a feasibility study. The reclamation programme has also seen an extension of the industrial zone to the old dockyard region, where new warehousing, light industrial units and ship-repair facilities unite under the name of Harbour View.

The third phase of Gibraltar's expansion caters to tourism and recreation on the Mediterranean side, at Catalan Bay. Here large hotel complexes are envisaged to promote the as yet limited tourist market. To facilitate easier access to this side of the Rock, a three-laned road tunnel will be drilled through its base—the kind of ambitious project at which Gibraltarians have traditionally excelled. It is scheduled to be completed by the mid-1990s, and the spoil will be used for further land reclamation.

These programmes for housing, industrial and commercial enterprise, and tourism are part of an overall government strategy to create a strong economy underpinned by foreign investment, and to double the present population from 30,000 to 60,000. It is a strategy that, if successful, will allow Gibraltar to box above her weight and achieve financial independence from both the UK and Spain, which it is determined to do, though without cutting off its strong cultural ties with the UK.

Getting Around

by air

There are at least three daily flights to London Gatwick, run by GB Airways; twice-weekly flights to Manchester and regular flights to Casablanca and Tangier. GB Airways has check-in facilities at Victoria, meaning you don't see your luggage again till you arrive. **Information**: GB Airways, ✆ (350) 79 300.

by sea

There are two ferries a week from Gibraltar to Tangier (Mon and Fri); three ferries a week from Tangier to Gibraltar (Mon, Fri and Sun). The fares are expensive, like everything else in Gibraltar (one way: £16, child £8; return: £27, child £13.50; day trip: £35, child £17.50). You'd be slightly better off doing it from Algeciras. **Information**: TourAfrica, ✆ (350) 79 140.

There is a direct **bus** service between Gibraltar and the Costa del Sol. Gibraltar's tiny buses, and **taxis**, serve the frontier which is only 800m (½ mile) from the town centre. If you are coming by **car,** leave it in La Línea as there are frequently long delays as customs check the day-trippers' stash of goodies. There is a **taxi tour** of the Rock, taking in all the sites and lasting about 1½ hours. The charge is £8 per person including adm to Nature Reserve; £32 minimum. **Information**: Gibraltar Taxi Association, 12 Waterport, ✆ (350) 70 027.

Tourist Information

Gibraltar Information Bureau: Duke of Kent House, Cathedral Square, ✆ (350) 74 950.

Local information bureaux: Market Place, ✆ (350) 74 982; Gibraltar Museum, 18–20 Bomb House Lane, ✆ (350) 74 289 (all open weekdays 10–6 and Sat 10–2). There are booths within the airport terminal and at Waterport coach park.

The Gibraltar National Tourist Board has recently introduced the **Privilege Key Card**, which allows free unlimited entry to the tourist sights, plus various discounts about town. The card is only available to visitors staying overnight in Gibraltar, and is designed to encourage would-be day-trippers to stop over on the Rock rather than cross back into La Línea, where accommodation is much cheaper.

Currency

The enclave has its own currency (the Gibraltar pound which is tied in value to the pound sterling) and stamps—don't be stuck with any currency when you leave, as it's hard to get rid of anywhere else. These days, most shops and restaurants in Gibraltar are perfectly happy to take British, Spanish or Gibraltarian money.

The Town

... a cosy smell of provincial groceries. I'd forgotten how much the atmosphere of home depended on white bread , soap and soup squares.

Laurie Lee, *As I Walked Out One Midsummer Morning*

Despite a certain amount of bad press, Gibraltar is still much more than just a perfect replica of an English seaside town. The town is long and narrow, strung out along **Main Street** with most of the shops and pubs. The harbour is never more than a couple of blocks away, and the old gates, bastions and walls are fun to explore

The short tunnel at **Landport Gate** will probably be your entry point if on foot; dating from the 18th century, it was for a long time the only entrance by land. It leads to

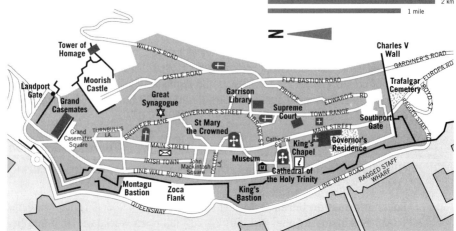

Casemates Square, one-time parade ground and site of public executions, and now an active trading centre. **Grand Casemates** itself, part of the town's defences and barracks, provides seedy accommodation for Gibraltar's 4,000-strong Moroccan labour force, but there are plans to revamp the whole area. **King's Bastion** is now used as an electricity generating station, but probably started out as an ancient Arab Gate, added to by the Spanish in 1575, and further extended in the 18th century by the British under General Boyd. It played an important defensive role at the time of the Great Siege, and it was from this spot that General Elliott commanded during the fierce fighting in 1782. **Ragged Staff Wharf** takes its name not from the sartorial deficiency of its troops, but either from the flagstaff that marked safe passage into the harbour, or from an emblem on the arms of the House of Burgundy.

Near the centre of town, off Line Wall Road, you should spare a few minutes for the small but excellent **Gibraltar Museum**, 18–20 Bomb House Lane, which offers a painstakingly detailed room-sized model of the Rock as it was in the mid-1800s, and a thorough schooling in its complicated history. The museum is built over the remains of a **Moorish bath**, with Roman and Visigothic capitals on its columns. It also contains a replica of the female skull found in Forbes Quarry in 1848, a find that predates the Neanderthal skull found in Germany by 8 years. (Perhaps Neanderthal Man should be known as Gibraltar Woman.) Other exhibits include archaeological finds from Gibraltar's caves; an Egyptian mummy found floating in the Bay by local fishermen, dating from 750 BC and probably from Thebes; a natural history collection; and a gallery devoted to Gibraltar artists— among them Gustavo Bacarisas, Mania and Olimpia Reyes (*open Mon–Fri 10–6, Sat 10–2; closed Sun*). In Library Street, in the grand building that was once the Governor's Residence, is the **Garrison Library**, built during the Great Siege in the hope of preventing boredom in sieges to come. Here there are extensive archives on Gibraltar's history. Nearby are the offices of *The Chronicle*, which reported Nelson's victory at Trafalgar. The **Supreme Court** looks diagonally across the street to the former 16th-century Franciscan convent, now the **Governor's Residence**, where the changing of the guard takes place (*check with tourist office for times*). If it's bucketing down, an occurrence frequent in winter months, you can watch these serious proceedings from the warmth and comfort of the *Angry Friar*, the pub on the corner. **Southport Gate**, at the top of Main Street, was built in 1552, during the reign of Charles V and has additions from the 19th century; the wall stretching east from the gate is **Charles V's Wall**, which ends just short of the water catchments at **Philip II's Arch**. Beyond the gate you can wander through shady little **Trafalgar Cemetery**, where sad little inscriptions tell of children killed by disease, and of young men who met their bloody end at sea. The **Alameda Gardens**, a few yards away, are more cheerful; you can stop in to see the exotic flora before taking the **cable car** up the Rock to the Apes' Den (*leaves every 15 mins 9.30–6; £4 inc adm to nature reserve; children half-price*).

The cathedral of **St Mary the Crowned** (between Main Street and Cannon Lane) stands on the site of the chief mosque of Gibraltar, of which some remains can still be seen. The Anglican cathedral of the **Holy Trinity** (off Main Street, near the museum) was consecrated in 1838, and in Engineer Lane the **Great Synagogue**, rebuilt in 1768, is attended by Gibraltar's 700-strong Jewish community. **King's Chapel**, part of the Franciscan convent, was one of the few buildings left standing at the end of the Great Siege, and was an earlier sanctuary for those sheltering from the attack by Barbarossa and his pirates, although the place itself was looted. Legend has it that the chapel is haunted by the grey nun, Alitea de Lucerna, whose family forced her into convent life because they disapproved of her lover. He, however, managed to sneak into the convent, dressed as a Franciscan friar, and the two continued their relationship until, inevitably, they were discovered. The lover drowned as they tried to escape, and poor Alitea remained to stalk the cloisters, bemoaning her lost (if not unrequited) love.

The Rock

The famous silhouette, surprisingly, does not hang over the seaward edge, but faces backwards towards La Línea. From 427m (1,400ft) up, the views from the upper part of the Rock are magnificent: the Costa del Sol curves away to the east, the mountains of Morocco sit in a purple haze across the narrow straits to the south; and way below, where the Mediterranean opens out into the wide and wild Atlantic, tiny toy-like craft plough through the waters in full sail. The Rock's entire eastern face is covered by the **water catchment system** that supplies Gibraltar's water—an engineering marvel to equal the tunnels. The upper part of the Rock has been turned into a nature reserve, which can be reached by cable car or through the entrance at Jews' Gate, on the hairpin bend where Engineer and Queen's Roads meet (*open daily except Sun, 9.30 to sunset; adm £3, children under 12 half-price, children under 5 free; cars £1.50*).

Apart from views of a panoramic variety, admission to the reserve will get you a look at Gibraltar's best-known citizens. The **Apes' Den** is halfway up the Rock where you can see Barbary apes, a species of tailless macaque. These gregarious monkeys are much more common on the African side of the straits and in Europe are unique to Gibraltar. There is an old saying that as long as they're here, the British will never leave. Understandably, they're well cared for, and have been since the days of their great benefactor, Winston Churchill. The Gibraltarians are fond of them, even though (as a local guidebook solemnly notes) they 'fail to share the same respect for private property' as the rest of us. Now that most of their feeding grounds have been built over, they are on the dole, and it's fun to watch them when the official Keeper of the Apes comes round at feeding time. Legend has it that the apes, two packs of them numbering 60 in all, travel to and from their native Morocco by an underground tunnel in the rock.

Nearby are remains of a **Moorish wall** and, a short walk to the south, **St Michael's Cave**, a huge cavern of delicate stalactites, now sometimes used as an auditorium. In the 19th century wealthy merchants would rent it out for extravagant parties; it was also a favourite venue for illegal duels, away from the censorious eye of the authorities; and during the second world war it was converted for use as a hospital. It's now used for concerts and fashion shows, but do bring a waterproof hat if you attend one of these—the roof leaks (*son et lumière shows at 11 and 4; free*). At the northern end of the Rock, facing Spain, are the Upper Galleries, now called the **Great Siege Tunnels**, an extensive section of the original British tunnels, which were hacked and blown out of the rock during the Great Siege—the work of Sergeant Major Ince, who was rewarded for his labours with a plot of farming land and a racehorse. (Horseracing and hunting were extremely popular; the airport was once the site of a racecourse.) Open to visitors, the Galleries have wax dummies of 18th-century British soldiers hard at work digging and blowing up Spaniards. From here it's a short walk down to the **Moorish castle** probably founded in the 8th century by Tariq ibn-Ziyad, but its best-known feature, the **Tower of Homage** dates from the 14th century when Abd Hassan recaptured Gibraltar from the Spanish. At present Gibraltar's **prison** is housed (and occupied) in the keep, but hopes are that this will be moved to a new military building. Unfortunately, some rather short-sighted town planning allowed a housing estate to be built within the castle's boundaries, again highlighting Gibraltar's acute need of space.

Away from the nature reserve, to the south of the promontory is the **Shrine of Our Lady of Europa**, adopted as a Catholic chapel in 1462, after which a flame was kept continuously alight—a predecessor to the present lighthouse at Europa Point. Close to the shrine fragments of a Moorish pavement can still be seen. **Gorham's Cave**, by the shore near Europa Point, was almost certainly inhabited by Neanderthal man. Extensive digs have uncovered important archaeological finds, largely of the animal remains variety.

If you want to sit on a beach, Gibraltar has a few, but they're all on the eastern side, opposite from the town, and accessible by bus. **Catalan Bay** and **Sandy Bay** are both a little built-up and crowded, the former slated for even greater development in the near future. Eastern Beach (dubbed 'Margate' in the 19th century) is better, though unfortunately it's next to the airport. The Bay of Gibraltar is a favourite playground of schools of dolphins, who on a good day will put on a show for the camera-toting bipeds on the shore. For sports enthusiasts the waters are ideal for activities ranging from windsurfing to scuba-diving. In Marina Bay you can charter yachts or cabin cruisers.

Where to Stay

expensive

For the businessman the **Holiday Inn (Whites)**, Governor's Parade, ✆ (350) 70 500, fax 702 43, offers sterile anonymity, along with air conditioning, sauna and jacuzzi (£90). The **Rock Hotel**, Europa Road, ✆ (350) 73 000, fax 73 513, a quality resort hotel of long standing, is up on the heights—about halfway up, under the cable car and near Gibraltar's casino. Visiting dignitaries and the occasional celebrity stay here. There's a pool, beautifully landscaped gardens and rooms with sea view and balconies (£85–90 for a double with balcony, £70 without, depending on land or sea view).

moderate

The **Bristol**, 8–10 Cathedral Square, ✆ (350) 76 800, fax 77 613, is in the heart of town, with swimming pool, and TV in all rooms (£60 for double with bath, £53 with shower). In the same price range, though not quite as comfortable, the **Continental**, 1 Engineer Lane, ✆ (350) 76 900, fax 41 702, is just off Main Street (£50), with a tacky fast-food restaurant on the ground floor. The **Queen's Hotel**, just outside the old city walls on Boyd Street, ✆ (350) 74 000, fax 40 030, is pretty characterless but has less expensive accommodation and there are good views of the Rock and Bay (£38 for a double with bath, £33 without). If you need a beach, the other resort hotel is the very modern **Caleta Palace**, Sir Herbert Miles Road, on Catalan Bay, ✆ (350) 76 501, fax 71 050 (£60–70 for a double, depending on the view).

inexpensive

In La Línea, if you're on a budget. Prices in Gibraltar are two to four times what they would be for comparable hotels in Spain. There is one opportunity for a cheap room in Gibraltar, the **Toc H Hostal**, Line Wall Road near the harbour, ✆ (350) 73 431, which will put you up for £6 a person. Understandably, it is usually full.

Eating Out

This isn't such a problem. Main Street is lined with pubs, fish shops, and cafés, and there are plenty of little places around Catalan Bay and the other beaches. Nearly all the hotels have restaurants.

The **Rock Hotel** is arguably the best place for lunch; colonial decor and discreet waiters help to set the scene for Gibraltar's answer to Raffles in Singapore, and the steaks are flown in fresh from the UK daily. Popular among the locals is the restaurant in the **International Casino Club**, 7 Europa Road, ✆ (350) 76 666, and you won't find a better place for five-star service; concerned with maintaining high standards, the management has a strict ruling on dress—even local celebrities have been turned away for inappropriate attire; there's a wide range of international dishes, and the terrace has great views overlooking the Bay and Algeciras—a perfect place to watch the sun go down on the Atlantic, if not the Empire (full meal with wine £25–35). In a lane off Main Street is the quaint **Country Cottage**, 13–15 Giros Passage, ✆ (350) 70 084, complete with antique furnishings and Olde Worlde atmosphere, although even the locals agree that it's a bit twee; the reliable and well-presented menu includes sole mornay, shrimp, scampi, and meat dishes from *brochettes* to Angus steaks (£20–30).

moderate

El Patio, 54 Irish Town, ✆ (350) 70 822, is a good spot; even Spaniards cross the border to sample its excellent Basque cuisine and Mediterranean fish specialities— rare delights considering the British culinary traditions around here; particularly popular with the business community, which jokingly refers to it as the 'Canteen', this place fills up at lunchtime; for a real treat telephone a day ahead and put in your order for *bacalao pil-pil*, delicious cod cooked slowly in garlic and olive oil (about £15–20 per head; closed Sat lunchtime and Sun). **La Bayuca**, 21 Turnbulls Lane, ✆ (350) 75 119, is a long-time favourite; Gibraltar's oldest and best-loved, not least for owners Tita and Johnnie; the walls are lined with photos of its more famous customers, and the decor is pleasantly rustic; the menu is first-rate: steaks, chicken, fish, and some Mediterranean dishes (£10–15; closed Tues and Sun lunch). Just off Main Street, **Bunter's**, 1 College Lane, ✆ (350) 70 482, provides welcome relief from some of the noisier establishments nearby; no blaring music or sloppy pints of ale here; the company is jovial and civilized, and the bar an ideal place for a cocktail while you decide on your meal: potted shrimps, pies, fresh salmon and steaks, rack of lamb and ribs, the more exotic boned duck and monkfish kebabs, and some truly great traditional English desserts—apple pie and cream, or sherry trifle; most main courses are under £10 and the three-course lunch is particularly good value at £9.50 (£25 including wine; closed lunchtime Sat and Sun, and Aug). Reservations are a must at **Strings**, 44 Cornwalls Lane, ✆ (350) 78 800, a small and intimate restaurant serving a decent selection of international dishes: smoked salmon, gravadlax, shrimp in wine sauce, grilled fish and meats, cheesecake (£10–15; closed Mon). **Sax** piano bar and restaurant, International Commercial Centre, attracts a young crowd; expect queues at weekends; the fare is mixed—English, Mexican, Italian—and the lunchtime menu particularly recommended; light snacks are also available, and there's live music two evenings a week (around £15 for full meal; closed Sun lunch). A little off the beaten track, **Jim's Den**, 25 Prince Edward's Road, © (350) 71 289, has a simple English menu, with simple whitewashed walls; it's a big hit with expats, and a popular place to drop in for a chat and a bite to eat (£10–15 for a full meal). There is a handful of Indian restaurants around; the **Maharaja**, 5 Tuckey's Lane, © (350) 75 233, with the simplest furnishings of the lot, offers some of the best food. The service is efficient and friendly, and all the old Indian favourites can be found on the menu (£10–15). In Marina Bay, you can sit out and watch the yachts or plane-spot at **Bianca's**, © (350) 73 379, which has reasonably priced fish, meat and pizza (around £12–15 for a full meal). Next door, **Da Paolo**, © (350) 76 799, has well-prepared fish specialities, such as fillet of John Dory in dill sauce, and a particularly good Spanish wine list (a little more expensive at about £15). Danish business interests in the area contributed to the opening of **The Little Mermaid**, Marina Bay, © (350) 77 660, a refreshing addition to the ethnic culinary scene. The interior is sleek and modern in the Danish style, and all the usual Scandinavian specialities appear including marinated herring, salmon and prawns; help your open sandwiches down with an *Aalborg Acquavit* and *Tuborg* chaser, instead of wine (£10).

inexpensive

Cheers Brasserie, G1 Cornwall Centre, © (350) 79 699, fills up with tourists at lunchtime and is a popular meeting place, where you can enjoy the large terrace and soak up the sun. The tasty and inexpensive snacks include club sandwiches, a variety of salads, and chilli, as well as full English breakfasts (snacks £3–5, full meals £8–10). There are around 360 pubs in Gibraltar, many serving food in one form or another. The best are **The Clipper**, 787 Irish Town, popular with Gibraltarians and visitors alike for its good roast beef and lasagna; and **The Royal Calpe**, 176 Main Street, where the grub is authentically English and served piping hot. And for a parting memory of Gibraltar before you cross back into Spain, drop into the patriotic **Old Bull and Bush**, complete with portrait of Queen Elizabeth II; drinks are chalked up on a slate as in days of yore. Pictures of England and English pubs cover the walls, and there are no tapas in sight, just crisps and hard-boiled eggs.

Entertainment and Nightlife

Many companies offer **guided tours** of Gibraltar and its sights; Bland Travel, Cloister Building, Irish Town, © (350) 77 012, also runs a 'Trafalgar Tour' from Rosia Bay to Tarifa in Algeciras. There are large populations of whales and dolphins within the Bay and the Straits of Gibraltar, which makes it an excellent place to see these mammals as nature intended. Mike Lawrence's **Dolphin Safari** from Sheppard's Marina, © (350) 71 914, is particularly good (£15 June–Sept). Gibraltar's late-nightlife happens up at the **Casino**, 7 Europa Road, © (350) 76 666—dress well and take lots of cash.

Expats residing in Spain flock across the border to pick up familiar brand-name groceries and household items at British prices; the real bargains are to be had in the top range of luxury goods. Remember that Gibraltar is Vat-free, and savings can be considerable. Here is a selection—but shop around.

Antiques: Bensaquen Antiques, 290 Main Street.

Cashmere: Carruana, 181 Main Street (jerseys, suits and fabrics).

Cuban cigars and perfume: S. M. Seruya, 165 Main Street, and Stagnetto's, 56 Main Street.

Jewellery: Sakata, 92 Main Street and The Red House, 66 Main Street (cultured pearls, Cartier, Rolex)

Menswear: García, 190 Main St (Dax, Burberry, etc).

Porcelain: Omni, 3 Main Street.

Art & Architecture

Until the coming of the Moors, southern Spain produced little of note, or at least little that has survived. To begin at the beginning, there are the 25,000-year-old cave drawings at the Cueva de la Pileta, near Ronda, and Neolithic dolmens near Antequera and Almería. No significant buildings have been found from the Tartessians or the Phoenicians, though remains of a 7th century BC temple have been dug up at Cádiz. Not surprisingly, with their great treasury of metals, the people of the region were skilled at making jewellery and figurines in silver and bronze (also ivory, traded up from North Africa where elephants were still common).

Real art begins with the arrival of the Greeks in the 7th century BC. The famous Lady of Elche in the Madrid museum, though found in the region of Murcia, may have been typical of the Greek-influenced art of all the southern Iberians; their pottery, originally decorated in geometrical patterns, began to imitate the figurative Greek work in the 5th century BC. The best collections of early work are in the Archaeological Museum at Sevilla and the museum at Málaga.

During the long period of Roman rule, Spanish art continued to follow trends from the more civilized east (ruins and amphitheatres at Itálica, Carmona, Ronda; a reconstructed temple at Córdoba; museums in Sevilla, Córdoba and Cádiz). Justinian's invasion in the middle of the 6th century BC brought new influences from the Greek world, though the exhausted region by that time had little money or leisure for art. Neither was Visigothic rule ever conducive to new advances. The Visigoths were mostly interested in gaudy jewellery and trinkets (best seen not in Andalucía, but in the museums of Madrid and Toledo). Almost no building work survives; the Moors purchased and demolished all of the important churches, but made good use of one Visigothic architectural innovation, the more-than-semicircular 'horseshoe' arch.

Moorish Art

The greatest age for art in Andalucía began not immediately with the Arab conquest, but a century and a half later, with the arrival of Abd ar-Rahman and the establishment of the Ummayyad emirate. The new emir and his followers had come from Damascus, the old capital of Islam, and they brought with them the best traditions of emerging Islamic art from Syria. 'Moorish' art, like 'Gothic', is a term of convenience that can be misleading. Along with the enlightened patronage of the Ummayyads, this new art catalyzed the dormant but not entirely dead culture of Roman Spain, creating a brilliant synthesis; of this, the first and finest example is **La Mezquita**, the Great Mosque of Córdoba.

La Mezquita was recognized in its own time as one of the wonders of the world. We are fortunate it survived, and it is chilling to think of the literally thousands of mosques, palaces, public buildings, gates, cemeteries and towers destroyed by the Christians; the methodical effacement of a great culture, an act unparalleled in the history of Europe. We can discuss this art from its finest production, and from little else. As architecture, La Mezquita is full of subtleties and surprises (*see* pp. 100–103). Westerners have tended to dismiss the Moorish approach as 'decorative art', without considering the philosophical background, or the expression of ideas inherent in the decoration. Figurative art being discouraged by Islam, artists used other means: Arabic calligraphy, which soon became an Andalucían speciality; repetitive geometric patterns, mirroring a Pythagorean strain that has always been present in Islam; and a meticulously clever arrangement of forms, shapes and spaces, meant to elicit surprise and delight. The infinite elements of this decorative universe (*see* Topics, pp. 70–72) come together in the most unexpected of conclusions— a reminder that the basic principle of Islam is unity.

The 'decorative' sources are wonderfully eclectic, and easy enough to discern. From Ummayyad Syria came the general plan of the rectangular, many-columned mosques, along with the striped arches. From Visigothic Spain, the distinctive horseshoe arch. The floral arabesques and intricate, flowing detail, whether on a mosque window, a majolica dish or a delicately carved ivory, are the heritage of late-Roman art, as can be clearly seen on the recycled Roman capitals of La Mezquita itself. The Ummayyads in Syria had been greatly impressed by Byzantine mosaics, and had copied them in their early mosques. This continued in Spain, often with artists borrowed from Constantinople. Besides architectural decoration, the same patterns and motifs appear in the minor arts of al-Andalus, in painted ceramics, textiles and in metalwork, a Spanish speciality since prehistoric times—your English baron of the time might have traded a village for a fine Andalucían dagger or brooch.

Such an art does not seek progress and development, in our sense; it shifts slowly, like a kaleidoscope, carefully and occasionally finding new and subtler patterns to captivate the eye and declare the unity of creation. It carried on, without decadence or revolutions, until the end of al-Andalus and beyond. Under the Almohads, who made their capital at Sevilla, it created the **Torre del Oro** and **La Giralda**, model for the great minarets of Morocco.

The Christian conquest of Córdoba, Sevilla, and most of the rest of al-Andalus (1212–80), did not put an end to Moorish art. The tradition continued intact, with its Islamic foundations, for another two centuries in the kingdom of Granada. In the rest of Spain, Muslim artists and artisans found ready employment for nearly as long; their Mudéjar art briefly contended with imported styles from northern Europe to become the national art of Spain. Most of its finest productions are not in Andalucía at all—the churches of Toledo, the towers of Teruel and many other towns of Aragón. The trademarks of Mudéjar building are geometrical decoration in *azulejo* tiles and brickwork, and elaborately carved wooden *artesonado* ceilings.

Granada, isolated from the rest of the Muslim world and constantly on the defensive, produced no great advances, but this golden autumn of Moorish culture brought the decorative arts to a state of serene perfection. In the **Alhambra** (continued throughout the 14th century), where the architecture incorporates gardens and flowing water, the emphasis is on panels of ornate plaster work, combining floral and geometric patterns with calligraphy—not only Koranic inscriptions, but the deeds of Granada's kings and much contemporary lyrical poetry. Another feature is the stucco *muqarnas* ceilings, translating the Moorish passion for geometry into three dimensions.

Granada's art and that of the Mudéjars cross paths at Sevilla's **Alcázar**, expanded by Pedro the Cruel in the 1360s; artists from Granada did much of the work. Post-1492 Mudéjar work can also be seen in some Sevilla palaces, such as the **Palacio de las Dueñas** or the **Casa de Pilatos**. The smaller delights of late Moorish decorative arts include painted majolica ware, inlaid wood chests and tables (the *taracea* work still a speciality of Granada), and exquisite silver and bronze work in everything from armour to astronomical instruments; the best collection is in the Alhambra's Museum of Hispano-Muslim Art.

Gothic and Renaissance

For art, the Reconquista and the emergence of a united Spain was a mixed blessing. The importation of foreign styles gave a new impetus to painting and architecture, but it also gradually swept away the nation's Moorish and Mudéjar tradition, especially in the south, where it put an end to 800 years of artistic continuity. In the 13th century, churches in the reconquered areas were usually done in straightforward, unambitious Gothic, as with **Santa Ana** in Sevilla, built under Pedro the Cruel, and the simple and elegant parish churches of Córdoba. In the next century, Gothic lingered on without noticeable inspiration; Sevilla's squat and ponderous **cathedral**, the largest Gothic building anywhere, was probably the work of a German or Frenchman.

The Renaissance was a latecomer to Andalucía. In 1506, when the High Renaissance had already hit Rome, the Spaniards were building a Gothic chapel in Granada for the tombs of Fernando and Isabel. This time, though, they had an architect of distinction; **Enrique Egas**, who had already created important works in Toledo and Santiago de Compostela, made the **Capilla Real** Spain's finest late-Gothic building, in the lively style called 'Isabelline Gothic' or 'plateresque', roughly corresponding to the contemporary French Flamboyant or English Perpendicular. The Plateresque in the decorative arts had already been established in Sevilla (the huge cathedral **retablo**, begun in 1482), and would continue into the next century (the cathedral's **Capilla Real** and **sacristy**). Other noteworthy figures of this period are the Siloés: **Gil de Siloé**, a talented sculptor, and his son **Diego**, who began the cathedrals at Granada (1526) and at Úbeda.

Genuine Renaissance architecture arrived with **Pedro Machuca**, who had studied in Italy. Strongly influenced by the monumental classicism of Bramante, his imposing **Palacio de Carlos V** (1527–8), in the Alhambra at Granada, actually antedates the celebrated Roman palaces it so closely resembles. Andalucía's Renaissance city is Úbeda, with an ensemble of exceptional churches and palaces; its **Sacra Capilla de Salvador** contains some of the finest Renaissance reliefs and sculpture in Spain. In the stern climate of the Counter-Reformation, architecture turned towards a disciplined austerity, the *estilo* *desornamentado* introduced by **Juan de Herrera** at Felipe II's palace-monastery of El Escorial, near Madrid. Herrera gave Sevilla a textbook example in his **Lonja**, a business exchange for the city's merchants. His most accomplished follower, **Andrés de Vandelvira**, brought the 'unornamented style' to a striking conclusion with his **Hospital de Santiago** in Úbeda, and other works in Úbeda and Baeza; he also began the ambitious **cathedral** at Jaén.

Baroque and Beyond

This style, like the Renaissance, was slow in reaching southern Spain. One of the most important projects of the 17th century, the **façade** for the unfinished Granada cathedral, wound up entrusted to a painter, **Alonso Cano** (1664). The idiosyncratic result, with its three gigantic arches, shows a little appreciation for the new Roman style, though it is firmly planted in the Renaissance. Real Baroque arrived 3 years later, with Eufrasio López de Rojas's **façade** for Jaén cathedral. The most accomplished southern architect in the decades that followed was **Leonardo de Figueroa**, who combined Italian styles with a native Spanish delight in colour and patterns in brickwork; he worked mostly in Sevilla (**El Salvador**, begun 1699, **Colegio San Telmo**, 1724, and the **Convento de la Merced**, now the Museo de Bellas Artes). Baroque sculpture was largely a matter of gory realism done in wood, as in the work of **Juan Martínez Montañes** (Sevilla cathedral) and his disciple **Juan de Mena**.

The 17th century has often been described as a 'golden age' of painting in Andalucía. Giving ample room for exaggeration, there is still **Velázquez** (1599–1660), a native *sevillano* who left the region forever in 1623 when he became painter to the king. Almost none of his work remains in the south. Of those who stayed behind, there is **Alonso Cano**, whose work often has a careful architectonic composition that betrays his side career as an architect, but seldom ranges above the pedestrian and devotional. **Francisco Herrera** of Sevilla (1576–1656) shows a little more backbone, in keeping with the dark and stormy trends of contemporary Italian painting. Best of all is an emigrant from Extremadura, **Francisco de Zurbarán**, who arrived in Sevilla in 1628. He is often called the 'Spanish Caravaggio', and though his contrasts of light and shadow are equally distinctive, this is as much a disservice as a compliment. Set in stark, bright colours, Zurbarán's world is an unearthly vision of monks and saints, with portraits of heavenly celebrities that seem painted from life, and uncanny, almost abstract scenes of monastic life like the *Miracle of Saint Hugo* in the Sevilla museum. Seeing the rest of his best work would require a long trip across two continents; the French under Maréchal Soult stole hundreds of his paintings, and there are more than 80 in the Louvre alone.

In the next generation of southern painters, the worst qualities of a decaying Spain are often painfully evident. **Bartolomé Esteban Murillo** (1617–82), another *sevillano*, is the best of them; two centuries ago he was widely considered among the greatest painters of all time. Modern eyes are often distracted by the maudlin, missal-illustration religiosity of his saints and Madonnas, neglecting to notice the exceptional talent and total sincerity that created them. Even harder to digest is **Juan de Valdés Leal** (1622–90), obsessed with the Hallowe'en blood-and-bones side of Counter-Reformation Catholicism to an extent that will often evoke either laughter or disgust (these two artists can be compared in Sevilla's museum and Hospital de la Caridad).

If any style could find a natural home in Spain, it would be the **rococo**. Eventually it did, though a lack of energy and funds often delayed it. **Vicente Acero** introduced the tendency early on, with a striking **façade** for the cathedral at Guadix. He had a chance to repeat it on a really important building project, the new Cádiz cathedral, but the money ran out, and the result was a stripped-down Baroque shell—ambition without the decoration. The great **Fábrica de Tabacos** in Sevilla (1725–65), the largest project of the century in Andalucía, met a similar end, leaving an austere work, an unintentional precursor of the neoclassical. Whenever the resources were there, Andalucían architects responded with a tidal wave of eccentric embellishment worthy of the Moors—or the Aztecs. Pre-Columbian architecture may have been a bigger influence on Spain than is generally credited; judge for yourself at the chapel and sacristy of the **Cartuja** in Granada (1747–62), the most blatant interior in Spain.

Elsewhere, the decorative freedom of the rococo led to some unique and delightful buildings, essentially Spanish and often incorporating eclectic references to the styles of centuries past. José de Bada's church of **San Juan de Dios** (1737–59), in Granada, is a fine example. In Córdoba, there is the elegant **Convento de Merced** (1745), and the **Coro** of the Cathedral, inside La Mezquita, a 16th-century Gothic work redecorated (1748–57) with elaborate stucco decoration by **Juan de Olive** and stalls and overall design by **Pedro Duque Cornejo**. Sevilla, in its decline, was still building palaces, blending the new style with the traditional requirements of a patio and grand staircase; the best of the century's palaces, however, is in Écija, the **Palacio de Peñaflor** (1728). Many smaller towns, responding to the improved economic conditions under Felipe V and Carlos III, built impressive churches, notably Priego de Córdoba, Lucena, Utrera, Estepa and Écija.

For all Andalucía's troubles, it should not be surprising that little has been produced in the last two centuries. **Pablo Picasso**, of Málaga, was the outstanding example of the artist who had to find his inspiration and his livelihood elsewhere.

Despite the lack of significant architecture, Andalucíans hold on to the glories of their past with tenacity; splashes of *azulejo* tiles and Moorish decoration turn up in everything from bus stations and market houses to simple suburban cottages.

Language

Castellano, as Spanish is properly called, was the first modern language to have a grammar written for it. When a copy was presented to Queen Isabel in 1492, she quite understandably asked what it was for. 'Your majesty', replied a perceptive bishop, 'language is the perfect instrument of empire'. In the centuries to come, this concise, flexible and expressive language would prove just that: an instrument that would contribute more to Spanish unity than any laws or institutions, while spreading itself effortlessly over much of the New World.

Among other European languages, Spanish is closest to Portuguese and Italian—and of course, *catalán* and *gallego*. Spanish, however, may have the simplest grammar of any Romance language, and if you know a little of any Romance language you will find much of the vocabulary looks familiar. It's quite easy to pick up a working knowledge of Spanish; but Spaniards speak colloquially and fast, and in Andalucía they do it with a pronounced accent, leaving out half the consonants and adding some strange sounds all their own. Expressing yourself may prove a little easier than understanding the replies. Spaniards will appreciate your efforts, and when they correct you, they aren't being snooty; they simply feel it's their duty to help you learn. There are dozens of language books and tapes on the market; one particularly good one is *Teach Yourself Spanish*, by Juan Kattán-Ibarra (Hodder & Stoughton, 1984). If you already speak Spanish, note that the Spaniards increasingly use the familiar *tu* instead of *usted* when addressing even complete strangers.

Pronunciation

Vowels

a	short *a* as in pat	u	silent after *q* and gue- and gui-, otherwise long *u* as in flute
e	short *e* as in set		
i	as long *as e* in be	ü	*w* as in dwell
o	long *o* as in note	y	at end of word or meaning *and*, as **i**

Consonants

b	in the middle of a word, often pronounced as *v*
c	before the vowels *i* and *e*, it's a *castellano* affectation to pronounce it as *th*; many Spaniards and all Latin Americans pronounce it in this case as an *s*
g	before *i* or *e*, pronounced as the *ch* in loch
h	silent
j	*ch* as in loch
ll	*y* or *ly* as in million
ñ	*ny* as in canyon (the ~ is called a tilde)
q	*k*
r	usually rolled, which takes practice
z	*th*, but *s* in parts of Andalucía

Pronunciation is phonetic but somewhat difficult for English speakers

Stress is on the penultimate syllable if the word ends in a vowel, on the last syllable if the word ends in a consonant; exceptions are marked with an accent.

If all this seems difficult, consider that English pronunciation is even worse for Spaniards. Young people in Spain seem to be all madly learning English these days; if your Spanish friends giggle at your pronunciation, get them to try to say *squirrel*.

Practise on some of the place names:

Madrid	*ma-DREED*	**Trujillo**	*troo-HEE-oh*
León	*lay-OHN*	**Jerez**	*her-ETH*
Sevilla	*se-VEE-ah*	**Badajóz**	*ba-da-HOTH*
Cáceres	*CAH-ther-es*	**Málaga**	*MAHL-ah-gah*
Cuenca	*KWAYN-ka*	**Alcázar**	*ahl-CATH-ar*
Jaén	*ha-AIN*	**Valladolid**	*vy-ah-dol-EED*
Sigüenza	*sig-WAYN-zah*	**Arévalo**	*ahr-EV-vah-lo*

Vocabulary

Useful Words and Phrases

yes	*sí*	nothing	*nada*
no	*no*	It is urgent!	*¡Es urgente!*
I don't know	*No sé*	How do you do?	*¿Cómo está usted?*
I don't understand	*No comprendo*	Well, and you?	*¿Bien, y usted?*
Spanish	*español*	What is your name?	*¿Cómo se llama?*
Do you speak English?	*¿Habla usted inglés?*	My name is...	*Me llamo... / Mi nombre es...*
Does someone here speak English?	*¿Hay alguien que hable inglés?*	Hello	*¡Hola!*
Speak slowly	*Hable despacio*	Goodbye	*Adios / Hasta luego*
Can you help me?	*¿Puede usted ayudarme?*	Good morning	*Buenos días*
		Good afternoon	*Buenas tardes*
Help!	*¡Soccoro!*	Good evening	*Buenas noches*
please	*por favor*	What is that?	*¿Qué es eso?*
thank you (very much)	*(muchas) gracias*	What ...?	*¿Qué ...?*
you're welcome	*de nada*	Who ...?	*¿Quién ...?*
It doesn't matter	*No importa*	Where ...?	*¿Dónde ...?*
all right	*está bien*	When ...?	*¿Cuándo ...?*
OK	*vale*	Why ...?	*¿Por qué ...?*
excuse me	*perdóneme*	How ...?	*¿Cómo ...?*
Be careful!	*¡Tenga cuidado!*	How much?	*¿Cuánto / Cuánta?*
maybe	*quizá(s)*	How many?	*¿Cuántos / Cuántas?*
		I am lost	*Me he perdido*

I am hungry	*Tengo hambre*	it's all the same	*es igual*
I am thirsty	*Tengo sed*	slow	*despacio*
I am sorry	*Lo siento*	fast	*rápido*
I am tired	*Estoy cansado*	big	*grande*
I am sleepy	*Tengo sueño*	small	*pequeño*
I am ill	*No siento bien*	hot	*caliente*
Leave me alone	*Déjeme en paz*	cold	*frío*
good	*bueno/buena*	up	*arriba*
bad	*malo/mala*	down	*abajo*

Accommodation

Where is the ... hotel?	*¿Dónde está el ... hotel?*	... with 2 beds	*con dos camas*
		... with a double bed	*con una cama grande*
Do you have a room?	*¿Tiene usted una habitación?*	... with a shower/ bath	*con ducha/baño*
Can I look at the room?	*¿Podría ver la habitación?*	... for one person/ two people	*para una persona/ dos personas*
How much is the room per day/ week?	*¿Cuánto cuesta la habitación por día/ semana?*	... for one night/ one week	*una noche/ una semana*

Numbers

one	*uno/una*	twenty	*veinte*
two	*dos*	twenty one	*veintiuno*
three	*tres*	thirty	*treinta*
four	*cuatro*	forty	*cuarenta*
five	*cinco*	fifty	*cincuenta*
six	*seis*	sixty	*sesenta*
seven	*siete*	seventy	*setenta*
eight	*ocho*	eighty	*ochenta*
nine	*nueve*	ninety	*noventa*
ten	*diez*	one hundred	*cien*
eleven	*once*	one hundred and one	*ciento-uno*
twelve	*doce*	five hundred	*quinientos*
thirteen	*trece*	one thousand	*mil*
fourteen	*catorce*	first	*primero*
fifteen	*quince*	second	*segundo*
sixteen	*dieciséis*	third	*tercero*
seventeen	*diecisiete*	fourth	*cuarto*
eighteen	*dieciocho*	fifth	*quinto*
nineteen	*diecinueve*	tenth	*décimo*

Time

What time is it?	*Qué hora es?*	morning	*mañana*
It is 2 o'clock	*Son las dos*	afternoon	*tarde*
... half past 2	*... las dos y media*	evening	*noche*
... a quarter past 2	*... las dos y cuarto*	today	*hoy*
... a quarter to 3	*... las tres menos*	yesterday	*ayer*
	cuarto	soon	*pronto*
noon	*mediodía*	tomorrow	*mañana*
midnight	*medianoche*	now	*ahora*
month	*mes*	later	*después*
week	*semana*	it is early	*está temprano*
day	*día*	it is late	*está tarde*

Days

Monday	*lunes*	Friday	*viernes*
Tuesday	*martes*	Saturday	*sábado*
Wednesday	*miércoles*	Sunday	*domingo*
Thursday	*jueves*		

Months

January	*enero*	July	*julio*
February	*febrero*	August	*agosto*
March	*marzo*	September	*septiembre*
April	*abril*	October	*octubre*
May	*mayo*	November	*noviembre*
June	*junio*	December	*diciembre*

Shopping and Sightseeing

I would like...	*Quisiera...*	money	*dinero*
Where is/are...?	*¿Dónde está/están ...?*	museum	*museo*
How much is it?	*¿Cuánto vale eso?*	theatre	*teatro*
open	*abierto*	newspaper (foreign)	*periódico (extranjero)*
closed	*cerrado*	pharmacy	*farmacia*
cheap/expensive	*barato/caro*	police station	*comisaría*
bank	*banco*	policeman	*policía*
beach	*playa*	post office	*correos*
booking/box office	*taquilla*	postage stamp	*sello*
church	*iglesia*	sea	*mar*
hospital	*hospital*	shop	*tienda*

Do you have any change?	¿Tiene cambio?	supermarket	supermercado
		toilet/toilets	servicios/aseos
telephone	teléfono	men	señores/
telephone call	conferencia		hombres/caballeros
tobacco shop	el estanco	women	señoras/damas

Driving

rent	aquilar	speed	velocidad
car	coche	exit	salida
motorbike/moped	moto/ciclomotor	entrance	entrada
bicycle	bicicleta	danger	peligro
petrol	gasolina	dangerous	peligroso
garage	garaje	no parking	estacionamento prohibido
This doesn't work	Esto no funciona		
Is the road good?	¿Es buena la carretera?	narrow	estrecha
		give way/yield	ceda el paso
breakdown	avería	road works	obras
(international) driving licence	carnet de conducir (internacional)		
driver	conductor, chófer	Note: Most road signs will be in international pictographs	

Transport

aeroplane	avión	hydrofoil	hidroala
airport	aeropuerto	platform	andén
bus/coach	autobús/autocar	port	puerto
bus stop	parada	seat	asiento
bus/railway station	estación	ship	buque/barco/embarcadero
car/automobile	coche		
customs	aduana	ticket	billete
ferry terminal	estación marítima	train	tren

Travel Directions

I want to go to...	Deseo ir a...	Do you stop at ... ?	¿Para en... ?
How can I get to... ?	¿Cómo puedo llegar a... ?	How long does the trip take?	¿Cuánto tiempo dura el viaje?
Where is... ?	¿Dónde está... ?	I want a (return) ticket to...	Quiero un billete (de ida y vuelta) a
When is the next... ?	¿Cuándo sale el próximo... ?	How much is the fare?	¿Cuánto vale el billete?
What time does it leave (arrive)?	¿Parte (llega) a qué hora?	Good trip!	¡Buen viaje!
From which stop does it leave?	¿De dónde sale?	here	aquí
		there	allí

close	cerca	north (n./adj.)	norte/septentrional
far	lejos	south (n./adj.)	sur/meridional
full	lleno	east (n./adj.)	este/oriental
left	izquierda	west (n./adj.)	oeste/occidental
right	derecha	corner	esquina
forwards	adelante	square	plaza
backwards	hacia atrás	street	calle

Eating Out

Menu

Hors d'oeuvres & Eggs — Entremeses y Huevos

artichokes with mayonnaise	alcachofas con mahonesa	scrambled eggs	huevos revueltos
frog's legs	ancas de rana	rice soup	sopa de arroz
olives	aceitunas	asparagus soup	sopa de espárragos
broth	caldo	garlic soup	sopa de ajo
assorted hors d'oeuvres	entremeses variados	noodle soup	sopa de fideos
baked eggs in tomato sauce	huevos de flamenco	chickpea soup	sopa de garbanzos
		lentil soup	sopa de lentejas
shrimp in hot garlic sauce	gambas pil pil	vegetable soup	sopa de verduras
		Spanish omelette, with potatoes	tortilla
cold soup	gazpacho	French omelette	tortilla a la francesa
fried eggs	huevos al plato		

Fish — Pescados

small splaice	acedías	cuttlefish	chipirones
fish marinated in white wine	adobo	... in its own ink	... en su tinta
clams	almejas	crab	cangrejo
anchovies	anchoas	spider crab	centollo
eels	anguilas	whitebait	chanquetes
baby eels	angulas	baby clams	chirlas
crayfish	ástaco	sea bass	dorado, lubina
tuna fish	atún	pickled or marinated fish	escabeche
codfish (usually dried)	bacalao	prawns	gambas
sea bream	besugo	lobster	langosta
lobster	bogavante	giant prawns	langostinos
tunny	bonito	sole	lenguado
fresh sardines	boquerones	shellfish	mariscos
mackerel	caballa	mussels	mejillones
squid	calamares	hake	merluza

grouper	*mero*	anglerfish	*rape*
razor-shell clams	*navajas*	skate	*raya*
oysters	*ostras*	turbot	*rodaballo*
monkfish	*pejesapo*	salmon	*salmón*
barnacles	*percebes*	red mullet	*salmonete*
whiting	*pescadilla*	sardines	*sardinas*
swordfish	*pez espada*	trout	*trucha*
plaice	*platija*	scallops	*veneras*
octopus	*pulpo*	fish stew	*zarzuela*

Meat and Fowl   *Carnes y Aves*

meatballs	*albóndigas*	pork loin	*lomo*
roast	*asado*	blood sausage	*morcilla*
beefsteak	*bistec*	pigeon	*paloma*
tripe	*callos*	duck	*pato*
pork	*cerdo*	turkey	*pavo*
spiced sausage	*chorizo*	partridge	*perdiz*
chops	*chuletas*	spicy mini-kebabs	*pinchitos*
sucking pig	*cochinillo*	chicken	*pollo*
rabbit	*conejo*	bull's tail cooked with	*rabo/cola de toro*
heart	*corazón*	onions and tomatoes	
lamb	*cordero*	kidneys	*riñones*
pheasant	*faisán*	sausage	*salchicha*
cold meats	*fiambres*	salami	*salchichón*
fillet	*filete*	brains	*sesos*
liver	*hígado*	sirloin steak	*solomillo*
wild boar	*jabalí*	veal	*ternera*
raw cured ham	*jamón de York*		
baked ham	*jamón serrano*	Note: *potajes, cocidos, guisados, estofados,*	
tongue	*lengua*	*fabadas* and *cazuelas* are various kinds of stews.	

Vegetables   *Verduras y Legumbres*

artichokes	*alcachofas*	endives	*endibias*
celery	*apio*	salad	*ensalada*
rice	*arroz*	asparagus	*espárragos*
rice with saffron and	*arroz marinera*	spinach	*espinacas*
seafood		chickpeas	*garbanzos*
aubergine (eggplant)	*berenjena*	peas	*guisantes*
onion	*cebolla*	French beans	*judías (verdes)*
mushrooms	*champiñones*	lettuce	*lechuga*
cabbage	*col, repollo*	lentils	*lentejas*
cauliflower	*coliflor*	potatoes	*patatas*

(fried/sautéed)	*(fritas/salteadas)*	leeks	*puerros*
(baked)	*al horno*	beetroots (beets)	*remolachas*
cucumber	*pepino*	Spanish mushrooms	*setas*
pepper	*pimiento*	carrots	*zanahorias*

Fruits and Desserts — *Frutas y Postres*

apricot	*albaricoque*	apple	*manzana*
almonds	*almendras*	peach	*melocotón*
rice pudding	*arroz con leche*	melon	*melón*
cake	*bizcocho/pastel/ torta*	orange	*naranja*
		flan with ice cream	*pajama*
ice cream and coffee float	*blanco y negro*	pastries	*pasteles*
		pear	*pera*
cherries	*cerezas*	pineapple	*piña*
plums	*ciruelas*	banana	*plátano*
prune	*ciruela pasa*	cheese	*queso*
crème caramel	*flan*	cottage cheese	*requesón*
raspberries	*frambuesas*	watermelon	*sandía*
strawberries (with cream)	*fresas (con nata)*	fruit pie	*tarta de frutas*
		shortcake	*torta*
biscuits (cookies)	*galletas*	nougat	*turrón*
slush, iced squash	*granizado*	grapes	*uvas*
ice creams	*helados*		
figs	*higos*		

Beverages — *Bebidas*

mineral water (without/with fizz)	*agua mineral (sin/con gas)*	Spanish champagne	*cava*
		chocolate	*chocolate*
water with ice	*agua con hielo*	milk	*leche*
milkshake	*batido de leche*	tea (with lemon)	*té (con limón)*
orange juice	*zumo de naranja*	wine (red, rosé, white)	*vino (tinto, rosado, blanco)*
beer	*cerveza*		
coffee (with milk)	*café (con leche)*		

Other Words

(olive) oil	*aceite (de oliva)*	change	*cambio*
marinade	*adobo*	waiter	*camarero*
garlic	*ajo*	menu	*carta/menú*
lunch	*almuerzo/comida*	dinner	*cena*
sugar	*azúcar*	spoon	*cuchara*
sandwich	*bocadillo*	knife	*cuchillo*

bill/check	*cuenta*	ground pepper	*pimienta*
breakfast	*desayuno*	plate	*plato*
meat pie	*empanada*	grapefruit	*pomelo*
ice	*hielo*	(without) salt	*(sin) sal*
lemon	*limón*	sauce	*salsa*
butter	*mantequilla*	napkin	*servilleta*
marmalade	*mermelada*	cup	*taza*
table	*mesa*	fork	*tenedor*
honey	*miel*	toast	*tostada*
bread	*pan*	glass	*vaso*
roll	*panecillo*	vinegar	*vinagre*

Restaurant

Do you have a table?	*¿Tiene una mesa?*	Do you have a wine list?	*¿Hay una lista de vinos?*
... for one /two?	*¿... para uno/dos?*	Can I have the bill (check), please?	*La cuenta, por favor*
Can I see the menu, please?	*Déme el menú, por favor*		

Glossary

ajaracas:	trellis work brick design, often decorating Mudéjar apses
ajimez:	in Moorish architecture, an arched double window
alameda:	a tree-lined promenade
albarrani:	projected tower joined to main wall by a bridge
alcazaba:	a Moorish fortress
alcázar:	a Moorish fortified palace

Almohads:	group of puritanical Muslims, originally Berbers, who ruled Spain from about 1147 to 1213
Almoravids:	fanatical people of Berber origin and Islamic faith who founded an empire in North Africa that spread over much of Spain in the 11th century
arabesque:	decoration in the form of scrolling or interlacing flowers and leaves
arrabal:	quarter of a Moorish city
artesonado:	Mudéjar-style carved wooden ceilings, panels or screens
ayuntamiento:	city hall
azulejo:	painted glazed tiles, popular in Mudéjar work and later architecture (from the Arabic *az-zulaiy*, a piece of terracotta)
banderillero:	bullfighter's assistant who plants banderillas (sharp darts) into the base of the bull's neck in order to weaken the animal
barrio:	city quarter or neighbourhood
bodega:	wine bar, cellar or warehouse
bóveda:	vault
calle:	street
capilla mayor:	seat of the high altar in a cathedral
capilla real:	Royal chapel
Carmen:	a Carmelite convent, or Morisco villas with pleasure gardens outside Granada
carretera:	a main road
cartuja:	a Carthusian monastery
castillo:	a castle
castrum:	Roman military camp
churrigueresque:	florid Baroque style of the late 17th and early 18th centuries in the style of José Churriguera (1665–1725), Spanish architect and sculptor
ciudad:	a town or city
ciudadela:	a citadel
converso:	a Jew who converted to Christianity
coro:	the walled-in choir in a Spanish cathedral
coro alto:	a raised choir
corregidor:	chief magistrate
corrida de tros:	bullfight
cortijo:	Andalucían country house
cupola:	a dome or rounded vault forming a roof or ceiling
custodia:	tabernacle, where sacramental vessels are kept
diputacíon:	seat of provincial government
embalse:	reservoir
ermita:	hermitage
esgrafiado:	style of painting, or etching designs in stucco, on a façade
estilo desornamentado:	austere, heavy Renaissance style inaugurated by Felipe II's architect, Juan de Herrera; sometimes described as Herreran
fandango:	traditional dance and song, greatly influenced by the gypsies of Andalucía

feria:	major festival or market, often an occasion for bullfights
finca:	farm, country house or estate
fonda:	a modest hotel, from the Arabic *fonduq*, or traders' inn
fuero:	exemptions, or privileges of a town or region under medieval Spanish law
grandee:	a select member of Spain's highest nobility
hammam:	Moorish bath
Herreran:	see *estilo desornamentado*
hidalgo:	literally 'son of somebody'—the lowest level of the nobility, just good enough for a coat of arms
homage tower:	the tallest tower of fortification, sometimes detached from the wall
humilladero:	calvary, or stations of the Cross along a road outside of town
Isabelline Gothic:	late 15th-century style, roughly corresponding to English perpendicular
judería:	Jewish quarter
junta:	a council, or specifically, the regional government
khan:	inn for merchants
kufic:	very angular style of Arabic calligraphy originating in the city of Kufa in Mesopotamia, often used as architectural ornamentation
lonja:	merchants' exchange
Los Reyes Católicos:	The Catholic Kings, Isabel and Fernando
madrassa:	Muslim theological school, usually located near a mosque
majolica:	a type of porous pottery glazed with bright metallic oxides
mantilla:	a silk or lace scarf or shawl, worn by women to cover their head and shoulders
maqsura:	elevated platform usually with grills
matador:	the principal bullfighter, who finally kills the bull
medina:	walled centre of a Moorish city
mercado:	a market
mezquita:	a mosque
mihrab:	prayer niche in a mosque facing Mecca, often elaborately decorated
mirador:	a scenic viewpoint or belvedere
monterías:	hunting scenes (in art)
Moriscos:	Muslims who submitted to Christianization to remain in al-Andalus after the Reconquista
mozarábes:	Christians under Muslim rule in Moorish Spain
mudéjar:	Moorish-influenced architecture, characterized by its decorative use of bricks and ceramics; Spain's 'national style' in the 12th–16th centuries
muflón:	a wild, short-fleeced mountain sheep.
muqarnas:	hanging masonry effect created through multiple use of support elements
ojival:	pointed (arches)
parador:	state-owned hotel, often a converted historic building
paseo:	a promenade, or an evening walk along a promenade
patio:	central courtyard of a house or public building
picador:	bullfighter on horseback, who goads and wounds the bull with a pica or

	short lance in the early stages of a bullfight in order to weaken the animal
plateresque:	heavily ornamented 16th-century Gothic style
plaza:	a town square
plaza de toros:	bullring
plaza mayor:	main square at the centre of many Spanish cities, often almost totally enclosed and arcaded
posada:	inn or lodging house
pronunciamiento:	a military coup
pueblo:	a village
puente:	a bridge
puerta:	gate or portal
Reconquista:	the Christian reconquest of Moorish Spain beginning in 718 and completed in 1492 by the Catholic Kings
rejas:	iron grilles, either decorative ones in churches or those covering the exterior windows of buildings
retablo:	carved or painted altarpiece
romería:	pilgrimage, usually on a saint's feast day
sagrario:	reliquary chapel
sala capitular:	chapterhouse
sillería:	a choir stall
souk	an open-air marketplace in Muslim countries
stele:	a stone slab marking a grave or displaying an inscription
taifa:	a small Moorish kingdom; especially one of the so-called Party Kingdoms which sprang up in Spain following the 1031 fall of the caliph of Córdoba
taracea:	inlaid wood in geometric patterns
torero:	a bullfighter, especially one on foot
torre:	a tower
vega:	a cultivated plain or fertile river valley

General and Travel

Baird, David, *Inside Andalusia* (Lookout Publications). Background reading. Glossy, full of history and anecdote.

Borrow, George, *The Bible in Spain* (various editions, first written in 1843). A jolly travel account by a preposterous Protestant Bible salesman in 19th-century Spain.

Brenan, Gerald, *The Face of Spain* (Penguin, 1987). An account of his journey through central and southern Spain in the spring of 1949.

Brenan, Gerald, *South from Granada* (Penguin, 1987). A sharp-eyed, evocative account of Brenan's many years in the village of Yegen, first published in 1957.

Chetwode, Penelope, *Two Middle-Aged Ladies in Andalusia*. A delightful bosom-heaving burro-back look at the region.

Ford, Richard, *Gatherings from Spain* (Everyman). A boiled-down version of the all-time classic travel book *A Handbook for Travellers in Spain*, written in 1845. Hard to find but worth the trouble.

Hooper, John, *The Spaniards* (Penguin, 1987). A comprehensive account of contemporary Spanish life and politics. Well done.

Jacobs, Michael, *A Guide to Andalusia* (Viking). Informative and well-researched volume on history, culture and sights.

Luard, Nicholas, *Andalucía* (Century). Readable chronicle of life in an Andalucían village.

Lee, Laurie, *As I Walked Out One Midsummer Morning* and *A Rose for Winter*. Very well written adventures of a young man in Spain in 1936, and his return 20 years later.

History

Brenan, Gerald, *The Spanish Labyrinth* (Cambridge, 1943). Origins of the Civil War.

Carr, Raymond, *Modern Spain 1875–1980* (Oxford, 1985). A confusing period, confusingly rendered.

Castro, Américo, *The Structure of Spanish History* (E L King, 1954). A remarkable interpretation of Spain's history, published in exile during the Franco years.

Elliot, J H, *Imperial Spain 1469–1714* (Pelican, 1983). Elegant proof that much of the best writing these days is in the field of history.

Further Reading

Gibson, Ian, *The Assassination of Federico García Lorca* (Penguin, 1983).

Kanen, Henry, *The Spanish Inquisition* (out of print). The definitive history.

Mitchell, David, *The Spanish Civil War* (Granada, 1982). Anecdotal; wonderful photographs.

O'Callaghan, J F, *History of Medieval Spain* (Cornwell University, 1983).

Thomas, Hugh, *The Spanish Civil War* (Penguin, 1977). The best general work.

Watt, W H, and Cachia, Pierre, *A History of Islamic Spain* (Edinburgh University Press, 1977).

Art and Literature

Brenan, Gerald, *The Literature of the Spanish People* (Cambridge, 1951).

Burkhardt, Titus, *Moorish Culture in Spain* (Allen and Unwin). Indispensable for understanding the world of al-Andalus.

García Lorca, Federico, *Three Tragedies* and *Five Plays: Comedies and Tragi-comedies* (Penguin).

Goodwin, Godfrey, *Islamic Spain* (Penguin, 1991). From the informative Architectural Guides for Travellers series.

Irving, Washington, *Tales of the Alhambra* (various editions) and *The Conquest of Granada* (London, 1986).

Arberry, A J, *Moorish Poetry* (Cambridge, 1953). Arberry's translation of a 13th-century anthology, mostly of Andalucían poets.

Index

Prima de Rivera, Miguel and José Antonio 201
prison (Gibraltar) 222
property, buying 18
public holidays 33
Puente Genil 184
Puente Nuevo (Ronda) 178
Puerta de las Granadas (Granada) 191
Puerta de las Palmas (Sevilla) 101
Puerta del Perdón (Sevilla) 101
Puerta del Puente (Córdoba) 103
Puerta de Tierra (Cádiz) 131
Puerta del Vino (Granada) 192
Puerta de Elvira (Granada) 199
Puerta de Justicia (Granada) 191
Puerta de las Pesas (Granada) 199
Puerto Banús 152, 153
Puerto Sherry 135, 137
Puntilla 135
Pythagoras 70
Qaddafi, Colonel 145
Queipo de Llano, Gonzalo 56, 84
Quintilian 53

Ragged Staff Wharf (Gibraltar) 220
rail transport **4**, **9**, 11-13
  coasts, Andalucían 122, 131, 138, 141, 150,
    162, 170
  Guadalquivir valley 78, 92-3, 97, 113, 119
  interior of Andalucía 176, 180, 190
Reccared 49, 58
Reconquista **52-3**, 58-7
  Guadalquivir valley 75, 79, 97, 113
  interior of Andalucía 180, 184, 187, 201,
    207
Redonda de Miradores (Úbeda) 116
refugios 38, 44
Renaissance *see under* art and architecture
RENFE 11-12
Rescue of Animals of Sahara, Centre of
  (Almería) 171
Reserva Nacional de Sierra de Tejeda 167
restaurants *see* eating out
Reyes Católicos, Los **52-3**
  see also Fernando III; Isabel
Ribera, José 84, 105, 164, 184, 201
Río Tinto 48, 123, 126
Rivera, Francisco (Paquirri) 110, 142
road transport *see* bus; car; taxis
Rock of Gibraltar 221-2
rococo *see under* art and architecture
Rodriguez, Ventura 119
Roldán, Pedro 93, 119
Romans 48-9, 57, 63-4, 214, 228, 229
  coasts, Andalucían 129, 133, 142, 151, 156,
    163, 168
  Guadalquivir valley 75, 92, 93, 96, 103, 106
  interior of Andalucía 177, 179, 180, 181,
    182, 184, 186
  Roman Bridge (Córdoba) 103

Roman necropolis (Carmona) 93
Roman spa (Manilva) 151
Roman temple (Córdoba) 106
Roman temple (Fuengirola) 156
Roman theatre (Málaga) 163
Romero, Francisco and Pedro 62
Romero de Torres, Julio 105-06
Ronda/Serranía de Ronda 29, 38, 176, 177-8
  Alameda del Tajo 178
  Alcázar 178
  bullfighting 62
  Casa del Rey Moro 178
  Ciudad Nuevo 178
  eating out 178, 180
  festivals 23
  geography 26
  Mercadillo 178
  Mina 178
  Moorish bath 178
  Palacio de Salvatierra 178
  Plaza de Toros 178
  Puente Nuevo 178
  Santa María La Mayor church 178
  sport 38
  where to stay 179
Rooke, Admiral Sir George 215
Roquetas de Mar 170
Rota 135, 136
  eating out 136-7
  where to stay 136
Royal Palace (Granada) 192-6
rugby 36
Rute 184
Ryder Cup 34

Sacra Capilla del Salvador (Úbeda) 116, 230
Sacromonte 199-200
Saenz de Santa María, Lt Gen. José Antonio 34
St Michael's Cave (Gibraltar) 222
St Mary the Crowned (Gibraltar) 221
Salamanca 64
Salobreña **168**
  eating out 169
  tourist information 166
  where to stay 169
San Andres church (Córdoba) 104
San Bartolomé church (Montoro) 111-12
San Clemente monastery (Sevilla) 85
San Esteban church (Sevilla) 86
San Felipe Neri church (Cádiz) 132
San Gabriel church (Loja) 181
San Gil church (Écija) 94
San Ildefonso church (Sevilla) 86
San Isidoro del Campo monastery 92
San Isidro church (Los Barrios) 143
San Jerónimo church (Granada) 203
San José church (Granada) 199
San Juan Bautista church (Écija) 94
San Juan Bautista church (Marchena) 93

This Best of Southern Spain selection is admittedly subjective, but it may give you a start in planning your holiday.

Beaches: many quiet, undeveloped beaches on the windy Costa de la Luz, and sandy coves in Almería.

Bodegas you can tour: Alcazaba, La Tasca and González Byass in Jerez de la Frontera.

Bullrings: Ronda, Sevilla, Córdoba.

Castles: Alhambra (Granada), Almería, Baños de la Encina (near Bailén), Solera (near Huelma).

Curiosities: Gibraltar; cave dwellings in Guadix; Gruta de las Maravillas, a spectacular cave near Aracena; Mini Hollywood in Almería.

Golf courses: Torrequebrada (between Torremolinos and Málaga), Sotogrande (near Gibraltar).

Horse trekking/riding: Serranía de Ronda.

Hotels: the 18th-century splendour of the Alfonso XIII (Sevilla); the superb setting and gardens of the Puente Romano (Marbella); the grand but affordable Palacio Duques de Medina Sidonia (Sanlúcar de Barrameda); the old-world charm of the Reina Victoria (Ronda); and the pueblo-style La Bobadilla (Loja).

Paradores: Granada, Carmona, Úbeda.

Parks and gardens: the tropical plantlife and trimmed hedges of the Generalife in Granada; the Alameda gardens of Cádiz, and several in Sevilla.

Restaurants: El Caballo Rojo and El Churrasco (Córdoba), Egaña Oriza (Sevilla), Casa Bigote (Sanlúcar de Barrameda), El Bosque (Jerez de la Frontera), La Hacienda (Las Chapas, near Marbella).

Scenery: mountains around Ronda and Las Alpujarras (Granada); the Pass of Despeñaperros, and the rugged heights of the Sierra Nevada.

Towns and villages: Arcos, and the picturesque White Villages of Andalucía and their views; Cazorla and Baeza (both near Úbeda), Alhama de Granada, Montoro, Mojácar, Zahara, Nerja (especially for views).

Venta routes: through the mountains of Málaga along the old road to Granada, along the Guadalhorce river valley through Churriana, Cártama and Alhaurín; along the road to Ronda from San Pedro de Alcántara; along the road to Ojén from Marbella; the road from Mijas to Alhaurín el Grande.

Wild country: Sierra Nevada and Las Alpujarras (Granada); the marshlands of Las Marismas and Parque Nacional del Coto de Doñana (near Huelva); the hiking country of the Sierra de Cazorla (near Úbeda); Almería desert; and the twisted rock formations of El Torcal.

Windsurfing: off Tarifa.